The British Slave Trade:
Abolition, Parliament and People

'The House of Commons', c. 1806, by Augustus Charles Pugin and Thomas Rowlandson, published in *The Microcosm of London* (R. Ackermann, 3 vols, 1808-10). (© Palace of Westminster.)

The British Slave Trade: Abolition, Parliament and People

Including the Illustrated Catalogue of the Parliamentary Exhibition in Westminster Hall, 23 May–23 September 2007

Edited by

Stephen Farrell
Melanie Unwin
and
James Walvin

Edinburgh University Press
for
The Parliamentary History Yearbook Trust

© 2007 Edinburgh University Press

Edinburgh University Press,
22 George Square,
Edinburgh EH8 9LF

Typeset in Bembo and printed and bound in
Great Britain by Page Bros Ltd, Norwich

A CIP record for this title is available from the British Library

ISBN 978 0 7486 3314 2

This volume is a supplement to *Parliamentary History*, vol. 26 (2007)

CONTENTS

NOTES ON CONTRIBUTORS

Hilary McDonald Beckles is principal and pro-vice-chancellor of the University of the West Indies, Cave Hill Campus, Barbados. He has researched and published extensively on the history of the Caribbean, including his recent book (with Verene Shepherd), *Liberties Lost. The Indigenous Caribbean and Slave Systems* (Cambridge, 2004). He is a member of the International Task Force for the U.N.E.S.C.O. Slave Route Project and is principal consultant for resource material in the schools programme. A keen cricketer, he has also written a two-volume history of *The Development of West Indies Cricket* (1999).

Caroline Bressey's research focuses on the presence of black people in Victorian Britain, particularly London. The aim of her research is to recover the experiences of life, and understandings of race and racism, among the black population. She is currently based in the Department of Geography, University College London, as an Economic and Social Research Council research fellow, working on a research project examining the historical geography of *Anti-Caste*, an anti-racist journal first published in the 1880s. She is also secretary of the Black and Asian Studies Association (B.A.S.A.).

Christopher L. Brown is associate professor of history at Rutgers University in New Brunswick, New Jersey, where he teaches British history, British imperial history, and the comparative history of slavery and abolition. He is the author of *Moral Capital. Foundations of British Abolitionism* (Chapel Hill, NC, 2006), which received from the American Historical Association the 2006 James A. Rawley Prize for the best book in Atlantic History and the 2006 Morris D. Forkosch Prize for the best book in British History. He received his D. Phil. in Modern History from Balliol College, Oxford in 1994.

Kathy Chater is a freelance writer and genealogist. She is the author of books and articles about tracing family history and has a special interest in black people because of her possible black ancestry. She is working on a Ph.D. at Goldsmiths' College, University of London, and as part of this has created the first large-scale database of black people in England and Wales during the period of the British slave trade.

Seymour Drescher is university professor of history and sociology at the University of Pittsburgh. He has held Fulbright, Guggenheim, National Endowment for the Humanities and Woodrow Wilson Center fellowships, and was founding secretary of the European Program at the Wilson Center. His publications include *Econocide. British Slavery in the Era of Abolition* (1977); *Capitalism and Antislavery* (1986), *From Slavery to Freedom. Comparative Studies in the Rise and Fall of Atlantic Slavery* (1999) and

The Mighty Experiment. Free Labor Versus Slavery in British Emancipation (2002). The last work was awarded the Frederick Douglass Book Prize in 2003.

Stephen Farrell is a senior research fellow at the History of Parliament in London, specializing in the early nineteenth-century house of commons. He completed his Cambridge Ph.D. thesis on the Rockingham whigs and the house of lords in 1993, and has since published articles in *Parliamentary History*. He is a member of the curatorial team for the parliamentary exhibition, for which he did extensive background research.

Mike Kaye has been working in the human rights' field for more than 15 years and currently manages Anti-Slavery International's communications and advocacy work. His previous jobs have included teaching in the University of Central America (Nicaragua); human rights field work in El Salvador, Guatemala and Mexico; policy officer for the Central America Human Rights Committees; and parliamentary officer for the Refugee Council. Recent publications include: *Contemporary Forms of Slavery in Argentina, Paraguay and Uruguay* (2006), *1807–2007: Over 200 years of Campaigning against Slavery* (2005) and *The Migration-Trafficking Nexus* (2003).

Gelien Matthews pursued undergraduate studies at the University of the West Indies, St Augustine Campus, Trinidad, where she also obtained a Diploma in Education. She read for her Ph.D. at the University of Hull. She has recently published her Ph.D. manuscript with Louisiana State University Press under the title *Caribbean Slave Revolts and the British Abolitionist Movement*. She is an adjunct lecturer in Caribbean studies at Caribbean Nazarene College, and has recently taken up a temporary post as lecturer of American history at the University of the West Indies, St Augustine Campus.

William A. Pettigrew is a lecturer at Lincoln College, Oxford, and former director of the University of Oxford and the University of Virginia's Atlantic history seminar. He is the author of forthcoming articles on seventeenth and eighteenth-century British Atlantic history. He is currently completing a study that examines how political changes at the turn of the eighteenth century accelerated Britain's involvement in the transatlantic slave trade.

Cassandra Pybus is currently Australian Research Council professorial fellow in history at the University of Sydney and has also held several research fellowships in the United States. She is the author of 11 books, of which the most recent are *Epic Journeys of Freedom. Runaway Slaves of the American Revolution and their Global Quest for Liberty* (Boston, 2006) and, as editor with Marcus Rediker, *Many Middle Passages* (Berkeley, 2007).

David Richardson is professor of economic history and director of the Wilberforce Institute for the Study of Slavery and Emancipation (W.I.S.E.), the University of Hull. He sits on the Scientific Committee of the U.N.E.S.C.O. Slave Route Project and is an adviser to the National Maritime Museum on Merseyside, the Bristol Empire and Commonwealth Museum, the Manchester Museum and the Wilberforce House Museum, Hull. His principal area of research is the Atlantic slave trade, where, among other things, he co-authored *The Atlantic Slave Trade. A Database on CD-Rom* for Cambridge University Press in 1999 and has published numerous articles in leading journals. His current work focuses on networking and institutional change in the context of the slave trade and on the demography and medical treatment of enslaved Africans.

Melanie Unwin M.A. (R.C.A.) is a member of the curatorial staff at the Palace of Westminster and the project manager for 'The British Slave Trade: Abolition, Parliament and People' exhibition.

James Walvin is the consultant curator for the parliamentary exhibition. He taught for many years at the University of York, where he is now professor of history emeritus. He also held visiting positions in the Caribbean, the U.S.A. and Australia. He won the Martin Luther King Memorial Prize for his book *Black and White*, and has published widely on the history of slavery and the slave trade, including more recently *Black Ivory. A History of British Slavery*. His book *The People's Game* was a pioneering study of the history of football and remains in print 30 years after its first publication. His recent books are *A Short History of Slavery* (2007), and *The Trader, The Owner, The Slave* (2007).

Marcus Wood is a painter, performance artist and film maker. He is also professor of diaspora studies at the University of Sussex. His most recent books on slavery are *Blind Memory. Visual Representations of Slavery in England and North America, 1760–1865* (2000), *Slavery, Empathy and Pornography* (Oxford, 2002) and *The Poetry of Slavery. An Anglo American Anthology 1764–1865* (Oxford, 2003).

EDITORIAL NOTE

The editors would like to emphasize that they have made every effort to use appropriately sensitive vocabulary and to avoid phraseology which is now considered unacceptable. Variations on 'enslaved African' has been our preferred term, though the (still ubiquitous) word 'slave' is unavoidable in certain contexts, particularly that of historical usage and when linked to the word 'trade'. Although 'negro' only appears where it is quoted from an historical source, 'creole', 'coolie' and similar terms have been retained, a precise meaning being specified on each occasion. For consistency, 'black' is always given in lower case.

In footnotes, the place of publication is London, unless otherwise stated.

The editors wish to express their gratitude to Clyve Jones, editor of *Parliamentary History*, for agreeing to publish these essays together with the catalogue of the parliamentary exhibition. They are grateful to Alisdair Hawkyard for his copy-editing and indexing, and to Ian Davidson and Ann Vinnicombe of Edinburgh University Press for seeing this project through to publication. Thanks are also due to Malcolm Hay, curator at the Palace of Westminster, and Paul Seaward, director of the History of Parliament Trust.

Foreword

PROFESSOR THE BARONESS YOUNG OF HORNSEY

In 2007, the passing of the act that abolished the British slave trade will be commemorated in a wide variety of ways across the United Kingdom and internationally. Numerous organizations from arts groups to churches are working on, for example, the political and social legacy of the slave trade, the work of prominent abolitionists such as Olaudah Equiano and William Wilberforce, the generation of wealth through the slave trade in cities such as Bristol, Liverpool, Birmingham, Lancaster and London. Agencies and organizations such as English Heritage and the Victoria and Albert Museum are taking a fresh look at the objects in their care, stimulated at least in part by the activities and debates that will be taking place in the commemorative year.

Across the country signs of empire are inscribed on the city and landscape. The Blackboy Lanes, Jamaica Streets, Pretoria Avenues, West India Quays and so on give an indication of the extent to which Britain has been shaped by and is inextricably linked to its colonial history. Much of that history remains hidden from public view in as much as its meaning is rarely discussed–unless there is a contentious move by a local authority or a community based organization to have a street or public house renamed. By and large, unless there is a personal, intellectual or emotional investment in developing that understanding it seems most people are content to go no further than mild curiosity about how and why their environment has been named with an eye on centuries old historical connexions.

The commemorative events and activities planned for the 200th anniversary of the passing of the Abolition of the Slave Trade Act have the potential to alert people to those signs of history that surround them. The planned memorials; the artists' commissions; the exhibitions, conferences and literature; the media coverage–all these acts of commemoration have the potential to make a significant impact on the ways in which we think about Britain and the long period of transatlantic enslavement.

No doubt some of this work will be contentious and make for impassioned debate–that is part of the point and we should not shy away from it even though it might prove to be uncomfortable for many of us. Even for organizations whose job it is to present objects from the past, the bicentenary poses a substantial set of challenges. Historical material relating to African–and indeed Asian, Jewish and Irish peoples and people with disabilities–which are deemed offensive by today's standards abound in our museums and archives. How is that material to be handled without distorting either the historical truth or the reality of attitudes to those communities? Such images and objects can pose a real threat to a community's sense of itself, especially if it feels it is under siege. I hope that far from trying to avoid the potential difficulties, the political, community, cultural, educational sectors will join together to embrace the challenge. We need to move towards a better understanding of how history is shaped, its impact on, and legacy in contemporary life, and the difference we can make for the future, especially in relation to issues of 'race', ethnicity and identity. That is, perhaps, a heavy burden for the bicentenary to carry but it seems to me to be implicit in the overall project whether we wish to acknowledge it or not.

The objects, artefacts and documents that are to be exhibited in Westminster Hall focus on the role of parliament in the struggle to end the slave trade. Although it concentrates on parliamentary involvement, this is not a story exclusively about the members of the house of commons and the house of lords. The title of the exhibition, *The British Slave Trade: Abolition, Parliament and People* makes this point clear and also suggests some of the layers of complexity involved in such a project. There are many different ways of constructing the unfolding of events, the list of key actors and significant moments in this tragic narrative: no single display or volume can capture all the nuances. In particular, the role of parliament itself in sustaining the inhuman trade in enslaved Africans ought to be examined alongside the passing of the act to abolish it. The whole story cannot be contained in one exhibition however: we hope the display in Westminster Hall will be viewed as complementary to other events and activities. Indeed the exhibition itself is one of a number of key elements of parliament's contribution to the bicentenary commemorations: we have, for example, appointed a writer-in-residence to work alongside the exhibition, an on-line resource and a schools programme.

Whilst the normal constraints of time, space and resources mean that the exhibition cannot give a comprehensive account of the history of Britain's enthusiastic and profitable participation, the essays in this publication contextualise and give more details of specific aspects of the slave trade. As well as providing invaluable material illuminating the backdrop against which the saga of legislative change was performed, the essays discuss life for the formerly enslaved Africans after abolition. Due to the perception that the act was an endpoint, the perspective of the millions of Africans stuck in a life of poverty and continued brutality after abolition is a subject which has not received enough attention within and outside academic circles. The actuality was that the 1807 act did not end slave trading, and, of course, slavery itself was not officially ended in the British empire until the act of 1833.

The omission of African perspectives and accounts in Britain's colonial and imperial history is a cause for concern as is the notion that slavery was a footnote in British history rather than one of its defining narratives. The role of enslaved Africans in hastening the end of the trade in humans has been omitted from populist, mainstream accounts of the abolitionist movement, which consequently serve to construct Africans as victims, aided by a few good white people.

In the popular imagination, William Wilberforce is the dominant figure in the abolitionist movement: indeed, he's often the only person mentioned. As an M.P., Wilberforce was responsible for putting the bill through parliament and it is right that he is recognized for taking up the cause over a period of almost 20 years. Sadly, the names of Olaudah Equiano, Ottobah Cugoano, Granville Sharp, Hannah More, Ignatius Sancho and Thomas Clarkson may be known to a small, dedicated group of activists and scholars but have little resonance for the wider public. Little is also known of the thousands who signed petitions, attended meetings and read and absorbed abolitionist literature: this lack of knowledge makes it all the more important that the essays in the journal testify to the breadth of the abolitionist movement.

The commemorations in 2007 present us with further opportunities to recognize the achievements of the African and British women and men who united across class and racial divides to participate in what was arguably the first great grassroots political movement for change in this country. The role of Thomas Clarkson, along with Olaudah Equiano, Ignatius Sancho, Hannah More, Granville Sharp and William Wilberforce will be commemorated in a special issue of stamps, and the impact of the abolitionists will be marked by a specially minted £2 coin.

It's worth reflecting on one of the wider meanings of the bicentenary for a moment. Within the parliamentary exhibition, a section has been curated by Anti-Slavery International, revealing insights into the relevance of the history of enslavement to our current situation. Over 180 years after its establishment, the organization's campaign against enforced labour and the denial of human freedom and rights is still necessary in our contemporary globalized world.

That the exhibition and the accompanying volume of essays–which also serves as a catalogue–are being produced at all is testament to the drive and commitment of several individuals. I would like particularly to pay tribute to the late Tony Banks, Lord Stratford, for his early support for the project. Thanks are also due to The Lord Great Chamberlain, Mr Speaker, The Lord Speaker, Black Rod and Yeoman Usher in the House of Lords, and the Serjeant-at-Arms in the House of Commons, the House of Commons Commission, the House of Commons Advisory Committee on Works of Art, and the House of Lords Information Committee.

The curatorial team of James Walvin, Melanie Unwin, Stephen Farrell and Machel Bogues, and the designers of the exhibition, Metaphor, have all risen to the difficult challenge of creating an exhibition for this most significant commemorative event. The Advisory Board has played an active role in this project and thanks are due to them for their engagement and constructive critiques; thanks also to John Benger, Tim Jarvis and the project board who have helped to ensure that the project remained on track.

Those who know their history are aware that Britain has for centuries been a multi-layered, multi-textured nation, and multi-cultured too. Principled, informed leadership at all levels is a crucial element in effecting successful change and social justice. I hope that 2007 can maximise opportunities for a wide range of people to appreciate that history belongs to us all, and that the people's engagement in the political process can effect real change.

Introduction

JAMES WALVIN

The act to abolish the slave trade in 1807 was, by any standards, a remarkable piece of legislation. First, it marked the end of British dominance in the Atlantic slave trade. Second, it ushered in a new phase in British overseas history: after 1807 Great Britain became, at a stroke, the world's leading abolitionist power. The act of 1807 represented a decisive shift in Britain's dealings with the outside world. But behind this apparently simple change, from slaving to abolition, there lurked a complexity of issues, and this special supplement to *Parliamentary History* is designed to address many of those questions. The essays in this volume bear testimony both to the significance of 1807 and to the broad-ranging historical and intellectual challenges posed by the abolition of the slave trade in 1807.

1

The Atlantic slave trade was the largest single enforced movement of people in the pre-modern world. There had been other slave trades, notably in the world of Greek and Roman antiquity. But the shipping of Africans across the Atlantic has no parallel in numbers, or organized brutality, until the totalitarian regimes' transportations of people in the twentieth century. It was a trade which spanned almost four centuries, from the age of Columbus through to the 1860s, and it involved all the major maritime powers and states of Europe and the Americas. Though the British came to dominate the trade, it was pioneered by the Spaniards, Portuguese and Dutch. They were eagerly followed by the British and the French – even by the Danes and Germans. It was a trade which yielded potential profits that few could resist. From an early date, European (later North American and Brazilian) shippers and merchants had no qualms about buying Africans and shipping them to the Americas. There was, it is true, an early and persistent religious criticism of the Atlantic slave trade, but such criticisms were easily drowned or ignored by the sound of successful and expansive commerce. Profits ensured that morality was silenced. The end result was that the slave trade developed almost as if it were morally neutral: a form of trade the benefits from which silenced any adverse critic. This was true of all European slave trading nations and of all the American colonies.

The images of the Atlantic slave trade remain embedded in modern popular memory: the brutal packing of Africans below decks, the manacles and chains, the guns trained on the decks – all remain potent images in popular recollection two centuries later. They were also images which after 1787 were used to great political effect by the abolitionist campaign. But, even more than the imagery, it is perhaps the numbers which leave the most indelible impression. We know of 34,000 slave voyages, some 5,000 from Liverpool: of 12 million Africans loaded on to the slave ships, and more than ten million survivors stumbling ashore in the Americas. They had no idea where they were. Year after year, Africans greatly outnumbered European settlers arriving in the Americas. By the 1820s, for example, of the people who had crossed the Atlantic to settle in the Americas, only 2.5 million were white – the rest were Africans. And they, of course, had been forced across the Atlantic in the slave ships. Until the 1820s the enslaved African was, in many respects, the typical pioneer of American settlement.

The British (initially the English) came relatively late to the slave trade. But the establishment of their own colonies in the Americas and the shift to sugar production proved a turning point. The Brazilians had already shown that sugar plantations were labour intensive, and European settlers could never secure enough labour among local indigenous people, or European settlers (free or unfree). But Africa had already yielded an abundance of labour to Europeans. Enslaved Africans had, for centuries, been traded along the overland caravan routes to North Africa. Existing forms of African slavery had been eagerly exploited by early Europeans traders and explorers on the West African coast. The Spaniards and Portuguese for example had used Africans as slaves in Spain and Portugal and in their Atlantic islands *before* they settled their colonies in the Americas. But it was above all sugar which became the engine behind the early slave trade. In fact, something like 70 per cent of all Africans shipped across the Atlantic were destined to work in the sugar fields.

Though Africans dominated the plantations (sugar in Brazil and the West Indies, tobacco in the Chesapeake, later rice in South Carolina) Africans and their descendants could soon be found everywhere. They worked in all corners of the American economies, and by the end of the eighteenth century they were even scattered across the face of Europe. But the largest concentration of Africans was to be found in the sugar colonies.

Wherever we look in the sugar islands, there we see legions of Africans working to produce the sugar which transformed the tastes and habits of the western world. Sugar sweetened the naturally-bitter drinks of tea, chocolate and coffee, while rum from the sugar cane made life more tolerable for men in the royal navy. Tobacco smoke became an inescapable feature of western life. Yet both these products – sugar and tobacco – were cultivated by Africans labouring on the plantations. But how many people spotted the connexion as they enjoyed their sweet tea or coffee, or relaxed with a pipe of tobacco? Did anyone ponder that it was all made possible by the Africans toiling thousands of miles away across the Atlantic? And who contemplated the terrible sufferings of the Africans on board the slave ships? For much of their history, the enslaved Africans were generally out of sight and out of mind. But, as the following essays make clear, all this began to change from the mid-eighteenth century onwards.

2

To secure so many Africans, Europeans developed complex and highly competitive trading systems on the west coast of Africa. These were linked to local traders, rulers and systems which, in return for imported goods from European ships, exchanged growing numbers of enslaved Africans. At myriad locations, slave ship captains haggled, bartered and negotiated for their human cargoes. To secure the best trading spots and conditions, the British, like all other nations, did their utmost to enhance their position. From the first, the British state involved itself in this process. The royal court, parliamentary legislation, military power – all were used to promote national interests against other competitors. It is important then, when remembering parliament as an abolitionist legislature, that we also recall parliament as a slave trading legislature. Parliament regularly passed acts to secure and enhance the best ways of promoting British slaving interests on the African coast, at sea and in the Americas. Were British interests best served, for example, by creating monopoly companies (the Royal African Company for instance) or by throwing open the trade to all comers? This earlier legislation, advancing the slave trade, is the subject of William Pettigrew's important essay. Also acting as a backcloth to the story of abolition itself is Christopher Brown's valuable article on the period between 1713 and 1783. During these years the African trade rarely intruded on public notice, but Brown's study of the occasional investigations and discussions that took place in the Commons sheds light on the motivations of its supporters in parliament.

The slave trade had massive ramifications for the British and their economy. We know of about 12,000 British slave voyages. Many thousands of sailors served on the slavers (and many lost their lives on them). The British economy thrived on the goods packed into the holds of the outbound slave ships: textiles, metalwork, firearms, implements. The whole financial structure of slavery, of credit and debt, of maritime insurance, flowed in and out of the booming merchant and trading houses, and banks of London and provincial towns. The complexity of the economics of the slave trade, and of the wider world of Atlantic slavery, are captured in David Richardson's masterly essay. Here was a massive economy which brought together the diverse peoples and economies of three continents. And, as Richardson shows, there was little evidence, on the very eve of abolition, that any sector in that system (European, African or American) was keen to abandon slave trading as uneconomic. Why then should the British defy their own economic self-interest, and turn against the slave trade?

The slave trade was, above all, a trading system which yielded material bounty on all hands – except, of course, to its millions of victims. Yet here lies a historical conundrum: why should the British turn against a business which continued to yield such material well-being to the British people?

The rise of the British abolition movement had complex and slowly developing origins, although in the event, after 1787 the political unfolding of abolition was relatively swift. Although abolition appears at first glance to have emerged out of the blue in the wake of the British defeat in North America in 1783, there were signs of unease about slavery much earlier. From the 1760s for example there had been a string of cases in English courts about slavery in England. They had attracted the outraged attention of Granville Sharp, whose dogged and unwavering commitment to black freedom in England was a one-man campaign which eventually developed into an important legal and political campaign. Sharp was indefatigable in pressing the case for black freedom, and in exposing the outrages which lay at the heart of the slave system. He pestered the great and the good, with letters and pamphlets, aided by black victims who provided personal testimony about slavery. Best-remembered perhaps by the Somerset case of 1772, Sharp's efforts lasted from the 1760s to the formal foundation of the abolition movement in 1787. Long before it was expedient or fashionable to doubt the slave trade, Granville Sharp had pursued a vigorous and influential campaign on behalf of its victims.

The turning point for abolition was the war in America (1776–83). For a start, the question of slavery was embedded within the conflict itself. Many of the prominent American revolutionaries were major slave holders, and were anxious to maintain slavery. The British, however, used the offer of freedom to win runaway slaves to the British side of the conflict. Caught in the middle were the American quakers, long uneasy about slavery, but they were now in a difficult position and could not afford to appear unpatriotic in wartime. For their part, the enslaved voted with their feet, thousands escaping to the British side. Unfortunately, they had opted for the losing side. When the defeated British finally left North America, they took with them thousands of ex-slaves, shipping many to Florida, Nova Scotia and to London. For those who stayed behind, the new United States of America offered not freedom but a tightening of slavery itself. The enslaved population of the United States was to provide the expanding labour force which was shifted from their old locations in the east to the new cotton plantations of the south after 1800.

The American war unleashed a major debate about slavery. In fact North American planters no longer needed slaves from Africa. The black population of North America was increasing of its own accord, and American planters could fill the ranks of their labour force, not by purchasing Africans from the ships, but by buying slaves from the eastern in seaboard. Thomas Jefferson denounced the slave trade, but continued himself to use slave labour throughout his lifetime. But it was to be American voices raised against the slave trade which proved influential in the launching of abolition in Britain itself.

American quakers had long denounced the slave trade, and their objections took root among Friends in England. British quakers were always in close correspondence with American Friends (many of whose prominent spokesmen were regular visitors to London) and became increasingly assertive about the trade. Though relatively few, the quakers exercized an influence out of all proportion to their numbers. They also influenced other dissenting groups, most notably the methodists, themselves increasing in numbers, especially in areas of Britain beyond the reach of the anglican Church. It is clear that the origins of the campaign against the slave trade in Britain are to be found long before the formal establishment of an abolitionist organization in 1787. There was a longer germination of abolitionist ideals and culture than historians have generally recognized.

The one group traditionally overlooked by historians of abolition was the slaves. In the campaign to secure black freedom, the enslaved were generally regarded as 'noises off stage', victims of the system waiting for their masters to grant freedom. Today, the story looks quite different. It is clear that, from the first, there was an important black role in the politics of abolition. Africans fought against enslavement from the moment of initial capture, through the horrors of the slave ships, to the daily life of the plantations. It took its most spectacular form in slave uprisings. And, in the American Revolution, resistance manifested itself in flight to the British side. In joining the colonial power they hoped to find the freedom unobtainable in the company of the revolution's great leaders George Washington, Thomas Jefferson, *et al.* who could offer local slaves nothing but a continuation of their perpetual bondage. Yet the British were, whatever their strategic offers of freedom to North American slaves, also the masters of the greatest slave empire the world had yet seen. At the time, British slave ships were ferrying an annual 40,000 Africans into bondage in other parts of the Americas.

Those ex-slaves who sailed to England soon found themselves trapped in uncertainty and poverty. They formed the core of 'the black poor', living in abject conditions in London. Many had lost everything by siding with the British, and their wretchedness attracted charitable help. Finally, when charity proved inadequate, the government intervened. The decision to establish a new colony in Sierra Leone for London's black poor (joined later by others from Nova Scotia) seems at first sight a harsh move. To encourage ex-slaves to relocate, once again, to an area of West Africa deeply enmeshed in the slave trade, seems a heartless decision. In fact, its organizers, including Granville Sharp, were naïve rather than heartless, and looked on the scheme as a means of creating a 'province of freedom' in Africa: a place where independent and free blacks could thrive economically and politically. The outcome, as Cassandra Pybus illustrates in her essay in this volume, was altogether different from the founders' intentions. The initial optimism foundered in the harsh circumstances of life in Sierra Leone, and the miseries of the black settlers were beyond endurance.

One man who narrowly avoided that fate was the African Olaudah Equiano. An ex-slave, Equiano was an acquaintance of Sharp's and had alerted him to the *Zong* massacre in 1781. Appointed commissary to the Sierra Leone fleet, Equiano had quit at the last minute, amid accusations of corruption and ineptitude in 1787. There followed a highly-public argument which gave Equiano a public prominence which he subsequently used to launch his autobiography published in 1789. The book proved to be an instant and widespread best-seller. It also added a new dimension to the proliferation of abolitionist sentiment in Britain.

Black people had been increasingly notable in Britain, especially in London, in the course of the eighteenth century. A black presence had been a striking feature from the early years of maritime explorations and trade to West Africa. Sailors, traders and officials returning from Africa returned with Africans, often as slaves. But it was the expansion of the slave trade which saw a growing number of Africans land in Britain as slaves, hence the legal disputes about slavery in English courts. As far as we know, most were employed as domestics or, like Equiano, at sea. The time-consuming complexities of recovering the history of Britain's black population are well illustrated in Kathy Chater's essay, based on painstaking work on many unyielding sources. But what Chater's work confirms is the presence of a black population at the heart of English (largely metropolitan) society. She also raises important questions about the comparative treatment of immigrant and migrant groups by the host society.

Historians are agreed that the British black population 'peaked' in the late eighteenth century, at about the time of the arrival of black loyalists from North America. It used to be thought that thereafter there was a marked decline in the black population. In many respects this seemed logical. The end of the slave trade in 1807 dramatically reduced the movement of Africans across the Atlantic Ocean. Caroline Bressey's essay is a timely reminder of a different story. She writes of a continuing black presence, though one sustained by different migratory patterns. New shipping routes to Africa and new generations anxious to secure a British education, ensured the continued arrival of Africans and West Indians into Britain. Theirs was a different story from the struggles of the enslaved generations. They had to wrestle with newer forms of oppression, spawned by a different set of imperial attitudes towards black people. What linked these very contrasting black experiences was the theme of dissent and opposition, and it was here that we can begin to appreciate a generally overlooked theme in the campaign against the slave trade.

Black agitation against the slave trade and slavery was part of the history of slavery itself. The African victims of enslavement did their best to resist their bondage, and a black voice of protest was audible throughout. It was generally ignored or silenced by a slave system which was draconian and brutal. Though black dissent often prompted a violent reaction it was none the less a voice which refused to be silenced and, in the late eighteenth century, took on a new and ultimately corrosive form.

The emergence of mass literacy was a prominent feature of the consumer revolution of the eighteenth century. As ever more people were able to read and write, and as cheap print flew off the presses in ever increasing volumes, the questions posed by slavery became a matter of ever-wider debate. More than that, literacy seeped into the slave quarters. Black writers, whose literacy was generally encouraged by christian conversion, emerged to offer a new and distinctive literary account of slavery. Whatever its literary flaws, this black voice of experience had a power and persuasion which no outsider, however critical, could hope to match. On both sides of the Atlantic, slaves and ex-slaves emerged who were able to challenge a fundamental principle of the pro-slavery lobby: namely the belief that Africans and their descendants were incapable of learning and attainment, and were suited solely to be labourers on the plantations. A number of black writers not only described their lives, but added their voice to the early demands for black freedom. The most notable, in England, was Ignatius Sancho, whose letters, published posthumously in 1782, put down an important marker. It was, however, Olaudah Equiano whose words had the most important impact on the course of abolition. Despite a continuing debate about his origins, Equiano remains an emblematic figure. His had been an extraordinary life, even by the standards of Atlantic slavery.

After a lifetime at sea and in the plantation economies, Equiano had secured his own freedom, by industry and application, to become a man of literary and social ambition, and fired by a confused christianity. His autobiography of 1789 gave abolition an African dimension which in effect complemented the growing clamour for an end to the slave trade. Equiano's personal testimony was only the latest of a stream of literary and political objections to the slave trade which had emerged since 1783.

As we have seen, the American war had profound consequences for slavery and for the political debate about slavery. What evolved after 1783 was a gradual coalescing of men of abolitionist sentiment who felt the need to formalize their outrage against the slave trade. But the political movement which was, quite rapidly, to transform the British political landscape, had a longer germination than is sometimes thought.

The small band of men who came together between 1783–87 to *do* something about the slave trade did not at first glance appear a threat to the all-powerful pro-slavery lobby. Quakers, a small band of anglicans, Granville Sharp, Thomas Clarkson and William Wilberforce did not seem a body of people to give the planters and traders too much to worry about. In fact they were to shake the slave system to its foundations – even they were amazed at the way popular abolition quickly took root.

The founding of the Society for Effecting the Abolition of the Slave Trade, otherwise known as the London Committee, transformed everything. It did so at two levels. Abolitionists first of all stirred up public agitation against the slave trade, largely via Thomas Clarkson's untiring efforts, while at the same time, its parliamentary spokesmen, notably William Wilberforce, pressed home demands for an act to end the trade. It was however the *popular* politics of abolition, which Seymour Drescher analyzes in his study, which proved to be the seminal abolitionist tactic. Drescher's work has established beyond doubt the ubiquity, originality and the persuasiveness of popular agitation in the abolition campaign.

As many authors in this volume show, there had been a growing tide of publications directed at the outrages of the slave trade. Quakers, methodists, some anglicans, a small band of people of sensibility, men with experience on the slave ships and plantations, groups of local women, all had taken up their pen against the slave trade. What they wrote was shocking and persuasive, but their tracts and essays had limited, often sectional, circulation. The London Committee determined to move beyond this small interested readership and take the abolitionist message to a wide, national readership. For this, they had to hand a ready-made network.

Quaker businessmen, organizations, printers and meetings formed a highly efficient and willing network for the task. Letters and articles were placed in the newspapers, pamphlets flew off the quaker presses, authors were commissioned to write, and after 1787 there was a veritable deluge of abolitionist literature. There was a parallel drive to establish local abolitionist societies, linked to London, but each generating its own swirl of local activity. Linking them all was the figure of Thomas Clarkson, the indefatigable foot soldier of the movement, criss-crossing the country on horseback, lecturing wherever he went, urging local people (who flocked to hear him) to commit themselves to vigorous abolition. The most immediate and remarkable response was a flowering of abolitionist petitions sent to parliament. Everyone was surprised by the number of petitions, and by the number of signatures they contained. The petition emerged as a powerful means of directing public opinion to the legislature; the public spoke direct to parliament through the abolitionist petitions. Crowded lectures across the country, a massive growth in abolitionist societies, tens of thousands of publications, churches and congregations adding their own voice to the clamour, all and more, added to the rising crescendo of abolition. Moreover, it was clear from the start that demands for abolition came from all sorts and conditions of people. Ordinary working men and women joined the abolition chorus. There had been nothing like it, in terms of political ferment and socially inclusive agitation, since the turmoil of the seventeenth-century Revolution. But this time it had a specific focus and aim. The focus was parliament – and how to direct public opinion to parliament – and the aim was to persuade parliament to ban the slave trade.

In May 1789, the young Wilberforce, encouraged by his friend, the prime minister, William Pitt the Younger, began what became an annual ritual: bringing a motion to the House for abolition. Thereafter the parliamentary and governmental politics of abolition were confused and uneven. Despite disappointments, periodic rebuffs, both in the Commons and especially the Lords, Wilberforce stuck to the task of promoting abolition in parliament. The evidence from the slave ships, from ships' surgeons, captains, preachers to the slaves and others, was presented to parliament and to its various committees. It catalogued the horrors which formed the commonplace experience of life on the slave ships. In the general process of the development of abolitionist agitation, there emerged the indelible images of anti-slavery which survive in the public memory to this day as icons: the kneeling slave, the phrase 'Am I not a man and a brother?', the plan of the crowded slave ship, the *Brookes*, all and more came to form a popular visual and durable imagery of abolition. But as Marcus Wood argues in his essay, here is an imagery which raises some disturbing questions. The memorialization of abolition, the artefacts and iconography of the movement are troublesome, cultural items which can conceal and deceive. But in the 1780s and 1790s, these abolition artefacts seemed to drive forward a powerful public outrage.

From 1787, through this tumult of abolition activity, the powerful West India lobby was assailed and reduced in power and influence. For a century past the slave planters, merchants and traders had effectively been unopposed in parliament. There were, of course, arguments about how best to promote the slave lobby's interests. But no one had seriously challenged the West Indian interest's rationale, or disputed its economic arguments. Abolition utterly transformed all that, not only confronting the morality of the slave trade, but increasingly casting doubt over the entire slave enterprise. It was not so much that the abolitionists disputed the West Indians' accountancy of slavery, but that they assaulted their entire legitimacy. More than that, abolition quickly stole the political and moral high ground. The West Indian interest was quickly and comprehensively outmanoeuvred. Although their spokesmen were always on hand in parliament and in the corridors of power to promote the case for slavery and the slave trade, after 1787 fewer and fewer people actually believed what they said. Even if it were true that the slave trade continued to deliver widespread material bounty, more and more people looked to other, non-economic views of the slave system. Thus it was, in the very years when the slave trade remained in the ascendancy, when British ships were delivering record numbers of Africans to the colonies, the British people turned against the slave trade in huge, hostile numbers. It was as if, as Seymour Drescher has argued, the nation had turned against its own self interest. In the process the West Indian interest found itself relegated. Despite upsets, failures and long periods of inactivity, abolition was never to be dislodged from its dominant position.

All this must have seemed hopelessly optimistic in 1787, though it was very soon apparent that there was a national tide running in favour of abolition. It was clear enough that the victims of the system – the Africans and their enslaved descendants – wanted nothing less than an end to their miserable slavery. The question of what the enslaved wanted, and what role they played in abolition has remained oddly elusive, not least because the ending of the slave trade was for many years studied primarily as a British and a parliamentary issue. At one level, it was. The debates for and against abolition took place in parliament, and the decision to pass the Abolition (and later the Emancipation) Act was taken by parliament. But extra-parliamentary pressures were critical in persuading politicians and ministers to move towards abolition. It is now clear that foremost among those pressures were the slaves themselves.

Historians of the enslaved in the Atlantic world have recently discussed the role of the enslaved people in the move towards abolition. Hilary Beckles, for many years a prominent interpreter of the historical voice of the enslaved in the Caribbean, illustrates the role of the enslaved in the era of abolition. Beckles also addresses the dissonance between slave visions and the expectations of British abolitionists. To put the matter simply, what was happening in Britain, and especially in parliament, looked very different in the slave quarters of the Caribbean. What, for example, would an end to the slave trade do for the slaves already resident in the West Indies? Their status and their daily grind would remain unaffected: they would continue to be slaves, subject to the same masters, on the same plantations. The joy expressed in Britain when abolition was passed was not so readily appreciated by plantation slaves whose only change was not having to accommodate, welcome, train and care for, new (and generally sick) Africans just off the slave ships. Slave expectations, and disappointments, were then often quite different from those of British abolitionists, even though they might have parallel long-term hopes of ending the entire slave system.

3

Even allowing for extra-parliamentary pressure, and even when slave visions and agency are incorporated into the formula of abolitionist politics, it was ultimately a parliamentary change. Precisely *how* parliament came to that momentous decision is analyzed here by Stephen Farrell. His forensic analysis of perceived voting intentions – which M.P.s were thought to have opted for abolition and why – provides a unique explanation of the parliamentary process of abolition itself. Farrell's essay also offers a genre of historical analysis, detailed parliamentary scrutiny, which acts as a foil to other essays in this volume, many of which discuss broad, more sweeping issues in the story of abolition.

In 1807 no one could have predicted what the end of the slave trade would bring. It was assumed that the enforced movement of Africans across the Atlantic would stop, but even that was only partly true. Demand for enslaved labour remained high after 1807, especially in Brazil and Cuba, and there were plenty of traders willing to run the risk of being impounded by the British and the American navies, to engage in profitable trade shipping Africans across the South Atlantic. Some three million Africans crossed the Atlantic as slaves *after* 1807. In addition, slavery itself continued in the British colonies. The impact of the 1807 act differed from colony to colony. Some recently-acquired islands (for example, Trinidad secured from the Spanish) had barely been touched by the massive settlement of Africans. This meant, as Gelien Matthews shows, that Trinidad's subsequent experience of slavery, between 1807 and emancipation in 1833, was quite different from, say, Jamaica (which had absorbed the largest number of Africans among the British islands). Trinidad, unable after 1807 to buy new Africans, had to find an alternative source of labour for its development. Thus is was that Trinidad (like Demerara/Guyana) turned to large-scale settlement of Indian indentured labour. It was an irony, not lost on her enemies, that Britain's much-vaunted attachment to abolition after 1807 went hand-in-hand with a reliance on indentured Indian labour which was both less than free and which looked suspiciously like slavery itself. The British did not end indentured labour until 1919, by which time some one and a half million people had left India under an indenture.

The history of Indian indentured labour in the West Indies is, of course, not the history of slavery. Yet it does raise troubling questions about Britain's attachment to freedom. Britain took great pride in ending the slave trade in 1807 (and slavery itself in 1833). Thereafter it became the world's most aggressive abolitionist power, obliging others to stop trading in slaves. It did this via foreign office negotiations and the power of the royal navy. Yet, as we have seen, this was not totally successful, even across the Atlantic, nor from East Africa to Arabia.

Slavery survived, thrived even, in any number of places after 1807. The United States was the most spectacular example of a nation which turned its back on slave trading (1808) but which continued to use slave labour. Thanks to the cotton plantations of the South, American slavery boomed as never before. Britain moreover remained involved. Cotton from the South was shipped through New Orleans and Mobile to feed the voracious appetite of Lancashire's cotton mills. Slavery in the United States ended in the bloodshed of the Civil War. In Cuba it survived until 1886, and in Brazil until 1888.

Abolitionists, then, had much to think about after 1807. More immediately they wanted to know: what were the effects of abolition? Would it work? Would it undermine slavery in the Caribbean? But how could anyone actually know or judge the effects of abolition without suitable data? This led after 1813 to the introduction of slave registration, a form of slave census. To ensure international compliance after 1814 Britain forced the question of the abolition into European diplomacy, keeping up diplomatic pressure, often to the irritation of other European powers, in order to enforce international agreement. There were areas of the world where slavery, was so endemic and deeply entrenched, that abolition seemed a lost cause. Yet the British maintained their effort right through the nineteenth century and into the twentieth. The story of that persistent pressure is told in the essay by Mike Kaye of Anti-Slavery International.

Today, Anti-Slavery International is a fearless campaigner the world over against forms of slavery and human trafficking. The very fact that an anti-slavery organization founded in 1823 continues to campaign in 2007 is a salutary reminder of the persistence and scale of the problem. Prostitution rackets, global trafficking, child slavery, unfree and bonded labour, all continue to surprise and shock the public. The Atlantic slave ships have long gone but a global demand for imported, unfree labour continues on a massive scale, and causes enormous human suffering. Hence the work of Anti-Slavery International. All this may seem far removed from the work of that small band of well-meaning men and women who after 1787 set out to end the Atlantic slave trade. However there is a direct and unbroken link between the events which in 1807 culminated in abolition and modern anti-slavery activities.

Abolition in 1807 marked a dramatic break in British history and in British economic practice. Before 1807 the British were *the* greatest maritime slave traders, linking Africa and the Americas. After 1807, the British transformed themselves into the world's greatest and most aggressive abolitionists. Precisely why and how this happened forms the concern of the different essays in this volume. The two hundredth anniversary of the Act of 1807 gives us an opportunity not merely to address some of the puzzling historical questions behind abolition, but it also allows us to think about the role of slavery and the slave trade in the broader setting of British history. If abolition in 1807 was an important reflection of parliamentary will and intent, it was also a function of some dramatic and far-reaching changes in British life itself. And parliament responded to those changes. But 1807 also allows us to look back to the period before abolition, and to remind ourselves that while in 1807 parliament ended the slave trade, for many years it had played a vital role promoting the nation's highly profitable slave interests. Parliament, once so complicit in the slave trade, decided in 1807 that enough was enough: it heeded the views of the British people and ended the slave trade.

Parliament and the Escalation of the Slave Trade, 1690–1714

WILLIAM A. PETTIGREW

There was as pronounced a parliamentary dimension to the escalation of England's slave trade as there was to its abolition. Between 1690 and 1714, and absorbing about the same parliamentary time as discussions of its abolition, parliament persistently debated how the slave trade should be managed. Would a joint-stock monopoly company, the foundering Royal African Company, better promote the export of English goods to Africa and satisfy the colonies' demand for slave labour than an open trade in which any British subject was free to trade in slaves?[1] By 1714 the British slave trade had become entirely deregulated, and its capacity dramatically increased, and the origins of slave trading voyages altered.[2] There are remarkable similarities between the parliamentary debates about the escalation of the slave trade and those concerning its abolition. Both discussions sought to mobilize and respond to public opinion. Both proceeded against the backdrop of war that often delayed proceedings and encouraged, in respective cases, policy-makers to consider the imperial implications of their proposals. There are also similarities between the movement that expanded Britain's slave trade, 'the separate traders', and the group who achieved its abolition. Both movements had a distinctive transatlantic aspect, and both appealed to ideas of free trade. Although the escalation of Britain's slave trade resulted from a legislative vacuum while abolition required a statute, parliamentary consideration contributed equally to both outcomes.

This essay analyzes the effect of parliamentary consideration on the development of the British slave trade. It has two overlapping aims. The first is to offer a better sense of the intentional, parliamentary aspect of slave trade escalation to complement all we know about the parliamentary dimensions of abolition, and to show how, in particular, slave trade escalation depended upon the emergence and interaction of those two historiographical shibboleths of the post-1688 period, the public sphere and parliamentary sovereignty. It argues that notions of political reform and liberty proved as instrumental to the acceleration of England's slave trade as they were to its abolition. Second, this essay aims to show how the legislative process is better examined beyond the narrow confines of statute, the annual session, and parliament itself. The legislative process produced non-statutory results, such as the deregulation of the British slave

---

[1] Strictly speaking, English to 1707.

[2] In 1690, English slavers assembled six Africa trade cargoes, by 1713 they managed 43. See *The Transatlantic Slave Trade. A Database on CD Rom*, ed. David Eltis, David Richardson and Herbert Klein (Cambridge, 1999). I derive all figures relating to slave trade volumes from this dataset. The company's demise allowed Bristol and then Liverpool to later dominate the slave trade.

trade that could be as significant as statutory outcomes. Legislative failure could be a constructive process.[3] The legislative process often involved multiple parliamentary sessions, and what occurred and resulted from activity outside the chamber proved critical to its outcome. Effective policy makers, like the separate traders, had to employ the means to influence both public opinion and its representatives in parliament to ensure the success of their proposal. Extra-parliamentary public opinion was not, on its own, sufficient. This public opinion had to be subjected to the legitimating gaze of formal parliamentary consideration before a legislative vacuum could be tolerated. The essay begins by describing why the Royal African Company brought the Africa trade issue before parliament; it then examines how changes in the political landscape in England after 1688 encouraged opposition to the company, and then compares the company and its opponents as interest groups by analysing their various constituencies, as well as their lobbying tactics.

The demise of absolutist monarchy in England did much to liberate the British slave trade. More than any other monopoly company, the Royal African Company depended on royal patronage. Charles II founded the company in 1672. Its motto *'Regio floret patricionio commercium, commercioque regum'* (Commerce flourishes due to royal protection, and the kingdom due to commerce) made explicit the perceived link between monarchical protection and commercial prosperity. Parliament offered a platform for those who opposed the company's monopoly. In 1679, interlopers in the African trade used parliament to undermine the company as part of a movement to exclude the duke of York, the company's governor, from the succession. But King Charles intervened and prorogued parliament. Other opponents of the company had attempted to lobby the privy council complaining that the company restricted trade and fixed prices. But again, the monarch protected the company by dismissing their petition.[4] After James II's flight from England in 1688, the company became an easy target for anti-monopolists. In 1689, in *Nightingale* v. *Bridges*, Chief Justice Holt ruled that the company's seizure of the cargo of an interloping ship owned by Nightingale was unlawful because its monopoly derived from the prerogative and had been executed through admiralty courts. Holt added that any future enforcement of monopolistic privileges must derive from statute.[5] The company, as a result, paid Nightingale damages and dispatched warnings to its colonial agents not to seize or detain interlopers fearful that doing so would bring about further costly legal reprisals.[6] Depriving the company of the means to enforce its monopoly appeared to many of the company's opponents to offer an official endorsement of independent slave trading. Interloping slave voyages increased dramatically as a result.[7]

---

[3] The constructive implications of legislative failure would serve to embellish the work of Julian Hoppit and Joanna Innes in *Failed Legislation, 1660–1800*, ed. Julian Hoppit (1997).

[4] See Roger Coke, *Reflections upon the East-Indy and Royal African Companies with Animadversion, concerning the Naturalisation of Foreigners* (1695), p. 10.

[5] W. Darrell Stump, 'An Economic Consequence of 1688', *Albion*, VI (1974), 26–35.

[6] T.N.A. (P.R.O.) Treasury Series, 70 Records of the Royal African Company (hereafter T70) vol. 57 (unfoliated): Royal African Company (hereafter R.A.C.) to Henry Carpenter and Thomas Belchamber, 10 Mar. 1691.

[7] In 1690 there was a single interloping voyage. In 1691 there were 11. The total volume of the British slave trade increased from 1,556 in 1690 to 8,336 in 1692.

In January 1690, on the last day of the Convention Parliament, the company therefore petitioned the house of commons to have its monopoly confirmed by statute. This petition inaugurated the Africa trade debates that were to last on and off for nearly a quarter of a century. Between 1690 and 1714, M.P.s discussed the future of the company in 16 parliamentary sessions. The issue produced 206 parliamentary petitions. These arrived from 49 locations covering the length and breadth of Britain and its Atlantic colonies.[8] Over 17,000 signatures appeared on these petitions.[9] The debates also generated close to 200 printed pamphlets circulated by the company and its opponents around coffee houses in the capital, in the provinces, in the colonies, and in the lobby of parliament.[10] The Africa trade issue generated more petitions and pamphlet material and absorbed more parliamentary time than any other economic issue of the period. Out of 16 sessions, however, parliament produced a single temporary statute in 1698 opening up the Africa trade to all on payment of a duty to maintain the company's forts which lasted until 1712. The House ordered ten bills of which, only three progressed beyond a second reading.

Acknowledging the extent of interest in the Africa trade debates need not make parliament's failure to produce a statute surprising. The persistence of legislative failure helps explain the quantity of petitions and pamphlets. But legislative failure also resulted from extensive lobbying. Realizing that an open trade required no statutory backing, the company's opponents lobbied parliament to sustain a legislative vacuum. In relation to economic legislation, statute became synonymous with regulation.[11] Monopoly and other forms of state intervention in the economy required statutes to prescribe the rights of monopoly companies, their jurisdictions and their powers of enforcement. After 1688, parliament became the forum not only for the defeat of monopolies whose charters derived from royal prerogative but also for proposed statutes of regulation branded tyrannical by M.P.s. In 1692, during a discussion concerning the future of the East India Company, Gilbert Heathcote, the scourge of several monopoly companies during this period (including the African company), obtained a motion in the house of commons declaring that all English subjects enjoyed the right to trade to the East Indies unless restricted by statute.[12] Statutes of regulation would therefore be difficult to achieve and the Africa Trade Act of 1698 should be understood as a rare and fragile hybrid that confirmed the right of all English subjects to trade in slaves while temporarily endorsing the importance of regulation to finance the company's forts. Parliament was, in relation to trade, as much a vehicle for public opposition to regulation as an organ that allowed oligarchic interests to govern through statute. If such opposition was successful and deregulation was upheld

---

[8] The debates and petitioning can be followed in *C.J.*, XI–XVI.

[9] These calculations are based on extrapolations from transcriptions of a series of Africa Trade petitions preserved in T70/175.

[10] The company printed about 300 copies of its pamphlets. See T70/58, f 167. Tim Keirn, 'Monopoly, Economic Thought, and The Royal African Company', in *Early Modern Conceptions of Property*, ed. John Brewer and Susan Staves (1995).

[11] Historians' attempts to describe a legislating free trade movement in parliament during the 1690s have not been successful. See for example, George Cherry, 'The Development of the English Free-Trade Movement in Parliament, 1689–1702', *The Journal of Modern History*, XXV (1953).

[12] *C.J.*, XI, 50.

by legislative inertia, the sovereignty of parliament within the reformed constitution increased the likelihood that this legislative vacuum was sustained because other parts of the constitution, like the monarch and privy council, were now less likely to be called upon to resolve disputes like that surrounding the African trade.

Other alterations within the British political landscape after 1688 aided the separate traders. The growing importance of parliament spread the location for political initiative. Government became more responsive to the interests of a more assertive provincial and colonial periphery which wished to prevent the confinement of the lucrative trade in human beings to what they regarded as an over-privileged metropolis. Increased use of petitions to record grievances and to legitimize requests for reform saw the company under siege from multiple interests. The separate traders obtained 61 petitions from the English provinces in comparison to 11 for the company.[13] Similarly, the Act of Union and the expectations it produced amongst Scottish commercial interests encouraged them to lobby parliament when they believed the capital engrossed economic opportunity. Scottish boroughs submitted nine petitions, all against the company. Widespread colonial opposition to the company also became more effective as more means for colonial interests to influence the metropolitan political process emerged. Colonial interests began to cultivate particular M.P.s and petition the House as parliament became the undisputed arbiter of overseas commercial concerns. The company's deputy governor, Thomas Pindar, wrote to its colonial agents informing them: 'it will be difficult to preserve this Trade unless the Plantations make application that it may be done'.[14] Thirty colonial petitions in favour of open trade appeared in contrast to the three received in favour of monopoly. Throughout the dispute, the reformed board of trade gathered colonial and domestic opinion about the future of the slave trade. In 1708, the board asked the colonial governors for information about the African trade in their respective colonies and to canvass colonial preference in the debate between company and open trade.[15] Despite being an adjunct of the executive, the board operated like a select committee of the house of commons and wrote reports which, in channelling anti-company colonial opinion, provided authority for the separate traders' cause. Metropolitan interest in colonial affairs evolved symbiotically with greater colonial means to influence the metropolitan political process.[16] Both favoured the company's opponents.

Because the company required a statute to confirm its monopoly and its opponents did not, the most important distinction between the two interest groups is that the company was a proactive lobbyist and its opponents were usually reactive. One pro-company pamphleteer pointed out that before the 1698 act, separate traders preferred obstructing African company bills to submitting their own:

> Ever since the Parliament voted that it was the undoubted Right of all the subjects of England to Trade to Foreign Parts – none of those Free Traders have ever

---

[13] For the increased incidence of provincial petitions see Perry Gauci, *The Politics of Trade* (Oxford, 2000), pp. 214–15.

[14] T70/58, ff.332–5: R.A.C. to Gawin Corbin.

[15] The inquiry can be followed in, *Documents Illustrative of the History of the Slave Trade*, ed. Elizabeth Donnan (4 vols, Washington D.C., 1930–5), II, 44.

[16] See Alison Olson, *Making the Empire Work* (Cambridge, Mass., 1992), pp. 51–75.

brought to the Parliament a Bill to settle this Trade, but still opposed what was offered by the Company . . . because those free traders . . . had just cause to believe that under such a Regulation, whatsoever it should be, they must pay towards what by the Parliament should be thought necessary for the general interest of that trade whereas if they continue that heavy load upon the African Company only by opposing this bill, they should then enjoy their trade without that expense.[17]

The company's opponents initiated proceedings in parliament in only three out of 17 sessions. Daniel Defoe argued that when the separate traders did propose legislation, they formulated schemes sufficiently outlandish to prevent success and maintain the legislative vacuum: 'they car'd not whether the Parliament did any thing or no, provided they did but delay the company; for then they knew the thing would fall into their hands of course, the company not being able to stand of themselves, without some act was passed in their favour, which they had nothing to do but to prevent.'[18]

Whether proactive or reactive, both the company and the separate traders' parliamentary clout depended upon their success at mobilizing support. Both interest groups had three potential constituencies: first, the membership constituency of those whose economic concerns were inseparably and indefinitely tied to both organizations; the beneficiary constituency of those who chose to trade with each as either suppliers or customers; and the sympathizing constituency of economically disinterested individuals who could be compelled or persuaded to lobby on behalf of each group.

The company's membership comprised four separate groups: its directors (the court of assistants), its other shareholders, its creditors and its debtors which gave the company a potential membership constituency of several hundred. The court of assistants included 24 prominent shareholders. Eighteen were also M.P.s during the Africa trade debates, twice the equivalent for the separate traders. The company had a hierarchical management structure that could compel directors or company servants to arrange petitions and write pamphlets. In 1707, at the beginning of the second phase of the African trade debates, the company had just over 400 shareholders. The shareholders provided a capital pool from which the company could divert cash to finance the writing and printing of petitions and pamphlets and the various backhanders to parliamentary servants and lobbies attending parliament on their behalf.[19] The company requested that its shareholders cultivate M.P.s to support it in parliament. On occasions, however, shareholders acted on behalf of the company without direction from the court of assistants.[20]

The weakness of the company's economic position enlarged its membership constituency. Inability to collect debts in the colonies enabled the company to compel their debtors to lobby on its behalf.[21] Because the company ceased from

---

[17] *Considerations relating to the African Bill* (1698), p. 3.

[18] Daniel Defoe, *An Essay Upon the Trade to Africa*, (1711), p. 25.

[19] For details of the charges involved see T70/112, ff. 16, 34.

[20] T70/9, (unfoliated): Richard King to R.A.C., 13 Nov. 1708.

[21] T70/57 (unfoliated): R.A.C. to Prideaux, 23 Feb. 1697.

1708 to pay interest on their bonds, its creditors became powerful pro-monopoly lobbyists. They numbered approximately 200 at the height of the Africa trade dispute. When short of funds, the company paid its suppliers in bonds. This expanded its network of creditor lobbyists. Many of the creditors were former suppliers of the company, especially shipwrights and gunsmiths.[22] The creditors petitioned parliament on ten occasions in favour of the company and helped stall legislation to dissolve it by convincing parliament such moves were contrary to its traditional role as the protector of property.

In terms of size of group membership the company dwarfed the separate traders. Between 1707 and 1713 those separate traders actively trading ranged in number from 50 and 100.[23] Neither the company's nor the separate traders' membership constituencies, however, could be relied upon to lobby on their behalf. The company used its political campaigns as an opportunity to request further subscriptions from its shareholders. They rightly believed that their cause looked more convincing to M.P.s when they enjoyed a sound financial footing. By advertizing the effect that parliamentary establishment would have on its share price, the company could encourage shareholders to lobby on its behalf, increasing its capital at the same time as strengthening its political base. Only half of the independent slave traders acted as lobbyists by either signing separate trader petitions or appearing on their behalf in parliament or at the board of trade.[24] Many traded only once and therefore did not need to defend the interests of independent slave trading. Others sometimes traded with the company and did not wish to jeopardize this relationship by publically supporting its opponents. Without a means of compelling independent slave traders to contribute, the separate traders concentrated on cultivating their suppliers and customers.

Among the leadership of the politically active separate traders, there was some division of labour. Robert Heysham, a prominent Barbados sugar trader and M.P. for Lancaster, oversaw petitioning and parliamentary affairs, and Richard Harris and Humphrey Morice (both Jamaica sugar merchants), wrote pamphlets, reports, and appeared before the board of trade. Their members' firms offered infrastructure for the separate traders' political operation. Richard Harris and Co. served as the deposit account for funds submitted by provincial interests to help finance the company's parliamentary lobby.[25] They appeared collectively to lobby at Westminster in both chambers and in the Court of Requests.[26] They were a more diffuse, flexible organization that better suited their reactive remit.

As a petitioning interest, the company relied on its membership constituency. Of the 74 pro-company petitions, member constituents signed 44. The separate traders, by comparison, proved more effective at mobilizing others to support their cause. Only five of the separate traders' 135 petitions were signed by the separate traders themselves. Their beneficiary constituency was far larger than the company's because their collective trade was so much more impressive in scale. This was essential for a

---

[22] T70/88, f. 270.

[23] T70/1199.

[24] T70/175; *Journal of the Commissioners for Trade and Plantations*, I–IV *passim*.

[25] Bristol R.O., Merchant Venturers Hall Books: 6 Oct. 1710 and 8 Oct. 1711

[26] T70/9: John Hooks to R.A.C. 16 Nov. 1709.

good parliamentary reception because the larger the beneficiary constituency the more difficult it was for opponents to brand the movement self-interested which, because they were independent traders, often happened.[27] The separate traders enjoyed the support of 130 independent petitions in comparison to the company's 30. The geographical reach of the separate traders' petitioning constituency was far larger than the company's. Seventy-three of their petitions arrived from the provinces compared with eight for the company. The separate traders benefited from 27 from the colonies compared with the company's 11. Although the company enjoyed a network of representatives in all of the major outports and all British American colonies, its poor trading record prevented them from gathering signatories for the petitions that the company dispatched to them. Its colonial respondents described how much easier it would be to gather signatories if the company supplied sufficient quantities of slaves.[28] The company relied excessively on petitions from its metropolitan suppliers. Its support emanated from the manufacturing and planting interests as opposed to the overwhelmingly mercantile profile of the separate traders' petitioning interest.[29] Parliamentary consideration served to publicize the breadth of opposition to the company.

The separate traders placed more value on the number of signatures than their 'quality' as the company did. In September, 1709, the Royal African Company's agents in Barbados enclosed a petition 'of ye Best Characters and Estates in ye Island and are now owners of $\frac{2}{3}$ of ye Land and Negroes'. They went on to recount how the governor bowed to William Heysham's (Robert's brother and business partner in Barbados) interest and had his militia officers rally their 'common soldiers' to sign a separate trader petition which was 'Kept out of Town and signed by Servants and Such'. 'Had we thought', they went on, 'the number of hands and not the quality we could easily out done them . . . [and] could had all the sailors in the five men of war which are in much better circumstances than [r]ough servants hardly a degrees above slaves.'[30] Whether this was true or not, by 1711 the company, perhaps desperate, perhaps enlightened by the separate traders' approach, advised its agent in Exeter: 'if the Governing part of the city will not join with the Company get the hands of the workmen concerned in you manufactures and return it . . .'[31] Excluding their own petitions, those that supported open trade contained nearly 8,000 signatories compared to the company's 2,500. The separate traders' political repertoire better suited the post-1688 political climate in which appeals to broadly-based public opinion legitimized proposals for change.[32]

Defoe believed that the separate traders imposed on their provincial contacts and watched with amazement: 'the clamours of the petitions which they have rais'd, (as

---

[27] Charles Davenant, *Reflections Upon the Constitution and Management of the African Trade* (1709), p. 130.

[28] T70/8, f. 116: John Hussam to R.A.C.

[29] A minute from a house of lords discussion in 1713 reads: 'The rich men seem for an open trade, the planters for a separate trade because the company trusted them.' H.M.C., *Lords MSS*, X, 173–4.

[30] Bodl., Rawlinson MSS, A312, f. 7: 3 Sept 1709.

[31] T70/44, (unfoliated): R.A.C. to Matthew Barrett, 1 Mar 1711.

[32] For the emergence of an idea of the public and the ensuing tension between quality and quantity of signatories to petitions see Mark Knights, *Representation and Misrepresentation in Later Stuart Britain* (Oxford, 2005), pp. 5, 96, 137.

witches do the Devil) from the several counties of England, and made the poor people say any thing they bid them'.[33] The separate traders, however, received 33 petitions from provincial civic bodies such as borough corporations and mercantile interest groups like the Bristol Society of Merchant Venturers that were likely to resist attempts by metropolitan interests to represent them. Such groups often sent their own interests to monitor the progress of the Africa trade debates.[34] Their petitions purported to be responses to hearing of African Company attempts to achieve a monopolizing statute. It is unclear whether this was the sound of separate trader cultivation or not. Robert Heysham, however, wrote to both colonial and provincial civic bodies to arrange petitions. In January 1709, the company's agent in Liverpool informed Africa House 'that this post Mr Heysham has written to Captain Clayton to Get a petition from that Town against the Company'.[35] The following February the company wrote back expressing their surprise that Heysham could have orchestrated William Clayton, Liverpool's M.P, to gather a petition from its corporation 'which is a thing very uncommon'.[36] Heysham also wrote to several other M.P.s and obtained a petition from Chester in February 1709. Such lobbying helped the separate traders to recruit sympathizing M.P.s to their banner while gathering beneficiary petitions. The separate traders proved more imaginative and successful as cultivators of influential petitioning interests than the company.

Not all petitions came from beneficiary constituents. Some interests needed persuading. The company wrote letters and circulated pamphlets to colonial contacts to convince planters that it represented their interests and suggested that they send their own petitions to parliament, perhaps because it did not receive any petitions spontaneously from civic bodies. This proved fruitless. So the company began to send its own petitions, for which it hoped its colonial and provincial agents would gather signatures. Conscious of the importance of appearing to cultivate rather than co-ordinate petitions, a company official chastized one of its agents for failing to alter the texts of a series of petitions which because of their similarity suggested a lack of sincerity.[37] To give the impression of disinterested support, the great majority of the petitions that the company sent to the colonies to be signed did not explicitly support the company but, instead, argued that the 1698 Act raised the price of slaves and reduced their supply. These neutral petitions helped the company to deflect charges that its campaign appeared self-interested in the absence of any spontaneous petitioning. The company put considerable energy into cultivating petitions but its requests, because of its trading inanity, fell largely on deaf ears.

Cultivated and spontaneous petitions had different effects once presented in parliament. The company was unable to cultivate sufficient petitions to catalyze its own legislative proposals. Cultivated counter-petitions from the separate traders often

---

[33] *Review*, 22 Mar. 1712.

[34] T70/45: Jacob Reynardson to R.A.C. 26 Feb. 1713. See also Merchant Venturers Hall Books, 10 Nov. 1713 which describes how the Bristol Merchant Venturers provided the Bristol M.P., Joseph Earle, with 'a butt of sherry wyne' to be distributed to further the interests of the company's opponents.

[35] T70/9: Jasper Mauditt to R.A.C., 28 Jan. 1709.

[36] T70/44: R.A.C. to Jasper Mauditt, 8 Feb. 1709. This petition appeared in parliament on 20 Dec. 1709. William Clayton's was the first signature on the petition.

[37] T70/58, f. 501: R.A.C. to John Hussam.

ensured the defeat of company measures.[38] Spontaneous petitions in support of open trade, however, often complicated legislative measures because they had not been assembled to co-ordinate with existing legislative action in parliament.[39] This was especially true for the Africa trade dispute because it affected so many interest groups. In this way, parliament's remit as a vehicle for representation impeded its newfound role as the most important organ of government. Petitioning then, although critical to the commencement of the legislative process in this case, usually served to directly defeat or inadvertently to complicate proceedings. In both cases, the greater incidence of petitioning to parliament increased the chances of legislative failure and therefore favoured the company's opponents.

Mobilizing this petitioning beneficiary interest offered one means of accruing sympathy within parliament by convincing it that their cause represented a broadly-based, 'national interest'. Persuasion offered another avenue. Both sides sought to cultivate particular M.P.s. The support of powerful individuals or groups of individuals could prove critical to the fortunes of each movement. The company worked hard to cultivate the favour of the monarch, giving shares to William III and seeking the support of Queen Anne. But neither intervened conclusively on its behalf in the parliamentary debates. The company benefited from the care of Robert Harley who during the 1690s had presented a pro-company petition. But his support later resulted from his connexion with the South Sea Company whose existence confirmed the company's demise, although its directorate could be relied upon to lobby against legislation that might intrude on the Royal African Company trading opportunities.[40] In the end, no company proposal received the favour of the sort of personnel who could guarantee its realization.

Pamphleteering was another method used by both sides to persuade disinterested individuals inside and outside the parliament to support their cause. Both parties exploited the press to mobilize the opinion of an emerging critical public whose contribution increasingly legitimized requests for reform such as the desire to liberalize the African trade. The resultant Africa trade literature ranged from tomes to single-sided briefs. Of those that were clearly partisan, the company produced the majority. As a proactive lobbyist in need of a statute, the company had more of a case to make and employed experienced pamphleteers including Daniel Defoe and Charles Davenant to write in support of its monopoly.[41] The separate traders wrote their own pamphlets.[42] The company's literature was longer and more theoretical in contrast to the separate traders who prided themselves on their direct experience of trade and often simply reproduced the facts of their superior trading record. The company achieved some success as a propagandist. On its sending pamphlets to Portsmouth in March 1709, its agent reported that he had 'placed them in noted Coffee houses

[38] This occurred in 1690, 1693–94, 1694–95, 1707–8 and 1708/9.

[39] This seems to have occurred in 1709–10 and 1710–11.

[40] T70/52, f. 332: R.A.C. to John Clark, 14 Aug. 1713: 'By this interest we have now acquired you may rest assured no act of Parliament will ever pass in favour of interlopers for an open trade.'

[41] Defoe received payment from the R.A.C. See T. Keirn, 'Daniel Defoe and the Royal African Company', *Historical Research*. LXI (1988), 243–7. It is not clear whether Davenant was paid.

[42] Bank of England Archives, Morice Papers: Nicholas Morice to Humphrey Morice, 25 Mar. 1709 T70/52, f. 332.

where the trading People are, which they find much to the satisfaction of Several Gentlemen who before concurd with ye private Traders printed Pamphlets'.[43] But this satisfaction did not translate into either sufficient public support for the company to obtain a statute or enough public resentment of the ensuing legislative vacuum to prevent the deregulation of the slave trade after 1712. The separate traders used parliament as a means to publicize the financial and economic failings of the company which lessened the value of its stock, and to broadcast the economic and political benefits of an open trade. Parliamentary deliberation authenticated these conclusions and, in being printed and circulated, they entered the public sphere and influenced public opinion which proved critical to the acceptance of the legislative vacuum after 1712.

The company and its opponents debated in print which of their respective positions better suited the 'people', or the 'publick', or the 'national interest' and both argued that they represented broadly based interests.[44] These tracts often inflected the narrow debate between the company and the separate traders with ideological flourishes designed to associate the dispute with broader concerns that might grab the attention and support of disinterested parties. The strength of the company's ties with the displaced regime led its critics to couch their opposition in constitutional terms. One pamphleteer described how the interlopers' political wing: 'have now broken in upon [the company] . . . under a pretence of their zeale for the publick rights and liberties of the subject'.[45] These rights and liberties included the right to pursue one's own economic self-interest. Without any appreciation of the irony of the language, another pamphlet asserted that monopolies were 'the Badges of a slavish People, . . . nothing hitherto but an English Freedom has been wanting to extend the Trade'.[46] The company argued that such unrestrained pursuit of self-interest would compromise the public good.

Such rhetoric need not, however, attribute a party aspect to the dispute between the company and the separate traders with the tories favouring the former and the whigs the latter, as one historian has argued.[47] Both factions used similar language. Of the membership constituencies, a third of the company directors in parliament were whigs and nearly half of the parliamentary separate traders were tories, including their leader, Robert Heysham. Party networks did not provide a decisive means for either faction to mobilize sympathetic constituents. When cultivating M.P.s, the company lobbied M.P.s of both party persuasions.[48] Twenty-eight per cent of those supporting the company in parliament were whigs and 41 per cent of those supporting the separate traders were tories. The separate traders received support from staunchly tory boroughs like Totnes as well as whig constituencies. The company failed to fasten its cause to a party majority to gain a parliamentary statute. The separate traders therefore

[43] T70/9: James Arnold to R.A.C., 15 Mar. 1709.

[44] For emphasis on the importance of the 'publick' see *Considerations Upon the Trade to Guinea* for the importance of appeasing the 'people' see *The Case Between the African Company and the People of England*. For the company's argument that it was broadly based see: *A Proposal for settling the trade to Africa*.

[45] B.L., Harleian MS 3710, f. 238.

[46] *A Letter to a Member of Parliament Concerning the African Trade* (1709).

[47] Keirn, 'Monopoly', p. 430.

[48] T70/9: 5 Feb 1709.

did not need to incite the rage of party to counter the company. The expansion of Britain's slave trade, like its abolition, had cross-party appeal.

Because they provided its best argument in favour of a statute, the company, in the pamphlet and petition debate, sought to focus parliamentary attention on its African forts. This also enabled the company to distract M.P.s from the weakness of its record as an exporter of English goods and an importer of slaves in the plantations and also prevented the company from straying into territory that would leave it vulnerable to attack from an increasingly assertive plantation interest. The company supposed that its forts were indispensable to trade and mandatory for preserving the British interest on the African coast by preventing the encroachment of rival European nations' African operations. Such notions appealed to M.P.s during wartime. The company deliberately over-dramatized the condition of its African forts in the hope that this would compel parliament to act. The company informed its agents in Africa of its strategy:

> Our application to Parliament the last year was almost over before any notice was taken of the African Trade, which occasioned us to represent the danger of its being lost. Upon which the house of commons addressed her maj[esty] praying her care of the settlements and the trade, till some other provision be made by Parliament for the same, whereupon her majesty has been pleas'd to direct that two men of war should be forth with sent to the coast, and to be followed by two others.[49]

Frustrated by their lack of success in parliament, the company welcomed the opportunity to appeal to its traditional constitutional ally, the monarchy. In implementing this arrangement, the company also achieved a higher profile with ministry figures.[50] Realizing the public support that the company had accrued for its forts, the separate traders did not, by the end of the Africa trade dispute, propose to dissolve the company, which experience had taught them involved many legislative pitfalls. The separate traders allowed the company to survive without statutory protection to offer further evidence, when needed, of the disadvantages of a monopolistically organized Africa trade, until it was dissolved by act in 1750 and the government took control of the African forts. It made far more sense for the separate traders to allow the company to survive knowing that it did not represent serious competition.

The proposed content of legislation offered means to gather extra support or alienate members concerned about the practicality of proposed legislation. Impractical legislation could derail a movement that appeared convincing by virtue of being broadly based. This occurred in 1712, the only session when M.P.s voted on a regulated company bill. The company's creditors lobbied to convince M.P.s that the separate traders' bill appeared inadequate because it failed to take account of those interests that would be dispossessed by its terms. However such oversight could be deliberate. Defoe accused the separate traders of formulating legislative proposals that aimed at failure by being over-ambitious and/or vague: 'I cannot say the vigour of the Company has gain'd the victory; but the difficulty, or rather impossibility of the

---

[49] T70/52, f. 254: R.A.C. to Seth Grosvenor and James Phipps, 4 Oct. 1711.
[50] T70/44: R.A.C. to George Mason, 26 July 1711.

chimerical settlements some men have proposed, has given the death blow to all their attempts.'[51] The company echoed Defoe in a petition to Queen Anne on 3 December 1710: 'some few Private Traders for selfish and particular ends had the art of propagating and imposing impractical notions on some members of the legislature in such a manner and possessing them with very groundless prejudice against the Company, that both the sessions terminated without any actual care being taken for the preservation of the Trade'.[52] Such filibustering helped ensure a legislative vacuum once the 1698 act expired in 1712.

Nevertheless, the Africa trade was in a confused state after the expiration of the 1698 act. Despite both sides believing that expiration favoured their cause, both remained uncomfortable about the legislative vacuum in the short term. The expiration appeared to favour the separate traders, because the ten per cent duty had expired with the act of 1698. But the separate traders attempted further legislation in 1713. In a pamphlet supporting their 1713 Open Trade Bill the author remarked: 'Without this bill the African trade remains very precarious; and no man can tell whether to enter into it, or to continue it when he is in.'[53] Company officials, however, argued that the act allowed a unification between the company and its creditors and offered clear parliamentary countenance to its charter, and therefore its monopoly. The company dispatched warnings to separate traders not to interlope in the African trade without license from the company citing an infringement of the royal prerogative now that the management of the Africa trade, as they saw it, reverted back to its charter.[54]

It became apparent, however, by the summer of 1713 that the company was in no position to enforce its monopoly and that there existed widespread public support for an open trade, without any statutory confirmation. A company pamphlet recorded the effects of a separate trading explosion on the coast of Africa despite the failure of their open trade bill: 'These gentlemen have, with a high hand, taken their swill of liberty, and have made a full experiment what they can do for the nation and themselves, even as much as if they had had their Darling Act.'[55] Thomas Stewart, a company official, reported in June 1713 that there appeared on the African coast 'more interlopers and other ships than have been known at one time, that they were neither encouraged nor molested by the factors'.[56] Other Royal African Company agents in the colonies confirmed that the separate traders had vowed to continue trading without license from the company due to 'encouragement from England' that combined extra-parliamentary acceptance of open trade with a refusal (inside and outside the legislature) to sustain the company's monopoly.[57] By June 1714 company stock dropped to 37 pence 'which is lower that at any time hither to it has been and

---

[51] *Review*, 8 June 1710.

[52] T70/175, ff. 200–1: petition to the queen, 3 Dec. 1710.

[53] *The Present Case of the Africa Trade Truly Stated*.

[54] For the belief that the Creditors' Act supported the company's charter see *The Case of About One Thousand Africa-creditors now united with the company, by virtue of the late Act of Parliament* (1713). For the company's warning to interlopers see T70/58, ff. 418–19: loose sheet print mark 214.

[55] *A Letter from one of the Royal African Company's Chief Agents on the African Coasts*.

[56] T70/8, 135: Barbados agents to R.A.C.

[57] T70/8, 128: Barbados agents to R.A.C.

declining'.[58] Distracted by the misplaced expectation that the ill-fated contract it had obtained from the South Sea Company in 1713 would solve its financial problems, the Royal African Company hardly watched as the separate traders, buoyed by broad public support, destroyed its market share. In 1686, prior to the Africa trade debates in parliament, the company's market share of England's slave trade had been 86 per cent. By 1730, the separate traders had eroded that figure down to one per cent.

The separate traders' triumph over the company resulted partly from a lobbying strategy that reflected an astute appreciation of the post-1688 political process and partly from constitutional changes that underpinned that process. They sought sufficient support from their constituents to influence the legislative vacuum but not so much that they prevented a vaccuum from existing by achieving a statute in their favour. The separate traders encouraged parliamentary deliberation but discouraged parliamentary resolution. They steered a middle course in parliament that aimed at achieving non-statutory legislative concessions that would modify public opinion in favour of open trade and ensure that the legislative vacuum was tolerated. These concessions accrued more public significance the more interest in parliament increased after 1688. They were meaningful because of the ritualized nature of parliamentary deliberation. Once a legislative proposal had reached a certain stage, it gathered legitimacy even if the proposal ultimately failed. But because the company would require the juridical as opposed to legitimizing control of a statute, these concessions were of less use to them and were, because of the weakness of their position both economically and politically, less frequent. Several parliamentary resolutions in support of the forts, however, informed the separate traders' strategic decision to shy away from dissolving the company completely.

These non-statutory legislative concessions came in several forms. First, and perhaps most important, was the precedent established by the act of 1698 which could be deemed a non-statutory concession after its expiration in 1712. The Africa Trade Act proved that open trade expanded British exports to Africa, imports of enslaved Africans to America, and the Atlantic colonial commodity trades. One separate trader pamphlet argued that this act had been designed to prepare the way for unregulated trade.[59] The second were the board of trade reports. Charles Davenant noted how the board's findings in early 1709 offered much needed legitimacy to the separate traders' cause and 'the Transcribing them by way of report and intermixing them with such accounts as were demanded of ye Royal African Company, has happened to give them some more seeming authority than can reasonably be supposed to have been ever intended by the Lords Commissioners'. Davenant observed how such legitimacy proved influential with public opinion and helped, in turn, to influence the political process 'for the Separate Traders have taken occasion, from thence to print certain paragraphs of there [sic] own base allegations by way of Extracts out of the said report, as vouchers to gain Credit to the very same allegations again without doors'.[60]

---

[58] T70/45: 3 June 1714.

[59] *The Case of the Separate Traders to Africa with Remarks on the African Company's Memorial.*

[60] T70/175, ff. 87–96: *Some General Observations and Particular Remarks on the Report made by the Lords Commissioners for Trade and Plantations the 3rd February, 1708 Touching the Contents of the Royal African Company's Petition Referred to them by her Majesty.*

The third were the parliamentary votes and resolutions, which occurred throughout the debates and allowed the separate traders to convince many outside parliament that they enjoyed parliamentary favour.[61] Such resolutions were often printed which made them more influential outside the chamber. They conferred pseudo-statutory legitimacy on parliamentary proposals in the absence of a statute. A petition from Exeter cited how a resolution in favour of a regulated company in a previous session had: 'so far encouraged the petitioners, that it gave a new life to their trade, and some thousands of pieces ... made more than usual, and the price advanced from eleven shillings and six-pence per piece to fifteen shillings and six-pence per piece'.[62] One separate trader described the effect that non-statutory legislative concessions would have on the company's share price: 'a bill ... to be read once or twice in the house of Parliament, [would affect the stock] as well if it should not pass as if it should'.[63] The resolutions confirmed, especially when originating from the committee of the whole House, that there existed broad parliamentary approval for the proposed scheme and that its translation into statute would be undone by disagreement over the legislation's fine print. One pamphlet complained how the company's assumption that the law of the African trade revert to its 1672 charter after the expiration of the 1698 act proceeded 'without any regard to the many resolutions of this honourable house repeated last session, viz. that the African trade ought to be free and open to all her majesty's subjects', and went on to admit: ''Tis true the bill for the National Trade did not pass last year, but even the adversaries thereto did agree, 'twas not because they were against an open Trade, but that some clauses in that bill were excepted against.'[64] This pamphleteer believed a non-statutory legislative concession from parliament commanded more public authority than a charter derived from royal prerogative. The separate traders also used these concessions on the African coast to convince African traders not to deal with the company.[65] The open trade bills themselves offered further evidence of parliamentary support and provided some of the information about how the trade might function without a statute. The separate traders' victory was to convince the public at large that they could operate the trade, unlike the company, without statutory approval. These non-statutory legislative concessions helped them achieve this outcome.

Parliament therefore proved as instrumental to the escalation of Britain's slave trade as it was to the trade's abolition nearly a century later even though escalation received no statutory endorsement. The full-scale British slave trade began as well as ended with a flood of pamphlets and an army of lobbyists. The separate traders operated more effectively within the post-1688 constitution than the Royal African Company. Political reform therefore helped to escalate the British slave trade. A revolution associated with a Declaration of Rights celebrating the 'indubitable rights and liberties of the people' proved critical to the development of an open trade

---

[61] T70/8, f. 106: 'The inhabitants think it in Vain to Sign Any More Papers in favour of the Company Since ye Parliament Countenance ye Separate Traders'.

[62] *Petition of Mayor, Aldermen, and Common Councilmen of the City of Exon 9th December, 1691.*

[63] T.N.A., CO 388/11, f. 16: Richard Harris to the board of trade.

[64] This view was commonplace. See *The Case of the National Traders to Africa* (1714); see also *The Anatomy of the African Company's scheme for carrying on that trade in a joint-stock exclusive.*

[65] T70/52, f. 223: R.A.C. to Sir Dalby Thomas.

in human beings. Acknowledging the similar part played by public opinion and parliament in the escalation and abolition of Britain's transatlantic slave trade need not taint the history of parliament. It confirms that parliament could be responsive to shifting public opinion and celebrates the achievement of the abolitionists in affecting that shift.

The Africa trade debates also shed new light on the late Stuart legislative process. They show how the public sphere and the sovereign parliament interacted in the context of state regulation of the economy. The British slave trade evolved without regulation because more broadly-based interests lobbied parliament to defeat the company's attempts to restrict the trade, because parliamentary sovereignty made it more likely that such legislative failure would mean legislative vacuum and because the separate traders used parliament to influence public opinion to ensure that the legislative vacuum and the resultant unregulated slave trade would endure.

The Africa trade debates also prove that parliament was a forum that offered the means to defeat statute as much as an institution of legislation. Statute, the traditional measure of legislative success, usually resulted from parliament acting as an institution of *government*. Statute often derived from monarchical or oligarchic interests who wished to regulate and restrict the economy. Legislative failure either resulted from parliament's failure to govern or, as in the case of the African trade debates, its success as a *representational* body for diverse interests. Parliamentary sovereignty decreased the chances of other branches of the constitution resolving an issue left unresolved by parliament and non-statutory legislative concessions helped ensure acceptance of the legislative vacuum. Parliamentary consideration offered a means for groups to preserve the legislative vacuum and with it, in this case, their economic interests. If it had not been instrumental to the escalation of the enslavement of human beings, legislative failure might, in this case, be rebranded as a victory for representation and consent.

The British Government and the Slave Trade: Early Parliamentary Enquiries, 1713–83

CHRISTOPHER L. BROWN

In what ways did parliament influence the British slave trade during the eighteenth century? How did the politics of the Atlantic slave trade figure in parliamentary politics in the years when the British seized the largest share of the international traffic in African labour? In the present state of research, such questions remain surprisingly difficult to answer for most of the eighteenth century, in between the prolonged controversies that shaped the slave trade in its early years and at its close. The British slave trade became the subject of sustained controversy twice in its history, as most scholars long have known. In the first instance, in the quarter-century after the Glorious Revolution of 1688, the central questions concerned the organization of the trade to Africa. Who would have the right to participate in the slave trade and under what terms? Did the Royal African Company, which had enjoyed a monopoly in the Africa trade, best serve the interests of the nation and the state?[1] In the second, more famous instance, between 1788 and 1806, the opponents of the slave trade and its defenders contended over its fate.[2] That preoccupation with the Africa trade, both in its early years and during its last, contrasts markedly with the state of public and official debate in the intervening decades. From 1713 to 1787, when the British slave trade reached its apex, the traffic in African captives only rarely became the subject of sustained discussion in parliament.

For this reason, perhaps, the political history of the British slave trade for most of the eighteenth century remains almost wholly unknown. Instead, when studying these years, scholars justifiably emphasize how the slave trade worked – who participated, how it was organized and financed, where it was conducted, and with what consequences for Africa, Africans, and the colonial societies in the Americas. The place of parliament – and the British imperial state more generally – in the development

---

[1] K. G. Davies, *The Royal African Company* (1957), pp. 122–52; Tim Keirn, 'Monopoly, Economic Thought, and the Royal African Company', in *Early Modern Conceptions of Property*, ed. John Brewer and Susan Staves (1996), pp. 427–66. 'Between 1689 and 1714,' Kenneth Morgan observes, 'Parliament debated legislation or enquired into the organization of the British trade to Africa in fifteen separate sessions and the printed literature on the company's monopoly generated 198 titles.' *The British Atlantic Slave Trade, Volume 2: The Royal African Company* ed. K. Morgan (2003), p. xviii. Also see William A. Pettigrew, 'Parliament and the Escalation of the Slave Trade, 1690–1714', in this volume.

[2] From a very large literature, see in particular, Roger Anstey, *The Atlantic Slave Trade and British Abolition, 1760–1810* (1975), parts III and IV; Seymour Drescher, *Capitalism and Antislavery. British Mobilization in Comparative Perspective* (1987); J.R. Oldfield, *Popular Politics and British Anti-Slavery. The Mobilisation of Public Opinion against the Slave Trade, 1787–1807* (Manchester, 1995); Judith Jennings, *The Business of Abolishing the British Slave Trade, 1783–1807* (1997); and Adam Hochschild, *Bury the Chains. Prophets and Rebels in the Fight to Free an Empire's Slaves* (Boston and New York, 2005), parts II and III.

of the Atlantic slave trade receives only the most cursory acknowledgment. So we are left in the odd position of knowing that the British slave trade mattered to the emerging wealth and power of the British empire, but not how, or even if, it mattered to the governing *élite*.

This is, in part, the fault of how the politics of the slave system, and commercial and imperial questions more generally, tend to be treated by historians of eighteenth-century Britain. Practices like the slave trade, it sometimes is assumed, have a political history only when they become embroiled in political controversies. And so the measure of their political importance is often judged by the intensity of public debate and the time and effort devoted to a topic in parliament. In this conception, political history takes place when political change occurs, or the prospects for political change appear. Political stability, the absence of debate or political controversy, by contrast, marks the terminal point of political history, or alternatively the space from which to track the emergence of new political controversies, but only rarely itself becomes the subject of historical analysis. Yet, political stability should interest us as much as political change, not only for what it reveals about earlier and later political controversies, but also because political stability, too, results from political processes. The forces, conditions, and interests that sustain a set of practices, the circumstances that prevent a subject from becoming controversial, should also become the subject of political history. What accounts, then, for the lack of public and official interest in the Africa trade during the middle decades of the eighteenth century? On the rare occasion that the British slave trade did draw comment, what were the context and the content of these concerns?

An answer to these two questions may further elucidate the peculiar place of the Atlantic slave trade in eighteenth-century British culture, as well as in Hanoverian politics. For the apparent tension between the importance of the slave trade to the empire and the limited official interest in its operation would seem to mirror a larger ambivalence about what the Africa trade meant to the nation as a whole. Most knew of its importance to imperial wealth and power. And many knew of its contribution to mercantile fortunes in London, Bristol, and Liverpool. Yet the institution, as a conventional and routine aspect of overseas enterprise in the eighteenth century, elicited few public reflections, discussion, or comment. It never became a regular subject of praise or condemnation among novelists, or poets, or chroniclers. It did not become enmeshed in narratives of imperial greatness or, until the very end of the period, fears of national decline. That absence from the cultural imagination stands in contrast to the treatment of colonial slavery, which inspired verse, fiction, and song in Britain by the middle decades of the eighteenth century.[3] By comparison, in the cultural realm, the Atlantic slave trade almost seemed not to exist. One could savour the fruits of slave labour, witness the wealth generated by slaving fortunes, count the ships headed to African waters, and encounter Africans on the street, and yet not muse at all upon the international trade in African labour that made such experiences possible. For most of the British nation, as well as for most members of parliament, the African slave trade was at once fundamental and almost entirely invisible.

---

[3] See, for example, the excerpts assembled in James G. Basker, *Amazing Grace. An Anthology of Poems About Slavery, 1660–1810* (New Haven, 2002).

Typically, during the eighteenth century, there were a few in the house of commons who took a special interest in the African trade. Two who entered parliament after the Seven Years' War had worked as British agents in Africa earlier in their careers. The merchant William Devaynes, member of parliament for Barnstaple, served as director of the East India Company and a principal government contractor during the era of the American Revolution. Before then, though, from 1751 to 1762, Devaynes had been employed as a factor on the African coast, primarily at Whydah. Richard Worge entered parliament in 1768 as a representative for Stockbridge. During and immediately after the Seven Years' War, however, he had served as the first British governor of Fort Louis in the Senegal River, which in 1758 a British naval squadron had captured from France.[4] At least two members of parliament had traded in slaves extensively. In the 1720s Humphry Morice transported hundreds of African captives to the Americas. When Henry Lascelles entered parliament in 1745, he had been trafficking in slaves from Africa for more than three decades.[5] At least three merchants with seats in the house of commons after the Seven Years' War, George Aufrère, Anthony Bacon and Samuel Touchet, enjoyed lucrative contracts to provision the British castles and trading forts in West Africa during the 1760s or 1770s. Four others served on the executive committee of the Company of Merchants Trading to Africa between 1750 and 1764, in the same years that they held seats in the house of commons. These were Samuel Dicker, Charles Pole, Peregrine Cust, and Edward Lewis.[6]

In addition, there were others in parliament who found reason to care about the British slave trade, even if they had no direct role in its operations. William Beckford, the absentee Jamaica sugar planter and London politician, led a coalition of West Indian lobbyists in the 1740s and 1750s that tried to ensure that the British slave trade continued to meet the needs of Caribbean estate owners. The members of parliament for Bristol and Liverpool sometimes served as the spokesmen for the British slave traders, both in the house of commons and in the offices of state. The African traders at times could also count on those members of parliament that represented neighbouring boroughs in Lancashire or near Bristol.[7] To this group of returned African factors, British slave traders, African contractors, West Indian planters, and slave ship delegates, should be added the many members of parliament who served on the board of trade in these years, and, through this experience came to know the character of the African trade and its politics. As with most overseas trades in this era,

[4] Dennis Klinge, 'The African Company in British Politics, 1748–1783', Cornell University Ph.D., 1973, pp. 267, 270; Sir Lewis Namier and John Brooke, *The History of Parliament. The House of Commons, 1754–1790* (3 vols, 1964) II, 319; Eveline C. Martin, *The British West African Settlements, 1750–1821. A Study in Local Administration* (1970), p. 58.

[5] James A. Rawley, 'Humphry Morice: Foremost London Slave Merchant of his Time', in *London, Metropolis of the Slave Trade*, ed. *idem* (Columbia, MO, 2003), pp. 40–56; 'Lascelles, Henry (bap. 1690, d. 1753)', *O.D.N.B.*, online edn., May 2005.

[6] Klinge, 'African Company in British Politics', pp. 196, 200; *ODNB*, I, 942; III, 121–2; LV, 81. James Rawley notes that several London merchants with seats in the house of commons also had an investment in the Africa trade. Among them were Slingsby Bethell, Rose Fuller, Alexander Grant, George Hibbert, Richard Oliver, Richard Oswald and Barlow Trecothick. See James A. Rawley with Stephen D. Behrendt, *The Transatlantic Slave Trade. A History* (Lincoln, Neb., 2005), p. 204.

[7] Klinge, 'African Company in British Politics', pp. 69–70, 110.

the number in parliament engaged in and knowledgeable about African affairs was not large, but neither was it negligible.

Moreover, throughout the middle decades of the eighteenth century, a small few outside parliament attempted to bring the British slave trade to public attention and declare its national importance. Rhetorically, it sometimes helped to describe the British slave trade as the creature of the British state and as the project of the British nation, as well as a business operated by British merchants, even if the facts tended to suggest a more complicated reality. Virginia planter and lawyer Thomas Jefferson adopted this view in June 1776 when constructing the case for American independence. In a controversial passage subsequently deleted from the Declaration of Independence, he described the British slave trade as licensed and operated by the agents of George III.[8] Such comments presented an ironic echo of claims long favoured by the British promoters of the trade to Africa in preceding decades, who described the commerce as a national undertaking when hoping to secure financial assistance from the state.[9] Years later, the abolitionists in England, such as Granville Sharp, would appropriate such proclamations to make a very different point, that because the slave trade was a national project, it was also a national sin.[10] These declarations represented attempts to persuade as much as to describe. They aimed to expand the circle of those who cared about the African trade, though they knew that very few did, or would. For, as men like Thomas Jefferson, Malachy Postlethwayt, and Granville Sharp understood, both parliament and the public found it difficult to think about the trade to Africa as the collective enterprise of the nation. British merchants, not the British state, directed the traffic, and with very little intervention from Whitehall or Westminster between 1713 and 1787. In the years when the British slave trade reached its peak, the British government and the British nation, more generally, showed only the most passing interest in its conduct, its dimensions, its results, or its character.

The important exception lay with the management of the British trading forts that dotted the West African coast from James Island in the Gambia River to Fort William at Whydah on the 'Slave Coast', in present day Benin. The Royal African Company owned and operated these forts until 1750. After its dissolution in 1752, parliament established the Company of Merchants Trading to Africa, to oversee the forts which, with a few important exceptions retained control of them until 1821, more than a decade after slave trade abolition. Although the trading forts became decreasingly important to the operation of the British slave trade over time, the British government, and many British traders as well, considered them vital to sustaining the nation's influence in West Africa, and acted accordingly. At the direction of parliament, the treasury awarded an annual subsidy first to the Royal

---

[8] *A Necessary Evil? Slavery and the Debate over the Constitution*, ed. John P. Kaminski (Madison, 1995), p. 7.

[9] This perspective is most apparent in the works of Malachy Postlethwayt. See, among other works, *The African Trade, the Great Pillar and Support of British Plantation Trade in America* (1745); *The Importance of Effectually Supporting the Royal African Company of England* (1745), and *The National and Private Advantages of the African Trade Considered* (1746).

[10] Christopher Leslie Brown, *Moral Capital. Foundations of British Abolitionism* (Chapel Hill, NC, 2006), pp. 155–206.

African Company and then to the Company of Merchants Trading to Africa to maintain and provision the British establishment on the coast. Those grants, which commenced in 1730, and continued, with important exceptions, until the early nineteenth century, sparked intermittent debate and controversy among those with an interest in Africa and, at times, though less frequently, within parliament as well.

It was in this way, through the annual appropriation of public money to sustain the British forts in the Gambia River, on the Gold Coast, and on the Slave Coast, that the slave trade became the subject of sporadic government interest and action during the middle decades of the eighteenth century, in the era before the abolitionist movement first took shape in the 1780s. After 1730, in most instances, parliament simply authorized the annual request, usually in the final days before it adjourned for the summer and with little discussion or comment. But, in other instances, the petition for funds occasioned a more searching inquiry into the state of the African trade. The house of commons wanted to know how public money had been spent, and if it had been spent well. Those questions sometimes then led to more fundamental issues regarding who should manage the African forts, under what terms, and with what kind of oversight. The pattern repeated itself throughout the century. Those who operated and provisioned the forts insisted that the subsidy needed to be increased, that the British establishment on the coast would go bankrupt without a more sizable contribution from the treasury. Those who resented the operators of the British trading forts in Africa contended, in turn, that public money was being misused, that officials on the African coast had diverted the subsidy to serve their own purposes, that the existing mode of oversight did not, and would never, work.

In sorting through these rival claims, the debate within the house of commons sometimes touched upon much broader questions about the relationship between private enterprise and the national interest. Why have forts in Africa? What purposes did they serve? Might those purposes be achieved through some other means? And were coalitions of merchants best equipped and most likely to pursue these ends? The inconclusive resolution to this perennial tension between state needs and private profit-taking came to characterize the politics of the African trade through most of the eighteenth century. There often was a sense in parliament that the objectives of the imperial state and the agendas of the traders to Africa were not in perfect alignment. But those intimations of concern tended to fade before the more powerful inclination to treat the Africa trade as the special province of those merchants directly engaged in the business, rather than an ongoing subject of public interest.

1. *The Case of the Royal African Company*

Establishing an infrastructure that would nurture and sustain the English commerce in Africa had been a concern from the start. The Royal African Company had received from Charles II an exclusive right to trade on the coast in exchange for the investment required to establish a lasting presence in the region. When in 1672 the Royal African Company received its charter, the English had two forts in Africa, Cape Coast Castle on the Gold Coast, and James Fort in the Gambia River. During the subsequent years, before 1698, when they would lose their monopoly to the English African trade, they constructed six more.[11] Even as parliament came to favour the claims of the separate traders, it repeatedly asserted that maintaining the coastal establishment remained a high priority. When opening the Africa trade to all English merchants in 1698, parliament required that the separate traders pay a ten per cent duty to the Royal African Company so as to provide sufficient funding for the African forts, as, in the words of the act, the 'Forts and Castles are undoubtedly necessary for the Preservation and well-carrying on the said Trade'. In the years of the contentious and largely inconclusive debates on the Africa trade that followed, the house of commons declared the forts essential to the English interests in the region on seven occasions, even as they refused to extend the privileges of the company that kept those forts at work.[12]

That history figured prominently in the pamphlet of 1730 *The Case of the Royal African Company*, a text that would help lead to the establishment of an annual parliamentary subsidy for the upkeep of the British forts in Africa. For that history of service to the imperial state at once established the utility of the Gold Coast trading forts, parliament's long-standing commitment to them, and the state and the nation's obligation to underwrite their upkeep. Why have forts? Without them, the company spokesman explained, British merchants would be driven from the slave trade along the Gold Coast. They would find it impossible to compete with the French and the Dutch for African captives, without a coastal establishment that provided ready and open access to the coast. Britain's rivals in Europe understood the importance of these trading forts, so that while the British outposts were in decline, the company's spokesmen argued, the Dutch and French invested heavily in sustaining and supplementing their coastal establishment. It was not just the slave trade that would suffer if the condition of the British forts declined further. Without them, there would be no chance to develop an inland trade and build diplomatic relationships with commercial and military *élites* beyond the coast. In any case, some solution had to be found as in the years after 1712 the Royal African Company had acquired an unmanageable debt in maintaining the forts.

Who, then, should bear the cost? The spokesman for the Royal African Company accepted that the separate traders now had won unfettered access to the coast. The company denied any interest in taxing the merchants engaged in the Africa trade as a way of maintaining the forts. Indeed, they professed concern for the prospects of the separate traders. The declining profit margins in the slave trade, they argued, would render such a tax a prohibition in effect. The only alternative, then, was an alternative source of funding. The Royal African Company recognized that state subsidies for a trade or a trading company were unusual and might set a dubious precedent. Yet, in practice, these forts were strategic outposts, as much as commercial entrepots. Functionally, they resembled the various fortified garrisons stationed at the perimeter of British influence around the Atlantic that annually received money from parliament. The Royal African Company would accept financial compensation

---

[11] These were Accra, Anomobu, Kommenda, Sekondi, Dixcove and Winnebah. In this period, the Royal African Company also purchased Frederixborg from the Dutch in 1685. Davies, *Royal African Company*, pp. 247–9.

[12] *Ibid.*, p. 152.

for the surrender of their forts, if parliament determined that they no longer served a useful purpose, as the separate traders sometimes argued. But, to the company, it seemed wiser to invest in the coastal establishment, not surrender it, as, in making the slave trade possible, they served the needs of the colonies, the nation, and the empire as a whole. 'There is not a Man in this kingdom', *The Case of the Royal African Company* declared, 'who does not more or less partake of the Benefit and Advantages of the Royal African Company's Forts and Castles in Africa; and who would not be a Sufferer or a Loser, in Proportion to his Rank and Circumstances, should the said Forts and Castles be abandoned, or come under the Power, or Fall into the hands of any Foreign Nation.'[13]

These were the arguments that in the spring of 1730 the defenders of the Royal African Company made on the floor of the house of commons.[14] And, in one way or another, every text published on behalf of the Royal African Company during the next two decades reiterated these same key points, that the African forts were a commercial asset and a strategic necessity, and that the Royal African Company for providing a public service needed public assistance. The argument persuaded parliament in 1730 to authorize an annual grant of £10,000 to the Royal African Company to maintain its forts. The house of commons rejected the suggestion that the forts were necessary for the trade, but agreed their maintenance as 'Marks of Possession of Great Britain in those Parts'.[15] On the declaration of war with France in 1744, parliament increased the subsidy to £20,000. Three years later, the government reverted to its previous level. From 1748, though, these awards were suspended entirely, as parliament grew increasingly dissatisfied with the performance of the Royal African Company and its drain on the public purse.[16]

Between 1748 and 1750, desperate for funds, and facing the prospect of dissolution, the company tried to persuade sceptics in parliament of its continuing relevance to commerce in Africa. The purportedly reduced state of the Gold Coast trade indicated the likely consequences of abandoning the forts altogether, the Royal African Company spokesmen declared. The slave trade from the Gold Coast had declined, they claimed, because of inadequate support for the coastal establishment that promoted good relations with African merchants. Instead, increasingly the British slave traders from the outports of Liverpool and Bristol, in particular, looked beyond the Gold Coast, to Bonny or to Calabar to purchase slaves for sale to the Americas. Therefore, the more desirable Gold Coast slaves increasingly ended up on French or Dutch ships, while English merchants, in competing with each other, bid up the cost for captives of an inferior quality. It did not have to be this way, insisted the African Company's propagandists. If the Royal African Company received sufficient annual funding from parliament, and if it received some assistance in reducing the debt accumulated since 1713, the corporation would be well positioned not only to

[13] *The Case of the Royal African Company of England* (1730), in *The British Transatlantic Slave Trade*, ed. Morgan, p. 91. An adequate assessment of these arguments would require a more sustained analysis than this article can provide, in part because of space limitations. My aim here and in what follows is to provide an overview of the political debate, rather than to render judgments on their respective claims.

[14] H.M.C., *Egmont MSS*, I, 51.

[15] *C.J.*, XXI, 522–3 (26 Mar. 1730).

[16] Morgan, *Transatlantic Slave Trade*, pp. xxx–xxxi.

restore the forts to their proper conditions but also to assist the independent merchants who now predominated in the slave trade. These defenders of the Royal African Company saw the two sets of entrepreneurs in complementary roles. The Royal African Company could provide military support for the traffic, preventing incursions from foreign rivals, and cultivating peaceable relations with African *élites*. It could keep a stock of captives at the forts, so that merchants trading along the coast could fill their ships with enslaved men, women, and children, in weeks rather than in months. And Britain, in the process, would be supplied with the natural productions of Africa that the company would ship home directly. These were the tasks that independent merchants could never take on themselves since their interests, necessarily, lay with the profit of individual voyages, not the diplomatic work of promoting open access to distant markets or the long-term investment required to sustain them.[17]

These arguments informed the suggestions that the Royal African Company presented to the board of trade and, through them, to the house of commons, in the parliamentary session of 1750, when the government intended to complete the reorganization of the African trade once and for all. In the spring of 1749, the house of commons had consented to a bill for the establishment of an open, regulated trade, the dissolution of the Royal African Company and the transference of its possessions to an administrative body guided by representatives from Liverpool, Bristol and London. The house of lords blocked the passage of this bill on discovering that, under its terms, the creditors of the Royal African Company would never recover the outstanding debt. Before adjourning in the summer of 1749, the house of commons addressed George II with a request for a plan for reorganization from the board of trade.[18] The board of trade collected evidence during the remainder of the year, and received testimony from interested parties in the first weeks of 1750.[19]

The Royal African Company and its allies insisted that transferring control of the forts to a committee of independent merchants would have dire consequences, both for the British trade to Africa and for the British plantation colonies in the Americas. In its memorial, the Royal African Company reiterated its belief that the joint-stock company and the independent merchants could assist each other, if 'each party appl[ied] themselves to the Branches of the Trade that suit them best'. They held out hope for a permanent allowance, not subject to annual renewal, which would allow the corporation to make long-term investments in its operation, reduce its debt, and attract more investors. To the London merchants sympathetic to the Royal African Company's plight, the Africa forts were more than 'marks of possession', they were, or, at least could be, commercial assets, and potential seats of power. But, in 1750, the defenders of the Royal African Company concentrated their energies

---

[17] For these claims, see the following texts published to shape public opinion and consideration in parliament. *A Letter to a Member of Parliament Concerning the African Trade* (1748); *Answers to the Objections Against the Proposals of the Royal African Company for Settling the Trade to Africa* (1748); *An Antidote to Expel the Poison Contained in an Anonymous Pamphlet, Lately Published* (1749); Mr O'Connor, *Considerations on the Trade to Africa Together with a Proposal for securing the Benefits Thereof to this Nation* (1749); *Considerations on the African Trade* (1750).

[18] This history is presented most lucidly in Martin, *British West African Settlements*, pp. 8–12. For further detail, see Klinge, 'The African Company in British Politics', pp. 54–142.

[19] *Journal of the Commissioners of Trade and Plantations*, V, 1–35.

on what they regarded as the wholly impractical plan to place a state interest in the hands of private entrepreneurs. The company could not believe that the independent merchants would embrace the laborious, time-consuming, and unrewarding work of maintaining buildings and managing employees. The separate traders, they asserted, 'had been raising great fortunes upon their Ruins'. Was it likely that they would invest energies in those projects of empire that they long had professed to despise? 'May not selfinterest prevail in this Case, as in other Cases, and encourage such neglect, or Misconduct, as may hazard the whole Gold Coast?' The committee of sugar planters from Jamaica and Barbados that sided with the Royal African Company thought such proposals absurd. Parliament must not grant control of these valuable possessions to such 'temporary, mutable, and transient Set of Men ... who might renounce it at Pleasure, and who would be answerable each for his own Acts only, and not one for the Acts of another'. Instead of persisting in the difficult work of preserving the British interest on the Gold Coast, they soon would only provide 'the worst kind of Negroes that can be purchased cheap, at Calabar, Congo, Angola, and other parts of Africa ... notwithstanding the only proper Negroes for the Preservation of our Sugar-Colonies are to be provided nowhere but on that Part of the Coast of Africa'.[20] For these petitioners, the likely consequences of reorganization were clear, the enrichment of individual merchants, and the sacrifice of what they regarded as the national interest.

2. Parliamentary Politics and The Company of Merchants Trading to Africa

By 1750 such arguments inspired little sympathy within parliament, a consequence of the growing influence of the independent traders and the government's impatience with the Royal African Company. As the chronicler of economic affairs, Adam Anderson, has expressed it, the house of commons 'did not seem inclined to trust that Company with any more money'.[21] For, by the end of the 1740s, the company not only lacked friends in parliament. It also carried the burden of its undistinguished record as a commercial concern. Unable to enforce its monopoly effectively from the first, the Royal African Company had struggled throughout its history to generate consistent revenue. Disappointment with its poor performance in supplying slaves to the British colonies in America, when combined with its close ties to the court before the Glorious Revolution, had helped to end its monopoly in 1698. The perceived importance of the forts had helped the company retain a privileged position in the trade until 1713. But, by then, and during the remaining decades that followed, it became increasingly apparent that the individual traders had proved most successful in conveying enslaved labour to the colonies, the complaints of certain Jamaica and Barbados sugar planters about price and quality notwithstanding. These traders received their fondest wish when in 1713 the ten per cent duty expired. Still, they remained watchful and suspicious of the Royal African Company,

---

[20] *Papers Laid before the Honourable House of Commons By the Commissioners for Trade and Plantations pursuant to the An Address of the House of Lords to his Majesty, the 8th of June, 1749 for the better Securing, Improving, and Extending the Trade to Africa* (1750), pp. 7, 17, 49, 51.

[21] Anderson cited in Klinge, 'African Company in British Politics', p. 72.

thereafter, concerned that the corporation would, at some point, reassert itself in the slave trade.[22]

For this reason, the independent traders mobilized opposition in parliament when in 1730 the Royal African Company first sought a public subsidy. The traders failed in this attempt to stop the grant, and in the years that followed they chose not to contest the annual awards to the Royal African Company. Still, at this early date, they articulated the themes that not only had informed their previous campaigns against the Royal African Company, but that also would figure again in their attempt to guide parliamentary reorganization in the late 1740s. They warned that a revived Royal African Company would soon go broke again; that, in the process, this would also bankrupt a whole new set of investors; disappointing them as they had others in the past; that the forts served little purpose to the African trade, that security for the trade would be better arranged through the positioning of war ships on the African coast, and that the company succeeded only in undermining the commercial operations of independent traders, who since 1713 had brought the trade to new heights.[23]

Although in 1730 these warnings made little difference, they proved decisive when in the late 1740s, parliament at last seemed inclined to reorganize the African trade. If the Royal African Company mobilized the most talented publicists, the separate traders rallied the more extensive list of petitioners. Prominent among them were the African merchants from Bristol and Liverpool, as well as some from London, who described the annual subsidies to the Royal African Company as throwing good money after bad.[24] It was true, they volunteered, that the company had gone bankrupt, but this was because its directors mismanaged the trade, because they had misapplied funds intended for the upkeep of the forts, and because they had contracted loans on behalf of the company at exorbitant rates. 'In short,' as one opponent of the company put it, 'nothing throve that they undertook, and by a Series of plundering Misfortunes and Bad Management, both at Home and Abroad, they were most deservedly sunk to their present contemptible situation.'[25] At the very least, parliament should not award another shilling to the company without first scrutinizing how the earlier grants had been spent. By the 1740s, however, the separate traders were prepared to go further. They suggested that parliament dissolve the Royal African Company entirely. Its directors and their agents served no interest but their own, the company's opponents maintained. The absurd fantasy of establishing an inland trade, which, they noted, the company had failed to accomplish in the previous half-century, only demonstrated just how detached its advocates had become from the realities of the African traffic. Now the separate traders chose to acknowledge the importance of the trade forts not only as marks of possession but also as political assets. Here they seemed to accept the inclination of most members of parliament to think of the African trade in strategic

---

[22] Davies, *Royal African Company*, pp. 97–152, remains the most thorough published account of the company's decline and fall.

[23] *Remarks on the Supplement to the African Company's Case* (1730); H.M.C., *Egmont Diary*, I, 51.

[24] Klinge, 'African Company in British Politics', pp. 118–22. For the Bristol petitions, see *Politics and the Port of Bristol in the Eighteenth Century*, ed. Walter Minchinton, (Bristol Record Society's Publications, XXIII 1963), pp. 67–76.

[25] *A Detection of the Proceedings and Practice of the Directors of the Royal African Company of England* (1749), p. 30.

as well as commercial terms. The opponents of the company insisted, however, that the forts should operate only as military and administrative centres, rather than as sites for commercial enterprise. With this in mind, they proposed either vesting the coastal establishment in the crown or, even better, assigning their management to the separate traders themselves.[26]

In April 1750 the separate traders received what they long had sought. The Act for Extending and Improving the Trade to Africa divested the Royal African Company of its possessions on the West African Coast. It asserted the liberty of all British subjects to trade to Africa 'as he or they shall think fit, without any Restraint, whatsoever'. It established a regulated company, formally known as the Company of Merchants Trading to Africa, which any trader could join with an annual 40-shilling subscription. It granted to this company all of the former possessions of the Royal African Company, and placed their oversight in the control of a committee of nine persons, three each from Liverpool, Bristol and London, who were to be elected annually by the members of the company. This committee would see to the upkeep of the coastal establishment, utilizing the funds acquired through subscriptions and the subsequent grants received from parliament. However, as a purely administrative body, this new company was expressly forbidden from trading on its own account. The act assigned the board of trade the responsibility of monitoring the company and, in cases of violations, removing committeemen or their agents on the coast from office. In another statute, enacted two years later, parliament compensated the Royal African Company, and their creditors, for a portion of their losses.[27]

This was the first parliamentary statute in more than a half-century to address the African trade comprehensively. It aimed to resolve the long-standing tension between a joint-stock corporation that had long since lost its commercial standing and the individual traders who conducted the commerce but lacked the institutional recognition regarded as essential to sustaining their interests. For the vast majority of members of parliament who had no commercial or political interest in the Africa trade, the prospects for the British forts on the coast remained the primary concern. And this new administrative structure seemed to instil some confidence that a solution to their maintenance at last had been found. That confidence seems most apparent in the comparative generosity of the house of commons when receiving the annual petitions for funds from the Company of Merchants Trading to Africa. The annual subsidy of £10,000 was revived, and continued to 1761, when it was increased by £3,000. Thirteen thousand pounds remained the standard grant, until abolition in 1807. More revealing than these annual supplies, though, were the extraordinary grants in the 1750s and 1760s. For example, authorized for specific purposes were grants of £6,000 in 1753 and again in 1755 to reconstruct the fort at Annamaboe (where French encroachments during the Seven Years' War seemed to threaten the British position on the Gold Coast), and £7,000 for a new set of buildings at Appolonia to counterbalance the growing presence of the Dutch. Supplementary

---

[26] *Papers Laid Before the Honourable House of Commons by the Commissioners for Trade and Plantations* (1750), pp. 37–52.

[27] *Documents Illustrative of the Slave Trade to America* ed. Elizabeth Donnan (4 vols, Washington, D.C., 1930–5), II, 474–85.

awards like these, typically, had come less easily and less frequently to the Royal African Company in the first half of the eighteenth century.[28]

The Act for Improving and Extending the Trade to Africa did not, however, bring an end to the controversy over the organization of the trade. Those devoted to the idea of a joint-stock corporation became virulent critics of the new Company of Merchants Trading to Africa and looked for ways to undermine its position. Some of these opponents had held important positions in the Royal African Company in its final years, such as John Roberts, the governor of Cape Coast Castle from 1749 to 1750, a perpetual irritant to the Company of Merchants Trading to Africa during the three decades that followed. Others, outside the company, had regarded the joint-stock corporation as most amenable to the advancement of their own economic interests. This was particularly true of William Beckford, an absentee Jamaica planter and member of parliament for Shaftesbury from 1747 to 1754, and, thereafter, for London until 1770. From 1753 to 1758, he led a contingent of the West Indian interest in a concerted campaign within parliament to bring the new company into disrepute. Ironically, many of the charges that these critics levied echoed the accusations that individual traders long had directed to the Royal African Company. They insisted that the forts on the coast had deteriorated further under the charge of Company of Merchants Trading to Africa. They claimed that funds had been misapplied, particularly the grants intended to rebuild the fort at Annamaboe. And they reported that the employees of the new company had engaged in private trade on the Africa coast, directly contravening the spirit of the 1750 act.[29]

These charges led parliament to conduct a series of investigations into the affairs of the Company of Merchants Trading to Africa during the 1750s, in the decade after the new company received parliamentary authorization. The most serious challenges to the position of the new company came in 1756 and 1758, as parliament took an interest in how the funds allocated for Annamaboe had been spent. Harbouring suspicions about the accuracy of the new company's reports, parliament asked the crown to send out an engineer from the board of ordnance to make an independent assessment of the forts and their condition. This report, which proved unflattering to the company, seemed to provide incontrovertible evidence of malfeasance by the company's employees. The spokesmen for the West India interest and the deposed officers of the Royal African Company seized on the report as proof of the new company's corruption. Yet, after conducting an extensive investigation in the spring of 1758, parliament reached the opposite conclusion, resolving 'that the Company of Merchants trading to Africa, have faithfully discharged the Trust reposed in them'. Insofar as the forts remained in an inadequate condition, those faults should be attributed to the poor management of the Royal African Company.

This vindication in the house of commons marked the high-water mark for the influence of the African merchants in parliament. Confronted with an unflattering report on their activities, and facing a small but powerful interest committed to its overthrow, the Company of Merchants Trading to Africa emerged victorious from

---

[28] Martin, *British West African Settlements*, pp. 16–18.

[29] This paragraph and the two that follow draw largely upon Klinge, 'African Company in British Politics', pp. 195–217.

the hearings of the 1750s. Their success in part resulted from the contributions of key members of parliament who had close ties with the new company. On commercial matters such as the African trade, the house of commons tended to defer to those members who had knowledge and experience of the traffic, in particular the representatives for Bristol and Liverpool. In the last two decades of its existence, in the 1730s and the 1740s, the Royal African Company no longer possessed useful connexions within the House. The new Company of Merchants Trading to Africa, by contrast, through its well-placed committee members, could both fend off challenges from its rivals and lobby effectively for additional funding.

None the less, there were limits to how far parliament would trust the Company of Merchants in the management of African affairs. In 1758, during the Seven Years' War, the secretary of state, William Pitt, authorized a British naval expedition to capture the French forts at Goree and in the Senegal River. Although British merchants had long been excluded from the region by the French government, the Senegambian coast formally lay within the boundaries of the jurisdiction assigned to the Company of Merchants in the act of 1750. As a consequence, the new possessions were placed under their control in 1764. That same year, though, French attempts to assert claims to the Gambia River trade raised fears regarding the security of the new acquisitions. The convenient solution of vesting the former French possessions in the management of commercial traders seemed like an unreliable way to ensure the preservation of British interests in the region. Two years earlier, the erstwhile proponents of an African joint-stock company had made exactly this point, that is before the forts had been awarded to the Company of Merchants. In 1765 the board of trade and then parliament concluded that there was some wisdom in this view. But rather than establishing a new corporation to conduct trade on the Upper Guinea Coast, parliament instead placed the new possessions under the authority of the crown. The new royal colony of Senegambia represented the first instance in which the British state attempted direct government of any of the trading stations along the African coast. Significantly, the spur to this innovation lay in concerns with security, and the possibility of French encroachments. The establishment of the colony represents one of the very few instances in which the direction of British affairs in Africa were decided by the state itself, rather than one or another set of commercial interests.[30]

If the creation of wealth most concerned the traders to Africa, parliament tended to focus on the prospect of war. In most instances, after 1713, parliament's engagement with African questions tended to arise alongside broader concerns regarding the conditions of strategic outposts at the peripheries of the empire. The extraordinary appropriations for the Royal African Company in 1744 coincided with the outbreak of war. The supplements awarded in the 1750s to the Company of Merchants Trading to Africa came at a time of increased fears for British possessions on the coast during the Seven Years' War. And the Senegambia colony took shape as a direct response

---

[30] Martin, *British West African Settlements*, pp. 80–102; J. M. Gray, *A History of the Gambia* (1966), pp. 234–75; H.A. Wyndham, *The Atlantic and Slavery* (1935), pp. 51–8; *Select Documents on the Constitutional History of the British Empire and Commonwealth. The Foundations of a Colonial System of Government, Vol. III, Imperial Reconstruction, 1763–1840. The Evolution of Alternative Systems of Colonial Government*, ed. Frederick Madden and David Fieldhouse (Westport, Conn., 1985), pp. 491–505.

to the fear of French incursions into territories acquired in the Seven Years' War. For this reason, the management of the African forts became an issue once again during the years of the American Revolution, as it became clear that suppressing the American rebellion would require an unusual outlay of money and men. In these years, the state of the African trade never became of more than secondary interest to parliament or to the ministry of Lord North. At the same time, their growing discomfort with the Company of Merchants Trading to Africa signalled a growing decline in its standing among the governing *élite*.

As before, the 1777 parliamentary inquiry into the African trade arose in response to a request for money. In its annual petition of 1777, the Company of Merchants asked for more than £7,000 of supplementary funds to offset debts incurred by its employees on the coast and to cover expenses associated with preparation for war. A fractious spirit within the company that had developed during the early 1770s ensured that, for the first time, critics of the company would come from within the organization, as well as from without. Bamber Gascoyne, member of parliament for Liverpool and president of the board of trade in 1777, had figured among the several Africa traders suspicious of the committee that directed company affairs. From his seat of power at the board of trade, he conducted a searching investigation into company affairs, drawing substantially on the revelations provided by Richard Camplin, the company's former secretary. This investigation by the board of trade turned up the types of behaviour that the African traders long had attributed to the Royal African Company in the years before – embezzlement, the misapplication of funds, and private trading under the aegis of officialdom.[31]

The scathing report produced by the board of trade briefly inspired a flurry of activity in parliament. Temple Luttrell, scourge of the North ministry, used the occasion to embarrass the administration, by claiming that the dilapidated state of the British establishment in Africa reflected the broader mismanagement of imperial affairs that, he argued, had led to the American war. Outside parliament the remaining devotees of a joint-stock corporation, John Roberts in particular, tried to bring down the Company of Merchants Trading to Africa once and for all. The African traders, however, were fortunate in their only important friend in the house of commons, Edmund Burke, who articulated an eloquent defence of the Company of Merchants Trading to Africa in 1777 and 1779. Burke was helped by the clearly partisan spirit of the 1777 report presented by the board of trade and of the one-sided process that produced it. The African merchants were helped even more by parliament's preoccupation with the far more important questions pertaining to public finance, the war in America, and the defence of the nation. No one wished a reprise of the last years of the Royal African Company, when the suspension of all grants to the African forts left the coastal establishment devoid of all supplies for two years from 1748. At the same time, the new revelations of wrongdoing within the Company of Merchants increasingly left it in a similar position to the Royal African Company during its last two decades of existence. Parliament treated the annual grants to the

---

[31] 'Minutes of Enquiry into the Administration of the African Trade', in *Journal of the Commissioners of Trade and Plantations*, V, 15, 126–146. *Return from the Commissioners for Trade and Plantations to the Honourable House of Commons relating to the general state of the Trade to Africa* (1777).

Company of Merchants as a necessity, but showed no inclination to trust it with additional assistance, or to have much confidence in its choices. Temple Luttrell's failure to hang the mismanagement of the African forts upon the ministry of Lord North because, in part, it was clear that neither North nor anyone else in power much cared for the Company of Merchants.[32]

In the closing years of the American war, the Company of Merchants Trading to Africa lost whatever political capital it had once possessed. The campaign to overthrow it failed in the early 1780s, in part because its most powerful institutional opponents, the board of trade, was abolished in 1782, chiefly owing to the efforts of Edmund Burke. No one in office, and no interest in parliament, much cared about the Africa trade in the 1780s. In the treaty of peace that settled the American War of Independence, Britain returned Goree and the forts on the Senegal River to France. The Senegambia colony was extinguished with little discussion and with little regret. The African trade flourished in the years after the American war. The slave trade recovered rapidly to meet the pent-up demand inadequately met during the several years of fighting in the Caribbean. Yet the decreasing importance assigned to African questions, and the lowered standing of the Company of Merchants, had mixed consequences for the African traders. If they no longer had to defend the behaviour of their employees, they also no longer had the institutional strength to advance or defend their interests. This vacuum in political leadership on African questions, in the end, would present an opportunity for an emerging abolitionist movement outside parliament to place questions of morality, not organization and finance, on the public agenda.

---

[32] This interpretation draws primarily upon Klinge, 'African Company in British Politics', chs 5-6, as well as *Cobbett's Parliamentary History of England. From the Norman Conquest, in 1066, to the Year 1803* (36 vols, 1806–20), XIX, 1–3, 291–314.

Public Opinion and Parliament in the Abolition of the British Slave Trade

SEYMOUR DRESCHER

Before the end of the war of American Independence the possibility of abolishing Britain's Atlantic slave trade had never been raised in parliament. No pressure group from without had urged its consideration. No member had moved its investigation. By the end of the French wars three decades later, parliament had shut down Britain's trade. Its government had begun a process of internationalizing abolition. For fully half a century after Waterloo every major initiative would be advertized to the world as the desire of both the government and the nation.

This dramatic change was embedded in far larger transformations in British political culture and practice. The evolving dialogue between people and legislators was increasingly nationalized by the thickening network of provincial newspapers. Parliamentary debates and governmental initiatives were now the daily grist of provincial readers. Letters, advertisements for public gatherings, political pamphlets and news items about activities of political leaders in London provided fare for ongoing public conversations which linked provincial readers, not only with the centre in London, but with interested actors from all parts of the island. When parliamentary debates extended over weeks and months, newspapers, associations, libraries, debating societies and public meetings offered parallel venues for ongoing discussions and petitions to the national legislature.[1]

Within this broader process abolition came to occupy a distinctively innovative position. As we shall see, it combined new techniques of propaganda, petitioning and association with the organizational networking techniques of mercantile and manufacturing lobbyists. Between its emergence as a national political movement in 1787 and the internationalization of slave trade abolition at the end of the Napoleonic wars, political abolition became a pioneering organization in mobilizing hitherto untapped groups as actors for philanthropic and social reform. The movement's fortunes in parliament during those three decades were also emblematic of the difficulties entailed in converting public pressure into law and policy.[2]

---

[1] See Joanna Innes, 'Legislation and Public Participation 1760–1830's', in *The British and their Laws in the Eighteenth Century*, ed. David Lemmings (Woodbridge, 2005), ch. 5. For an analysis of Britain's path to new forms of mass politics and relationships to the state, see Charles Tilly, *Popular Contention in Great Britain, 1758–1834* (Cambridge, MA, 1995).

[2] See Seymour Drescher, *Capitalism and Antislavery. British Mobilization in Comparative Perspective* (1986) ch. 4; J.R. Oldfield, *Popular Politics and British Anti-Slavery. The Mobilisation of Public Opinion Against the Slave Trade, 1787–1807* (Manchester, 1997) ch. 4; and Judith Jennings, *The Business of Abolishing the British Slave Trade* (1997), chs 3–5.

1. *Antislavery Sentiment before Mobilization*

One of the distinctive qualities of British political abolitionism was its emergence in conjunction with a massive wave of popular support in 1787–8. Christopher Brown has meticulously traced the long history of abolition's protohistory down to the eve of popular mobilization. Two themes stand out in this story. The first is the steady stream of articulated distaste and revulsion that the overseas slave system continually evoked in eighteenth-century writings. Few travel accounts, imperial histories or geographical compendia failed to mention its striking brutality and its deviance from metropolitan behavioural, legal and religious norms. Some commented upon the ease with which most participants accepted the indifference to human suffering entailed in its perpetuation.

Eighteenth-century culture was therefore saturated with casual references to the violence done to social norms by the slave trade. By the mid-1780s apologists for the trade would have found most lines of defensive rationalization closed except those grounded on the sanctity of private property, the economic value of slave labour and the national interest in sustaining valuable Atlantic trades and products.[3] The bad news for pioneer abolitionists was that these reasons, all linked to the need of African labour for staple agriculture in the tropics, were precisely those that had easily sustained the system against sporadic hostility for nearly a century.

Arguments for the maintenance of the British transatlantic system were always fundamentally grounded in the necessity of the slave trade to sustain the wealth and power of the empire in a highly competitive world. From the early eighteenth century, writers also occasionally deplored the unexplored opportunities for greater development in Africa hindered by the slave trade. They almost invariably returned, however, to the premise that one had to develop trades based upon the world 'as it stands'.[4]

Throughout the century it was apparent that the British legislature held the key to restricting or prohibiting the slave trade. Britain's first abolitionist, Granville Sharp, exemplified the pervasive sense of helplessness when imagining attempts to influence parliament toward that end. In 1772, flush from his own judicial victory in the Somerset case, Sharp was delighted by Anthony Benezet's assurance from Philadelphia that 20,000 to 30,000 signatures could easily be amassed to petition the British government to end the slave trade to some of the colonies. Sharp assured Benezet that even a tenth of that number would furnish vital leverage in favour of outcomes they both intensely desired. Sharp's enthusiastic response indicated the hopes

---

[3] Christopher Leslie Brown, *Moral Capital. Foundations of British Abolitionism* (Chapel Hill, 2006), p. 369. On changing moral perceptions see also David Brion Davis, *The Problem of Slavery in Western Culture* (New York, rev. edn, 1988), pt III. The security of the system was often revealed in the instances of its casual condemnation. Just ten years before the emergence of abolitionism the author of *The Present State of the West Indies* (1778), p. 11, noted, in passing, 'this [slave] trade, to the disgrace of the age, has so deeply taken root, it is become so *necessary* to the present state of affairs, and our wants have justified it in a manner so absolute that it is almost common-place to cry out the barbarity and cruelty of it'.

[4] See Malachy Postlethwayt, *The Universal Dictionary of Trade and Commerce* (1757, 1766 and 1774), entry on Africa. *The Monthly Review* echoed Postlethwayt's concluding phrase in its initial review of October, 1757 (XVII, 311–12). Postlethwayt's conclusion remained unaltered through the *Dictionary's* last edition in 1774: 'This [slave] trade, as it stands, is as *good* as any we have.'

he placed in the potential power of petitioning. However, to another correspondent he indicated his fear that he might not find 50 righteous men in London itself willing to petition against a potential West Indian initiative to undermine the Somerset decision against the deportation of blacks from England.[5] Sharp's individual appeals to Prime Minister North and Lord Dartmouth, another cabinet member, against the slave trade proved fruitless.

Two years later Sharp's political pessimism was echoed by John Wesley, certainly no mean mobilizer of his fellow Britons. Stimulated by Anthony Benezet's writings Wesley wrote a tract against slavery. There he publicly mused, 'Should we appeal to the English nation in general? ... This also is striking wide and is never likely to procure any redress for the sore evil we complain of. As little would it in all probability avail, to apply to the Parliament. So many things, which *seem* of greater importance lie before them.'[6]

These assessments of the parliamentary scene seemed to be verified a decade later. In June 1783, the quakers submitted the first public petition to parliament against the slave trade. Lord North complimented the petitioners on their generous feelings. He politely added that, unfortunately, all the European maritime powers had to make use of the African trade. Many of the future legislative luminaries of abolition debates were present in that session. Not one of them took issue with the prime minister's assessment. The bill that had occasioned the quaker petition, regulating the African trade, passed through parliament without further discussion.

The following year a quaker abolitionist committee obtained an audience with the new ministry, led by the young William Pitt. Once again there was praise for the principle, but the committee were told that 'the time was not yet come to bring the affair to maturity'.[7] The quakers continued to canvass the commercial and imperial *élites*, to subsidize pamphlets and to place notices on the subject in the London and provincial press. They were not encouraged by the parliamentary response. By 1785 their distribution of 11,000 copies of Benezet's principal pamphlet to all M.P.s, justices of the Peace and clergy had resulted in 'an approbation of our benevolence ... but little prospect of success'.[8]

Based upon the evidence available in the public sphere even the eye of faith would have had difficulty discerning an imminent political threat to the slave trade in the three years following peace with America. A voracious reader of the press between 1783 and the formation of the London Committee in May 1787, would have been

[5] See, York Minister Library, Granville Sharp Letterbook, p. 65: Sharp to Anthony Benezet, 21 Aug. 1772; pp. 56–7: Sharp to John Fothergill, 27 Oct. 1772.

[6] John Wesley, *Thoughts upon Slavery* (3rd edn, 1774), pp. 24–7.

[7] Brown, *Moral Capital*, p. 425.

[8] Drescher, *Capitalism and Antislavery*, pp. 63, 206 n. 42. As late as 1785 an item in the London *Public Advertiser* (21 Jan. 1785), warned that to expect any relief from parliament was to expect the impossible 'till Negroes, by having boroughs for their property and loans at their disposal, shall have a party in the House of Commons at their command'. The most important anti-slavery tracts published between 1783 and 1787 were the writings of James Ramsay. Ramsay's detailed attack provoked a series of polemical exchanges in a correspondence that kept the issue of slavery before the reading public. Until 1788 the *Monthly Review* scored 'points' for each side, and converted the issue into a debate between personalities. Only after the first great wave of petitions did the periodical casually announce that abolition was 'a good old *Monthly Review* sentiment'. See *ibid.*, April 1788, p. 342.

hard put to conclude that the quakers had stimulated a rising tide of discussion, much less an expectation of agitation.[9]

Other evidence also points in the same direction. Until 1786 the handful of active abolitionists were still working in virtual isolation from each other. While writing his prize essay against slavery at the university of Cambridge in 1785 the young Thomas Clarkson was oblivious of Granville Sharp's decades of activity. Only on reaching London, early in 1786, did Clarkson discover that a quaker anti-slave trade committee had been functioning for three years. The broader significance of the quaker organization would become apparent only in 1787, when they furnished cadres for the provincial, informational and financial networks of the initial abolitionist movement.[10]

Before 1787 the small band of evangelicals who were also to play so large a role in the abolitionist process had furnished only one writer, James Ramsay, to the abolitionist cause. Clarkson was unaware of Ramsay too, until he met the quakers. The very limited visibility of pre-political abolitionists may well account for the relative unconcern of their opponents before the summer of 1787.

In any event, neither the public nor the slave traders appear to have been particularly impressed by abolition's political potential. As late as the winter of 1787 the colonial agent for Jamaica in London counted William Pitt as 'a great favorite' with the West India interest.[11] It was, after all, the quakers' own sense of their failure to obtain any parliamentary leverage that made them merge into a non-denominational successor organization and to begin the search for at least one committed member of parliament.

William Wilberforce's adhesion to abolition in 1787 came with a priceless bonus, his close friendship with the prime minister. As a politician who prided himself on his responsiveness to public opinion, William Pitt actually offers us the most important bit of evidence that the quaker campaign had scored at least one strategic success in the parliamentary sphere. The leader of a government that in 1784 had told the quaker lobby that the time was not ripe for pressing the issue had within three years re-evaluated the matter. Pitt not only urged Wilberforce to take up the issue of the slave trade but warned his friend that someone else might otherwise seize the initiative.[12]

---

[9] As late as the 33 months between Jan. 1785 and Sept. 1787 *The Times* contained only four reports with anti-slavery overtones, an average of one every four months. By comparison, during the 27 months between Oct. 1787 and Dec. 1789 the newspaper printed 210 such reports, or twice as many a month as in the entire previous period of 33. See Drescher, *Capitalism and Antislavery*, p. 208.

[10] See Thomas Clarkson, *The History of the Rise, Progress, and Accomplishment of the Abolition of the Slave Trade by the British Parliament* (2 vols, 1808), I, ch. 7.

[11] Duke University, Perkins Library, Stephen Fuller Letterbook I, 20: 20 Feb. 1788.

[12] Robin Furneaux, *William Wilberforce* (1974), p. 72. It is not unimaginable that Pitt saw the slave trade as an excellent counterweight to another *cause célèbre*, the emerging impeachment of Warren Hastings. The attack upon Hastings was launched in 1786 by the opposition and captivated the public. The ministry's responsibility for Britain's imperial behaviour in India was implicitly under scrutiny. Launching a simultaneous demonstration of humanitarian concern in Britain's western empire reduced any moral capital that the opposition might have hoped to reap from the east. Michael Duffy considers Pitt to have been 'the first Premier to bring public pressure on Parliament by means of petitions demanding reform for which he acted as spokesman'. One of Duffy's two examples is Pitt's motion against the slave trade. See Michael Duffy, *The Younger Pitt* (2000), p. 143.

2. *The Breakthrough 1787–8*

Contrary to one important historiographical tradition, British abolitionism did not emerge at a moment of chastened anxiety or national humiliation arising from the loss of the North American colonies. It was not an attempt to resuscitate Britain's threatened image as the torchbearer of liberty in comparison with the new American republic.[13] Nor was it a direct response to heightened internal class conflict or to the devaluation of the British slave system in relation to the empire or the economy.[14] To the extent that moral self-scrutiny became an aspect of the post-war imperial discourse, it did so in the context of revived national self-confidence. By almost every empirical measure popular abolitionism emerged at one of the most benign conjunctures of British history in the century between the Seven Years' War and the American Civil War. A survey of London's newspapers in 1786–7 evidences a nation revelling in its prosperity, security and power. From Cornwall to Aberdeen came reports that indicated the most abundant harvest in a decade, and, in some places, in living memory. Industry was thriving and the cotton industry in particular was expanding at an unprecedented rate. Labour disputes had diminished in the coal mines and artisan friendly societies were congratulated on their performance. Pitt was given full credit for the administration's successful financial planning and for the anticipation of a budgetary surplus.[15]

Prospects beyond the seas seemed equally bright. British goods were winning out everywhere. The new French treaty was throwing open a new market for British manufactures. British trade dominated entrepots from Canton to America. The West Indies was sending a fine crop of sugar. The French islands were producing cotton wool for English industry and expanding British West Indian output promised future imperial self-sufficiency.

What the press found most exhilarating was Britain's transformed international position. Plagued by aristocratic revolt and popular rioting, France was verging on bankruptcy and military impotence. The Netherlands was descending into revolution. The Dutch East and West Indian Companies were both foundering. Britons were most fascinated by unfolding developments in the new American republic. In 1786 and 1787 newspapers offered an unending flow of bad news from New England to Georgia: rebellion in Massachusetts; inflation in Rhode Island; stagnation in Philadelphia; ferment in New York; problems in Georgia and Carolina. The American confederation itself seemed to be disintegrating. When William Grenville presented a

---

[13] The most clearly argued case for this perspective is Robin Blackburn's *The Overthrow of Colonial Slavery* (1988), ch. 4. This does not, of course, mean that class conflict did not impinge upon public opinion and the parliamentary response to abolitionism during the twenty year struggle that followed.

[14] The classic statement of the economic decline thesis and slave trade abolition is Eric Williams's *Capitalism and Slavery* (Chapel Hill, 1944), ch. 6. For a recent overview of the implications of the debate over the Williams thesis and its opponents, see David Brion Davis, *Inhuman Bondage. The Rise and Fall of Slavery in the New World* (New York, 2006) ch. 12. For the most extensive discussion of attempts to link British abolitionism to the class tensions of the early industrial revolution, see *The Antislavery Debate. Capitalism and Abolitionism as a Problem in Historical Interpretation*, ed. Thomas Bender (Berkeley, 1992). For a commentary on this debate, see Seymour Drescher, 'The Antislavery Debate', *History and Theory*, XXXII (1993), 311–29.

[15] See Drescher, *Capitalism and Antislavery*, pp. 140–2, 247–8, for this and the following paragraph.

new bill on rules to govern trade between the United States and the British West Indies, he emphasized that the provisions had to be temporary, as it was difficult to decide whether Americans were 'under one government or no government at all'.[16]

For Britain's fledgling abolitionists in 1787 there was some good news from America: the ending of the slave trade by Rhode Island; and the Pennsylvania Abolitionist Society's memorial to the constitutional convention in Philadelphia, requesting a national abolition of the slave trade. The bad news was that the new constitution placed a 20-year prohibition on any implementation of abolition. American slavery itself seemed secure. Britain was hardly threatened by moral comparison as regards the slave trade in particular. While some American seamen were again sailing to West Africa to load slaves for the West Indies, others were themselves being enslaved by the corsairs of North Africa. The London press smugly listed the high prices demanded for Americans in Algiers alongside accounts of the dey's brutal punishments to any corsair who dared to capture Britons in violation of Anglo-Algerian treaties. Never since Yorktown had British self-satisfaction been so spiced with *Schadenfreude*.[17]

Whatever may have contributed to transforming abolitionism from a popular sentiment to a political movement in 1787, it was not any widespread notion that the British needed to snatch the role of liberty's champion back from the United States. Popular abolitionism proceeded from a different premise: how could the world's most secure, free, religious, just, prosperous and moral nation allow itself to remain the premier perpetrator of the world's most deadly, brutal, unjust and immoral offences to humanity? How could its people, once fully informed of its inhumanity, hope to continue to be blessed with peace, prosperity and power?

3. *Popular Mobilization 1788–92*

Organized abolitionism began in May 1787 with the formation in London of a Society for Effecting the Abolition of the Slave Trade (hereafter the London Committee). As J.R. Oldfield has demonstrated, London would thereafter remain the nation's headquarters and co-ordinating centre for popular mobilization. From the quakers, who formed its original majority, the London Committee inherited experience in business organization, sources of funding, and a publishing and distribution network for books, pamphlets, reports and letters. Its members hoped that provincial contacts would support an anticipated parliamentary intervention by local communications and petitions to representatives.[18] The committee's first priority was to gather first-hand evidence for an anticipated parliamentary inquiry. Thomas Clarkson was quickly dispatched on a journey to Bristol and Liverpool, the two towns that were least likely to take the lead in furnishing abolitionist pressure on their M.P.s. In other towns along the way Clarkson raised the possibility of petitions, but his account offers no

---

[16] *Morning Chronicle,* 15 Mar. 1787.

[17] See, *inter alia, Morning Herald,* 25 Jan.; *Public Advertiser,* 2 Mar.; *General Advertiser,* 3 Mar. 1786; *Public Advertiser,* 3 Jan.; *Morning Chronicle,* 14 May, 8 Nov. 1787.

[18] Oldfield, *Popular Politics,* ch. 3.

evidence that he considered dispensing suggestions for producing a wave of petitions with converging appeals and demands.[19]

On his way back to London Clarkson was surprised and delighted to find that the town of Manchester had already formed its own abolitionist committee and intended to submit a mass petition to parliament. Manchester's contribution was particularly valuable to the London Committee. It undercut the traditional morality/policy dualism in British political culture that had discouraged or undermined earlier appeals against the Anglo-Atlantic slave system. Manchester was the epitome of a booming hard-nosed manufacturing town. Although not dominated by the Afro-Caribbean trades some of its inhabitants had a tangible stake in them, larger, perhaps, than that of any other inland city in Britain. One-quarter of the town's insatiable appetite for raw cotton came from Britain's own slave-purchasing colonies, and altogether 70 per cent from the slave colonies of the Caribbean. While some of Manchester's leading cotton manufacturers, like the Peels, would be able to muster smaller-scale petitions against abolition they were never to come close to matching the 10,600 signatures supporting Manchester's abolition petition, much less the larger ones that followed.[20]

These 10,000 signatures, the largest of the 1787–88 campaign, offered striking evidence that Manchester's workers were also aligned with the abolitionist cause. The Manchester signatories represented about two-thirds of the town's adult males. That forestalled any argument that abolitionism lacked a mass base. The slave interest initially assumed that the populace of industrial and commercial towns would be aligned with the slave interest.[21] Along with Birmingham's later petition, Manchester was given pride of place in affirming that the broadly popular and economically informed portion of the nation had opted for abolition. Its petition did not concern itself with the policy or economic aspects of the abolitionist case, setting a general pattern that was to be followed throughout the next 50 years. Petitioners focused first and foremost on the need for political action against an offence to humanity, justice and national honour. Subsequent petitions against the trade also stressed moral grounds for reform under the same triad of 'humanity, religion and justice.' Less than five per cent of those to come added any promise of economic advantage.

To a lesser degree, the parliamentary debates were to replicate the same rhetorical profile between 1788 and 1807. Antagonists could not of course afford to ignore the

[19] For Clarkson's account, see *History*, I, chs 15–19. From its minutes of correspondence, the committee does not seem to have taken a co-ordinating role in the wording of the first petitions. Drescher, *Capitalism and Antislavery*, pp. 67–76, credits Manchester with the primary role in the nationalization of petition appeals for abolition in 1788. It follows Roger Anstey's approach, comparing Clarkson's account of his first journey with E. M. Hunt's account of Manchester's early mobilization. See, Roger Anstey, *The Atlantic Slave Trade and British Abolition 1760–1810* (Atlantic Highlands, NJ, 1975), pp. 263–6; and E. M. Hunt, 'The North of England Agitation for the Abolition of the Slave Trade, 1780–1800', University of Manchester, M.A., 1959. Oldfield, in *Popular Politics,* pp. 47–8, correctly demonstrates that the London Committee, from the outset, saw petitions as integral to their general quest for the support of public opinion. On the quaker background to the mobilization, see especially Jennings, *Business*, chs 2–3; and Brown, *Moral Capital*, ch.7.

[20] Drescher, *Capitalism and Antislavery*, pp. 67–75.

[21] See 'Trebor Tnappilo's' letter, 'A Friend to the African Trade,' in the *Public Advertiser*, 7 July 1787.

strong points of the opposition, nor the usually large number of M.P.s who wanted to hear both sides of the argument. Nevertheless, a systematic study of parliamentary rhetoric in the major debates until 1807 indicates that, by ratios of two and three to one, abolitionists consistently emphasized moral over other reasons for action. Their opponents conversely emphasized economic and security reasons, by the same ratios. This indicates that the moral versus economic dichotomy inherited from the pre-political period remained remarkably stable throughout the two decades before abolition was enacted.[22]

The Manchester petition of December 1787 was also innovative in another major respect with repercussions on public opinion. Newspapers were especially significant in the first national mobilization. There is no evidence that the local petitioning committees were in direct contact with each other during the 1788 campaign. Based upon Manchester's prior efforts at mobilization on economic issues, its abolitionists used some of their subscription funds to advertize copies of their petition in every major newspaper in England while calling for similar petitions from local readers. This summons probably helped to ensure that petitions for abolition composed more than half the total sent to parliament in the 1787−8 sessions. Manchester's initiative was echoed by London. When early in January 1788 the London Committee circularized a general call for petitions, it was published in the form of a copy of the Manchester petition.[23]

At a conservative estimate at least 60,000 individuals signed the abolition petitions of 1788.[24] The London Committee was elated by the massiveness of the reaction to its original appeal. Newspaper accounts stressed the diversity of the supporters, including universities, quakers, dissenters, bishops, merchants and poets. On 7 January 1788, only ten days after the Manchester petition was published London's *General Evening Post* claimed that the attack on the slave trade had already excited public opinion as much as the anti-catholic agitation of 1780 and the Wilkes affair ten years before that.

The first campaign caught allies of the slave interest by surprise. They appeared to be overwhelmed by the speed and breadth of the national mobilization. The slave interest was as dismayed by the adhesion of prelates, universities and other corporate communities as by the large popular base.[25] Liverpool was the only locality that seemed capable of responding with a large counter-petition to parliament in the name of its inhabitants. The shock of Liverpool's merchants was especially severe. Its response was filed among the home office files on threats of popular violence. The

[22] Drescher, 'People and Parliament: The Rhetoric of the British Slave Trade,' *Journal of Interdisciplinary History*, XX (1990), 561−80.

[23] See *Society for the . . . Abolition . . . (1788)*, containing the Manchester petition of December 27, 1787. See University of London, Senate House Library, Goldsmith's Library 13719.

[24] One contemporary source claimed 100,000 signatories (see Drescher, *Capitalism and Antislavery*, p. 82). This compared quite favourably with estimates for other major petition campaigns of the previous two decades: those related to the Wilkes affair in 1769−70; to the American colonies in the mid 1770s; and to the dismissal of the Fox-North coalition in 1784. See James E. Bradley's estimate in *Religion, Revolution and English Radicalism. Nonconformity in Eighteenth Century Politics and Society* (Cambridge, 1990), pp. 319−21. In none of these did the numbers of petitioners exceed those for abolition in 1788.

[25] See Gilbert Franklyn, *Observations Occasioned by the Attempts made in England to Effect the Abolition of the Slave Trade* (1789), p. 21.

government was requested to take account of how far the people had been perverted and inflamed by abolitionists, thereby increasing the danger of 'flames of rebellion' and the 'torch of civil contest'. Various economic interests in London likewise resisted abolition from 1787 right up to its final passage, in 1807.[26]

Disoriented opponents searched for historical perspective. One writer was reminded ominously of 1772, the year of the Somerset case in England and of Virginia's appeal for the ending of the slave trade to the colony. More general were the terms thereafter applied to popular supporters of abolitionism by distressed defenders of the trade: 'general clamour', 'popular emotion', 'phrenzy', 'fanaticism', etc. All these terms implicitly recognized that the appeal for action was both widely and emotionally shared. Published appeals against the new movement almost always acknowledged that their own 'side has scarce found a single defender'.[27]

From the outset the slave interest made no attempt to initiate a broad counter-petition drive or to reach beyond their traditional interest network. Over the next two decades the slave interest would have ample opportunities to claim that the intensity of public feeling had cooled. They would never assert that the public had repudiated its original judgment. Anti-abolitionists therefore focused their collective political energies on pamphleteering, parliamentary lobbying and private appeals to sympathetic governmental officials.

The first wave of petitioning quickly lifted the slave trade onto the political agenda. In February 1788 the prime minister, invoking intense popular interest, launched an inquiry of the privy council committee for trade and plantations into the slave trade. Its very mission marked a paradigmatic break with more than a century of governmental attention to the African trade. Instead of seeking ways to protect and enhance trade, this investigation signalled a fundamental shift in the relationship between the metropolis and its overseas slave system. For the first time the British political system was asked to treat Africans as fellow human beings in a foreign land rather than as factors of trade and production.[28]

In May 1788 the issue of abolition was formally introduced into the house of commons as part of an implicit dialogue between parliament and people. Standing in for the ill Wilberforce, the prime minister framed his motion as a necessary response to 'the great number and variety of petitions' that bespoke an engaged public. Pitt was powerfully seconded by other luminaries in the House. Charles James Fox and Edmund Burke drew attention to the table of the House, loaded with petitions. Fox noted that he would have moved for consideration of abolition himself in the absence of Wilberforce's commitment. Public opinion, in its activist sense, had ensured parliamentary consideration on both sides of the House. Burke rhetorically outbid the two other orators in highlighting the imperative created by national agitation. If the House 'neglected the petitions of its constituents it must be abolished'. To forestall any acrimony Pitt requested only that the subject be committed to full discussion in

---

[26] T.N.A. (P.R.O.), HO 42/13: 25 May 1788. On opposition in London, see James A. Rawley, 'London's Defense of the Slave Trade, 1787–1807,' *Slavery and Abolition*, XIV (1993), 48–69.

[27] *Morning Chronicle*, 5 Feb. 1788.

[28] Drescher, *Capitalism and Antislavery*, pp. 87–8.

the following parliamentary session. He 'studiously avoided' revealing his own views and the opposition chose to remain silent.[29]

The dimensions of the struggle became clear a few weeks later when Sir William Dolben introduced a bill to regulate the conditions of the middle passage. Faced with a specific challenge, the opposition showed its distress in the house of commons and its strength in the house of lords. Further removed from the pressures of public opinion, the peers saw no reason to put a hitherto unchallenged component of the nation's commercial and naval supremacy at risk. Lord Chancellor Thurlow sarcastically dismissed the popular agitation as a 'five days fit of philanthropy', and the Lords seemed poised to eviscerate the bill. Pitt even found himself faced with a hostile majority within his own cabinet. Only his threat of resignation succeeded in retrieving a heavily amended bill just a few hours before the end of the session.

The fate of the Dolben Bill foreshadowed the parliamentary struggle to come. During the next 18 years the abolition of the British slave trade would be moved 12 more times in parliament, but always as an open question not a government measure. Twice before 1807 abolition bills would succeed in the Commons only to be stymied in the upper house. Before 1806 partial bills for eliminating British transportation of slaves to foreign colonies, or from certain parts of the African coast would suffer a similar fate in the Lords. Stephen Fuller, the colonial agent for Jamaica, had anticipated the situation: 'The stream of popularity runs against us', he wrote as early as January 1788, 'but I trust nevertheless that common-sense is with us, and that wicked as we are when compared with the abolishers, the wisdom and policy of this country will protect us.'[30] 'Common sense' was institutionalized in the Lords. Until 1806 the peers would usually invoke their prerogative of independent examination to prevent the abolition bills passed by the Commons from moving on to a definitive vote. Almost 20 years later abolitionists would have to develop a two-session, two-house, strategy to achieve total victory.

During the three years following the 1788 campaign the London abolitionists focused their energies on procuring witnesses and evidence to be laid before a Commons select committee on the slave trade obtained by Wilberforce in 1789. The abolitionists had to find funding for witnesses and Clarkson's journeys. The propaganda and the organization of the movement had to be sustained. In addition to its official seal with the kneeling slave the committee circulated the famous print of the slave ship *Brookes*. As a cheap mass produced product it endured as the most widely disseminated image of the slave trade.

The provincial committee system remained 'the heart of organized anti-slavery'.[31] It was the network through which popular mobilization was organized. However,

---

[29] *Cobbett's Parliamentary History of England. From the Norman Conquest, in 1066, to the Year 1803* (36 vols, 1806–20), XXVII, 495–505 (9 May 1788); and John Ehrman, *The Younger Pitt. The Years of Acclaim* (New York, 1969), p. 393.

[30] Duke University, Perkins Library, Stephen Fuller Letterbook: Fuller to the Jamaica Committee of Correspondence, 30 Jan. 1788; also quoted in Roger Anstey, *Atlantic Slave Trade*, pp. 288–9, 364–402. See also Michael W. McCahill, *Order and Equipoise. The Peerage and the House of Lords, 1783–1806* (1978), p. 210.

[31] Oldfield, *Popular Politics*, ch. 5; Jennings, *Business*, ch. 3; David Turley, *The Culture of English Antislavery, 1780–1860* (1991), ch. 5, esp. pp. 118–21.

one should not lose sight of the distinctive ways in which abolitionism deepened its base and intensified its appeal far beyond the affluent and educated urbanites who always constituted the majority of local committees. Abolitionism continually opened up new horizons for participation in the national movement. During Clarkson's first venture out of London on behalf of the abolition committee in the summer of 1787, he turned to common sailors for the bulk of his information. The brutality and mortality suffered by the crews of slave ships became an effective abolitionist argument. Clarkson's informants included a black sailor, John Dean, who had been abused aboard a slaver. Although no African slaves were allowed to give evidence before the select committee, one of Clarkson's informants was called to the house of commons hearings. An observer wrote that the 'whole committee was in a laugh', and Wilberforce was asked, 'Will you bring your ship-keepers, ship-sweepers, and deck cleaners in competition with our admirals and men of honor?'[32]

Clarkson's initial expansion of participants in the movement foreshadowed a broader pattern. Women appeared on the first publicized list of abolitionist subscribers in Manchester in 1787, constituting 68 out of a total of 302. Another list from London in August 1788 included the names of more than 200 women, about ten per cent of the total number of subscribers.[33] Their extensive participation was singled out for newspaper comment. As Clare Midgley observes, such lists affirmed the legitimacy of women's role in the public sphere. Another legitimizing link was provided by the slave trade's assault on the family. On this account women were welcomed to add their voices and pens, if not their signatures, to the abolitionist cause. Women responded abundantly as poets and public speakers.[34] As early as February 1788 abolition was discussed in 'a ladies only' meeting in London. Newspapers commented upon the astonishing talent of one woman speaker, who won the decision in favour of abolition. By the following month the *Monthly Review* casually noted the appearance of an anti-slave trade work as that of another anti-slavery woman 'joining the benevolent band'.

Just two days before the 'talented woman' displayed her prowess, the same newspaper took note of the appearance of 'a native of Africa' in a public debate on the slave trade.[35] Before the late 1780s the black presence made itself felt in England chiefly through freedom cases in England, or in accounts of anonymous victims: those brutalized on the Atlantic voyage or in the colonies, those freed during the American Revolution, or those rescued from poverty on the streets of London and those sent to found a new settlement in Sierra Leone. Well-known writers like Phyllis Wheatley and Ignatius Sancho might tangentially attack the slave trade, but they served primarily as celebrated evidence of African potential for cultural achievement.

The advent of political abolitionism opened up new public space for Africans. In quick succession Ottobah Cugoano and Olaudah Equiano became mobilizers

---

[32] Quoted in Marcus Rediker, 'Thomas Clarkson and History from Below', *Naked Punch*, VIII (2006), 16–23. See also Clarkson, *History*, I, chs 14–18.

[33] Clare Midgley, *Women Against Slavery. The British Campaigns, 1780–1870* (1992), pp. 18–19; and Oldfield, *Popular Politics*, pp. 135–41.

[34] See Midgley, *Women Against Slavery*, pp. 29–35; Moira Ferguson, *Subject to Others. British Women Writers and Colonial Slavery, 1670–1834* (New York, 1992); and *Morning Herald*, 27 Feb. 1788.

[35] *Morning Herald*, 25 Feb. 1788.

of opinion rather than voiceless victims. To the themes of brutality published by Ramsay, Clarkson and the quakers, Cugoano's *Thoughts and Sentiments on the Evil of Slavery* (1787) boldly added arguments for the total abolition of the slave trade and the creation of a maritime blockade against slavers.[36] Two years later the *Interesting Narrative of the Life of Olaudah Equiano, or Gustavus Vassa, the African written by himself*, made its author the most widely known African in Britain. Equiano's best-selling book and nationwide lecture tours provided Britons with the most personalized experience of the Atlantic slave system most were ever to receive. Equiano epitomized an astonishing journey from captivity to freedom, conversion and celebrity.[37]

4. *The Second Wave: The Triumphs and Perils of Popular Mobilization 1791–2*

The first wave of abolitionism enlarged the opportunities for new actors in the public sphere. The second expanded the public sphere still further. Three years of investigation and manoeuvring from 1788 to 1791 revealed the parliamentary influence of the mobilized slave interest. During the presentation of evidence the London Committee continued to organize, but it did not mobilize. As early as July 1788 Wilberforce had advised the London Committee to 'avoid giving any possible offence to the legislature by forced or unnecessary associations'.[38] There was no further collective intervention before Wilberforce's motion on abolition finally came on in April 1791. Pitt, Fox and Burke again fully supported the bill. From the beginning the abolitionists attempted to minimize the potential impact of abolition. They focused parliament's attention on the £600,000 to £900,000 annually invested in the slave trade itself. Their opponents, by including all West Indian capital, maximized the risk more than a hundredfold. At the end of the debate a backbencher concisely summed up the situation: 'The leaders, it was true were for the abolition; but the minor orators, the pygmies, would, he trusted, carry this day the question against them. The property of the West Indians was at stake.' Abolition was defeated by a vote of 163 to 88. Whatever the merits of their argument, Roger Anstey concluded, the abolitionists lost resoundingly.[39]

The London Committee quickly resolved that the time had come to appeal once more to the justice and humanity of the nation for 'that redress which was denied by

---

[36] See *Unchained Voices. An Anthology of Black Authors in the English-Speaking World of the Eighteenth Century*, ed. Vincent Carretta (Louisville, 1996), pp. 145–84, esp. 170–1. For a detailed analysis of the role of blacks in the emergence of British abolitionism, see Brown, *Moral Capital*, pp. 282–98.

[37] See Vincent Carretta, *Equiano the African. Biography of a Self-Made Man* (Athens, GA, 2005); and James Walvin, *An African's Life. The Life and Times of Olaudah Equiano, 1745–1797* (1998). In view of the public's focus upon the African slave trade, Equiano may have fictionalized his narrative to maximize its marketability in Britain by claiming an African rather than an American childhood. See also James Sidbury, 'Early Slave Narratives and the Culture of the Atlantic Market', in *Empire and Nation. The American Revolution in the Atlantic World* ed. Eliga H. Gould and Peter S. Onuf (Baltimore, 2005), pp. 260–74, 364 n. 7. On the historiographical controversy over Equiano's African or American birthplace, see Vincent Carretta, Paul E. Lovejoy, Trevor Burnard and Jon Sensbach, 'Olaudah Equiano, The South Carolinian? A Forum', *Historically Speaking*, VII (2006), 2–16.

[38] B.L., Add. MS 21255: minutes of 1, 15, 29 July 1788. See also Robert Isaac and Samuel Wilberforce, *The Life of William Wilberforce* (5 vols, 1838), I, 183–4.

[39] *Cobbett's Parliamentary History*, XXIX, 358 (19 April 1791); and Anstey, *Atlantic Slave Trade*, p. 273.

the policy of parliament'. This time the mobilization was not left to the hazards of local initiatives. It was orchestrated from the centre. Clarkson systematically toured England. Another agent, William Dickson, covered Scotland. The emissaries were no longer seeking but dispensing evidence in the form of a carefully selected abstract of the testimony before the select committee. They also offered cautionary advice on the timing of petition meetings. The agents' function was to 'excite the flame', but delay its flaring forth until the mass of petitions could simultaneously converge on parliament.[40]

The results far exceeded the committee's expectations. Even two decades later Clarkson's sober *History* allowed itself a moment of awe:

> Of the enthusiasm of the nation at this time none can form an opinion but they who witnessed it. There never was perhaps a season when so much virtuous feeling pervaded all ranks ... The current ran with such strength and rapidity that it was impossible to stem it ... [No petitions] were ever more numerous, as far as we have any record of such transactions ... The account stood thus. For regulation there was one; against all abolition there were four; and for the total abolition of the trade five hundred and nineteen.[41]

Upwards of 400,000 names flowed into London just in time for the opening of Wilberforce's second motion. These were probably the largest numbers of both petitions and signatures ever simultaneously reaching parliament on a single subject. In some parts of the country between a quarter and a third of the adult male population petitioned for abolition, with Manchester's proportion reaching nearly 50 per cent.[42]

Geographically, the committee received positive responses from one end of the country to the other. No boundaries were drawn between backwaters and large towns, or between 'principal' and 'general' inhabitants. Clerical assemblies, universities, chambers of commerce took their places modestly beside trades organizations and workers' friendly societies. The committee emphasized that it favoured popular petitions.

Polemics could, of course, be matched by opposition propaganda. Signatures could not. Anti-abolitionist attempts, first in the press and later in parliament, to devalue or denigrate the signatories actually reinforced the evidence of popularity. Open public signing at guarded sites was recommended in order to catch or minimize groups, like schoolboys, who were considered illegitimate signatories. Paupers on public welfare were not sought out by sponsors since the open nature of their adhesion made their signatures vulnerable to the charge of coercion.[43]

The popular response to the great campaign of 1791–2 indicates that the abolitionists requested and received almost unlimited support within the contemporary boundaries of legitimate signers. The organizers were clearly less worried about too little popular enthusiasm for abolition than too much. Their most important concern

[40] B.L., Add. MS 21256: minutes of 27 May 1791; London, Library of the Religious Society of Friends, TEMP MS 10/14: William Dickson's Diary of a visit to Scotland, 5 Jan.–19 Mar. 1792.

[41] Clarkson, *History*, II, 352–5.

[42] Drescher, *Capitalism and Antislavery*, p. 80; and Oldfield, *Popular Politics*, pp. 114, 123 nn. 83, 84.

[43] Drescher, *Capitalism and Antislavery*, p. 82.

was actually the danger to their own popular mobilization from linkage with other or more radical programmes. Clarkson's first warning to William Dickson, *en route* to Scotland, was to urge him that it was 'impossible to be too earnest in professing the distinction between emancipation and abolition'. The committee was burdened by the memory that the less coordinated petitions in 1788 had resulted in simultaneous denunciations of both slavery and the slave trade, subverting the abolitionists' tactical claim, that their target was the slave trade alone. Dickson was warned to steer the potential petition committees away from any discussion of policy except the most general idea, that 'what is unjust must be impolitick'.[44]

Most members of the London Committee also feared that other political issues might impinge on the abolitionist mobilization. Clarkson, very sympathetic to the French Revolution, was explicitly warned by Wilberforce to steer clear of discussing it for fear of damaging the cause. When Dickson made two contacts who lacked any connexion 'with the French Revolution club', he charged them to 'beware of any allusion to it; or even to *liberty*'. Dickson also encountered evidence that opponents were making efforts to use the St Domingue slave uprising of 1791 against petitioning and had already succeeded in terrifying at least one sympathizer in Perth.[45]

There was also another mass anti-slavery mobilization that the committee approached with caution. Following the parliamentary defeat of abolition in 1791 a new abolitionist strategy emerged outside the orbit of the London Committee. A nationwide campaign was launched to abstain from the consumption of slave-grown sugar. This 'anti-saccharite' movement was more than just a symbolic means of pollution avoidance. It was meant to be an instrument of direct economic coercion against the whole slave interest and it dramatically broadened the public sphere. Special appeals were directed towards women, as managers of the household budget. They stressed women's sensitivity to family destruction and offered them a means of compensating for their exclusion from the petition campaign. Children too were also urged, and volunteered, to become part of this national consumer mobilization. On his speaking tours, Equiano distributed pamphlets against consuming slave sugar. Although Clarkson privately favoured the anti-saccharite agitation in hopes of increasing the turnout for petitions, Wilberforce feared abstention as likely to alienate moderates.[46]

Thus, alongside the carefully crafted and targeted appeal of the London Committee appeared a parallel movement involving hundreds of thousands of other participants. Although we have no breakdown of the abstainers by age or gender, women and children, the majority members of most families, clearly lay outside boundaries envisioned by most of the provincial petition committees. Some abstentionist polemics explicitly identified the British legislature, as constituted, as an institution that was unlikely to abolish the slave trade. Since parliament had failed to heed the express will of the people, the people had to 'manifest to Europe and the World that public spirit,

[44] Library of Religious Society of Friends, William Dickson's Diary of a visit to Scotland, instruction, 1.

[45] *Ibid.*, 5: 14 Feb. 1792.

[46] Clarkson, *History*, II, 349–50; *Life of Wilberforce*, I, 338–9. See also Shropshire R.O., Plymley diaries 5: 27 Feb. 1792.

that virtuous *abhorrence* of SLAVERY, to which a British SENATE is unable – or unwilling to aspire'.[47]

The language of this radical voice of abolition resonated with other voices calling for fundamental political reform in Britain. In the winter of 1792 the anti-saccharite movement appeared to be but one more symptom of many radical challenges sweeping across the Atlantic world. Every British radical political organization hailed the surge of abolitionist petitions as the harbinger of still greater transformations. They happily incorporated 'the end of the slave trade' into their toasts and resolutions. The Society for Constitutional Information and the London Corresponding Society found a natural affinity in the plight of enslaved Africans and oppressed Britons. The British press noted the French National Assembly's award of honorary citizenship to Wilberforce. As the flow of petitions peaked early in 1792 anti-abolitionists widely advertised publications detailing the horrors of slave revolution in St Domingue. Clarkson felt impelled to publish a denial of membership in the Jacobin club of Paris. The counter-abolitionist strategy broadened to conflate abolitionism not only with slave emancipation, but with every potential threat to public order, foreign and domestic.

During the extended parliamentary debates on abolition in April 1792 the news coverage of abolition reached a crescendo. For want of space some daily newspapers ran full verbatim reports of the debates in parcels extending over days and even weeks. The house of commons spent much of the month of April analyzing the petitions and their significance. Fox reiterated the premise of 1788 – a table loaded with petitions indicated that the whole people of England felt a legitimate grievance. The unprecedented pile of sheets on the table in 1792 emboldened some abolitionist M.P.s to welcome the charge that schoolboys and people of the lowest status had signed on: 'What did this prove but that individuals of all sorts, conditions and ages, young and old, master and scholar, high and low, rich and poor, the risen and the rising generation, had unanimously set every nerve on stretch for the overthrow of the ... abominable and the indefensible?'[48]

For a few weeks the new wave of public opinion seemed to have succeeded in reversing the defeat of 1791. The house of commons voted for gradual abolition by a vote of 230 to 85, and for an immediate end to the British trade to foreign colonies. By a far smaller margin, the Commons voted to set the date of total abolition at 1796. Yet within months the abolitionist tide receded both in parliament and in the country. In 1788 the Lords had barely assented to the Dolben regulatory measure. Now they insisted upon hearing their own evidence and put off beginning the hearings until the following session. By then the political window for agitation had closed. Fear of domestic radicalism was compounded by the twin threat of revolutionary slave

---

[47] See Drescher, *Capitalism and Antislavery*, pp. 56–60; Carretta, *Equiano*, p. 355; *Considerations addressed to Professors of Christianity* (1792), p. 2; and W[illiam] A[llen], *The Duty of Abstaining from ... West India Produce ... January 12, 1792* (1792) p. iii, 'advertisement'.

[48] *The Diary* [a newspaper published in London], 14, 24 April, 4 May 1792. In moments of major conflict with abolitionists the colonists in the West Indies also petitioned parliament, but in far smaller numbers. They later shifted their pleas towards the crown, reflecting the 'increasingly unpopular nature of the pro-slavery cause'. See David Lambert, 'The Counter-Revolutionary Atlantic: White West Indian petitions and Proslavery Networks', *Social and Cultural Geography*, VI (2005), 405–20.

emancipation in the Caribbean and French revolutionary expansion in Europe. By 1793 'odium had fallen on collective applications' to parliament for any reform.[49]

5. *The Third Mobilization 1806–7: Abolition*

Nothing resembling the great popular agitation of 1792 was repeated before the passage of slave trade abolition acts in 1806–7. This has led many historians to conclude that the larger public played little or no role in these last parliamentary initiatives. Accounts written on this phase of the struggle focus almost exclusively on the interaction of the parliamentary saints and the governmental leadership. Some historians see parliamentary abolition as having occurred within a long lull in popular participation, stretching from 1792 until the 1820s.[50]

If one looks beyond mass petitioning, the role of public opinion, in 1806–7 is abundant. In accounting for its changed form, one must bear in mind both the magnitude of the reactionary culture of the 1790s and abolition's relatively rapid reappearance as the first successful reform movement after the French revolutionary decade. Even in the 1790s, for all of the innuendos about Wilberforce and jacobinism, the Commons never refused to consider his annual motions for abolition. By 1804 fears of popular radicalism had subsided. The British Volunteer Movement had demonstrated, in the view of Prime Minister Addington, that 'the people', continually assembled and armed, had indicated a collective determination to defend British independence that 'transcended the divisions between social classes'.[51] In these large associations, regularly gathered together, slave trade abolition was deemed quite compatible with the broader struggle for national liberty. Preachers told the volunteers that they were fighting to decide whether there should be any more freedom on earth and made an explicit connexion with the moral imperative to welcome abolition.

The dissociation between abolition and French radicalism was eased by Napoleon's reinstitution of colonial slavery in 1802. With the resumption of Anglo-French hostilities the following year, the French ruler became the potential enslaver of two worlds. Toussaint L'Ouverture, 'torn like a felon from Domingo's plain' and shipped to Europe to die in captivity, suffered a fate that loomed over Britons too. The invasion scare of 1803–4 stimulated speculations that French conquest would result in able-bodied Englishmen being 'turned out in gangs, like galley slaves', or turned into factory and mining slaves.[52] Correspondingly, the struggle of ex-slaves against

---

[49] *Life of Wilberforce*, II, 18.

[50] See James Walvin, 'Abolishing the Slave Trade: Anti-Slavery and Popular Radicalism, 1776–1807', in *Artisans, Peasants and Proletarians, 1760–1860* ed. Clive Emsley and James Walvin (1985), pp. 32–56. Turley, *Culture*; David Brion Davis, 'Capitalism, Abolitionism and Hegemony', in *British Capitalism and Caribbean Slavery. The Legacy of Eric Williams* ed. Barbara L. Solow and Stanley L. Engerman (Cambridge, 1987), pp. 209–28; and Oldfield, *Popular Politics*, p. 186.

[51] Linda Colley, *Britons* (New Haven, 1992), pp. 309, 319. Henry Addington, the prime minister least sympathetic to abolition, used the peace negotiations with France in October 1801 to sound out the possibility of a mutual prohibition on the further introduction of Africans into the Caribbean. See Yves Benot, 'Bonaparte et la Démence Coloniale (1799–1804)', in *Mouri pour les Antilles. Indépendance nègre ou l'esclavage (1802–1804)*, ed. Michel L. Martin and Alain Yacou (Paris, 1991), pp. 20–1.

[52] Austin Gee, *The British Volunteer Movement, 1794–1814* (Oxford, 2003), p. 186; and Stuart Semmel, *Napoleon and the British* (New Haven, 2004), pp. 46, 57, 112. Haiti's impact on British opinion is detailed

France shifted the role of St Domingue's revolutionary masses to a potential ally against a common enemy. With each passing year after 1804 Haiti's approach to British merchants for vital trade links made the new regime appear less threatening to both British colonial and national interests. This shift would ultimately be reflected in parliamentary debates. By 1807 the long absence of indigenous revolts among slaves in the British colonies became an abolitionist axiom: 'Look at the state of these islands for the last 20 years and say, is it not notorious, that there never were so few insurrections among the negroes, as at the very time they knew that such an abolition of this infamous traffic was under discussion?'[53]

The decoupling of abolition from these exogenous threats did not, of course, suffice to insure abolition's success in parliament. In May 1804, Pitt's return to office and the uncertainty about the impact of newly independent Haiti on the British islands encouraged Wilberforce to reintroduce his abolition motion, unaccompanied by any pressure from without. The bill successfully passed through the Commons late in June. The old hurdle then reappeared. The Lords again insisted on hearing evidence, and the lateness of the session caused Wilberforce's allies to advise postponement until the following year.

Relying solely on manoeuvring from within was not enough. In 1805 Wilberforce saw his majority in the Commons melt into an unexpected minority. As Anstey concluded, the victory of 1804 had been deceptive. 'Enemies had only to exert themselves more, and friends less, and the day was lost.'[54] Regrouping after the unexpected setback, the London Committee decided that renewed popular pressure was essential to break the stalemate. For the first time since 1792 Clarkson was dispatched on another tour to reconnect with the local communities. He reported on the relative ignorance of the younger abolitionists but was more struck by a widespread welcome that could be turned into activism. The energy of the new generation could furnish the movement 'with endless sources of rallying'.[55] Given the pitfalls of national mobilization, the Committee confined its tactics to localized mobilizations, but they began to have a serious effect. As early as 1805 the slave interest protested that the 'violent' propaganda being worked up in Yorkshire, Lancashire and London by their antagonists was becoming a serious deterrent to the flow of capital to the Caribbean. The West India Committee had to revive its dormant propaganda committee.

With the formation of the Grenville ministry early in 1806 the abolitionists returned to the 'partial' abolition tactic that had twice failed to gain traction in the Lords – the

---

[52] (*continued*) in David Geggus, 'British Opinion and the Emergence of Haiti, 1791–1805,' in *Slavery and British Society, 1776–1846*, ed. James Walvin (1982), pp. 123–49. On Haiti's diminishing role as a military threat before 1807, see Seymour Drescher, *Econocide. British Slavery in the Era of Emancipation* (Pittsburgh, 1977), pp. 167–9, 256 n. 11.

[53] Lord Howick led off the debate on the committal in the Commons on 23 Feb. 1807; *Cobbett's Parliamentary Debates* [hereafter *P. D.*] (41 vols, 1804–20), VII, 952. See also, Drescher, *Econocide*, pp. 169, 256 n. 11.

[54] Anstey, *Atlantic Slave Trade*, p. 346.

[55] Clarkson, *History* II, 502–3; on details of the mobilization, see Seymour Drescher, 'Whose Abolition? Popular Pressure and the Ending of the British Slave Trade,' *Past and Present*, No. 143 (1994), 136–66; and Peter F. Dixon, 'The Politics of Emancipation: The Movement for the Abolition of Slavery in the British West Indies, 1807-1833', Oxford University D. Phil. 1971, pp. 119–32.

Figure 1 A section of the petition of the inhabitants of the town and neighbourhood of Manchester for the Foreign Slave Trade Abolition Bill, presented to the Lords on 14 May 1806 (© Parliamentary Archives, HL/PO/JO/10/8/106).

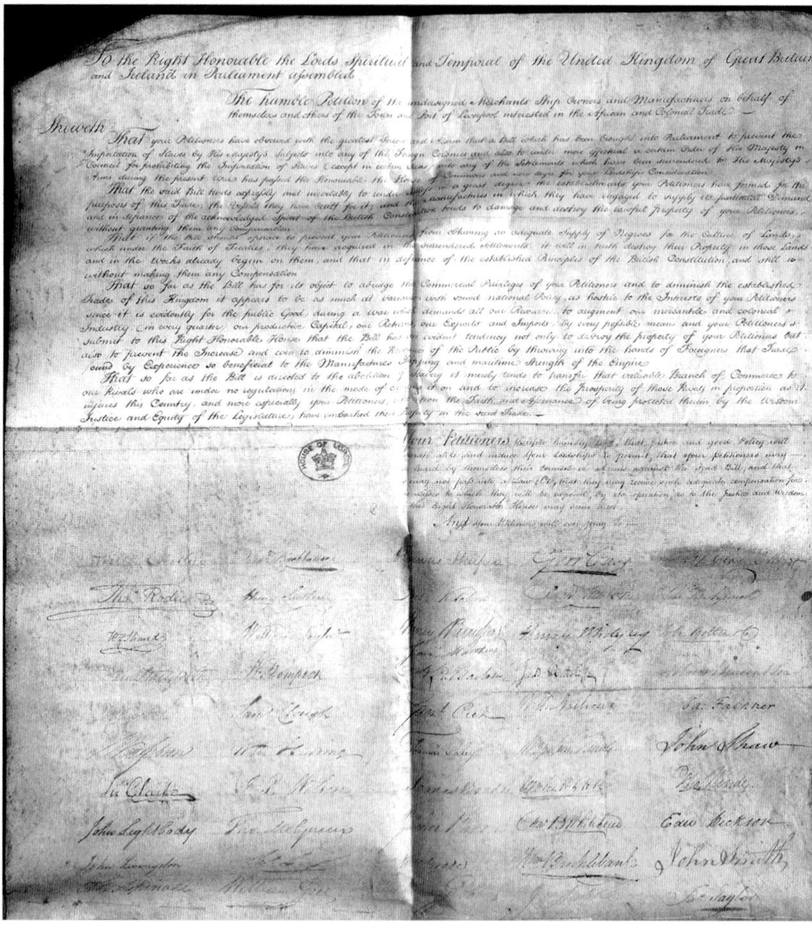

Figure 2   The top section of the petition of the merchants, ship owners and manufacturers of Liverpool against the Foreign Slave Trade Abolition Bill, presented to the Lords on 6 May 1806 (© Parliamentary Archives, HL/PO/JO/10/8/105).

abolition of the British trade to foreign and conquered colonies. By stealth tactics the bill made its way through the first two stages before its implications were discovered by Manchester's Robert Peel, who renewed his vigorous opposition to abolition of two decades standing. He quickly had a petition circulated in Manchester. Ultimately signed by 430 men, it was designed to reach the Lords in time to affect their decision. Clarkson, acting for the London Committee, countered with an emergency appeal to Manchester. In a matter of hours more than five times as many names were dispatched to London in favour of the bill. Clarkson's Manchester co-ordinator assured him that if he had had just a single day more he could have doubled the number of signatures. As it was the petition sufficed to show that Peel had spoken for a minority of the city and its cotton industry.[56] (Figs 1, 2, and see catalogue nos 24 and 25)

With the passage of the Foreign Slave Trade Bill in May 1806, attention turned to the question of total abolition. Grenville and the abolitionists were aware that they had passed the bill on the grounds that it would help the British colonies keep a wartime edge over their competitors. Final abolition would have to contradict that rationale and return to the original abolitionist grounds of 'justice and humanity'.[57] James Stephen urged Grenville to delay the final motion until after the autumn general election, so that M.P.s might be *'instructed by large bodies of their constituents to vote for an abolition of the slave trade'*. Grenville agreed, feeling that an increase in pro-abolitionist sentiment would also help to strengthen the ministry's position in parliament. His strategy worked. Grenville was especially pleased by the electoral result in Yorkshire, where Henry Lascelles, heir to a fortune based on Barbadian sugar was forced to withdraw, abandoning the county's seats to Wilberforce and another candidate pledged to vote for abolition.[58]

Wilberforce's campaign song offered incidental evidence of women's participation in a less well noted aspect of the abolitionist movement:

> O master your Charms on Humanity's Side,
> Your invincible Legion the cause will decide,
> [and the final line of the chorus]
> And Women and Wilberforce conquer again![59]

The last word of the last line indicates that, at least in Yorkshire, female election canvassers were hardly an innovation in 1806.

Early in 1807 the Abolition Committee attempted to estimate the relative strengths of its supporters and opponents in the upcoming debates. The Committee divided M.P.s into four groups: 'Staunch Friends', 'Friendly', 'Doubtful' and 'Adverse'. After careful analysis Stephen Farrell concludes that the numbers of 'Staunch Friends' oscillated between 145 and 177 M.P.s; the 'Friendly' ranged between 65 and 88; the 'Doubtful' between 274 and 307, and the 'Adverse' between 80 and 104. In the

---

[56] Drescher, 'Whose Abolition?', pp. 142–4.

[57] Anstey, *Atlantic Slave Trade*, pp. 395, 401–2.

[58] Drescher, *Econocide*, p. 218 (my emphasis). See also, Peter Jupp, *Lord Grenville, 1759–1834* (Oxford, 1985), pp. 388–9, and Drescher, 'Whose Abolition?', p. 145.

[59] *Leeds Mercury*, 14 Nov. 1806.

crucial debate in the Commons, on 23 February 1807, the actual margin of victory was 283 in favour and only 16 opposed.[60]

The 'noes' figure is intriguing. In the last previous vote on a total abolition bill in 1805, a far thinner house had produced 70 votes for abolition and 77 against. Two years later, in a House casting twice as many votes, the bill's opponents could produce no more than one-fifth as many votes as they had in 1805. Given the abolitionists' minimal estimate of 80 'adverse' M.P.s in 1807, and setting aside the whole list of up to 300 'Doubtfuls', why could anti-abolitionists not muster more than one in five of the 'Adverse' to vote against on 23 February? And why was the opposition, at that critical moment, reduced to less than a handful of M.P.s willing to speak to their colleagues?

One clue might be found in earlier words of Lord Sidmouth, abolition's major opponent in the cabinet. When he spoke in the Lords debate, earlier in the month he began by referring to 'the pain' that it gave him 'to differ from the great body of people in this country'. In the Commons, the most articulate of the three 'adverse' speakers was more explicit. Liverpool's General Gascoyne complained that:

> every measure that invention or art could devise to create a popular clamour was resorted to on this occasion. The church, the theatre, and the press, had laboured to create a prejudice against the Slave Trade ... The attempts to make a popular clamour against the trade *were never so conspicuous* as during the late Election, when the public newspapers teemed with abuse of the trade, and when *promises were required from different candidates* that they would oppose its continuance. There *never had been any question agitated* since that of parliamentary reform, in which so much industry had been exerted to raise a popular prejudice and clamour, and to make the trade an object of universal detestation. *In every manufacturing town and borough* in the kingdom, all those arts had been tried.[61]

It would be difficult to identify a more anguished register of the weight of public opinion in favour of abolition in the winter of 1807. One can also understand why the forlorn 'noes' in both the press and parliament complained bitterly that 'popular clamour' had displaced the debate into a framework of emotion rather than reason. As for public sentiment, the shrewd Josiah Wedgwood had measured it well in advance of the vote. He had the market sense to fire fresh batches of his classic cameo, for the first time since the spring of 1792, to coincide with the final parliamentary battle for slave trade abolition.[62]

---

[60] See below p. 176.

[61] *P. D.*, VIII, 718–19 (my emphasis). On Sidmouth's opposition to the 'popular cause', see also George Pellew, *The Life and Correspondence of Henry Addington, Viscount Sidmouth* (3 vols, 1847), II, 427–48. In his thorough analysis of abolition in 1807, Roger Anstey concludes that the 'immediate explanation' for its passage 'lies in systematic abolitionist lobbying'. He notes, however, that without exception the abolitionists were astonished that the negative position was so poorly supported by the opposition, despite their 'unusual *exertions*' to procure votes, and what Wilberforce described as a 'terrific list of doubtfuls' (*Atlantic Slave Trade*, pp. 396–400, my emphasis). The outcome conflicts with Anstey's logic for the abolitionists' parliamentary defeat in the previous balloting on abolition in 1805.

[62] Oldfield, *Popular Politics*, p. 159. See also Peter Spence, *The Birth of Romantic Radicalism. War, Popular Politics and English Radical Reformism, 1800–1815* (Aldershot, 1996), pp. 36–7; F. E. Sanderson, 'The

Both the overwhelming victory in parliament and the pressure of public opinion may have had another important effect. The Grenville government fell immediately after the bill received a reluctant royal assent. The new ministry was far less friendly to the act. Had the 'adverse' and the 'doubtful' M.P.s registered a stronger negative in the debates, the incoming ministers might have considered revocation. It is crucial to note in this regard that abolition did not become a symbol of national solidarity in 1807. The role played by Wilberforce and Grenville in its passage only increased the suspicions of a radical like William Cobbett, always hostile to 'negrophile' altruism. Other radicals argued, *ex post facto*, that Grenville's government had acted to relieve the West Indian planters, while Jamaican planters, decidedly of a different view, railed against the damage abolition had done to their future. In Liverpool, rioters terrorized William Roscoe, one of their M.P.s, into withdrawing from politics in 1807 because he had voted for the bill. Finally, within three months of the act's passage, Wilberforce himself came close to losing his Yorkshire seat because of a rumoured campaign alliance with the man on the West Indian interest whom he had forced to withdraw from the 1806 election.[63]

6. *The Fourth Mobilization – 1814: An Enduring Dialogue*

British public opinion did not approach a truly national consensus until the summer of 1814. Foreign minister Castlereagh's entrance into the house of commons, with the treaty of Paris in his hand should have been his moment of supreme triumph. According to *Hansard* he was received with loud cheers. Then Wilberforce rose to speak. He denounced the treaty as the death warrant for a multitude of innocent victims, men, women and children.[64] The treaty's 'Additional Article' reopened the French slave trade, with British sanction, for five full years. Other members were not backward in reminding the House that members of the government, including the foreign minister, notoriously had been among the diehard opponents of abolition seven years earlier.

The London Committee quickly determined to launch another petition campaign, while tactically avoiding a challenge to the government. They condemned the treaty's slave trade article and gave Castlereagh credit for having done everything he thought possible. But the message was clearly aimed at the government of Britain. For the fourth time in 27 years the public was called in against the Atlantic slave trade. The national response was resounding. Although some high tories saw an anti-ministerial challenge embedded in the campaign, not a single 'counter-petition' was sent up to parliament from any quarter. Newspapers quickly reported that signatures were being totted up

---

[62] (*continued*) Liverpool Abolitionists', in *Liverpool, the African Slave Trade, and Abolition*, ed. Roger Anstey and P.E.H. Hair (Bristol, 1976), pp. 126–56; Drescher, 'Whose Abolition?', pp. 149–52; and Marcus Wood, *Slavery, Empathy, and Pornography* (Oxford, 2002), ch. 3.

[63] Drescher, 'Whose Abolition?', pp. 149–152. See especially Paul Michael Kielstra, *The Politics of Slave Trade Suppression in Britain and France, 1814–48. Diplomacy, Morality and Economics* (New York, 2000), pp. 7–15, 23–33.

[64] *P. D.*, XXVIII, 274, 332, 352, 443.

in the hundreds of thousands. Once more abolitionists launched the largest petition campaign Britain had ever seen.[65]

In some ways it was the most impressive of the entire struggle. Clarkson and some quakers threw themselves back into their old routine of co-ordination, now eased by many other hands. Beginning in late June, the abolitionists presented parliament with 806 petitions before the session ended late in July. Ultimately, a total of 1,370 petitions arrived, well above the average annual number of all other petitions reaching parliament between 1811 and 1815. At one point abolitionists estimated that 750,000 people had signed up. Paul Kielstra has calculated the final total to have been 1,375,000, although this figure may include petitions sent up to both houses of parliament. In any event, for a nation with no more than four million males over the age of 16, between a fifth and a third of all those eligible to sign had added their names to the appeal.[66]

Castlereagh's own evaluation of the campaign was concise: 'the nation is bent upon this object. I believe that there is hardly a village that has not met and petitioned.' The duke of Wellington registered a similar impression on his way back to France to renegotiate the slave trade article: 'I was not aware till I had been some time here [London] of the degree of frenzy existing here about the slave trade. People in general appear to think that it would suit the policy of this nation to go to war to put an end to that *abominable* traffic.'[67]

When Clarkson wrote of the petitions, 'All England is moving', he could finally claim that this opinion was as close as Britons might ever get to consensus. Had he chosen to update his *History* in 1814, he might well have summed up public opinion as: in favour of revision, 1,370 petitions; against, nil. The West India interest aligned itself with the nation and against this clear foreign threat to its own competitive position. Most remarkable of all the petitions, however, was the monster document signed by 30,000 men in Liverpool. Just seven years after registering their fury over abolition its citizens placed Liverpool among the most signed-up towns in Britain. Indeed, John Gladstone, one of its major West Indian investors, was responsible for raising the town's total from 2,000 to 30,000. After having been attacked by a mob of unemployed seamen following his vote for abolition, William Roscoe was presented with the freedom of the borough.[68]

With this great surge of petitioning, abolition moved beyond registering a protest against an article in a peace treaty. It definitively launched Britain into a long-term international moral and political campaign against the transatlantic slave trade. It was a pioneering development in the link being forged between the terms of public discourse and the mobilization of public opinion. In the course of a single generation

---

[65] Kielstra, *Politics*, pp. 30–31; and Drescher, 'Whose Abolition?', pp. 160–2.

[66] This ratio is reached by comparing the estimated number of signers with the age ratios for the populations of England and Wales in 1816. See Drescher, 'Whose Abolition?', p. 164 and n; Kielstra, *Politics*, pp. 30–1; and E.A. Wrigley and R.S. Schofield, *The Population History of England, 1514–1871* (Cambridge, 1989), pp. 528–9, 591. For a different interpretation of the 1814 petition, see Turley, *Culture*, pp. 65–6.

[67] Drescher, 'Whose Abolition?', p. 164.

[68] Seymour Drescher, 'The Slaving Capital of the World: Liverpool and National Opinion in the Age of Revolution', *Slavery and Abolition*, IX (1988), 128–43, esp. 139–40.

abolition had evolved from the programme of an innovative public contender into a settled fixture of national policy. The first great reform movement to revive after the general eclipse of the 1790s, its power was successively ratified in legislative victories and governmental policy. By 1814 abolitionism had spawned the first human rights organization and altered the world's perspective on the future of slavery as an institution.[69]

[69] See Drescher, *Capitalism and Antislavery*, p. 67; and 'Whose Abolition?', pp. 162–6. For the effect of British policy on the transatlantic slave trade after British abolition, see David Eltis, *Economic Growth and the Ending of the Transatlantic Slave Trade* (New York, 1987). For an assessment of the ultimate cost of British abolition policy, see Chaim D. Kaufmann and Robert A. Pope, 'Explaining Costly International Moral Action: Britain's Sixty Year Campaign against the Atlantic Slave Trade', *International Organization*, LIII (1999), 631–68. For the long-term impact of the abolitionist process on liberalism and western culture in general, see David Brion Davis, *Slavery and Human Progress* (New York, 1984), pt II, ch. 1; pt III, ch. 3; and his *Inhuman Bondage*, pp. 238–9.

Black People in England, 1660–1807

KATHY CHATER

It was through genealogy that I became interested in the subject of black people in England during the period of the British slave trade. In 1998, suspecting that one of my ancestors had been black, I read the handful of books on their history in Britain before the twentieth century.[1] Most historians of black Britons concentrate on the issues of slavery and poverty, and some, particularly Folarin Shyllon, assume black people's experiences in England were similar to those in the North American and Caribbean colonies, especially in the area of prejudice and discrimination.

The picture that emerged from most of these earlier histories was not one I recognised from my genealogical research over some 25 years. During that time I had come across occasional references to black people in various sources. My impression was that they had not been treated any differently from the indigenous population, most of whom, it is important to remember, were also poor. What, I wondered, was life like for the average black person in eighteenth-century England?

I began to collect references to black people, mainly from parish records, but also from other sources: newspapers, coroners' inquests, wills, diaries and letters. Within a few months I had some 600, more than had been previously assembled. This formed the basis for an article for the *Genealogists' Magazine*, which prompted numerous references from fellow family historians. Systematically working my way through parish registers and other records, I created a database, the first and biggest of its kind, which now contains more than 4,000 entries and the information drawn from it has resulted in a thesis. This enabled me to draw some demographic conclusions about sex, age, places of origin and occupations but a great deal of work remains to be done. I went through every extant parish register in the cities of London and Westminster as well as many others held in the London Metropolitan Archives, the county record office for Greater London. In 2004 London Metropolitan Archives conducted a project to extract every baptism from the parish registers held there and the results were put on the internet, so I was able to use this to supplement my previous work.[2] Combined, this data gives almost complete coverage of baptisms between 1660 and 1807 in the

---

[1] In order of publication they are: James Walvin, *The Black Presence. A Documentary History of the Negro in England 1555–1860* (1971); Edward Scobie, *Black Britannia* (Chicago, 1972); James Walvin, *Black and White. The Negro and English Society 1555–1945* (1973); Folarin Shyllon, *Black Slaves in Britain* (Oxford, 1974); idem, *Black People in Britain 1555–1833* (Oxford, 1977); Peter Fryer, *Staying Power. The History of Black People in Britain* (1984); David Dabydeen, *Hogarth's Blacks. Images of Blacks in Eighteenth Century English Art* (Hebden Bridge, 1985); Rosina Visram, *Ayahs, Lascars and Princes* (1986); Gretchen Gerzina, *Black England* (1995); Norma Myers, *Reconstructing the Black Past. Blacks in Britain 1780–1830* (1996). I later read Kenneth Little, *Negroes in Britain* (1948) and Rosina Visram, *Asians in Britain. 400 Years of History* (2002).

[2] www.corpoflondon.gov.uk/Corporation/lma_learning/dataonline/lz_baproject.asp.

Greater London area and also of burials in the cities of London and Westminster. This work revealed that the largest concentration of black people in the London area, and probably the whole of England, lived in Westminster among M.P.s and peers attending parliament and among the rich and aristocratic people attached to the court. It is a substantial black presence largely ignored by parliament – and by historians who have concentrated their studies on poor blacks in riverside parishes.

The library of the Society of Genealogists yielded entries from several hundred published parish registers for places outside London and transcripts made by individuals and family history societies. Some county record offices have also put findings from their records on the internet and these have been included. Inevitably, however, the coverage for the rest of the country is far from complete. My research is confined to England and Wales, partly because Scotland had, and still has, a different legal system and partly because Scottish and Irish records are held locally. Although there are occasional isolated references to black people in Scotland and Ireland, their history is as yet largely unexplored.

1

John Hawkins is the first Englishman known to have dealt in slaves. He made three expeditions to Africa during 1562–3. Between Hawkins's third expedition and the founding of the Royal Adventurers into Africa a century later in 1663, there are occasional references in English records to black people. Some may have been acquired by merchants dealing in other goods from Africa. Others may have been enslaved Africans captured from the ships of Spain or other slave trading nations, or brought back from colonies in America or the Caribbean. There is some evidence of English trading in slaves before 1660,[3] but 1660 makes a suitable year to mark the beginning of the substantive English slave trade which was legally abolished in 1807. It therefore effectively occupied the period known as the long eighteenth century.

One of the most difficult questions to be answered is just how many black people there were in England during the period of the British slave trade. Historians generally estimate that it was between 10,000 and 20,000. This uncertainty is because there was never any form of legal discrimination against black people: their colour or ethnic origin was irrelevant and not always recorded in official documents. In many instances, the colour/ethnic origin of those on the database has to be deduced from other information. Adult baptism and birthplace are the most significant factors, but being born in a slave colony does not necessarily indicate ethnicity on account of the white population there. Other factors arise from whether the person concerned was a servant and whether master and servant had the same surname. It was, however, common for white people to take poor relations into a household as servants.

It is not always possible to distinguish between people of African origin and those who came from the East Indies. Both are often referred to as 'black', and birthplace is not habitually given. The links between Britain and India following the founding

---

[3] In 1651 the Company of Adventurers of London Trading into the Parts of Africa requested James Pope to purchase '15 or 20 lusty young Negers'. Fryer, *Staying Power*, p. 21.

of the East India Company in 1600 meant that a number of East Indians also came to England.[4] J.J. Hecht noted that not all of these people were slaves and that many of them refused to do anything beyond 'the highly specialised tasks which they were accustomed to at home'.[5] Some of the figures given below may therefore include both categories of people, African and Asian.

The chart below gives the number of people appearing in the database in each decade of the long eighteenth century. This does not, of course, indicate the total number but it shows how the black population grew, especially in the London area, from where the majority of the entries on the database come. As the same pattern appears in the number of black people appearing at the Old Bailey, it seems likely that these figures offer a reliable indication of the relative size of the black population in these years.

The peak years for the black presence in this period were apparently in the 1780s. By this time people bringing their black servants from the colonies were probably less willing to do so because the Mansfield judgement in the Somerset case in 1772 ruled that such people could not be compelled to return. However, this judgement, popularly believed to have freed slaves in England, meant, as W.J. Bolster argues that black people made determined attempts to come here, especially to London.[6] The end of the American War of Independence in 1783 brought a few thousand black people to England, some coming with their loyalist masters and some because they had been offered their freedom in return for fighting on the British side.[7] The French and Napoleonic Wars (1793–1815) also brought some black prisoners of war from the French colonies, who were persuaded to fight on the British side or who remained in England at the end of hostilities. These, however, were a small number.

Black people were not shipped directly from Africa to Britain and sold. No large-scale public slave auctions seem to have been held, although private sales at coffee houses and the like were occasionally advertized. Most black people seem to have arrived in England either as domestic servants to families from the Americas or as sailors. Sea captains, trading with Africa in slaves, were sometimes entitled to a few slaves to sell for their own profit. Many kept one as a servant. It is likely that African seamen were also recruited by slave traders to replace members of their crews who had died or deserted.[8]

The origin of most black people in England remains unclear. There is no place of origin given for the majority of people (almost 75 per cent) on my database. Nor is there usually any way of knowing whether those coming from the Americas were born there, or in Africa and then shipped to the colonies before crossing the Atlantic again. Where origin is given (in just over 25 per cent of cases), the majority of people came from the Caribbean, but again it is rarely possible to tell their original place of

[4] The East India Company was granted a royal charter in 1600 and wound up in 1858.

[5] J. Jean Hecht, *Continental and Colonial Servants in Eighteenth Century England* (Smith College Studies in History, XL, Northampton, MA, 1954) pp. 50–4. There was never any European slave trade with India.

[6] W. Jeffrey Bolster, *Black Jacks* (Cambridge, MA, 1997), pp. 19–21, 149.

[7] This migrant group formed the core of London's 'black poor' in the late 1780s and prompted the ill-fated Sierra Leone scheme of 1787. Stephen J. Braidwood, *Black Poor and White Philanthropists. London's Blacks and the Foundation of the Sierra Leone Settlement 1786–1791* (Liverpool, 1994).

[8] Emma Christopher has found evidence of black seamen involved in the slave trade. *Slave Ship Sailors and their Captive Cargoes 1730–1807* (Cambridge, 2006).

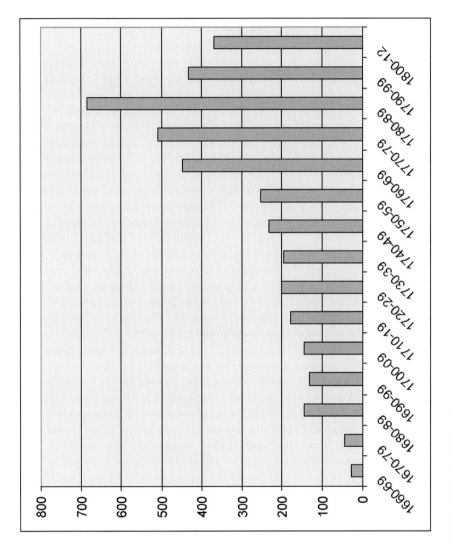

Figure 1 The Black Population in England.

birth. The next most common area of origin was Africa, followed by Asia, then North America. In addition, two (baptised on the same day) came from South America and one, a 'Spanish Indian', was either from Europe or South America or one of the Spanish Caribbean islands.

It is generally agreed that the ratio of men to women shipped from Africa to the Americas between the late seventeenth century and the first half of the nineteenth century was 64 per cent men and 36 per cent women.[9] Men were preferred for the hard physical labour on plantations. African traders were also less willing to sell women, partly because they produced children and partly because most agricultural work in Africa was, and still is in rural areas, largely a female occupation. In addition, it was women who were more likely to be kept as slaves in Africa. England had enough agricultural labourers of its own, so black people came from the colonies mainly as domestic servants. In this area of occupation men were preferred because the range of duties they could carry out was wider than that of women. The diary of John Baker, the solicitor general of St Kitts who in the 1750s came to England, includes references to his black servant, Jack Beef, carrying out tasks, like accompanying Baker's sons to school, conducting business deals for his master, riding ahead of the family when they were travelling to make arrangements for accommodation and food, all jobs that a female servant could not do at that time.[10] In addition, black servants in England were something of a status symbol, especially in highly visible positions, like footmen, pageboys or waiters at table.[11]

The evidence suggests that, up until the 1780s, the ratio of black men to women in England was approximately three-quarters to one-quarter. Thereafter, the overwhelming majority, about 80 per cent, of black people who came to England were men. As the imbalance is most notable in ports, especially London and Liverpool, these were probably mariners and may have been transient, although some undoubtedly did settle in England with wives and raised families.

The majority of black people seem to have been comparatively young when they enter the records (Fig. 2). Slave traders preferred younger people, partly because their youth meant they were more able to do the hard physical labour needed in the colonies, but also because they were considered to be more malleable. This also seems to be true of domestic servants brought to England. Age is not always given but, where it is, the largest cohort at baptism was between the ages of 10 to 19, followed by people in their 20s. No age is given for almost 36 per cent.

In addition, 328 were simply described as 'adult', 'of riper years' (this is the phrase used in the *Book of Common Prayer* for adult baptism) or 'at maturity'. Eight were described as 'man' and seven as 'woman', which also suggests over 21. There were five described as 'infant' (that is, under the age of two years old); nine as 'child'; 96 as 'boy'; 16 as 'girl'; six as 'youth'; five as 'young' and two as 'a lad'.

[9] P. Lovejoy, 'The Impact of the Atlantic Slave Trade on Africa', *Journal of African History*, XXX (1989), 378–9, quoted in James Walvin, *Black Ivory* (1992), p. 319.

[10] *The Diary of John Baker*, ed. Philip C. Yorke (1931), quoted in Gerzina, *Black England*, pp. 35–6.

[11] This visibility, incidentally, may have produced the over-estimate of black people in Britain made at the time of the Somerset case, which led to the Mansfield judgement. There were claims, apparently accepted by Mansfield, that there were some 15,000 black people in the country. T.B. Howell, *A Complete Collection of State Trials* (34 vols, 1816–28), XX, cols 1–6, 79–82.

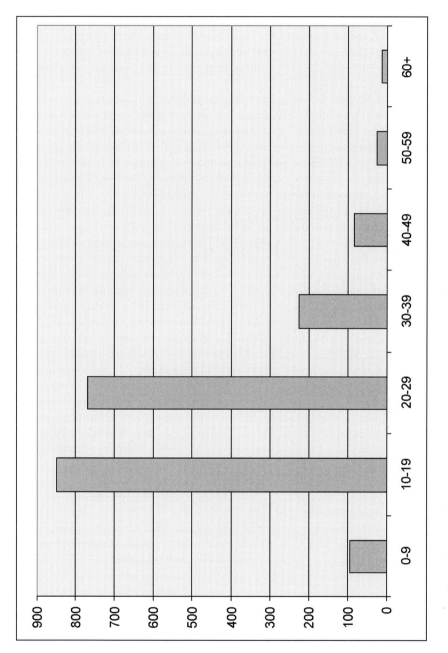

Figure 2 Ages of Black People in England.

2

The question of the legal status of black people in England is one that has been much discussed by historians, and has focussed on the handful of cases brought before the courts to determine whether they were slaves or free. There is still uncertainty about whether black people described as servants in official records during the long eighteenth century were paid, but there were also English servants who did not receive wages.

It is extremely rare, however, to find anyone called a slave: there are only 15 instances on my database. The legal cases culminated in the Somerset case in 1772 over which Lord Mansfield, the lord chief justice, presided. No ruling could be made on the laws in other countries, even British colonies, but while black people remained in England they could not be compelled to return to places where slavery existed (the law remains the same today), although there are examples of black people being kidnapped and returned to the colonies after this judgement.[12]

The Mansfield judgement has been widely misunderstood. At the time it was delivered, many believed that it freed black people in England,[13] and it is still occasionally accredited as such. Yet an article published in a legal journal in 1934 concluded that the judgement did not free black people, and it only prevented them being sent abroad against their will.[14] However, a close reading of the judgement shows that Mansfield concluded slavery had not existed in English law since the establishment of common law in the middle ages although he never explicitly said this. He began by observing that legislation passed overseas did not apply in England. He then reviewed various aspects of the laws relating to service in England without finding anything pertinent, and concluded that only the creation of 'positive law', i.e. specific acts of parliament, could define slavery in this country. The logical conclusion is that, though people legally enslaved in the colonies were brought to England by their masters, they were not slaves in England. However, masters bringing their slaves from the colonies to England genuinely believed slavery to be legal in England, and many of the black people must also have believed that they remained enslaved in England. What happened to them was, however, determined both by what both sides believed, and also how the law was applied during the eighteenth century before the 1772 judgement. There is also no suggestion that slave status was inherited in England and Wales as it was in the colonies: no case dealing with this particular issue seems to have come before the courts.

The area of the law which potentially affected most black people, however, was their status under the poor laws. At the Reformation, the responsibility for caring for those too ill to work or unable to support themselves and their families because of unemployment or poverty passed to individual parochial authorities. A succession of laws was passed to define which parish had responsibility for an individual (and

---

[12] Thomas Day's poem 'The Dying Negro' (1773) was inspired by a story in the press of a black man, taken on board ship, who shot himself rather than return to America.

[13] Wales would also have been covered, but Ireland, Scotland, the Channel Islands and the Isle of Man had their own laws.

[14] E. Fiddes, 'Lord Mansfield and the Somersett Case', *Law Quarterly Review*, L (1934), 499–511, quoted in Walvin, *Black and White*, p. 124.

his/her family, where applicable). The 1662 Poor Relief Act introduced the concept of settlement in a parish, i.e. the right to be supported should someone fall on hard times through poverty, illness or unemployment, a measure which remained on the statute books until 1876, although it was greatly altered by the Poor Law Amendment Act of 1834. The two key factors were the place of birth of a person and whether or not he or she had been employed and paid wages for a year by a master with settlement. These criteria applied to the majority of black people, most of whom were not born in England and some of whom (the percentage is not known) were not paid.

Later acts after 1662 added other ways of gaining settlement: by serving a full apprenticeship to a master who had settlement; by owning or renting property worth more than a certain amount (which also gave a man the franchise) or by serving as a parish official. These applied to a few black people. None of these laws, nor the numerous handbooks written for parish officials who had to implement them, specifically mentioned 'blacks'. This is partly a reflection of their comparatively small numbers but also of the rarity of their need to seek relief. It was not until the influx of black people from the American ex-colonies at the end of the War of Independence in 1783 that poor black people seem to have been perceived as a problem.[15]

Parish officials carried out settlement examinations before a local magistrate to determine which parish had responsibility for a person who was destitute or seemed likely to become a drain on parish resources. If they concluded that another parish was accountable, they obtained a removal order at the local quarter sessions and paid for the person to be taken to that parish. Naturally, parishes often disputed the decision, and the examinations and any subsequent legal wrangling provide some insight into a few individuals' lives. The survival of settlement examinations is patchy. Family and local historians have transcribed some of these. The biggest of such projects is for the parish of St Martin-in-the-Fields in Westminster. Between 1705 and 1795 there were some 60,000 examinations. There are eleven examinations of black men and six of black women. Another related to the child of a black couple, whose mother was dead and the father at sea. In addition, five references to the widows or white wives of black men with whom they were not living have been found and four to the mothers of illegitimate children fathered by a black man. Parish authorities were not much concerned with young men, who could usually find work of some kind, but they did keep a close eye on single women, who were at risk of becoming pregnant, as indeed two of these black women were. Three others had recently given birth to an illegitimate child. In a seventh case, ethnicity can be conjectured from other records. Nancy Lynch, born in Boston, Massachusetts, came to the notice of the parish officials in St Martin-in-the-Fields in 1788. Her colour was not mentioned in the settlement examination but her mulatto (that is mixed-race) child was sent to the workhouse in Greenwich, where she had been born, and thus gained settlement. It is possible that the child's father was black but, given Nancy's place of birth, it is more likely she was. Greenwich did not dispute responsibility for the child.

---

[15] The Sierra Leone project, detailed in Braidwood, *Black Poor and White Philanthropists*, was a response to this.

Bastardy examinations were also carried out to determine the father of an illegitimate child, who could then be pressured into marrying the mother or paying to support the child. Such examinations also provide some information about black people's lives, although these too have not survived in any great number and very few black people apparently appear in them. There are likely to be other black people in these records: married women, for example, took their husband's settlement status so their colour or ethnic origin were irrelevant and therefore not always mentioned.

Elsewhere in the country, there are a handful of surviving settlement and bastardy examinations related to black people. As far as can be determined, the same rules were applied to them as to the indigenous population, with one major difference. It was too expensive to return a black person to his or her last place of settlement if it were in the Americas, Asia or Africa. Thus efforts were usually made to trace the individual's last known master to get him or her to take responsibility. If this failed, the parish seems to have cared for the individual concerned, though such cases were rare. On the whole, masters seem to have had a strong sense of responsibility to their servants and this sense of duty seems to have continued in some cases even after servants had left their service. Benjamin Bowsey and John Glover were two black men who were tried for their parts in the Gordon Riots of 1780. Both men were sentenced to death but reprieved following strenuous efforts by their previous employers, although at the time of the riots Bowsey and Glover were no longer working for them.[16]

It has often been observed that colour and ethnic origin are only intermittently mentioned in parish registers. I argue that this is because clerks were recording facts that might later prove important should an individual (or his/her children) return to the parish to claim relief.[17] In terms of the poor laws, the most important factors were place of birth and paid service, which is why the occupation usually mentioned is that of servant. Marriage in a parish had no implication under the poor laws, so colour/ethnic origin are rarely included in marriage entries. They are recorded in baptismal or, less often, in burial registers. The inclusion of information about colour, ethnic origin or country of birth in burial registers is presumably because children were, in certain circumstances, entitled to claim relief from their parents' parish of settlement. Sometimes a person is recorded as black in a baptismal entry but not in a burial entry. I surmise this is because in the interim the individual had gained settlement in the parish. This theory also seems to account for the phrasing of references to people from other minorities, like French, Dutch and German immigrants, and therefore has implications for the study of these groups as well.

3

Occasional references to black people involved in criminal trials around the country are reported in newspapers. The original court records, which list name, crime, date of trial and outcome, almost never mention colour or ethnic origin, except where

---

[16] Marika Sherwood, 'Blacks in the Gordon Riots', *History Today*, XLVII (December 1998), 24–8.

[17] Kathy Chater, 'Hidden from History: Black People in Parish Records', *Genealogists' Magazine*, XXVI (2000), 381–4.

this relates to identification (Fig. 3). The only place where some analysis of the experiences of black people in the criminal courts is possible is in London, where trials at the Old Bailey were transcribed and published. Initially this was done as a commercial venture, but later these transcripts became accepted as official records.[18] I have done a complete analysis of all cases involving black people between 1674 and 1807.[19] Again, colour/ethnic origin are not consistently given, so using the online database alone does not pick up every black person who appeared at the Old Bailey. Sometimes this can be deduced by internal evidence or ascertained from other sources, but it is almost certain that not all black people who came before the courts at the Old Bailey have been identified.[20] With this caveat, I would agree with Norma Myers, who did a more limited study,[21] that there was no particular discrimination against black people, who appeared as prosecutors, defendants and witnesses. In the slave-owning North American states and in the Caribbean islands, where slavery was enshrined in law, black people could not testify against whites, but no such restriction applied in England and black people, in London at least, seem to have been confident about using the legal system to pursue crimes against them. Their evidence was also accepted against white people. The main witness against Captain John Sutherland, who in 1809 murdered a white cabin boy, was a black mariner, John Thompson. Sutherland was hanged on Thompson's evidence.[22]

Juries could, and often did, find a defendant guilty of a lesser crime than the one he or she was charged with in order to mitigate harsh sentences. There is a strong possibility that, in the absence of a support network of people to testify to their good character or take responsibility for ensuring their good behaviour in future, black men were less likely than white to have their crimes reduced by the jury. It also appears that white people committing crimes against black men were similarly less likely to have their crimes reduced, but because it is almost certain that not all black people in these records have been identified, these conclusions remain tentative. The reasons for these apparent differences must also be explored.

So few black women appear in the records that no valid conclusions about their treatment can be drawn. Even taking into account their smaller numbers in England, and the generally fewer appearances of women in criminal courts, they seem to have been an exceptionally law-abiding sector of the population.

Beyond the law, there is no evidence that black people in their everyday dealings with the general population were discriminated against more than any other immigrant minority. Certainly there are occasional references to the dislike of black people, but there are similar views expressed about the Irish, Jews and, especially, the French. Religion, rather than race or nationality, was the major source of discrimination, both

---

[18] *O.D.N.B.*, XXIV, 295 says Thomas Gurney was appointed official shorthand writer in 1748. The Old Bailey online website says that *Proceedings* was accepted as the official record only in 1778.

[19] The website www.oldbaileyonline.org contains both transcripts of the trials and statistical data, which makes it possible to compare the experiences of white and black people.

[20] There is, for example, a period between 1755–64 when no black person is stated to have appeared at the Old Bailey. Given the increasing number of black people on the database during this time, it is difficult to believe that no one fell foul of the law, either as the perpetrator or victim of a crime in this decade.

[21] Myers, *Reconstructing the Black Past*, pp. 82–103.

[22] *The Complete Newgate Calendar*, ed. J.L. Rayner and G.T. Crook, (5 vols, 1926), V, 42–4.

Figure 3 Undated print attributed to Thomas Rowlandson. The most common crime committed by and against black people was theft. Here two women contemplate a newly arrived sailor, whose pay and prize money make him a potential target. Both black and white sailors were frequently robbed by pairs of women working together. (Collection of the author.)

legal and social. Roman catholicism, in particular, inspired fear and loathing and it was not until the nineteenth century that legal bars on the entry into various areas of public life of catholics, protestant nonconformists and Jews were finally lifted. There was never any specific legislation against black people. A few, the mixed-race children of plantation owners by their slaves in the colonies who sent their children to England, achieved some success. So far, the one who attained highest public office seems to be Nathaniel Wells, who became deputy lieutenant of Monmouthshire.[23] Another, Brian Mackey, was rector of the parish of Coates in Gloucestershire,[24] and a third, Robert Laing, studied at Lincoln's Inn and was called to the bar in 1793.[25] In all these cases, their colour was not mentioned in official records but has to be recovered from private correspondence and diaries. It is likely that mixed-race women, especially rich heiresses, came to England from the colonies and married well but so far only fictional examples, like Miss Schwarz in Thackeray's *Vanity Fair* for example, have been found.[26]

These mixed race children tended to disguise their origins, as Robert Laing's descendants later did, by claiming Spanish or some other ancestry that accounted for their colouring. It was also believed by people in England at the time that their darker complexions were the result of the climate in the Caribbean.[27] In eighteenth-century England, their illegitimacy was possibly seen as more of a problem than the colour of their ancestors. The two became equally unacceptable in the later nineteenth century with the rise of what is called 'scientific racism', the belief that there was a hierarchy of races with Caucasians at the top and Negroes at the bottom.

4

Because the information easily recovered about black people mainly comes from parish registers, there is a tendency to assume that all were servants, but, as already indicated, there were legal reasons why the occupation of servant should be recorded in this particular type of record. In fact, just over 81 per cent of people on the database have no occupation recorded.

[23] J.A.H. Evans, 'Nathaniel Wells of Piercefield and St Kitts: From Slave to Sheriff', *Monmouthshire Antiquary*, XVIII (2002), 91–106. I am grateful to Eric Este, a descendant of a branch of Wells's first wife's family, for drawing my attention to him.

[24] *Alumni Oxonienses 1715–1886* (4 vols, Oxford, 1888–91), III, 895; J.D. Thorp, 'Rectors of Cotes or Coates', *Transactions of the Bristol and Gloucestershire Archaeological Society*, VIII (1929), 322–3; *Paupers and Pig Killers. The Diary of William Holland a Somerset Parson 1799–1818*, ed. J. Ayres (1984), p. 106; T.N.A. (P.R.O.), PROB 11/1422.

[25] Information from Lucy Richards, his great-great-granddaughter. He was not very successful there and became destitute. His son attended Christ's Hospital, a charity school, and after a brief, equally unsuccessful foray into the bar, became a teacher at his old school.

[26] There were also mixed-race children from the Indian subcontinent. Katherine Kirkpatrick, the daughter of James Achilles Kirkpatrick and his wife Khair um-Nissa, returned to England after her father's death. She married Captain James Winslowe Phillips. The family's story is told in William Dalrymple, *White Mughals* (2002).

[27] Edward Long, *The History of Jamaica* (2 vols, 1774), II, 274.

Some black people remained career servants, either with the same family, or moving from job to job.[28] One who did remain with the family until his death, some 19 years after obtaining his freedom and receiving a small legacy in his master's will, was John Scipio, servant of the slave trader William Snelgrave.[29] The fact that a black person would remain in service with the family of the man who had not only purchased him but also traded in hundreds of his compatriots may be difficult to understand today, but it is an indication that the concepts of service and slavery had different meanings in the past. Scipio was no downtrodden, abused wretch. When he died in 1760 his own will showed he was, by the standards of the day, better off than the average tradesman.[30]

Though a large proportion of black people in this country undoubtedly started their working lives as servants, as did the majority of the indigenous inhabitants before the First World War, there is evidence that some (the proportion is not known) left service for other jobs often in victualling. In the 1720s William Smith set up a sutler's booth in Hyde Park.[31] The best-known is Ignatius Sancho, who started life as a pageboy, was promoted to butler and then set up a grocery shop in Westminster. He is famous because he was acquainted with David Garrick, Lawrence Sterne and other figures in literary and artistic circles, and wrote a series of letters which were published after his death.[32] His life is known through his writings, but there are other black shopkeepers who lacked his literary talent and thus have remained obscure, like Africa Hunsdon of Hunsdon, Hertfordshire[33] and William Phipps of Westminster,[34] who were both, like Sancho, victuallers. These men are unlikely to be the only black servants who left their masters to set up businesses, just those whose occupations are mentioned in parish registers or other records.[35]

A few black people were apprenticed to a trade. Again, colour or ethnic origin are not regularly mentioned so it is impossible to know how many followed this route. For example, in 1725 a Scipio Affricanus [*sic*], described simply as 'a poor orphan',

---

[28] Some of those giving evidence at the Old Bailey remarked in passing that they were 'out of place' or 'between hirings'.

[29] Kathy Chater, 'Where There's a Will', *History Today*, L (April 2000), 26–7. Technically Snelgrave could not give Scipio his freedom: as the Mansfield judgement pointed out, slavery did not exist, and had not existed in England and Wales, but this is one of a number of examples where both master and servant were under a misapprehension.

[30] T.N.A., PROB 11/856. He left cash legacies totalling more than £200, as well as money for mourning rings, two watches, silver buckles, plate, china and other household goods.

[31] *Proceedings [of the Old Bailey]*, 7–12 Sept. 1722, p. 5.

[32] *Letters of the Late Ignatius Sancho, an African*, ed. Vincent Carretta (1998); Reyhahn King, Suhkdev Sandhu, James Walvin and Jane Girdham, *Ignatius Sancho an African Man of Letters* (1997).

[33] Hertfordshire R.O., Hunsdon parish baptismal register. He was baptized on 1 Apr. 1711, when he was noted to be 'a native of Africa' and the servant of Matthew Blucke. His son was baptized on 8 Sept. 1727, when his occupation, 'victualler', but not his ethnicity, was recorded. I am grateful to Dr Jill Barber of the record office for these references.

[34] City of Westminster Archives Centre, Registers of St Clement Danes: William babtized, 27 Nov. 1715.

[35] The *Proceedings* contain what appear to be shop assistants like Edward Thompson (*Proceedings*, 1785–6, IV, no. 325) and Thomas Wheeler (*Proceedings*, 22–25 Feb. 1727/8, p. 1) and a gardener John Commins (*Proceedings*, 1781–2, V, no. 664).

was apprenticed to John Highfield, citizen and cordwainer of London.[36] His name must indicate that he was black but how many others there were with less distinctive names is not known. By the time this Scipio Affricanus completed his apprenticeship (usually seven years), he would no longer have been eligible to become a citizen of London like his master and every other successful apprentice in the city. This was because in 1730 a black man called John Satia completed his apprenticeship, and thus became a freeman of the city with all the privileges that brought. The city of London authorities promptly passed a regulation forbidding the apprenticeship of black people. This has usually been cited as an example of racial discrimination but it should be seen as the latest in a long line of ordinances designed to reserve the privileges of the city to a small *élite*.[37] Jews were particularly restricted in what they could do in the city, a further example that religion was the main source of discrimination before the mid-nineteenth century.[38] Elsewhere in the country, other black men, like Bill Richmond (later famous as a boxer) in Yorkshire;[39] George John Scipio Africanus in Nottingham[40] and Edward Juba in Leicester[41] were apprenticed to a trade after periods in service and became freemen of the towns and cities where they served their apprenticeships.

Seafaring was the other occupational area in which black men are known to be strongly represented. The most famous black British writer is Olaudah Equiano. Although he is best known for his involvement with the abolitionist movement and the Sierra Leone project, Equiano spent much of his youth at sea in the royal navy.[42] It is not easy to find out how many black mariners there were. Eighteenth-century records of the royal navy include place of birth and where the individual entered the service, but there are no comparable records for merchant seamen at this time. Even a place of birth in the colonies does not necessarily indicate black ancestry: there were many white people involved in seafaring there. Descriptions of mariners may say that someone had a 'black' complexion, but this word was also applied to dark-skinned Europeans – and seafarers were often dark-skinned because of their

---

[36] Society of Genealogists, unpublished typescript, *The Apprentices of Great Britain 1710–1762*, I, taken from T.N.A., IR Book 10/159.

[37] Irene Scouladi, *Returns of Strangers in the Metropolis 1593, 1627, 1635, 1639* (1985), pp. 1–72, details the various restrictions and attempted restrictions imposed on aliens and strangers from all countries.

[38] Guildhall Library, London Information Leaflet 'Sworn Brokers Archives'. The number of Jewish and alien brokers was limited. Jews could not become freemen of the City until 1830, although a few had been admitted before 1738.

[39] en.wikipedia.org/wiki/Bill_Richmond. Richmond came from America as a servant of the duke of Northumberland, who arranged for his apprenticeship as a cabinetmaker. Yorkshire also had the first black man to become a freeman of a city; John Moore becoming freeman of York in 1687. I am grateful to Audrey Dewjee for drawing my attention to John Moore.

[40] Ray Gale, en.wikipedia.org/wiki/George_Africanus.

[41] Leicester is one of the boroughs where the freedom descends through the eldest son: currently one of Edward Juba's descendants is entitled to this privilege through his ancestor.

[42] *Olaudah Equiano. The Interesting Narrative and Other Writings* ed. Vincent Carretta (2003). He is also claimed as a black American writer: though as a 12-year-old boy he was baptised in St Margaret's, Westminster, he was brought to London from Carolina and may have been born there as the parish registers record rather than in Africa, as he says in his autobiography. City of Westminster Archives Centre, Registers of St Margaret, 9 Feb. 1759.

exposure to the elements. Contemporary pictures and prints attest to their routine presence on board ships.[43]

If black sailors seem not to have been promoted to the extent of their white counterparts in the royal navy, this is probably partly due to the system of promotion in operation at the time. Although the navy rewarded talent more readily than the army, some influential support was also necessary. Edward Young, one of the mutineers on the *Bounty*, came from St Kitts and was said to have black ancestry. He entered Captain Bligh's service as a midshipman (a starting point for a potential officer) because a Captain George Young requested that he be taken on.[44] It can be presumed that this captain was a relative of Young's to whom Bligh owed a favour. How many other black or mixed-race midshipmen or officers there were remains a matter for conjecture – Young's background was of public interest because of his involvement in the mutiny and was therefore mentioned at the time. The website detailing sailors involved at the battle of Trafalgar gives numerous examples of mariners born in the colonies but there are no references to colour or racial origin simply because this information was rarely entered in the original records.[45]

Service in the royal navy but not in the mercantile marine, brought the right to be treated or to live in Greenwich Hospital on retirement, and there are a number of examples of black men accorded this benefit. Briton Hammon, apparently the first black man to write his autobiography, spent some time recovering at Greenwich after being wounded at sea.[46] After their lives in the royal navy ended, some preferred not to live in the hospital but still received pensions in lieu just like their white counterparts.

The army also employed black soldiers. It is not always clear from early eighteenth-century records whether some were soldiers or servants of army officers. John D. Ellis has found that black rankers were rarely promoted.[47] As with the navy, promotion depended partly on influential contacts, but it was also possible to buy rank, a further barrier to black soldiers without rich connexions.

Many black soldiers were musicians. This was a highly visible position because musicians led the way on ceremonial duties, and this may be analogous to the aristocracy employing black servants as status symbols. However, some musicians had another duty. It was customary in the army for drummers to administer floggings. A black man flogging a white man was 'a new and disagreeable spectacle', as a Lincolnshire newspaper declared in 1768, but the army seems to have seen no problems with this.[48]

---

[43] Craig Spence, 'Seeing Some Black in the Union Jack', *History Today*, LII (October 2002), 30–9.

[44] Trevor Lummis, *Life and Death in Eden* (1999), p. 81–2.

[45] www.nationalarchives.gov.uk/trafalgarancestors.

[46] Briton Hammon, *Narrative of the Uncommon Sufferings and Surprizing Deliverance of Briton Hammon, a Negro Man, Servant to General Winslow of Marshfield, in New-England; Who returned to Boston, after having been absent almost Thirteen Years, etc* (Boston, 1760), p. 12.

[47] J.D. Ellis, 'The Visual Representation, Role and Origin of Black Soldiers in British Army Regiments During the Early Nineteenth Century', University of Nottingham, M.A., 2000.

[48] John D. Ellis, 'Drummers for the Devil? Black Soldiers of the 29th (Worcestershire) Regiment of Foot 1759–1843', *Journal of the Society for Army Historical Research*, LXXX (2002), 194–5.

Scipio Affricanus, mentioned above, was given what today is regarded as a name typical of black slaves.[49] It has been suggested that these classical names mocked their bearers. As Folarin Shyllon observed:

> The black ... was often made to bear an absurdly pompous classical name. The exalted associations of which contrasted sharply with his lowly estate as a chattel or plaything ... Why such classical names should have been bestowed upon these poor black lads is hard to say, unless the practice arose from a cruel inclination to mock at them by contrasting their grand appellations with their abject fortunes.[50]

Given the importance of servants in everyday life, this would seem to be a mistake on the masters' part. The opportunities for a mocked and humiliated servant to make disagreeable the lives of the members of the family he or she served were numerous. Classical names were in vogue in the eighteenth century, although they are found from the Renaissance onwards. Military men were particularly fond of Caesar, Hector and Hercules for their own sons, as parish registers in garrison towns attest. However, these names were given to only a small percentage of black men, usually servants of the aristocracy. Such black servants were a status symbol, and noblemen probably saw them as a kind of pet. This impression is reinforced by the fashion for silver collars, like dog collars, that were advertised in the press and are sometimes mentioned in advertisements for runaway servants. Heroic names are very rare for black women; there are only a few Didos[51] and Cleopatras on the database. Lower down the social scale, however, the names most commonly given to black people are identical to those of the general population. The most common name for a black man in the long eighteenth century is John Williams.

In the course of constructing my database, I came across a number of black people who married and reared families. So far it has only been possible to reconstruct the lives and descendants of individuals with distinctive names – tracking the descendants of a John Williams (black or white) is a virtually impossible genealogical task. Those with a name like Juba, given only to black people, are easier to find in records and descendants can often be traced for several generations and in a few cases down to the present day, like the freeman of Leicester mentioned above. It is very rare, however, to find the colour of a black person's child specified. It is the parent (almost always the father) whose colour or ethnic origin is stated. This is because, under the poor laws, children took their status from their father if their parents were married, so it is his that is recorded. The colour/ethic origin of women is only given if the child is illegitimate. After the first generation, however, black ancestry becomes invisible. Occasional references to mulattos is made, although I have only found adults, not children born in this country, described as such. Nor are there the fine gradations found in the slave-owning colonies of colour and ancestry, quadroon, octaroon, quintaroon, sambo, mustee, mustefino.

---

[49] Presumably a reference to the Roman senator.

[50] Shyllon, *Black People*, pp. 15–16.

[51] Presumably after the legendary founder and queen of Carthage.

The lives of black women are particularly hard to recover as they legally disappear on marriage. As mentioned above, colour or race are very rarely given in marriage registers. On marriage, women took not only their husbands' names but also their status under the poor laws, so their ethnic origin became irrelevant. The only eighteenth-century women about whom much is known are those whose lives were noteworthy. Black Harriott was the mistress of a Caribbean plantation owner who brought her to England around 1766 but died in 1772, leaving her and her children destitute. She ran a series of brothels in Westminster.[52] Ann Duck, the daughter of a black man who taught swordfighting to men of the inns of court, and his white wife, became a member of the Black Boy Alley Crew, a notorious criminal gang in Clerkenwell, London. She was tried and acquitted several times at the Old Bailey before being sentenced to death.[53] She was hanged in November 1744 and the ordinary of Newgate published her confession.[54] Her career was reported because crime is newsworthy. A law-abiding life is not.

So far the only respectable black women about whose lives much is known are Joanna Vassa, daughter of Olaudah Equiano (whose wife was white), and Dido Elizabeth Lindsay, the mixed-race great-niece of Lord Mansfield.[55] They are of interest and considered worthy of research because of the prominence of their male relatives. How many other black or mixed-race women were living quietly and unremarked has yet to be discovered.

Both Peter Fryer[56] and Gretchen Gerzina[57] conclude that black people and their descendants during the period of the British slave trade became part of the general population in Britain. I have reconstructed several generations of the family of a black man named John Juba, whose daughter Sarah married a man named Outlaw in Suffolk. This has been possible only because of her comparatively rare married name. Sarah's female descendants married men with more common names, like Dawson, and disappeared into the general population, just as their male counterparts did.

That black people were treated much like everybody else is not a very exciting story but it appears to be true of the long eighteenth century. Attitudes towards black people seem to have remained much the same until the rise of what is called scientific racialism in the mid-nineteenth century. However, research on individuals in the

---

[52] E.J. Burford, *Royal St James* (1988), pp. 201–4. What happened to her children is unknown.

[53] *Proceedings* 1743–4, II, nos 77, 297; *Proceedings*, 1743–4, VII, no. 448, *Proceedings*, 1743–4, VIII, no. 435. Another crime in which she was involved, but for which she was not tried nor did she mention in her own confession comes in the confession of Elizabeth Nash, Ordinary's *Accounts*, 24 Dec. 1744, p. 39 ff.

[54] Ordinary's *Account*, 7 Nov. 1744. This confession included other crimes which she committed but for which she was not tried.

[55] Joanna Vassa married a clergyman, Henry Bromley. She is buried in Abney Park Cemetery in north London. The couple seem to have had no children. (Information from Vincent Carretta, author of *Equiano the African. Biography of a Self-Made Man* (Athens, GA, 2006)). Dido Lindsay married a man named Davinier and her descendants can be traced down to the 1970s. Sarah Minney, 'The Search for Dido', *History Today*, LV (October 2005), 2–3.

[56] Fryer, *Staying Power*, p. 235.

[57] Gerzina, *Black England*, p. 183.

nineteenth century, such as that carried out by Professor David Killingray[58] and Dr Caroline Bressey[59] also reveal that at the level of individual black people's experiences, there is a far more complex and interesting story than popular assumptions would suggest.

The early books on black history in Britain were mainly written in the 1970s, a period when discrimination against black people was a major source of concern. In particular, Folarin Shyllon's two major works[60] are still influential, but they were the product of this particular intellectual climate. They were both published for the Institute of Race Relations and take as a starting point the assumption that during the long eighteenth century there was widespread discrimination on the basis of colour. He used examples from America to draw conclusions about life in Britain for black people, yet the legal and social factors were substantially different. Later research on individuals in England reveals considerably less hostility based on colour or race than is popularly believed, like Nathaniel Wells mentioned above; the musician and composer Joseph Emidy, who played a substantial part in Cornwall's musical life in the early nineteenth century,[61] and a host of other lesser-known black people.

Only the reconstruction of the lives of many more unremarkable individuals will make possible the production of demographic data, like age at marriage, average number of children, age at death, social and geographic mobility and the like. It may then be possible to draw comparisons between the experiences of the average black person and his or her white counterparts during the period of the British slave trade. There are other factors to be considered, such as potential differences between the experiences of black people in urban and rural areas. An experienced genealogist needs about a full working week to do the reconstruction of one person's life. There are thousands of individuals for whom this needs to be done and it will be a lengthy process, so this will require the involvement of many family and local historians.

---

[58] David Killingray, 'Tracing People of African Origin and Descent in Victorian Kent', in *Black Victorians, Black Victoriana*, ed. Gretchen Gerzina (New Brunswick, NJ, 2003), pp. 51–67.

[59] Caroline Bressey, 'The Black Presence in England and Wales after the Abolition Act, 1807–1930' see pp. 224–37.

[60] Shyllon, *Black Slaves* and *Black People*.

[61] Richard McGrady, *Music and Musicians in Early Nineteenth Century Cornwall. The World of Joseph Emidy – Slave, Violinist and Composer* (Exeter, 1991).

Trinidad: A Model Colony for British Slave Trade Abolition

GELIEN MATTHEWS

This essay presents an historical survey of the supply of enslaved African labour to colonial Trinidad during the era of Caribbean slavery. The central thesis of the study is that when Great Britain committed itself to the abolition of the slave trade, Trinidad, a relatively new British colony, was singled out for special treatment. The island became Britain's experimental colony; a position that was greatly facilitated by the fact that Trinidad was never tainted by substantial imports of enslaved Africans. The work chronologically examines the attempts made first by the Spanish colonists, followed by French and then by the British, to import African slave labour to Trinidad to man the various agrarian enterprises attempted in the colony. It is argued that, fortuitously for British slave trade abolition, under its Spanish colonizers economic activity in Trinidad was so stunted that no foundation was laid to create a sizeable enslaved African population. With the coming of French planters from neighbouring islands, and later the British, Trinidad did enter the embryonic stage of a slave plantation economy. Cocoa, cotton, coffee and, most significantly, sugar estates were established rapidly in various parts of the island. Trinidad's age of sugar and slavery in spite of its negligible beginnings had finally arrived in the nineteenth century. However, by that time, an enslaved society had still not been fully and firmly entrenched. Then, just before the British capture of the island, parliament, having already committed itself to the gradual abolition of the slave trade, approved several pieces of legislation from 1799 to 1806 which effectively curbed the import of enslaved Africans to Trinidad.

1

For most of its colonial history, Trinidad remained in the hands of the Spanish, becoming a British colony only in 1797, a mere decade before Britain decided to forego its involvement in the transatlantic slave trade. Abolitionists observed the fact that Trinidad never had a large slave labour force and thus was an ideal colony to begin its slave trade abolition project. For almost the entire three centuries of Spanish colonial rule the colony had been neglected because it lacked the mineral wealth of some of Spain's other Caribbean possessions. The Spanish did very little to stimulate either industry or the importation of enslaved Africans to the colony. Thus, British slave trade abolition meant that Trinidad planters were neither able to make do with the enslaved labour they had accumulated in previous years nor did they have the time to amass the numbers that could make the colony another viable British Caribbean enslaved plantation society. The British parliament under the influence of abolitionist agitators regarded the dearth of enslaved labourers in the new colony as advantageous to their general plans for slave trade abolition. Trinidad could be used to test the possible outcome of abolition in other parts of the British West Indies. Thus, the extended and woeful neglect of Trinidad by the Spanish unwittingly helped to secure for the colony the unique historical position of a model colony in the grand scheme of British slave trade abolition.

On 31 July 1498 Christopher Columbus had claimed Trinidad in the names of King Ferdinand and Queen Isabella of Spain. The Spanish monarch retained the island until 18 February 1797 when it was surrendered to the British. Throughout the extended period of Spanish colonial rule, however, Trinidad was nothing but a backwater within the Spanish Caribbean colonial empire. Trinidad's comparative insignificance to the Spaniards arose mainly from the fact that whereas territories like Panama, Mexico and Peru fed the coffers of Spain with precious silver and gold, Trinidad had no similar treasure to offer. The historian Eric Williams has appropriately concluded that 'A benighted, poverty stricken island like Trinidad could never hope to compete with this.'[1]

Apart from a few scattered glimpses of economic activity in Spanish Trinidad, the dominant picture was one of doom and gloom. Few Spaniards settled on the island. Few ships visited, and then only at irregular intervals. Settlers starved for supplies of food, clothing and other basic necessities. The first governor of the island, Antonio Sedeno, did little to make Trinidad an effectively occupied possession of Spain. Sedeno had been appointed to rule the island on 12 July 1530. He had arrived there in 1532 and left within two years. During Sedeno's brief governorship and for some 60 years thereafter, the Amerindians had a free hand in the colony.[2]

In the 1590s Antonio de Berrio was governor of Trinidad. In 1594 he oversaw the first landing of slaves on the island. Under his rule, only two structures gave some indication that a European nation had colonized the island. These were the town of San José de Oruña and the small fort at the mouth of the Caroni River. De Berrio did not personally supervise the establishment of San José. This was done in 1592 by Domingo de Vera acting on his behalf. Historians have commented, nevertheless, that San José, (or San Josef or St Joseph), was far from impressive: 'for decades it remained little more than a clearing in the bush'.[3] Such an uninspiring description of San José strongly suggests that the first set of enslaved Africans who, coincidentally, were imported into the colony specifically for the purpose of constructing the town, could not have been substantial in number.[4]

By 1635 the *cabildo*, a Spanish political structure initially intended to represent the democratic views of the townspeople, was complaining bitterly about the poverty of Trinidad. The *cabildo* lamented 'the thatched building which served as a church

---

[1] Eric Williams, *A History of the People of Trinidad and Tobago* (Port-of-Spain, 1962), p. 13.

[2] Carlton Robert Ottley, *Spanish Trinidad. An Account of Life in Trinidad, 1498–1797* (1971), p. 12.

[3] Bridget Brereton, *A History of Modern Trinidad, 1783–1962* (Kingston, Port-of-Spain, 1981), p. 2.

[4] C.A. Goodridge, 'Land, Labour and Immigration into Trinidad', University of Cambridge Ph.D., 1969, p. 10.

because there were no funds to erect a proper structure … the Cabildo's need to beg for a supply of oil in order to light the building for church services … there were only twenty-four settlers in the whole island, without arms or ammunition'.[5]

Trinidad languished under Spanish colonialism. The wealth of the colony, like most other West Indian territories, lay in the cultivation of the soil, but 'Spain had neither the managerial, financial, commercial, military nor population resources necessary to develop Trinidad'.[6] The Spaniards did not saddle its English colonial successors with the burden of an operational enslaved plantation economy. This dearth in Trinidad's colonial history prevailed almost right up to the era of the British abolitionist movement.

2

While metropolitan Spain did little to foster in Trinidad the model of the Caribbean servile regime that had taken firm root in other Spanish possessions as well as in many British and French colonies, Spanish colonists themselves made at least two significant attempts to introduce economic activities in the island. First, at the beginning of the seventeenth century under a new governor, Don Fernando de Berrio, Trinidad used the enslaved labour of native Indians, Caribs and Arawaks (also referred to as Kalinagos and Tainos respectively) to grow tobacco. The Indians were accustomed to the plant which they cultivated like a weed. Both groups of Indians had ascribed religious significance to tobacco. They believed that the trance they fell into after inhaling the smoke enabled them to communicate with their gods. Spanish cultivation of tobacco using Indian labour brought an interruption to the ennui that had settled on Trinidad right up to the end of the eighteenth century. Tobacco cultivation stimulated a bustling trade between the Spanish and the Dutch, English and French traders. Spanish colonists warmly welcomed this rare development for it provided a period when a fairly regular supply of their basic necessities was met at long last.

A consequence of Spanish tobacco production in Trinidad in the early seventeenth century was the introduction of enslaved Africans to the colony. About 1611 Sir Thomas Roe described to the earl of Salisbury the 15 ships of other nations seen by him in Port-of-Spain exchanging food, clothing and other essentials as well as a small number of enslaved Africans for tobacco.[7] In fact, the historian Johannes Postna records how the 'first successful Dutch slaving expedition was recorded for the year 1606 when Isaac Duverne delivered 470 slaves to the island of Trinidad … one of only two substantial landings by the Dutch before the 1630s.[8] The landing of enslaved Africans in Trinidad in 1606, though small, was far more substantial than the first landing in 1594 under Antonio de Berrio. A contemporary commented that:

[5] Williams, *Trinidad and Tobago*, p. 7; Michael Anthony, *Profile Trinidad. A Historical Survey from Discovery to 1900* (1975), p. 31.

[6] Ope Koyo, 'Labour Shortage in Trinidad, 1498–1797: The Scarcity of African Slaves', University of the West Indies M.A., 1992, pp. 1–2.

[7] Ottley, *Spanish Trinidad*, p. 21.

[8] Johannes Menne Postna, *The Dutch in the Atlantic Slave Trade, 1600–1815* (New York, 1990), p. 12.

Wee find nothing considerable at Trinidada vntill ye yeare 1606 at what time ye Spanyard bought of some Dutch merchants a quantity of Negroe slaues to be Delivered at ye River Carone on Trinidada, being resolved to Rebuild their citie of St. Joseph ... The Dutch Merchants sent their Negroes by one Isaac Duverne who Anno 1606 Landed 470 men & Women Negroes in Trinidada.[9]

The cultivation of tobacco in Trinidad opened up the colony's infant economy to the inhumane traffic in enslaved Africans. What chances there were, however, that the Spanish tobacco planters would lay a firm foundation for the development of African slavery in Trinidad were stifled. As Eric Williams has so clearly delineated in his work *A History of the People of Trinidad and Tobago*, Spain was firmly committed to the economic principle of mercantilism. Trinidad and all other Spanish Caribbean territories were to exist solely for the benefit of the mother country regardless of their state of development or underdevelopment. Spain translated the economic laws of mercantilism into what became known as the *exclusive*. Spain would not tolerate its settlers in Trinidad conducting trade with other nations. As early as 27 February 1610 the Spanish king issued a royal *cedula* to Governor Don Fernando de Berrio banning the purchase of slaves from foreign nations. As first de Berrio and the Spanish tobacco traders, desperate for an increased labour supply, ignored the *cedula*. Royal reaction was prompt. The king ordered an attack against the illegal traders. The tobacco ships in Port-of-Spain harbour were destroyed.[10] The initial show of force was followed by a *residencia*, an aspect of the Spanish system of government which functioned very much like an investigation of the political administration. De Berrio and the settlers put up no resistance against the *residencia*. They threw themselves at the king's mercy claiming that they had traded with the enemy for the sake of their very survival.[11] Spanish insistence on exclusive access to trade with its colonies effectively crushed not only the tobacco trade of the early seventeenth century, but also postponed Trinidad's participation in the transatlantic trade in enslaved Africans. It was the consensus among European colonists to the New World that the Caribbean colonies could only thrive through the importation of enslaved Africans.[12] Spanish colonial economic policy, however, while it crushed the aspirations of its colonists, augured well for making Trinidad a West Indian colony devoid almost entirely of the enslaved. It should be noted that in addition to Spain's effort to end the contraband trade in slaves to Trinidad, the tobacco industry of the island failed because, like other Caribbean producers of tobacco, Trinidad could not compete with the quantity and superior quality of tobacco produced in Virginia.

Another significant occurrence in Trinidad's economic history that might have gone a long way in establishing a substantial enslaved population long before the passage of the British slave trade abolition act of 1807 was the emergence of the

---

[9] V.T. Harlow, *Colonising Expeditions to the West Indies and Guiana, 1623–1677* (Hakluyt Society, 2nd ser., LVI, 1925), p. 125.

[10] Koyo, 'Labour Shortage', p. 7.

[11] Williams, *Trinidad and Tobago*, pp. 13–16.

[12] The historian James Millette has argued that the consensus among colonists was that the slave trade and slavery were indispensable to the material development of the colonial empire (*Society and Politics in Colonial Trinidad* (1985), p. 79).

cocoa industry in the first quarter of the eighteenth century. By 1717 Trinidad's Spanish settlers were producing and exporting from the valley of Santa Cruz, Maraval and the neighbourhood of San José the rich and highly valued forastero variety of cocoa. By the eighteenth century, Spain was the principal market for cocoa in the world and the Spanish appreciated the superior quality of cocoa produced in Trinidad. They willingly paid high prices for the agricultural product. The cocoa plantations of the Spanish farmers in Trinidad were initially worked by Amerindians but soon the demand for enslaved African labour grew steadily. Unlike the turn of events that contributed to the crippling of the tobacco trade of the seventeenth century, the French and the Spanish had entered into agreement to ensure that Spain's Caribbean territories including Trinidad would have the enslaved African labour they demanded to run their various economic enterprises by the eighteenth century . France had taken the initiative in approaching Spain with this proposition. Spain really had no qualms against using enslaved labour from Africa to develop its Caribbean empire although, throughout the era of Caribbean slavery, Spain desisted from direct involvement in the African slave trade. Political rather than humanitarian concerns were the underlying considerations of this policy. Spain adhered to the Treaty of Tordesillas of 1494 which had authorized Portugal's sole access to Africa. Spain, consequently, depended on the *asiento*, a special license, to permit foreign nations to supply her New World colonies with enslaved Africans. Interestingly, Spain thought little of the contradictory impact that the *asiento* would have on her commitment to the economic principle that her colonial empire existed only for her benefit. Thus, 'by a treaty that was entered into on the 27th August 1707 at Madrid between his most Catholic Majesty, by which it was allowed the Royal Company of Guinea, established in France, to supply the Spanish colonists with 48,000 Negroes, of both sexes and all ages, during ten years commencing 1st May 1708 at the rate of 4, 800 Negroes per year'.[13]

It was an ambitious project and had it been implemented a sizeable enslaved population would inevitably have been settled in Trinidad during the Spanish era. Very little was made of the Franco-Spanish slave trade treaty. No enslaved Africans arrived in Trinidad under it. Wars between European nations were largely responsible for obstructing its fulfilment.[14] Instead, between 1716 and 1718 some 40 enslaved Africans were introduced into Trinidad from Barbados and were exchanged for cocoa since colonists did not have the money to pay for them.[15] Furthermore, disaster struck. The Trinidad cocoa industry of the eighteenth century failed. In 1725, a mere 18 years after Trinidad's colonists had begun to export the crop, a fungus attacked the cocoa. No remedy for the disease was discovered. 'All forms of revenue disappeared and commerce came to a sudden halt. The island was suddenly cut off from contact with the outside world, and was to languish in that state for fifty years.'[16] The folding of the cocoa industry meant that the pattern of importations of enslaved African labour to Trinidad would not be altered. The demise of cocoa made enslaved labour redundant. Planters abandoned their enslaved workers. The historian E.L. Joseph

[13] E. L. Joseph, *History of Trinidad* (1970), p. 143.

[14] Linda Newson, *Aboriginal and Spanish Colonial Trinidad* (1976), p. 148.

[15] Koyo, 'Labour Shortage', p. 14.

[16] Brereton, *Modern Trinidad*, p. 3; Ottley, *Spanish Trinidad*, p. 43.

observes that 'In spite of the importation of slaves from the beginning of 1701 ... by 1733 no account is taken of the slaves ... there were so few of them on the island.'[17] Many settlers abandoned Trinidad for the Spanish mainland, taking with them their enslaved labourers and other valuables. Things were so badly off economically that others sold their enslaved Africans to outsiders to get money to buy necessities.[18] Joseph goes on to comment that by 1750 'The prosperity of the colony had by this time sunk to its lowest ebb, and indolence and apathy had seized the inhabitants to a decree that is most incredible.'[19] A hardier variety of cocoa was introduced in Trinidad by 1756 but its quality was inferior to forastero, and the revived industry never approached the promise that was evident in the first quarter of the century.

Under Spanish rule Trinidad experienced at least two major sparks in its economy via tobacco and then cocoa. Had these industries blossomed to their fullest potential, there is little doubt that the colony would have been converted into a regular enslaved plantation entity. Spanish rulers and their policies as well as war and nature, however, all conspired to keep Trinidad at the periphery of the inhumane traffic of enslaved Africans. Consequently, when Britain gained possession of the territory, just a decade prior to the abolition of slave trade, abolitionists had no great difficulty in persuading parliament that Trinidad was the ideal place to begin the process of limiting the imports of the enslaved to the island.

3

It is possible that Trinidad could have become a fully enslaved plantation economy in the 1770s when Spain was persuaded of the dire need to increase Trinidad's scanty population. A royal decree signed by King Charles III on 3 September 1776 permitted under certain restrictions the people from neighbouring islands to go to Trinidad.[20] It was a French planter from Grenada, Philippe Roume de St Laurent, who took full advantage of the royal decree. He travelled back and forth between Grenada and Trinidad as well as to French Caribbean islands and Spain from 1779 to 1783. Roume de St Laurent made it his goal to seek to enhance the benefits migrants would enjoy under the 1776 royal decree. His explorations of Trinidad's landscape left him fully impressed with the rich possibilities for agricultural development in the island. In comparison to the exhausted soil of Grenada, St Lucia, Guadeloupe and Cayenne, Trinidad was a paradise for French West Indian planters who wanted a fresh start in the production of tropical cash crops. One historian comments that St Laurent was 'struck with the beautiful appearance and fertile soil of the island and was astonished at it being unaccountably neglected, considering the comparatively sterile and exhausted soils of neighbouring islands'.[21] Eric Williams has also pointed out

[17] Joseph, *Trinidad*, p. 143.

[18] *Ibid.*, p. 145.

[19] *Ibid.*, p. 153.

[20] Gertrude Carmichael, *The History of the West Indian Islands of Trinidad and Tobago, 1498–1900* (1961), p. 35; Ottley, *Spanish Trinidad*, p. 65.

[21] Joseph, *Trinidad*, p. 158.

that Trinidad's value as prime agricultural land extended to include the fact that even other British West Indian possessions such as Barbados, Jamaica, Antigua and St Kitts, could not possibly compete against the virgin soils of Trinidad.[22] Furthermore, while the soil in Trinidad was tempting and fertile, many estates in Grenada were afflicted with ant infestations. Another consideration for Roume de St Laurent and other French planters was the political, religious and social discrimination they experienced at the hands of the newly arrived British settlers after Grenada passed from French to British hands at the end of the Seven Years War in 1763. These unbearable conditions in Grenada prompted the first substantial demographic and economic changes in Trinidad since the initial Spanish settlement.[23] Roume de St Laurent had also speculated how the *cedula* would stimulate the growth of the enslaved African population of Trinidad. He advocated that 'slaves and skills were exactly what Trinidad badly needed, and that 383 families with 33,000 slaves were on the verge of leaving for Trinidad'.[24]

Roume de St Laurent's efforts resulted in the *cedula* of population of 1783 which offered bountiful benefits to migrants to Trinidad. The *cedula* guaranteed that the new settlers would be exempted from taxation for ten years, unencumbered by the requirement to pay tithes for ten years, entitled to bequeath property, permitted to claim naturalized status after five years of residence and exempted from militia duty and public office. The most irresistible attraction of the *cedula* of 1783 to French Caribbean planters was the provision that rewarded the importation of African slave labour with the acquisition of land. The greater the quantity of slaves the new arrival brought to Trinidad, the greater the acreage of land allotted. Clearly the major objective of the *cedula* was not merely to increase Trinidad's population on the whole but to increase the size of the enslaved labour force. Three and a half acres of land was given to every white settler who took up the offer of the *cedula* and an additional half acre was granted for every slave who accompanied his or her master or mistress. Free coloured migrants were allotted half the quantity of land that was set aside for the new white settlers.[25] The Spanish decision to open up Trinidad to foreigners brought the first wave of migrants as early as 1777. They came from St Lucia and the migrants brought with them their slaves. By 1777 the population of Trinidad was approximately 1,410 with about 200 slaves.[26] A regular trickle of enslaved labour arrived in the island in the 1780s and 1790s. For the first time in its historical experience under the Spanish, enslaved Africans were slowly beginning to become the only significant source of labour in Trinidad.

Apart from the slaves who were brought to Trinidad from the French islands, the Spanish crown took measures to augment the enslaved population. In 1784 a contract was awarded to an Irishman, Edward Barry, to bring enslaved Africans to Trinidad. The result of Barry's contract, however, was negligible. By 1785 Barry had brought 40 enslaved African labourers but only five or six were alive three days later. Around

---

[22] Williams, *Trinidad and Tobago*, p. 66.

[23] Koyo, 'Labour Shortage', p. 21.

[24] Newson, *Aboriginal and Spanish Colonial Trinidad*, p. 179.

[25] Ottley, *Spanish Trinidad*, p. 65; Louise Horne, *The Evolution of Modern Trinidad and Tobago* (Chaguanas, 2003), p. 23.

[26] Horne, *Evolution of Modern Trinidad*, p. 23.

this time also, the Liverpool firm of Baker and Dawson received a Spanish contract to supply 4,000 African slaves per year to Trinidad as well as to other Spanish Caribbean colonies. Trinidad did not become the recipient, however, of the bulk of the Baker and Dawson consignment. In October 1784 Dawson and Baker shipped 640 slaves to the Spanish Caribbean but only 51 were landed in Trinidad. The rest went to La Guiara. On this occasion lack of port facilities and food succeeded in keeping down the enslaved African population of the island.[27]

The year 1784 saw another mad scramble for African slave labour for Trinidad. This time the source was within the Caribbean region. A minor but significant traffic in stolen enslaved Africans had developed between Trinidad and Grenada. The trade, however, was not permitted to grow out of control. The Grenada legislature passed stringent legislation to stop this illegal traffic and was particularly vigilant and suspicious of all persons arriving from Trinidad. Under the 1784 legislation visitors from Trinidad were generally regarded as vagabonds who were liable to be thrown in goal if they could not secure a bond and securities from some respectable person in Grenada.[28]

Fighting against the odds to secure a sizeable enslaved population, the Spanish government declared in 1789 that the trade in African slaves to its colonies was open and that for ten years importation of enslaved labourers was free of import duties. This was an extremely generous concession at the time considering the stringent taxation system that was in force in colonial Spanish America. The concession was a reflection of the extent to which the Spaniards were now intent on boosting their African servile labour supply. These combined efforts produced a limited increase in the enslaved population of Trinidad in the years from 1789 to 1791 when about 3,307 enslaved Africans were transported to the colony.[29]

While imports of enslaved labour to Trinidad were slowly and steadily increasing following French immigration to the island, however, mortality rates among the labourers in this period were extremely high. It seemed as if it was Trinidad's destiny to be devoid of servile labour. The labourers were worked to death during the genesis of the slave plantation economy of the island. The demands of clearing virgin forest for the cultivation of tropical produce through non-technological methods, with limited draft animals and exposure to harsh tropical conditions, ravished the lives of the newly growing enslaved African labour force. One estimate claims that from 1789 to 1791 the total enslaved population declined from 6,451 to 5,916.[30] Overwork was not the only factor responsible for the mortality rate among the enslaved. Many died from unfamiliar diseases, poor food, insanitary housing and improper medical care.[31] The *cedula* of 1783 provided a powerful stimulus for imports of slaves but it was also followed by the wasteful and destructive abuse of human lives involved in the establishment of European type plantation economies in the Caribbean. Despite the generous provisions the *cedula* made to encourage the importation of enslaved

---

[27] Koyo, 'Labour Shortage', p. 39.

[28] *Trinidad and Tobago Historical Society Publications*, no. 605 (July 1984).

[29] Brereton, *Modern Trinidad*, p. 26.

[30] Koyo, 'Labour Shortage', p. 47

[31] *Ibid.*

Africans, in the long run it did not prove to be a great obstacle in the attempts of British abolitionists to limit imports of the enslaved to Trinidad.

4

By the end of the eighteenth century, Trinidad had been captured by the British. The capture was an incidental part of the outcome of Britain's involvement in the first revolutionary war against France. When Spain entered the war on the side of France, military operations spilled over to the Caribbean. Leading the British expedition to seize Trinidad from the Spanish was Sir Ralph Abercromby. He came up against Don José Maria Chacon, the last Spanish governor of Trinidad. Chacon and his forces put up no resistance to Abercromby, and the Spanish capitulated in 1797.

British acquisition of Trinidad coincided with the era of British abolitionism, launched with the formation of the Society for Effecting the Abolition of the Slave Trade (or the London Committee) a decade earlier in 1787. The main advocate of slave trade abolition operating within the British parliament was the humanitarian William Wilberforce. By 1792 Wilberforce and his few parliamentary colleagues, with the assistance of anti-slave trade agitators outside the house of commons, succeeded in committing the British parliament to the gradual abolition of the slave trade.

Abolitionist activity in Britain was the final but most significant dimension of the continuum of Trinidad's demographic pattern of scarcity in African servile labour. While under the Spanish the importation of enslaved Africans was restricted, it was the expressed and deliberate object of British abolitionists to ban any further imports. The British anti-slave trade campaign was bad news for Trinidad planters, especially those of British origin, for they had recently invested great sums of money in opening new lands in the colony that had previously been uncultivated. Spanish, French and British planters in Trinidad were beginning to show interest in the cultivation of sugar cane for sugar prices on the European market at that time were artificially high. Between 1797 and 1801, the embryonic sugar industry in Trinidad grew from 159 sugar estates to 193. Sugar exports nearly doubled in quantity from 8.4 million lbs in 1799 to 14.2 million lbs in 1802.[32] The new pulse in Trinidad's economy was not only manifested in the strides that were achieved in the manufacture and export of sugar. By 1797 there were approximately 452 plantation concerns on the island. These comprised 59 sugar estates, 130 coffee plantations, 103 cotton plantations and 60 cocoa plantations.[33] British, French and Spanish planters alike naturally relied on and expected more and more enslaved Africans to supply the labour for their agricultural estates. By 1797 with the arrival of the British, the slave population of Trinidad had stood at just about 10,000. Within five years vigorous efforts on the part of the colonists almost doubled this figure to 19,709.[34] Striking as the increase may seem, it was hardly adequate to meet the demand that was necessary if Trinidad was to be cultivated to the fullest level of its agricultural capabilities. Historian Bridget

---

[32] Brereton, *Modern Trinidad*, p. 45.

[33] Anthony, *Profile Trinidad*, p. 54.

[34] Brereton, *Modern Trinidad*, p. 45.

Brereton appropriately points out that: 'In 1797 Trinidad was far from being a mature slave colony. It had then less than a sixth of the slave population of Barbados. Only the western lowlands and scattered peripheral areas were settled.'[35] A more detailed depiction of the labour supply and of the limited economic development of the island has been provided by Carlton Ottley. Ottley mentions that sugar estates on the colony usually had fewer than 100 enslaved Africans. By the beginning of the nineteenth century the sugar plantation in Marbella had 100, Union had 85, Harmony Hall had 66 and Les Champs Elysees Maraval had 60.[36] Trinidad's estate proprietors had only begun to scratch the surface of the archetypal plantation economy, but they had anticipated that enslaved African labour would have converted their investments into great fortunes. Anti-slave trade legislation passed by the British parliament under the influence of the abolitionists frustrated the planters' expectations.

As a prelude to the Slave Trade Abolition Act of 1807, the British government, under abolitionist pressure, in 1799 approved a policy which outlawed the practice in the colonies of transferring enslaved labourers from one island to another; a great blow to Trinidad's colonists for a high percentage of their enslaved labour force consisted of enslaved Africans brought from the French colonies and British islands as well. The 1799 decision was the outcome of feverish abolitionist agitation. Wilberforce, under the urging of fellow abolitionist James Stephen, approached Prime Minister Pitt in 1798 to thwart an order in council permitting the supply of slaves from the older British islands to Trinidad and other newly conquered British colonies.[37] The abolitionist rationale behind this project of limiting slave imports to Trinidad appealed to a wide cross section of interest groups in parliament. It went beyond the old humanitarian argument of the evils of the human traffic. The abolitionists proved that national interests necessitated the repeal of the 1798 order in council permitting the supply of slaves to the conquered islands from the older islands. Wilberforce explained that 'the British ought not to invest much capital in colonies which may probably have to be surrendered on the return of peace'.[38]

Nevertheless, despite the abolitionists' success in securing the 1799 change, because it made allowance for the transfer of domestic slaves attending their masters and mistresses, inter-colonial trade in enslaved labourers did occur in Trinidad.[39] The law stipulated that enslaved domestics who were migrating with their owners were not to be sold and their domestic status was not to be changed. In contravention of the law, however, slaves, whether house, field, factory or artisan, were brought and sold in Trinidad. All the newly arrived enslaved were registered as domestics but some were later alienated from their former owners and sold to plantations where they performed non-domestic tasks. Well after general abolition was established, between 1813 and 1821 Trinidad received 3,800 such enslaved of whom nearly 1,000 came from Dominica and nearly 1,200 from Grenada. In 1827, 266 'domestics' were

---

[35] *Ibid.*

[36] Carlton Robert Ottley, *Slavery Days in Trinidad* (Diego Martin, 1974), p. 36.

[37] Roger Anstey, *The Atlantic Slave Trade and British Abolition, 1760–1810* (1975), pp. 332–3.

[38] *Ibid.*, p. 333. See also R. I. and S. Wilberforce, *The Life of William Wilberforce* (5 vols, 1838), II, 377–8.

[39] Ottley, *Slavery Days in Trinidad*, pp. 37–8.

imported into Trinidad from Barbados. Of this number, 204 changed hands and 81 ceased to be domestics.[40] Apart from the passage of the British Abolition Act, another factor that impacted upon the contraband trade among the islands was the fact that slaves in Trinidad fetched very attractive prices. In Grenada, St Vincent and St Lucia slaves sold at approximately £30, in Barbados at £25, in Jamaica at £23, in St Kitts, Nevis and Montserrat at £20 and in Antigua at £17. On the other hand, traders reaching Trinidad enjoyed a distinct advantage for as much as £56 could be obtained from the sale of one enslaved African. The shortage of enslaved labour in the colony in relation to the availability of land made slaves a more valuable piece of property than in the other islands. The only exception to this general pattern was British Guiana which shared a similar predicament to Trinidad in terms of the ratio of enslaved labour to land availability. The average price obtained for enslaved Africans in British Guiana was £58.[41]

5

Following the revolutionary war involving Britain, and France and Spain, by the Treaty of Amiens of 27 March 1802, Britain retained Trinidad. The abolitionists were greatly alarmed. William Wilberforce anticipated that the acquisition of Trinidad with its abundant availability of virgin soil would inevitably lead to the increased demand for labour and an indefinite delay in the abolition of the slave trade. Consequently, he and his abolitionist supporters in the British parliament were resolved that crown lands in Trinidad should not be sold unless proper safeguards to prevent an increase in the African traffic in humans were put in place. The abolitionists questioned whether the new lands in Trinidad should be cleared and cultivated by the enslaved following the pattern in place in other West Indian territories.[42] Wilberforce had given such priority to the Trinidad question that he deliberately held back his motion for general abolition in the parliamentary session of 1802 to allow George Canning to press the crown land issue in Trinidad.

Canning's deliberations on the Trinidad question were lengthy. Canning advocated that the nation should gain maximum advantage from its acquisition of Trinidad. The slave based pattern of British West Indian economic development should be eschewed in the colony to avoid the shame and danger inherent in the system. Furthermore, he reasoned, to adopt the old system in the virgin territory of Trinidad would require a new trade in the enslaved. He demonstrated against taking this course for it would renege on the promise given in the Commons resolutions of 1792 not to create a new slave trade. He reminded West Indian representatives in parliament that in 1797 their spokesman Charles Rose Ellis had committed them to a pledge for gradual abolition, until such time as their present labour force should be adequate. Canning insisted that Trinidad's economy could be stimulated by alternative measures such

---

[40] *Ibid.*, p. 76.

[41] Horne, *Evolution of Modern Trinidad and Tobago*, p. 29.

[42] Patrick Lipscomb, 'Party Politics, 1801–1802: George Canning and the Trinidad Question', *Historical Journal*, XII (1969), 442–66. See also *Life of William Wilberforce*, II, 442–6.

as a vigorous local peasantry and free immigrant labour. To safeguard his motion that Trinidad should not be cultivated by enslaved Africans, he requested a delay in selling the colony's crown lands which if executed without proper legislations would unleash aggressive imports of enslaved Africans there.[43] The abolitionists won the day. Prime Minister Addington assured Canning that no decision had been taken to open Trinidad in the manner that he feared. Commissioners had been appointed to Trinidad to survey crown lands but no directive had been given to sell or allocate grants of land until thorough discussion on the subject had taken place in the House. Canning's misgivings had been assuaged and he felt safe to withdraw his motion. It should be noted that Canning's role on this occasion in protecting Trinidad from large imports of slave labour was not purely motivated by altruistic concerns for the enslaved. One of his uppermost objectives was to undermine the ministry of Addington.[44]

By the beginning of the nineteenth century, on the eve of British slave trade abolition, Trinidadian colonists were informed that Britain would not condone any increase in the number of slaves on the island. The colonists felt sacrificed and neglected by the new British policy just as the earlier colonists under the Spanish had felt. The circumstances, however, were considerably different. Spain had ignored the colonists' demand for enslaved labour because the island lacked the kind of wealth that attracted Spanish colonizers. Britain, on the other hand, denied the island slave labourers that were in great demand at a time when the prospect for economic growth appeared most promising because abolitionist pressure prevailed in dismantling the human traffic. Canning and other abolitionists held the view that Trinidad's population should not be supplemented by slave labour. The laws that were passed giving effect to their intentions perpetuated Trinidad's ancient tradition of a low population of enslaved Africans.

By the order in council of 15 August 1805, the British abolition of the slave trade came into effect in the crown colonies, which included Trinidad, in 1806. Thus, Trinidad's planters had less time to top up their supply of enslaved Africans than their counterparts elsewhere, who enjoyed the comparatively greater political freedom provided by legislative assemblies. The planters, nevertheless as mentioned earlier, had found a useful loophole in 1799 that allowed migrating masters and mistresses to travel with their unfree domestics. To curtail this fraudulent inter-island traffic, soon after the abolition of the slave trade to Trinidad in 1806, the British parliament, under abolitionist pressure, introduced the registration order of 1812. The order was issued to keep track of the census of the enslaved. Planters had vehemently denied abolitionist charges that servile labourers were being smuggled into the island. Yet statistics had proven that although the birth rate among the slave population had not increased markedly, there was significant increase in it. The registrar of slaves in Trinidad in 1813 listed 25,717, an increase of 4,429 over the previous two years. The controversy over the registry, as well as the evidence that substantiated the abolitionists' charges, reflected the desperate labour shortage in Trinidad. Despite the

---

[43] Anstey, *Atlantic Slave Trade*, pp. 332–40.
[44] Lipscomb, 'Party Politics', 442–66.

smuggling, however, there is no doubt that this piece of legislation continued to contain the numbers of the enslaved in Trinidad

The colony of Trinidad experienced a truly interesting and unique demographic history as far as its enslaved African population was concerned. Three hundred years of Spanish colonization established a continuum in which an island full of potential for exploitation via the importation of the enslaved never attained a settled economy based on slavery. The British, who took late possession of Trinidad, turned the scarcity of enslaved Africans to their advantage and made the colony a model for imposing pre-1807 slave trade limitation measures.

'A Less Favourable Specimen': The Abolitionist Response to Self-Emancipated Slaves in Sierra Leone, 1793–1808

CASSANDRA PYBUS

When on 23 February 1807 the bill to abolish the slave trade passed the house of commons, William Wilberforce was exultant. 'Well, Henry', he playfully demanded of his cousin and close colleague Henry Thornton, 'what shall we abolish next?' To which Thornton replied, 'The Lottery, I think.'[1] This scene of pious self-congratulation has been replayed over and over in the literature on abolition, yet rarely has it been questioned for what it reveals of the moral ambivalence of these two evangelical heavyweights. This exchange was not simply a rare moment of jocularity; the lottery *was* the institution most likely to galvanize the abolitionist zeal of the Clapham Sect, whereas the terrible institution of slavery was simply not on their agenda.[2]

The very next day Wilberforce spoke forcefully against a bill for the gradual abolition of slavery, arguing that slaves must first be trained for freedom. He reiterated the view that he had articulated in the Commons in 1804 that enslaved Africans were not 'fit to receive freedom', and so it would be 'madness to attempt to give it to them'.[3] Wilberforce spoke with conviction as a result of his experience as a director of the Sierra Leone Company, which had established a settlement for freed slaves on the west coast of Africa. Henry Thornton was the company chairman and several fellow evangelical abolitionists also served as directors. It is in their response to the emancipated slaves of Sierra Leone that their ambivalence toward enslaved Africans can most clearly be seen.[4]

A settlement for runaway slaves had been the brainchild of Granville Sharp, champion of James Somerset and the *Zong* case.[5] A passionate anti-slavery advocate,

---

[1] R.I. and S. Wilberforce, *The Life of William Wilberforce* (5 vols, 1839), III, 298.

[2] The inner circle of the Clapham Sect, engaged in abolition, moral reform and missionary work, were: Rev. John Venn, William Wilberforce, Henry Thornton, Charles Grant, James Stephen, John Shore (Lord Teignmouth), and Zachary Macaulay, who all lived at Clapham, as well Thomas Babington and Rev. Thomas Gisborne, who were frequent visitors to Clapham.

[3] *Cobbett's Parliamentary Debates* (41 vols, 1804–20), III, 521.

[4] The problematic Sierra Leone experiment is examined in detail in two recent books on the American Revolution: Cassandra Pybus, *Epic Journeys of Freedom. Runaway Slaves of the American Revolution and Their Global Quest for Liberty* (Boston, 2006) and Simon Sharma, *Rough Crossings. Britain, the Slaves and the American Revolution* (2005). An excellent earlier book that discusses the Sierra Leone settlement in exhaustive detail is Ellen Gibson Wilson, *The Loyal Blacks* (New York, 1976).

[5] The case of runaway slave James Somerset led to the decision by Lord Mansfield in 1772 that a slave could not be taken out of England, which all but destroyed the institution of slavery within England. For

Sharp was one of the founders of the anti-slavery committee in 1787, which became, rather to his dismay, the Society for Effecting the Abolition of the Slave Trade (or London Committee).[6] Into the creation of a 'Province of Freedom' he poured all his deepest convictions about humanity and justice among people of all races. Even though the people to be settled there were mostly illiterate and had suffered the demoralizing experience of slavery, Sharp believe they would be as capable of self-government as any. His plan for governance allowed all males over 16 a vote in the common council where power would reside. Households were divided into tens, called tithings, each of which would elect a tithingman, while every 100 households would choose a hundredor. Each person over 16, regardless of sex, was entitled to a one-acre town lot and a small farm, but overall the land was the responsibility of the community as a whole, with a majority vote to dispose of it. As he conceived it, the 'Province of Freedom' should be quite independent, where the settlers could make any laws not inconsistent with Britain's, hold their own courts and elect their own leaders.[7]

It was the Committee for the Relief of the Black Poor, under the chairmanship of Henry Thornton, which put Sharp's plan into action. In May 1787 it hastily settled some 340 black refugees from North America on land at the mouth of the Sierra Leone River, which had been 'purchased' from a local chief of the Koya Temne.[8] However this settlement did not turn out as Sharp had envisaged. It was an unmitigated disaster.[9] When early in 1791 a rescue mission arrived in Sierra Leone, it found only 46 survivors who had been driven out of the settlement by the local chief and were clinging to life on a swampy island in the river mouth. Sharp's anguished appeals for government assistance fell on deaf ears, so he then turned to his abolitionist friends to provide a stable economic base for his 'poor little ill-thriven swarthy daughter, the unfortunate colony of Sierra Leone'. The new plan was to establish a trading enterprise in Sierra Leone that would be an alternative to the abhorrent slave trade, as well as a base for spreading christianity throughout the heathen continent. He recruited Thornton, together with Wilberforce and other close associates from

[5] (*continued*) an excellent discussion of Granville Sharp and the Somerset case, see Schama, *Rough Crossings*, ch. 2. The *Zong* case in 1783 was Sharp's failed attempt to have the master of the slave ship *Zong* charged with murder for having thrown overboard 133 enslaved Africans the year before. The case inspired Turner's famous painting *Slave Ship*. It is discussed in detail in Folarin Shyllon, *Black Slaves in Britain* (1974).

[6] Sharp argued passionately that the committee should agitate for the emancipation of slaves, which the majority of the committee felt to be 'meddling with the property of the planters', see Thomas Clarkson, *The History of the Rise, Progress, and Accomplishment of the Abolition of the African Slave Trade by the British Parliament* (2 vols, 1808), II, 286

[7] Granville Sharp, 'Memorandum on a Late Proposal for a New Settlement to be Made on the Coast of Africa, August, 1783', in Sharp, *An Account of the Constitutional English Polity of Congregational Courts* (1786), pp. 263–81 and *A Short Sketch of the Temporary Regulations for the Intended Settlement on the Grain Coast near Sierra Leone* (1788).

[8] The idea of Sierra Leone as the site for the Province of Freedom came from the mercurial fly catcher, Henry Smeathman, discussed in Deirdre Coleman, *Romantic Colonization and British Anti-Slavery* (Cambridge, 2005).

[9] The first settlement in Sierra Leone is examined in-depth in Stephen Braidwood, *Black Poor And White Philanthropists. London's Blacks and the Foundations of the Sierra Leone Settlement 1786–1791* (Liverpool, 1994).

the Clapham Sect, as well as Thomas Clarkson, who was the powerhouse behind the campaign for the abolition of the slave trade.[10]

With Thornton's firm guidance, a bill to incorporate the Sierra Leone Company passed through the house of commons, on 6 June 1791. In defending the establishment of the company in parliament, Thornton stressed that its object was to promote the civilization of Africa; humanitarian concern for runaway slaves was not a primary consideration. The bill gave the company the right to ownership of the land in Sierra Leone, even though it had originally been granted to the black settlers and their heirs in perpetuity with Thornton successfully arguing that the original settlers had abandoned the settlement and so forfeited their claim.[11] It was telling that with regard to the rescue mission the company had sent to Sierra Leone, Thornton's most pressing concern was to get the company agent to bring the son of a local chief back to be educated in Clapham.[12] The few surviving settlers who had been located were offered new lots of land by the company, but at the same time they were stripped of their right to choose a governor and to exercise control over their affairs; the governance of the colony was solely now the responsibility of the directors. Granville Sharp was forced to accept this 'humiliating change' to his original scheme.[13] Having also been forced to relinquish the chairmanship to Thornton, Sharp had next to no influence on the colony's future.

In order for the Sierra Leone Company's commercial enterprise in Africa to prosper, more settlers needed to be found. It was serendipity, rather than intention, that the new settlers were also runaways from the American colonies. At just the time the company was being formed, a representative of the black loyalist refugees settled in Nova Scotia came to London to petition Pitt's government for his people to be resettled somewhere else. Nova Scotia was unacceptable, the petition argued, because of 'a degrading and unjust prejudice against people of colour that even those who are acknowledged to be free ... are refused the common rights and privileges of other inhabitants, not being permitted to vote at any elections nor serve on juries'.[14] In response to such embarrassing accusations of bad faith, the prime minister undertook to pay the necessary expenses to transport as many black settlers as wished to leave Nova Scotia, and the Sierra Leone Company offered free grants of 20 acres for every man, ten for every woman and five for every child, 'subject to certain charges and obligations'.[15]

---

[10] *Memoirs of Granville Sharp*, ed. Prince Hoare (1820), p. 313: Sharp to Lettsom, 31 Oct. 1787. Sharp has been often claimed as a member of the Clapham Sect (he is listed as such on a panel of the church in Clapham) but he was too individualistic and eccentric in his religious views to be a part of this close-knit evangelical group, see Michael Hennell, *John Venn and the Clapham Sect* (1958).

[11] T.N.A. (P.R.O.), T/669: Sharp to treasury, 18 May 1789. That the land was ceded to the blacks settler and their heirs was stipulated in two separate treaties with the supreme Koya Temne chief. The issue of the land tenure and treaties are discussed by Christopher Fyfe in *A History of Sierra Leone* (1962), p. 11.

[12] The son of the Koya chief Naimbana, baptized as Henry Granville Naimbana in Clapham in October 1792, caused great interest among the evangelical *élite*.

[13] *Memoirs of Granville Sharp*, ed., Hoare, p. 362: quote from Sharp, 5 Oct. 1791.

[14] T.N.A., FO 4/1/419.

[15] 'Free Settlement on the Coast of Africa' signed by the directors dated 2 Aug. 1791 and placed as an advertisement at Shelburne. University of Illinois, Chicago, Sierra Leone Collection: John Clarkson, 29 Oct. 1791.

John Clarkson, brother of Thomas Clarkson and friend of Wilberforce, was engaged as the company agent to collect the emigrants.[16] John Clarkson did a sterling job selling the company's offer in Nova Scotia, patiently explaining to his eager listeners that the expression 'subject to certain charges and obligations' did not signify that an annual rent would be levied on the land; rather it referred to 'a kind of tax for charitable purposes such as for the maintenance of their poor, the care of the sick, and the education of their children'.[17] Clarkson's black audience accepted his explanation, and they especially warmed to his promise that, unlike Nova Scotia, there would be no discrimination between white and black settlers in Sierra Leone.

Accepting Clarkson's assurances, nearly 1,200 people emigrated to Sierra Leone, most of them leaving behind freehold land grants of 40 acres. Wilberforce instructed Clarkson that he should call the new black settlers 'Africans', believing that this was 'a more respectable way of speaking of them', but this was emphatically not how they conceived of themselves.[18] In their eyes they were free British subjects and emphatically they were christians, having migrated as religious congregations. In March 1792 they were led ashore by their preachers, singing the old Wesleyan hymn:

> The day of Jubilee is come!
> Return ye, ransomed sinners, home.[19]

Reaching the land, they had to hack a path through the tangle of thorny bush and sharp-edged elephant grass to reach the site of the settlement. Once a site was cleared and named Freetown, they built temporary huts from green saplings woven together and plastered with mud to support a thatch of grass. Then the rainy season came, bringing with it catastrophic outbreaks of fever. Even so, once that first terrible year had passed, most of these settlers had survived. They began to adjust to the strange environment of Africa, but had less inclination to adjust to the changed political conditions that governed their new home.

The metropolitan fantasies entertained by the directors of the Sierra Leone Company, who envisaged vast profits from plantation crops and trading centres, bore no relationship to the harsh reality of creating a free community on the coast of Africa. None of the directors had ever been to West Africa and they could not begin to imagine what it was like living in mud huts during a torrential monsoon. Nor did they understand that the rugged terrain meant that only a limited amount of land was available for farming. When the settlers began to hack into the jungle, Clarkson realized that there would not be enough arable land to provide the large grants the settlers had been promised and persuaded them to accept only one-fifth of the land they had been led to expect. Clarkson softened the blow by agreeing that the settlers could hold elections for their own peacekeepers, reviving Sharp's

---

[16] For a biography of John Clarkson see Ellen Gibson Wilson, *John Clarkson and the African Adventure* (1980).

[17] New York Historical Society [hereafter N.Y.H.S.]: John Clarkson's Journal, 26 Oct. 1791.

[18] *Ibid.*, 19 May 1792.

[19] The account of this hymn singing is described in J. B Elliott, *Lady Huntingdon's Connection in Sierra Leone. A Narrative of Its History and Present State* (1851), p. 15. N.Y.H.S.: Clarkson's Journal, 11 Mar. 1792, also refers to the hymn being sung.

original concept of tithingmen and hundredors. However, he remained steadfast that the settlers would have no representation on the governing council, which consisted of himself as governor, supported by two white officers of the company, William Dawes and Zachary Macaulay.

In deference to the settlers' fears of further injustice at the hands of self-interested white people, Clarkson chose not to disclose the orders from the company directors to institute a quit rent of two shillings an acre on the land. The quit rent was a cornerstone of the directors' investment strategy and company profit predictions were based on the returns from this rent, which was a hundred times higher than the quit rent the settlers had successfully opposed in Nova Scotia. Clarkson believed that the directors would surely abide by his decision not to impose the tax and that their policies 'must give way to the general spirit of my promises'.[20] It was a high-risk strategy for a servant of the company who was about to go on extended leave.

Clarkson never returned to Sierra Leone. He was dismissed by the company and replaced as governor, first by William Dawes, and then by Zachary Macaulay, who was made of sterner stuff than either of his precursors. Macaulay's sole work experience as an overseer on a slave plantation in the West Indies made him an odd choice for a colony run by abolitionists, yet the directors set much store by this young man. He had repented of youthful wildness and excessive drinking to become an evangelical convert. Thornton described him in glowing terms as a zealous Christian who 'feels he is doing a duty to God by going out'.[21]

Of particular concern to Macaulay was religious observance among the settlers. In particular he was horrified by 'the reigning folly of Methodists of this place in accounting dreams, visions and the most ridiculous bodily sensations as incontestable proof of their acceptance with God and their being filled with the Holy Ghost'. This was *not* the christianity that the company envisaged taking root in heathen Africa. Macaulay instituted compulsory twice-daily sermons, where the company chaplain drove home the message that people could not commune directly with God since 'the Holy Spirit acted always in strict conformity to the word of God as delivered in Scriptures', which the mostly illiterate settlers could not read. Sermons of this nature became so unpalatable to the majority settlers of methodists and Huntingdon Connexion that they soon refused to attend.

Late in 1793, Isaac Anderson, who was a methodist elder, and Cato Perkins, the senior member of the Huntingdon connexion, travelled to London to make a direct complaint to the company directors. Expressing humble gratitude for all the company had done for them, they reminded the directors that the promise to better their conditions, which had induced them to leave Nova Scotia, had not been realized and they feared the promise would never be fulfilled. 'We have not the education which white men have', their petition read, 'yet we have feeling the same as other human beings and would wish to do everything we can for to make our children free and happy after us.' The problem, as they perceived it, was that they still had no land allocation and no option but to work for the company, which set both the

---

[20] N.Y.H.S.: Clarkson's Journal, 30 July 1792.

[21] Macaulay was converted through the influence of his brother-in-law Thomas Babington, who was a member of the Clapham sect. B.L., Add. MS 41262A: Thornton to Clarkson, 20 Nov. 1792.

price of their labour, which they thought too low, and the price for the goods they bought, which was artificially high. It was a form of labour exchange little better than bondage. Worse still, the governor 'seems to wish to rule us just as bad as if we were all slaves which we cannot bear'. At the heart of their concern was a palpable terror of losing the capacity for a sustainable, independent life, and as a consequence their children could be re-enslaved.[22]

These two earnest black men had not a hope in heaven of convincing the directors that injustice was a feature of their great scheme for Africa. A second petition written in formal English by a sympathetic ex-employee of the company, was presented to the directors in November 1793. This missive was much more direct: 'we have a right to a voice in naming the man who will govern us ... we *will not* be governed by your present agents in Africa'. The intention was to jolt abolitionist sensibilities in the directors, concluding 'the manner you have treated us has been just the same as if we were *slaves*, come to tell our masters of the cruelties and severe behavior of an *overseer*'. It did no good. Anderson and Perkins got no answer other than the offer of a return berth aboard a company ship sometime in February or March 1794, 'sent back like fools', they bitterly reported to John Clarkson.[23]

Clarkson was dismayed at the treatment of these two emissaries, observing sadly that the Clapham Sect was imbued with such a sense of religious superiority and moral righteousness that 'all those who may be said to be possessed of an independent heart and honest spirit, who would not *cringe* ... will be neglected'.[24] He was proved right when the directors released their annual report, which bristled with indignation that the settlers should make demands of them. Slaves who ran away from their masters, rather than 'emancipated on a prudent principle of discrimination', proved to be 'a less favourable specimen of the character', the directors explained. As self-emancipated people they did not understand obligations of 'respect and obedience', and were unable to exercise 'due regulation and command of their tempers'. Henceforth, the settlers must learn to curb their 'inadequate or enthusiastic notions of Christianity', and subordinate their 'false and absurd notions ... concerning their rights as freemen' to the long-term objectives of the company, which was the christianization of Africa.[25]

On 13 June 1794, when the slave ship *Thomas* tied up at the Freetown wharf, the captain taunted two black settlers working as porters, 'saying in what manner he would use them if he had them in the West Indies'. In response, a crowd of settlers attacked the captain and one of the porters tried to hit him with a hammer. The captain complained to the governor and the porters were dismissed. Within days Freetown was in uproar. Macaulay was so alarmed that he summoned all the white

---

[22] *Our Children Free and Happy. Letters from Black Settlers in Africa in the 1790s*, ed. Christopher Fyfe (Edinburgh, 1991), pp. 35–9: Perkins and Anderson to Chairman and Court of Directors, n.d.

[23] *Maiden Voyages and Infant Colonies. Two Women's Travel Narratives of the 1790s*, ed. Deirdre Coleman (1999), pp. 143–4. *Our Children Free and Happy*, ed. Fyfe, p. 41: Anderson and Perkins to Clarkson, 9 Nov. 1793.

[24] B.L., Add. MS 41263: Clarkson to DuBois, 1 July 1793.

[25] *An account of the colony of Sierra Leone, from its first establishment in 1793, being the substance of a report delivered to the proprietors* (1795), pp. 24–65.

employees to his house, together with the few baptist settlers who supported the company. Some kind of riot took place on 20 June 1784 when a mob of settlers plundered the company offices and threatened the governor's house.[26] On the third day of unrest, a Sunday, Macaulay distributed a statement to be read in church, which contained the awesome charge of 'the overthrow of God's altars in this place'. Macaulay fully understood the impact of such pronouncements issued on the Sabbath and reinforced his charge by asserting that Africa would 'cry loudly for vengeance on you, if not in this at least in another world'. His threats in relation to this world were no less terrifying. The settlers would be 'doomed to groan chained in the hold of a slave ship, or drag out a miserable life under the smart of a West Indian whip' without the company's protection, he told them. If they did not like the way the company ran Sierra Leone, they should go back to Nova Scotia. He had purchased a slave-trading brig for just such a purpose and any disaffected person was offered a free return passage.[27]

No one could face the prospect of repatriation to Nova Scotia. Protest sputtered out. Eight men were identified as ringleaders and marked out for exemplary punishment. All of these dissidents, Macaulay noted, were from 'that firm body of malcontents', the methodist congregation. Macaulay could see that the methodists self-validating religious experience, and their refusal to defer to ordained clergy, fed resistance to company rule. 'Their government is pure democracy', he noted with distaste, 'without subordination to anyone.' Youthful arrogance and his previous experience as overseer on a slave plantation prevented him from comprehending that faith itself made the methodist meetinghouse a seedbed of sedition. These were people who believed themselves to be God's chosen, living out the story of Exodus. When the preachers spoke about the delivery out of oppression and over the mighty waters into the land of Canaan, the congregation had a very firm idea of what that meant in their own lives. They were not going to be swayed from their goal by the dictates of a white man who believed that his ability to read Blackstone and the Bible gave him control over their lives. Macaulay noted in his journal that the methodist preachers compared the governor to pharaoh, whose oppressive rule must be endured until 'God in his own good time would deliver Israel.'[28]

Lacking the judicial powers to deal with sedition, Macaulay arranged, for the eight men to be taken to England to be tried under English law, sending a number of witnesses against them, but making no provision for any witnesses for their defence. They never were taken to court, nor even kept in prison.[29] By December 1794, Granville Sharp was imploring Thornton to arrange some kind of subsistence for the families left behind in Sierra Leone and to pardon the accused men so they could go home.[30] His advice was never heeded. After another two years had passed, it was John Clarkson who was pleading with Thornton on behalf of the accused men,

[26] The riot is discussed in Sierra Leone Council Minutes, T.N.A., CO 270/2: 16 June–9 July 1794.

[27] T.N.A., CO 270/2.

[28] Henry Huntington Library, San Marino, CA, [hereafter H.L.] MS MY 418: Macaulay Journal, 26 Nov. 1794, 13 Sept. 1793.

[29] Whatever decision the directors made with regard to them remains a mystery; the record of their deliberations was destroyed in a French attack on a company ship in October 1794.

[30] *Memoirs of Granville Sharp*, ed. Hoare, pp. 179–80: Sharp to Thornton, 26 Nov. 1794.

whom he considered were 'treated in a very unjust way'. The directors' abhorrence of Clarkson's jacobin sympathies completely prejudiced them against his views. It was assistance from the settlers themselves that eventually saw three accused men returned to Sierra Leone, while the others presumably 'hungered to death' just as Clarkson had feared.[31]

The persistent refusal of the settlers to subordinate their 'false and absurd notions . . . concerning their rights as freemen' to the economic objectives of the company remained a running sore for the next five years. 'The untoward disposition that which too many of the settlers have shown', Thornton wrote, 'proves but too plainly the importance of bestowing upon them an intelligent and protective government' of the kind provided by Governor Macaulay.[32] The settlers did not see the matter in that light. When one of the elected representatives suggested to the governor that kindness might reduce the level of confrontation at the settlement, Macaulay bluntly replied that if kindness meant acting on the basis of 'fanciful notions about your own deserving', then he was happy to be considered cruel.[33] The methodists tried reasoning with him. 'We are the people of the Methodist connection that are calld people of a ranglesome nature', they wrote to explain, adding that they were 'willing to be under the complement of any proposhall that is just', but they would not be ruled by dictatorial edict.[34] He ignored them. As far as he was concerned, all his trouble could be brought home to the headstrong preachers of these 'mad Methodists'.[35]

By 1796, Macaulay insisted the time had come for the settlers to pay the quit rent. Neither he, nor the directors in London, understood that the colonial government of Nova Scotia had been forced to abandon the concept because settlers, black and white, refused to pay a quit rent that was only 2s. for every 100 acres. When Macaulay cut the amount in half, requiring 1s. per acre, he naively believed that he was being generous and fully expected the settlers to be grateful to him. Accordingly, he redrafted all the titles for the allotments, to which the quit rent was added, to be paid from the beginning of 1797. To his chagrin, most of the settlers did not even bother to claim their new titles. A prominent member of the methodist congregation bitterly rejected the new claims, telling Macaulay that 'he looked on them just as he would on a claim that would bind him a slave forever'. Macaulay thought his statement absurd, failing to grasp that the man was expressing the view of the entire community.[36]

Macaulay also embarked on a calculated assault on the black churches. He regarded the settlers as supremely arrogant in substituting 'visionary and delusionary experience' for the received wisdom of the catechism and complained to his fiancée that these unlettered ex-slaves suffered 'a proud conceit of their own spiritual gifts', which led them to scorn religious instruction, 'fancying themselves wiser then their teachers'. He was hard pressed to decide which of the black sects was the worse: the rowdy

---

[31] T.N.A., CO 270/2: Clarkson to Thornton, 11 Dec. 1796, and Allison to Clarkson, n.d.

[32] *An account of the colony of Sierra Leone, 1795*, p. 22.

[33] H.L., MS MY 418: Macaulay to Directors, 16 Apr. 1795.

[34] *Our Children Free and Happy*, ed. Fyfe, pp. 45–7: Methodist petition, 19 Nov. 1795.

[35] H.L., MS, MY 418: Macaulay to Mills, 20 May 1796.

[36] *Ibid*.: Macaulay Journal, 19 Mar. 1796.

methodists appalled him with the creed of 'which shall bawl the loudest', while the 'rank antinomianism' of the countess of Huntingdon's connexion filled him with disgust.[37] The baptists were the least objectionable, he thought, though like the rest, their morality was extremely lax. Concerned to reform the loose sexual code of conduct that allowed partners to change at will, Macaulay instituted a law that removed the authority to marry from the black preachers and gave sole authority to an ordained minister in the anglican Church.

The result was pandemonium. Even the mild-mannered baptists were outraged at this attack on their religious freedom. One of the methodist elders dictated a letter to the governor, which was signed by 128 settlers, protesting that the new law was 'very disgusting to us, for we are dissenters ... and as such we consider ourselves a perfect church, having no need of the assistance of any worldly power to appoint or perform religious ceremonies for us'.[38] Macaulay took the opportunity of a day in court to lecture those assembled that the letter was seditious from beginning to end, not only disrespectful and insulting, but the 'spirit was that of rebellion itself'. With terror his listeners recalled that the last time the governor talked about sedition, eight men had been torn away from their families and sent to England. Macaulay was well aware of the terrifying effect his words had on his audience, later confiding in his journal that such harsh condemnation was necessary to prevent the methodist meetinghouse turning into 'a kind of Jacobin club'. Barely had he returned to his house on Thornton Hill when some of the methodists were at his door, 'almost dead with fear', to beg his pardon and explain that they had not understood the petition they had signed.[39]

Yet no matter how many times Macaulay lectured them, those of the methodist and Huntingdon persuasions remained obdurate in their resistance to his schemes. They would not allow their children to go to his catechism classes, even when he made it a condition of their access to the company school. Macaulay was enraged that the settlers did not trust him; they did not believe that the words he read to them were the same as the words written on any paper he wanted them to sign, and they were generally insolent toward him. He began to regret even the limited amount of settler representation the colony permitted. In an exasperated moment, he decided Sierra Leone was an object lesson in the folly 'of those who extol *vox populi*, as *vox Dei*'.[40] He derided the elected tithingmen and hundredors as ignorant and perverse, 'destitute of the capacity of joining together two ideas or comprehending the simplest proposal'. When they called on him to discuss their anxiety about a new constitution he was proposing, he told them 'they were disturbing themselves foolishly and to go home and mind their own business.' Not one of them was 'capable of reading or writing a sentence distinctly,' he scornfully recorded in his journal.[41]

Whether they could read or not, the settlers understood that the matter in question was one of huge significance. For more than 20 years, the defining issue for them

---

[37] *Ibid.*: Macaulay to Mills, 20 May 1796; Macaulay Journal, 13 Oct. 1793.

[38] Viscountess Knutsford, *The Life and Letters of Zachary Macaulay* (1900), p. 145: Methodist petition.

[39] H.L., MS MY 418: Macaulay Journal, 14–21 July 1796.

[40] *Ibid.*: Macaulay Journal, 16 Sept. 1796.

[41] *Ibid.*: Macaulay Journal, 16 Sept., 10, 15, 19, 21 Dec. 1796, 3 Jan. 1797.

had been to live as free people and not to submit to the indignities and deprivations that had marked their lives when they were enslaved. Owning land – not renting it or working it for somebody else – was critical in their self-definition, as was regulating their own community. The ownership of land was an essential element in the settlers' definition of freedom, yet they did not invest agriculture with any special mystique. Most were artisans, sailors or fishermen or were engaged in small trading ventures. Masons and carpenters had helped rebuild the nearby slave factory after the French destroyed it, while other settlers worked on visiting slave ships at the wharves. Even if their work was sometimes tainted with the odium of the slave trade, they were at liberty to choose their employment and set the terms of their labour. Macaulay did not understand why so few chose to grow the trade crops that the company needed. He believed they were simply too lazy to climb the hills to reach the farming lots that they had been allocated.

On 5 January 1797 the settlers met to discuss how to get rid of the quit rent, determined never to submit to a condition that reduced them to perpetual tenancy. Macaulay was not about to tolerate any dissent on the issue, warning that 'the smallest degree of clamour and tumult' would see them deprived of every service provided by the company.[42] Six months later the tithingmen and hundredors wrote to the governor to remind him that they had abandoned land in Nova Scotia in the expectation that they would receive land on the same conditions in Sierra Leone, and that they were never told that the land belonged to the company for which they must pay quit rent. 'Sir if we had been told that, we never could come here', they wrote; 'we are astonished why the company could not tell us after three years we was to pay a shilling per acre ... if the lands is not ours without paying a shilling per acre, the lands will never be ours'. Rather than pay, they said, the settlers would apply to the Koya Temne chief for more land that they could hold without such conditions.[43]

About two weeks after he received the letter, Macaulay called a public meeting. He denied that the black settlers had left freehold land in Nova Scotia and insisted that they had always known about the quit rent. The problem with ignorant people, he concluded, was that they were susceptible to 'every prating, malicious, designing talebearer' who wished to misrepresent the good intentions of the company. 'You have often been made to see the folly of acting thus', he told his stunned audience, 'yet you still return like the sow to flounder in the same dirty puddle.'[44] Very soon after this, all the methodists and most of the Huntingdon Connexion turned in their grants, saying that to accept the grant was to accept the status of a slave.

By this time Macaulay's disgust with the 'enthusiasm and bigotry' of his black charges had all but overwhelmed him. In the journal that he kept to send to Thornton, he confided that they were fast sliding into 'the wretched state of barbarism in which their African forefathers were sunk and from which we had fondly hoped they had now been rescued'.[45] So much had they regressed they had come to see themselves as indebted to the Koya Temne, rather than to the company. When Isaac Anderson

---

[42] *Ibid.*: Macaulay Journal, 5 Jan. 1797.
[43] T.N.A., CO 270/4: Sierra Leone Council Minutes, 17 Aug. 1797.
[44] H.L., MS MY 418: Macaulay Journal, 21 Aug. 1797.
[45] *Ibid.*: Macaulay Journal, 8 June 1797.

went to negotiate with the supreme chief who had originally ceded the land to the settlers, Macaulay suspected that the methodists 'cherished hopes of . . . throw'g off the jurisdiction of the company servants, and constituting one of their own number a kind of dictator, who assisted by a council, should rule them after the manner of the Natives around us'. He was sure that he would have to hang two or three of these troublemakers, despite having no legal capacity to enact a capital punishment, and was prepared 'to risk holding up my hand at the Old Bailey' in order to protect the company's interest.[46]

Single-minded in his devotion to the company, Macaulay duly informed the settlers that new titles had been drawn up incorporating the quit rent conditions, for which they must apply by 15 December 1798. About a dozen families accepted the grants and the rest refused, even though the refusal meant their children were barred from the free company school. A new grant register excluded the names of all those who refused their grants and listed their allotments under the designation of unallocated land. Among those whose land was reallocated in this fashion were some of the colony's most successful farmers. As always, the methodists fuelled the disaffection, but this time his action drove nearly every settler into the rebellious coalition, including previous supporters of the company.[47]

Macaulay left Sierra Leone in April 1799, leaving 23-year-old Thomas Ludlam to succeed him as the new governor. Macaulay took with him to England 25 young African children who were his sole source of satisfaction from his duty in Sierra Leone. He believed they, not the turbulent settlers, represented the future of the civilizing project in Africa. Thornton was delighted by the vision of Macaulay's 'triumphal entry into this island with a train of twenty or thirty little black boys and girls at his heels, the trophies which he brings with him from Africa'.[48] The children were installed in a house by Clapham Common to receive an evangelical education.[49]

As soon as Macaulay departed from Freetown, the settlers took matters into their own hands, with the tithingmen and hundredors forming into a bicameral parliament of sorts, passing resolutions about the day-to-day management of Freetown, quite independent of the company. In September this *de facto* government resolved that the back settlers were the proprietors of the colony since it was to these people that the Koya Temne had given the land. In making their bid for independence, the settlers were not to know that Macaulay had been appointed the permanent secretary of the Sierra Leone Company, and in that capacity had applied to the British parliament for a royal charter for formal jurisdiction over Sierra Leone, including full judicial power to 'repress the turbulence and assumption of the colonists'.[50]

In May 1800 Ludlam let it be known that a royal charter was being drawn up in Britain and that this meant all decisions about the management of the colony would be the king's prerogative. If settlers did not comply, they would be tried for treason.

---

[46] *Ibid.*: Macaulay Journal, 26 Aug., 30 Sept., 2 Oct. 1797.

[47] *Ibid.*: Macaulay Journal, 1 Dec. 1797.

[48] Thornton to More, 26 Oct. 1798 quoted in Wilson, *The Loyal Blacks*, p. 256.

[49] The African Academy closed down in 1806. Interestingly, Wilberforce, Macaulay and other evangelicals sent their own sons to the school for a brief period, see Bruce Mouser, 'The African Academy – Clapham 1799–1806', *History of Education*, XXXIII (2004), 87–103.

[50] *Sierra Leone Company Report for 1801*.

He had hoped to scare the settlers into compliance; instead they determined that they must move quickly to secure their independence. On 3 September 1800 nearly all the heads of black households in Freetown attended a gathering to formulate a new code of laws to regulate trading practices, animal husbandry and farming procedure, as well as domestic and social behaviour. The governor's authority was deemed to extend no further than the company's business. Two weeks later the new code of laws was displayed, drawing curious crowds. The frightened young governor overreacted and sent a group of loyal black settlers who he had armed and deputized as marshals to arrest several men on charges of treason. The marshals burst into the meeting just as it was breaking up and in the melee that followed, three men were arrested, while about 40 men escaped. In the following days they established a rebel camp near the bridge on the road out of town.[51]

Subsequently, the Sierra Leone Company tried to portray these rebel settlers as dangerous hotheads who wished to annihilate the company employees. Yet the men camped by the bridge were mostly all middle-aged or older and largely without arms, as all the ammunition was stored at Government House. Rewards were posted for the ringleaders who were charged with 'treasonable and rebellious practices'. After several tense days of failed negotiation, the rebel leader, Isaac Anderson, sent a note to the governor which read 'we de sire to now whether you will let our mens out if not turn out the women and children'.[52] Ludlam interpreted this ambiguous missive as a warning that the rebels intended to attack Government House 'and would give no quarter'. At that critical moment, a large British transport ship arrived in Freetown harbour carrying over 500 maroons and 47 soldiers of the 24th Regiment. Ludlam could not have prayed for a more timely 'intervention of providence'.[53] After months at sea the maroons were desperate for some physical activity, so they were pleased to be invited to 'stretch their legs a little', as Thornton later joked, and hunt the rebels down.[54]

Within a week, two men were dead and five had escaped, but Ludlam had the rest in custody. A court martial sat through October and each of the prisoners was tried for 'open and unprovoked rebellion'. Six men were banished for life to the British garrison at the slave fort of Goree, a sure sentence of death. Twenty-four others were banished across the Sierra Leone River to the Bullom Shore. All of those charged with rebellion lost their land in Sierra Leone, which was distributed to the maroons, along with the houses, stock and crops. A short time later, Isaac Anderson was captured. He was found guilty of sending a threatening letter and hanged with another settler found guilty of taking away a gun. There was no process for appeal.[55]

The personal tragedy and appalling loss in human resources that resulted from these dubious and draconian decisions – 40 of the colony's most respected settlers

[51] T.N.A., CO 270/5: Sierra Leone Company Report for 1800. Ludlam's *post facto* account of this whole episode was printed as Appendix. Eli Akim and John Kizell gave evidence about this episode to the Commission of Enquiry into Sierra Leone in 1826: T.N.A., CO 267/92.

[52] T.N.A., CO 270/5; *Our Children Free and Happy*, ed. Fyfe, p. 77: unsigned, undated letter said to come from Isaac Anderson.

[53] T.N.A., CO 270/5.

[54] Thornton to More 16 Feb. 1801, quoted in Wilson, *The Loyal Blacks*, p. 393.

[55] T.N.A., CO 270/5.

dead or banished – were of no consequence to the directors of the company. Exiling elderly ex-slaves to a slave factory was a grossly unfeeling response, but this heavy-handedness was driven by the belief that settler resistance to company rule was undermining the fundamental project to bring christianity to benighted Africa. None of the directors, except Thomas Clarkson, who had been effectively marginalized after the dismissal of his brother John, had concern for the aspirations for dignity and self-determination among these runaway slaves. The view was that the Sierra Leone enterprise would be much better off without them and 'the crude notions they had formed of their own rights'. Runaway slaves from America had made 'the worst possible subjects', Wilberforce complained in disgust, 'as thorough Jacobins as if they had been trained and educated in Paris'.[56] The company directors accepted Macaulay's proposition that the free settlers were so tainted by their delusionary religion, and so far sunk into the barbarism of Africans, that they could never be the frontline of the mission to Africa. Instead, the directors intended to train emissaries of civilization, removed from the vile degradation of their parents and the disgusting enthusiasm of the settlers, as represented by the 25 hand-chosen African 'trophies' Macaulay brought to be educated at Clapham, in true christian observance and civilized manners.

It is plain that the experience of Sierra Leone coloured the views of these evangelical abolitionists about the liberty due to enslaved Africans. Their stern paternalism was perfectly captured in Josiah Wedgwood's medal with its image of a semi-naked African supplicant in chains, while the record of the Sierra Leone Company shows how their humane concern for the African as 'a man and a brother' could evaporate if he got up off his knees without waiting for their permission. James Stephen's son recalled that all of the inner circle of the Clapham Sect believed that slaves were 'not fitted by education or moral discipline for that greatest and most refined state of liberty which is found under a social restriction of it, as secures an equal share to every member of the same community'.[57] No doubt this was what Wilberforce meant in 1804 when he assured the Commons that enslaved Africans were not fit to receive freedom. He need only look to Sierra Leone and shudder.

The Clapham Sect's deeply ingrained view that Africans were only fit to receive freedom after they had been fully indoctrinated into proper christian beliefs and tutored in their social obligations, encouraged them to define liberty for enslaved Africans in dubious ways. As David Eltis has observed, an overweening concern with freeing the African spirit from bondage to sin caused evangelicals to show a 'less fastidious' concern with the secular concepts of bondage and freedom.[58] Perhaps that was why Macaulay would encourage his successors in Sierra Leone to press Africans into a form of bonded labour that he euphemistically called 'apprenticeships', which looked to others very like slavery in another guise. There seems little reason to doubt the accusation that both governors, Dawes and Ludlam, purchased African labourers whom they worked without pay, hired out to others, and hunted down when they

---

[56] *Sierra Leone Company Report for 1801*, p. 8; B.L., Add. MS 41085: Wilberforce to Dundas, 1 Apr. 1800.

[57] George Stephen, *Anti-Slavery Recollections* (1854), pp. 21–2.

[58] David Eltis, *Economic Growth and the Ending of the Transatlantic Slave Trade* (New York, 1987), p. 103.

ran away.[59] In a letter to Ludlam, in 1804, Macaulay explained that while he was adverse to purchasing slaves in order to profit from their labour, he firmly believed that 'the most likely means of promoting civilization in that country would be by indenting the natives for a period not exceeding seven years, or until they achieved the age of 21'. Anecdotal evidence about the operation of such an apprenticeship scheme in Sierra Leone prior to 1808, suggests that none of these apprentices was ever liberated from servitude.[60]

The same concept of forced indenture was written into the 1807 bill to abolish the slave trade. In the heavily legalistic language of the bill, the enslaved African was constructed as a trade commodity, just as in the abhorrent trade. The slave cargo on ships could be 'seized and prosecuted, as forfeited to His Majesty ... as any Goods or Merchandize unlawfully imported' and were henceforth the property of the crown, whose appointees were empowered to 'enlist the same, or any of them, into His Majesty's Land or Sea Service, as Soldiers, Seamen, or Marines, or to bind the same, or any of them, whether of full Age or not, as Apprentices, for any Term not exceeding Fourteen Years'. Any apprenticeship was to have the same force 'as if' the person had voluntarily bound him or herself and upon the conclusion of the mandatory period the crown would determine where they went, in order to prevent a charge upon anyone to whom they had been bound. Equally, any African recruited into the military was to be treated 'as if he had voluntarily so enlisted', except that provisions to limit the period of service, or grant a pension on discharge did not apply.[61] Wilberforce stoutly defended these blatantly exploitative elements of the bill as 'the least objectionable way of rescuing slaves'.[62] As with his refusal to support a bill for the gradual abolition of slavery because the slaves must first be 'trained for freedom', he was being perfectly consistent.[63]

Three days after the bill received royal assent, Wilberforce and Thornton held the first meeting of the African Institution, an organization they had formed in order to ensure compliance with the new act. Having successfully lobbied the government to make Sierra Leone a crown colony, the African Institution, with Macaulay as its indefatigable secretary, seamlessly took on the role of government advisor on African matters. Viscount Castlereagh, now the colonial secretary, had opposed the abolition of the slave trade, but once the bill became law, he and Wilberforce 'shared the most unreserved and confidential contact' concerning the enforcement of the act and all dealings with Africa.[64] No longer troubled by the responsibility for Sierra Leone, Macaulay was able to keep a firm grip on power in the colony. 'I have little doubt', he wrote to Ludlam, 'that the government will accept any plan we propose to them with

---

[59] Much of the evidence was marshalled by Robert Thorpe, *A Letter to William Wilberforce Esq.* (1815); Gilbert Mathieson, *A Short Review of the Reports of the African Institution and the Controversy with Dr Thorpe* (1816).

[60] *Negro Emancipation Made Easy. With Reflections on the African Institution and the Slave Registry Bill by a British Planter* (1816).

[61] 47 Geo III Sess. 2, c. 44.

[62] University of Hull Archives [hereafter U.H.], DTH 1/61: Wilberforce to Thompson, 19 Oct. 1808.

[63] *Cobbett's Part. Debs*, IX, 142.

[64] Bodl., d17/1, f. 141.

respect to Africa'.[65] Wilberforce had shown the foreign secretary Macaulay's plans for Sierra Leone in August 1807, and Macaulay's memoranda to the privy council in March 1808 were the basis for the decision to designate Sierra Leone as the receiving depôt for captured slave ships. He also determined appointments, including several members of his family, to key positions in the colony and to the vice admiralty court established in Freetown. His instructions about the interception of slave ships were sent to commanders of his majesty's ships in West Africa.[66] In addition, he acted as agent for the captors of slave ships, taking a percentage of the not inconsiderable prize money for the slaves: £40 for a man, £30 a woman and £10 a child. To observe that Macaulay made a substantial amount of money from the suppression of the slave trade is, to echo David Eltis, 'to make an important ideological point rather than to be cynical'.[67]

It was Wilberforce, rather than Macaulay who chose the first governor of the crown colony: Thomas Perronet Thompson, son of his personal friend. Yet for all the Thompson family's close connexion to Wilberforce, they were wesleyan methodists and not of the evangelical fold. In Sierra Leone, Macaulay had a perpetual problem with methodists, be they white or black, and Thompson proved to be no different. Even before he left to take over the colony, Thompson had had a bitter argument with Macaulay about the morality of apprenticeships and on his arrival in Sierra Leone was horrified at what was happening to Africans 'liberated' from slave ships.[68] Thompson had no problem recognizing that forced recruitment into lifetime military service in the West India regiments, or 14 years bonded labour with no clear emancipation procedure, was a state of *non* freedom. If it was not slavery, he felt it could only be one step removed. 'Messers Wilberforce Thornton and Co have at last become slave traders with a vengeance in their old age', he wrote to his fiancée in horror.[69] He would have none of it and bombarded Castlereagh with strongly worded and imprudent letters of accusation and protest.[70] Enraged at the slur on his reputation, Wilberforce ordered Thompson to leave Sierra Leone and advised Castlereagh to immediately replace him with a Captain Columbine of the royal navy, who also happened to be a director of the African Institution.

This behaviour appears to be grossly hypocritical only if you choose to believe that Wilberforce and his allies were engaged in a 'fight to free an Empire's slaves', as the subtitle of recent book proclaims.[71] Yet this was not their fight at all. It was not the brutally enforced labour of enslaved Africans that concerned them so much as the condition of their own souls. These pious men had formed the Sierra Leone Company to christianize Africa, not to help emancipated slaves. In the same spirit of christian

---

[65] T.N.A., CO267/25: Macaulay to Ludlam, 4 Nov. 1807.

[66] T.N.A., PC2/175.

[67] Eltis, *Economic Growth*, p. 111.

[68] Evidence of the bitter dispute over apprenticeships can be found at U.H., Thompson Papers DTH 1/21: 'Narrative of Facts'. It is also discussed at length in Michael J. Turner, 'The Limits of Abolition: Government, Saints, and the "Africa Question", 1780–1820,' *E.H.R.*, CXII (1997), 319–57.

[69] U.H., DTH4/1: Thompson to Barker, 23 July 1808.

[70] U.H., DTH 1/61: Wilberforce to Thompson, 19 Oct. 1808.

[71] Adam Hochschild, *Bury the Chains. Prophets and Rebels in the Fight to Free an Empire's Slaves* (New York, 2005).

crusade, they took up abolition with such intensity because they believed complicity in the trade degraded the moral integrity of the nation. In these matters their politics and their morality were in perfect harmony. As Christopher L. Brown has suggested, rather than focusing on how the Clapham Sect gave rise to abolitionism, we would do better to consider the way that abolitionism gave rise to the Clapham Sect.[72]

[72] Christopher L. Brown, *Moral Capital. Foundations of British Abolitionism* (Chapel Hill, 2006), ch. 6.

The Wilberforce Song: How Enslaved Caribbean Blacks Heard British Abolitionists

HILARY McDONALD BECKLES

The process of ending the British transatlantic slave trade was politically acrimonious, socially divisive and long drawn-out. In 1787, the British, led by Thomas Clarkson founded a Society for Effecting the Abolition of the Slave Trade. The London Committee, as it was also known, agreed on a two-phased approach, separating the campaign to abolish the slave trade from general emancipation. First, it would seek to end the transatlantic slave trade, and second, it would urge the gradual abolish of slavery itself, both by legislative action in parliament. It was not until 1807 that any abolition action was authorized by parliament.[1]

Meanwhile, in the Caribbean, the enslaved community had moved further along with respect to its own course of abolition action. A successful rebellion of the enslaved community in the French colony of St Domingue in 1791 placed the colony firmly in the political hands of chief military commander, Toussaint L'Ouverture, who immediately sought to abolish the transatlantic slave trade and slavery. In 1804, the blacks unilaterally declared their constitutional independence from France, and by extension from Britain, which had made an ill-fated military attempt to capture the colony from L'Ouverture.

At the outset the Haitian state, confronting the slave-owning powers of Europe and the United States, proclaimed abolition the centre of its domestic and foreign policy, consistent with the ten-year anti-slavery revolutionary war from which it emerged. It was the first nation of its kind in the modern world, an inspiring expression of the endemic abolition movement that had long typified the Caribbean colonial experience.[2] The British parliament passed its legislation to abolish the slave trade on 25 March 1807, providing that as from 1 May 1807, except where ships had already been cleared to trade, it would be unlawful for British subjects to participate

---

[1] See Judith Jennings, *The Business of Abolishing the British Slave Trade, 1783–1807* (1997); James Walvin, *Questioning Slavery* (1997); *Slavery and British Society, 1776–1846*, ed. James Walvin (1982); *The Abolition of the Atlantic Slave Trade*, ed. David Eltis and James Walvin (Madison, 1981); Clare Midgley, *Women Against Slavery. The British Campaigns, 1780–1870* (1992); S. I. Martin, *Britain's Slave Trade* (1999); Stiv Jakobsson, *Am I not a Man and a Brother? British Missions and the Abolition of the Slave Trade and Slavery in West Africa and the West Indies, 1786–1838* (Lund, 1972); Seymour Drescher, *Capitalism and Anti-Slavery. British Mobilization in Comparative Perspective* (1986).

[2] See David Geggus, *Sugar, War, and Revolution. The British Occupation of Saint Domingue* (Oxford, 1982); Thomas Ott, *The Haitian Revolution, 1789–1803* (Knoxville, 1973); C.L.R. James, *The Black Jacobins* (1938); and Robin Blackburn, *The Overthrow of Colonial Slavery, 1776–1848* (1988).

in the transatlantic slave trade. Such ships would be allowed to operate until 1 March 1808.[3]

The abolition of the British slave trade has traditionally been presented as a benevolent act by the British state that acquiesced under the mounting pressure of opposing intellectual voices and the mass advocacy of religious and humanitarian activists. There is a substantial literature that details this rich history, but it does not, however, give adequate attention to the political role of enslaved communities in the Caribbean, who in the context of the wider Atlantic dimensions of the transatlantic slave trade, were its fiercest foes.[4]

Enslaved blacks everywhere focused their resistance politics upon both aspects of the crime against humanity, the transatlantic slave trade and slavery itself. The Haitian constitution, for example, reflected the precise thinking of the majority of the enslaved in the Caribbean. By providing that any enslaved person who arrived in Haiti would become automatically free and citizens, it set a benchmark in abolitionist politics for all nations. This legal facility was the most significant abolitionist development in the wider Atlantic world. By the time of the British act in 1807, L'Ouverture's revolutionary vision and policy had been operative for over a decade, gaining for him the status as principal abolitionist leader in the Caribbean, the Atlantic and beyond. Enslaved people from near and far were already fleeing to freedom in St Domingue before the state of Haiti was declared.[5]

The interactions between Caribbean and European abolitionists have not been fully researched, and certainly not recognized. Pride of place in the global abolition campaign has gone to the ideological and political leadership of the British, and to a lesser extent, the French. The British led the most persistent parliamentary campaign. But they also made the most money from the trade. The Portuguese may have shipped more enslaved Africans across the Atlantic but the British extracted the greatest per capita profits. This commercial circumstance had much to do with the timing and intensity of the British campaign.[6]

Recent research by David Eltis and Joseph Inikori has suggested that 12 to 15 million enslaved Africans were shipped to the Americas between 1492 and 1870. The transatlantic slave trade was the largest involuntary human migration in recorded history. It was big business, the largest commercial enterprise of its time. European

---

[3] Blackburn, *The Overthrow of Colonial Slavery*, pp. 131–58; D.H. Porter, *The Abolition of the Slave Trade in England* (1970); James Walvin, 'British Popular Sentiment for Abolition', in *Anti-Slavery, Religion, and Reform. Essays in Memory of Roger Anstey*, ed. C. Bolt and S. Drescher (Folkestone, 1980), pp. 101–18; David Geggus, 'British Opinion and the Emergence of Haiti', in *Slavery in British Society*, ed. Walvin, pp. 123–49.

[4] See Blackburn, *The Overthrow of Colonial Slavery*, pp. 213–60; David Geggus, 'The Cost of Pitt's Caribbean Campaigns, 1793–1798', *Historical Journal*, XXVI (1983), 699–706; Robert Debs Heinl jr and Nancy Gordon Heinl, *Written in Blood. The Story of the Haitian People* (Boston, 1978); David Nicholls, *Haiti in Caribbean Context. Ethnicity, Economy and Revolt* (1985); and idem, *From Dessalines to Duvalier. Race, Colour and National Independence in Haiti* (Cambridge, 1979).

[5] Nicholls, *From Dessalines to Duvalier*, pp. 35–60; Blackburn, *The Overthrow of Colonial Slavery*, pp. 228–60.

[6] See Joseph Inikori, *Africans and the Industrial Revolution in England. A Study in International and Economic Development* (Cambridge, 2002); David Eltis, *The Rise of African Slavery in the Americas* (Cambridge, 2000); and *The Atlantic Slave Trade. Effects on Economies, Societies, and Peoples in Africa, the Americas and Europe*, ed. Stanley Engerman and Joseph Inikori (Chapel Hill, 1991).

nations went to war against each other in order to dominate the market. As profits soared in the eighteenth century, and atrocities multiplied, no individual, government or group of people anywhere were able to stop its expansion. It encircled everything and everyone within the Atlantic world.[7]

The Caribbean was the largest single market for British traders. The debate over the numbers of Africans shipped into the region still rages, but the most reliable estimate suggests that the region accounted for some 40 per cent of the total. Of the British colonies, Jamaica, followed by Barbados, accounted for the majority. For the period 1655–1867, they received 11.2 per cent and 5.1 per cent respectively of the total trade, compared to 4.2 per cent for Guiana and 3.2 per cent for the British Windward Islands and Trinidad combined.[8]

Over two million Africans lost their lives in the capture, storage and shipment across the Atlantic, and maybe another three million died within five years of arrival in the Americas. Social and work-related brutality combined to produce a demographic disaster within the enslaved community. High death rates among survivors assured their inability to sustain themselves naturally. During the seventeenth, eighteenth and early nineteenth centuries the number of enslaved Africans in most colonies declined naturally. Slave-owners looked to the slave trade to assure a growing labour force.[9]

The British abolitionist campaign had a significant impact upon the Caribbean movement. First, there was George III's son the duke of Clarence (later William IV) going public in support of the slave trade; then there was the tragedy of the *Zong*; and finally the Wilberforce song that confirmed black Caribbean perceptions of the British movement. Captain Collingwood's decision to throw overboard, on grounds of their illness, 132 of the 430 Africans on board the *Zong en route* to Jamaica, knowing that his employer could claim on insurance for lost cargo, produced seismic waves in British society, though not in the Caribbean. The corresponding effects in the Caribbean came with the abolitionist pronouncements of L'Ouverture. The good news from L'Ouverture, like the bad news from Clarence, spread like fire among the communities of the canefields.[10]

The mass media that served the world of the enslaved, James Walvin notes, was driven by mostly illiterate persons who constituted news from the 'tittle-tattle gleaned at the planters' tables', and turned 'gossip and eyewitness accounts to their own ends'. But there were others. Some broadcasters could read, and many lived intimately with free persons, black, white, and coloured. What is certain, Walvin concludes, is that 'they used this information, gleaned from the most distant points of the vast Atlantic

---

[7] Eltis, *Rise of African Slavery in the Americas*.

[8] *Ibid.*

[9] See Thomas Phillips, *A Journal of a Voyage made in the Hannibal* (1746); Captain William Snelgrave, *A New Account of Some Parts of Guinea* (1734); Eric Williams, *Capitalism and Slavery* (Chapel Hill, 1944), pp. 81–2; John Atkins, *A Voyage to Guinea, Brazil, and the West Indies* (1735); Alexander Falconbridge, *An Account of the Slave Trade* (1788); Philip Curtin, *The Atlantic Slave Trade. A Census* (Madison, 1969); James Rawley, *The Transatlantic Slave Trade* (New York, 1981); Herbert Klein, *The Middle Passage* (Princeton, 1978); J.R. Ward, *British West Indian Slavery, 1750–1834* (Oxford, 1988).

[10] See Sir Reginald Coupland, *The British Anti-Slavery Movement* (1964), pp. 59–60; Folarin Shyllon, *Black Slaves in Britain* (1974), pp. 184–209; and Moira Ferguson, *Subject to Others. British Women Writers and Colonial Slavery, 1670–1834* (1992), pp. 134–5.

system' to inform and construct an oral culture to foster clear ideological views of their own.[11]

Throughout the Caribbean, Wilberforce ran second to L'Ouverture as the abolitionist leader. The enslaved knew of no other persons. Wilberforce was an iconic figure, and while he was vilified, demonized and burnt in effigy by slave-owners, the enslaved secretly drank to his good health. Not surprisingly, the interactive response from the enslaved took the form of a song. Crafted in the creative minds of enslaved Jamaicans, it was as subtle and politically astute a song ever composed within a moment of mass mobilization. It openly celebrated and skilfully analyzed Wilberforce's contribution, while pointing to its effective limitations.

There was no song about the *Zong* incident – just cold silence bred of contempt. The Wilberforce song was a discursive device, meant to illustrate how and where the Caribbean struggle differed with the British campaign. The enslaved had evolved an understanding, crude as well it might be, of British abolitionist politics, and clearly expressed their opinion. Wilberforce did not shape their political expectations. The logic of their comprehension was guided by the realization that neither he nor they had it within their power to end the transatlantic slave trade, though it was up to them to resist it to the death.

This reading began with the perspective that their presence as victims within the slave trade had much to do with *élite* commercial and political interests in their homelands. As such, it was an accurate comprehension of the Atlantic dimensions of their entrapment and enslavement. By situating their capture and sale within the context of the power politics of European military superiority and subordinate African *élite* interests, they read the transatlantic slave trade as a structure with tentacles far beyond their reach. If, as a result, they took the view that only Europeans could destroy the monster they created and unleashed, it did not follow that they were prepared to be passive in the face of it.

If elements within the enslaved community seemed resigned to life-long captivity, it was a state of consciousness driven by individual despair rather than collective defeat.[12] The turning of the black mind against the transatlantic slave trade constituted an endemic political posture that sustained the abolitionist ethos that informed everyday life. This state of being sustained an epistemic infrastructure upon which multiple patterns of opposition thought, attitude and behaviour, described narrowly as 'slave resistance', was passed on through generations. Somewhere within the Africans' vast and growing reservoir of experience with the transatlantic slave trade and enslavement, the sounds of British abolitionists were heard and recorded.

British-produced news about the slave trade, like Caribbean-generated rumours of black rebellion, traversed the Atlantic at hurricane speed. The enslaved in the islands had a saying, derived from an ancestral proverb, that 'if you wish the truth to be known, you must tell it to the winds'. The *Zong* was another line in the silent tune the enslaved whispered to the wind. Ships would arrive. The news was always bad. With the *Zong* the number told was 132 more or less; with other ships it might have been 20, 30,

---

[11] Walvin, *Questioning Slavery*, p. 130.

[12] See Robin Law, *The Oyo Empire* (Oxford, 1977); and *idem, The Slave Coast of West Africa, 1550–1750. The Impact of the Atlantic Slave Trade on an African Society* (Oxford, 1991).

more or less. Numbers could not measure the magnitude of grief when it was the sight of ships carrying chained souls for sale on a bloody shore that was the cause of pain. The event, however, led to a parliamentary debate that signalled the onset of professional persistence in the national campaign.[13]

Sections of the British public rose in moral indignation at the news of mass murder on the high seas by one of their subjects. For thousands of the enslaved in the Caribbean the tragedy broke the silence surrounding the frequency of middle passage massacres. It certainly helped in consolidating a popular perception of the Atlantic Ocean as a mass burial site within the black community. Many had witnessed or heard of similar murders, in captivity, on the West African coast, and during the 'passage' across the Atlantic.

Blacks knew that in the financial world of slavers, ocean deaths were rationalized as inevitable collateral damage. Moira Ferguson notes that the 'narratives that followed on the heels of the *Zong* murders took place in the Caribbean and promoted rebellion'. How closely-knit were the relations of these events remains to be known, but the *Zong* case did serve to indicate how far apart were enslaved communities and British public with respect to knowledge and emotional reactions to the transatlantic slave trade.[14]

British abolitionists were not as single-minded as their Caribbean counterparts. They were part of a wider movement dedicated to forging an agenda for domestic political reform. For some, the slave trade was an expression of what had gone wrong with public governance, and opposition to it was expected to serve as a moral barometer and political catalyst. The enslaved in the Caribbean focused on the singular importance of opposition to the slave system, of which the transatlantic slave trade was a part. While the enslaved heard much about the campaign in Britain, and observed closely the reactions of the white community around them, they had no reason to consider that it would bring them any meaningful solace or security.

Most enslaved Africans were extracted from societies ruled by monarchs, and were socialized to read political environments by privileging the ideas and actions of kings. Within their cosmology the transatlantic slave trade could not exist were it not for the concurrence of kings. Many of them were sold by their own kings and as a consequence understood their experience in terms of royal agreement and participation. The pro-slavery stance of English kings was known in the colonies. What could anyone in England do, the enslaved thought, when their king had spoken? To oppose the king was an action of lunatics, a conclusion that spoke to the courage, or lunacy, of Wilberforce and his comrades, but simultaneously reduced them as effective agents within the black world.

Wilberforce, then, was read and received within the enslaved community of the Caribbean, as an important but constrained ally in the struggle against the slave trade. His role was valued, but there was no expectation of him so long as his king opposed his efforts. Their song in tribute to him summed up their view that success could

[13] See Coupland, *British Anti-Slavery Movement*, pp. 59–60; Walvin, *Questioning Slavery*, p. 130.

[14] Ferguson, *Subject to Others*, p. 135.

be achieved with the power of God, the will of Wilberforce, and the strength of their collective will and force:

> Oh me good friend Mr Wilberforce mek we free
> God Almighty thank ye!
> God Almighty thank ye!
>
> Buckra in dis country no mek we free!
> Wa negro fe do? Wa negro to do?
> Tek force wid force
> Tek force wid force![15]

It speaks to their understanding that Wilberforce had stated the case but was unable to enforce his will upon the unwilling, including West Indian slave-owners. It affirmed their political thinking that it was necessary to take up arms in order to secure abolition and emancipation. While they did not question whether Wilberforce possessed the 'will' to win, they had determined that he was without the 'force'.

Historical experience played a central role in shaping why enslaved Africans persisted in their opposition to the transatlantic slave trade. Individual and group experience in Africa determined the varied paths to sale and transhipment. Some viewed the terrorism of their enslavement as an extreme extension of their prior social subjugation. For others the slave trade interrupted their lives through modalities that ranged from prisoner recruitment warfare to organized and random kidnapping. In all instances enslavement was an unfamiliar and culturally unacceptable system of ethnic degradation and social exclusion.

With these perspectives the enslaved community did not erect its opposition to the transatlantic slave trade on a platform of moral outrage consistent with the way of British abolitionists. First they had to overcome the fear associated with the widespread notion in West Africa that they were captured by Europeans for the purposes of being eaten. Then they had to comprehend the social and economic practice of chattel enslavement, and the political implications of the universal weakness of opposition to the slave trade.[16]

As the enslaved endured and internalized the inner workings of the transatlantic slave trade, particularly the mentality and modalities of its traders, they found no compelling reason to believe that the British abolitionists could overwhelm it with moral arguments. As news and rumours of the efforts of abolitionists increased during the last quarter of the eighteenth century so did the numbers of enslaved Africans arriving at Caribbean ports. As more among the enslaved heard of the name Wilberforce the greater was the number that had not. Only in L'Ouverture's St Domingue was the trade ended. This suggested to blacks that it would only be abolished by their armed resistance. The best they expected from white allies was their understanding of this circumstance.

---

[15] Cited in Blackburn, *The Overthrow of Colonial Slavery*, p. 293.

[16] See for example Olaudah Equiano, *Equiano's Travels. His Autobiography. The Interesting Narrative of Olaudah Equiano, or Gustavus Vassa, the African*, ed. Paul Edwards (1967), pp. 25–6, 30–1. Also, Michael Mullins, *Africa in America. Slave Acculturation and Resistance in the American South and the British Caribbean, 1736–1831* (Urbana, 1992), p. 35.

The enslaved Caribbean community, then, did not build its campaign with the notion that the transatlantic slave trade was a moral problem within trading nations. They understood that the slave trade was driven by an alignment of political power by African and European *élites* in order to generate wealth and prestige. Many knew that African rulers often times supported or opposed the trade based on calculated notions of self-interest. Some knew that rulers, and entire communities, fought against it on philosophical and moral grounds, and were destroyed in the process. The general understanding amongst them was that African rulers adopted over time pragmatic postures in the face of the growing militarization of the trading environment, and that states, like individuals, exercised choices.

During the eighteenth century no African government was able to sustain an active opposition to the transatlantic slave trade and survive. Some enslaved persons in the Caribbean had found their way into slave ships on account of the resistance of their rulers and communities. They arrived in the Caribbean with the understanding that government could not be the primary source of successful abolition. While they came to realize over time that the British and colonial governments did not always agree on matters in relation to the trade, they understood that it took just a rumour of anti-slavery rebellion to forge a common military vanguard for their violent suppression.

By the beginning of the nineteenth century blacks knew that only successful anti-slavery rebellion could inflict meaningful defeats upon agents of the slave trade. Such efforts began in Africa, continued into the middle passage, and flourished at sites throughout the Caribbean. As the most tenacious abolitionists, enslaved Africans fought battles long before the British campaign took formal shape. The rise of L'Ouverture, therefore, served as a validation of this truth, and confirmation of the efforts of millions who constituted themselves at the centres of the Atlantic effort.

According to Eltis, popular opposition in Africa took several forms and was shaped by complex forces in different places over time. He points to determined efforts by some African *élites* to contain geographical encroachment and settlement by Europeans, in order to determine and limit the scope of their control over slave trading. In some instances, he suggested, such political action was a part of the resistance network, in others it represented acquiescence and conformity.[17] Resistance differed from traditional forms of social protest. The underlying principles of chattel enslavement, particularly the racist European notion of black cultural inferiority, deepened African resolve.[18]

Europeans were able, however, despite this opposition, to establish trading arrangements with many West African kings and nobles. Philip Curtin's research has shown that some African rulers restructured their systems of governance in order to enhance their new interest in the transatlantic slave trade. He also showed that the development of a client relationship with European slave traders became the economic foundation of some new states.[19] As clients they conducted military operations against neighbouring and distant societies for the sole purpose of procuring persons for sale.

---

[17] See Eltis, *Rise of African Slavery in the Americas*.

[18] Richard Rathbone, 'Some Thoughts on Resistance to Enslavement in West Africa', *Slavery and Abolition*, VI, no. 3 (1985), 173–84.

[19] See Philip Curtin, *Economic Change in Pre-Colonial Africa. Senegambia in the Era of the Slave Trade* (Madison, 1975).

Curtin has described client states as predatory, and noted how they increased their business efficiency over time. European slavers sometimes found it necessary to sponsor directly their own violent recruitments against communities. But this was often not necessary. Client states sprung up within the vicinity of coastal slave forts, and also in the interior. The Bambara state of Segu, for example, formed about 1712, is described as 'an enormous machine to produce slaves'. Slave raiding and trading were crucial to its structure and behaviour. The Europeans provided guns to its leaders who supplied enslaved persons for shipment to the Caribbean and elsewhere.[20]

Robin Law has shown that for about 20 years after the Dahomey conquest of Ouidah in 1727, the king sold large numbers of political prisoners to the Europeans as they were all considered his personal property. After a military campaign soldiers would deliver all captives to the king for which they received a money payment. The royal monopoly of slave trading with Europeans, however, could not generate enough captives to meet the demand, forcing the king to resort to purchasing persons from independent slave raiding agents for resale to Europeans.[21] On arrival in the Caribbean these persons were well informed about the working of the slave trade.

African subjects, then, whether they lived within or beyond such client states were exposed to the raiding forces of professional warriors. From Sénégal to Angola, these states sprung up, or were recreated from old states. One of their primary functions was to subvert and displace states and their leaders that were opposed to the transatlantic slave trade. Communities, however, learnt how to defend themselves within this new context, and developed a culture of resistance against both the Europeans and African collaborators. Captain William Potter of the ship *Perfect*, a Liverpool slaver, experienced the impact of community opposition to the slave trade in 1758 while on the River Gambia. His crew and ship were attacked by men, women and children who had witnessed the sale of some of their families. Potter had almost completed the purchase of over 300 persons and was preparing for sail.[22]

The records of the English Royal African Company are replete with incidents of community attacks on slavers along rivers and on the coast.[23] The 1999 data base on the transatlantic slave trade compiled by Eltis and others contains references to 382 slave-ship revolts, two-thirds of which took place at the port of lading or within a week of setting sail. It is possible to identify the African region of departure for 342 of these revolts. These data show that an average of 57 Africans per incident died in 18 revolts on ships in the Senegambia region compared to 24 per incident in 49 revolts elsewhere on the coast.[24] Africans, then, before arrival in the Caribbean, were already dying in large numbers in opposition to the slave trade.[25]

In 1765, Captain Hopkins of the *Sally* arrived in Antigua, and told the story of an insurrection aboard his vessel four hours after leaving Calabar. The chained men were

[20] *Ibid.*

[21] Law, *Slave Coast of West Africa*, pp. 262–3.

[22] Winston McGowan, 'African Resistance to the Atlantic Slave Trade in West Africa', *Slavery and Abolition*, XI (1990), 5–29.

[23] See Hugh Thomas, *The Slave Trade. The History of the Atlantic Slave Trade, 1440–1870* (1997), p. 403.

[24] David Eltis, Stephen D. Behrendt, David Richardson and Herbert S. Klein, *The Atlantic Slave Trade. A Database on CD-Rom* (Cambridge, 1999).

[25] Thomas, *Slave Trade*, pp. 424–5.

vomiting from sea sickness, he reported, and were allowed on deck. A few healthy ones were allowed to cater to them on deck, but conspired to secure the freedom of the entire group. The struggle to take the vessel took several hours. Hopkins reported winning and forcing 80 Africans overboard to their deaths. Such incidents were a part of the common knowledge of enslaved West Indians and foretold the *Zong* incident within community consciousness.[26]

The middle passage was as violent and bloody a place as Caribbean plantations.[27] It was a life and death struggle. One well-documented rebellion took place at Calabar in 1767. Seven English ships, five from Liverpool, one from Bristol, and one from London, were awaiting enslaved Africans on the Old Calabar River where captains and agents had established trading relations with nobles in New Calabar. An armed contingent of over 30 Africans from Old Calabar attacked the English. They were unsuccessful because the king's soldiers came to the rescue of the English.

The leader of the Old Calabar warriors was beheaded, and survivors sold into slavery in the West Indies.[28] It should not be surprising, then, that they would continue their abolitionist actions during their enslavement. The 1752 experience of the *Marlborough* of Bristol had a different ending. The 400 captives on board, from Elmina on the Gold Coast and Bonny on the Niger Delta, rose up and killed all but two of the 35 crew; the pair kept alive were to assist returning the ship to Bonny.[29]

All Africans, whether in their roles as community raiders, ruling class collaborators, or captives, were adversely affected by the transatlantic slave trade. The central theme of British abolitionist rhetoric did not engage this understanding. Rather, it used character stereotypes of Africans to promote both extreme sympathy for, or fear of, the enslaved. Blacks were presented as either hopelessly dependent upon the compassion of whites to escape enslavement, or angry, rash, and easily moved to bloody violence. There were other representations, but none that was as appealing to the general public opinion. The politics of Caribbean abolition suggest the absurdity of such images.

The enslavers, on the other hand, in defence of the transatlantic slave trade, focussed on what they considered the ethnic peculiarities of Africans. There were good and bad slaves, they said, and the key to their effective governance was to determine what type you had, and then to fashion appropriate responses. J.B. Moreton, for example, writing from Jamaica in the 1790s, asserted the view held by slave-owners that 'there is a vast difference in the tempers and dispositions of the negroes, according to the coast they come from'.[30]

The behaviour of new arrivals, especially, suggests the naivety of these under-standings. One example of how the Africans swiftly restructured their behaviour in response to the transatlantic slave trade is to be found in the manner in which they fashioned the 'shipmate' concept. Persons who 'crossed' together became family on

---

[26] *Ibid.*, p. 425.

[27] Eltis, *Rise of African Slavery in the Americas*.

[28] Thomas, *Slave Trade*, pp. 403.

[29] *Ibid.*, p. 422.

[30] See J.B. Moreton, *West India Customs and Manners ... with the Methods of establishing and conducting a Sugar Plantation* (1793). Also Mullins, *Africa in America*, p. 281.

arrival and were expected to respect the emotional norms of kinship relations. Sexual relations between shipmates was taboo, for example. It was perhaps the most politically profound, socially far-reaching response to the transatlantic slave trade imaginable. One effect was to counter the slave-owners' view that Africans cared little for family life and kinship. By creatively reconstituting domesticity from the natal alienation inherent in the slave trade, Africans struck a telling blow to the boast of those who defended the slave trade.[31]

The 'Blacks are wiser now, massa', Matthew 'Monk' Lewis reported being told by one of his enslaved workers in Jamaica. He had reason to believe it, as their attitudes suggest hardening anti-slavery consciousness. Refusing to be fooled by their civility in his presence, Lewis observed that their desire for freedom was woven into social relations of attitudes to work. Similarly, the governor of Dominica reported in the 1790s that the 'idea of liberty' has taken over the enslaved community rendering both the transatlantic slave trade, and slavery in the island, a source of discontent.[32]

By the 1790s Barbados slave owners were satisfied that the slave trade was no longer important to sustain slavery on account of the positive growth performance of the enslaved community. They considered it tantamount to the importation of dynamite. Keen to turn away from African imports, they tried as best they could to suppress anti-slavery sentiments by seeking to improve the social and material well-being of the enslaved. That is, by removing 'new' Africans from the society, and hence a major source of political opposition, they could urge (Caribbean-born) 'creoles' to settle with reformed slavery as an acceptable way of life.

In 1795 manager Wood of the Newton Estate in Barbados wrote to Thomas Lane, his employer in London, informing him that the effectiveness of his strategy of estate management entailed his responding positively to the reasonable requests of the enslaved community. The Newton estate papers show, both before and after Wood's administration, that there was an established social hierarchy among the slaves based on the selective granting of privileges.

The *élite* were described as 'officers of the estate'. These were mostly skilled artisans, ranking domestics, and drivers of field gangs, who were distinguished from marginalized field hands.[33] It was assumed and sometimes said that these so-called privileged few were not opposed to the transatlantic slave trade because it was the means that enabled them to live a life superior to the 'salt water' (newly arrived) Africans who occupied the lowest ranks of the labour regime.

The same was also said of free blacks many of whom owned and used enslaved Africans in forging their individual and family advancement projects. For these and such like reasons, pro-slavery West Indians asserted that blacks were divided with respect to the abolition of the slave trade. British abolitionists were out of touch with

[31] Mullins, *Africa in America*, pp. 38, 42.

[32] *Ibid.*, p. 102; Matthew 'Monk' Lewis, *Journal of a West India Proprietor, 1816–17* (1929). See T.N.A. (P.R.O.), C.O. 71/19: Bruce to Lt. Gov. Sir John Orde, 15, 24 Jan. 1791, enclosed in Orde to Lord Grenville, Dominica, 3 Feb. 1791.

[33] University of London, Senate House Library, Newton papers: Sampson Wood to Thomas Lane, 19 Oct. 1798, no. 381(1), cf. 343.

Caribbean realities, they argued. 'Go tell it to the Wilberforces!', Wood suggested to Lane; it was 'amiable care' the blacks needed rather than abolition.[34]

Wood may have presented his employer with a persuasive argument until Betsy, one of the enslaved at Newton ran away to Bridgetown, and with help found her way to London. Once there she went to Thomas Lane, her titular owner, to protest about Wood's ill-treatment of her family and colleagues. When Lane brought these facts to Wood's attention he soon realised, like many whites in the West Indies, that the idea of blacks' self-liberation was at the top of their agenda, and that it had little to do with the speeches of Wilberforce. Rather, that it was home-grown, rooted amongst creoles and African-born alike, and sustained over generations by the 'shipmate' values and blood ties.[35]

The enslaved broke conceptually with British abolitionists on matters of family. During the eighteenth century eminent white male abolitionists did not centre the devastating impact of the transatlantic slave trade and enslavement upon African family life. This came later. Africans, however, had moved to the fore in rejecting slave-owners' legal definition of them as domestically demeaned, socially uprooted and therefore perfectly mobile chattels.

Females within the campaign did formulate opposition to the transatlantic slave trade in the area of domesticity that resonated with the African experience. Hannah More's poem *Slavery*, for example, represented a link to the heartbeat of black abolitionist writers such as Olaudah Equiano, who described the pain of being torn from his family, his sister especially. Hannah More wrote:

> See the dire victim torn from social life,
> The shrieking babe, the agonizing wife!
> She, wretch forlorn! Is dragg'd by hostile hands,
> To distant tyrants sold, in distant lands!
> ...
> By felons hands, by one relentless stroke,
> See the fond links of feeling Nature broke!
> The fibres twisting round a parent's heart,
> Torn from their grasp, and bleeding as they part.[36]

But even in the finest writings of female abolitionists, Moira Ferguson shows, the racial arrogance and contempt for Africans, considered dependent inferiors, tinged the ideological itinerary of the campaign. Black writers, public speakers, and campaign advocates, despite their important contributions to the British movement, did not escape the net that was cast over the entire race. Ferguson notes: 'Put in terms of realpolitik, the garnering of some cultural power for British white women was won at the expense of African material reality because the closer the country came to an abolitionist politic, the more imperative writers found it to denote racial difference'. Phyllis Wheatley, Ignatius Sancho, Olaudah Equiano, and Ottobah Cugoano would

---

[34] Mullins, *Africa in America*, p. 94.
[35] Lewis, *Journal*, p. 291.
[36] Quoted in Ferguson, *Subject to Others*, pp. 150–1.

have understood this all too well as it coloured the social relations they encountered daily.[37]

All Africans were entrapped within the web of the transatlantic slave trade. If large numbers escaped bondage by flight or manumission, thereby reducing the number of enslaved persons, this only stimulated demand within the trade, which as it was the main source of replacement. But the intention of escapees to return to Africa speaks to the depth of the resolve that sustained black abolitionism. Michael Mullins describes the case of a new arrival who ran away from an estate and was believed to be in Kingston looking for the ship that brought him from Africa. It was his intention to board the ship for what he hoped would be its return voyage to Africa. The data on runaways in Kingston show that many were sustained by 'shipmate' ties. In assessing shipmate support systems Mullins describes the case of 'two Ibos, a Coromantee, and a Congolese', who attempted 'to leave Jamaica in a canoe', and of 'five Bonny Country men and a Congolese who went to sea in a twenty-four-foot canoe' in efforts to return home.[38]

The 1790s, Michael Mullins notes, witnessed both the spectacular growth of Caribbean and British abolitionism. It also brought more Africans into Jamaica than any other decade. The effectiveness of African resistance strategies reached its highest point with Toussaint's reputation as the great abolitionist and liberator. Robin Blackburn observes, also, that the abolitionist crescendo in England coincided with maturing anti-slavery revolution in the Caribbean. The 'years 1795–1804', he commented, witnessed in addition to parliamentary seriousness about abolitionism, 'the publication of several accounts of war and revolt in the Caribbean, most of which stressed the dangerous mixture represented by spontaneous African rebelliousness and creole trouble making'.[39]

Heightened anxiety about abolitionism in the British colonies, however, was not linked in a positive way to Wilberforce's emergence, since the movement had suffered a number of setbacks in the mid-1790s. Rather, it drew sustenance directly from L'Ouverture's campaign, and to a lesser extent from the French movement that had signalled in 1794 its greater resolve in securing abolitionist objectives.

French abolition policy focused on Martinique and Guadeloupe, but news of French policies spread to all neighbouring islands. Illustrating the disconnexion between the Caribbean and English movements, Blackburn quotes abolitionist Henry Brougham's admission that the survival of black freedom in St Domingue, and the rise of free Haiti, which he called a 'negro commonwealth', meant that it would be 'folly to overlook the possibility of new insurrection' in the Caribbean intending to end both the slave trade and slavery.[40]

No British abolitionist, unlike the French, offered public support to the black abolition campaign in the Caribbean. Wilberforce denounced black self-liberation and by extension condemned Caribbean anti-slavery leaders. He was therefore unwilling to forge an alliance between his own public agenda and the daily sacrifices of life

---

[37] *Ibid.*

[38] Mullins, *Africa in America*, pp. 38, 37.

[39] *Ibid.*, p. 302.

[40] See Blackburn, *The Overthrow of Colonial Slavery*, p. 302.

that typified the abolitionist efforts of the enslaved. And, despite his grounding in morals, religious mores, and philosophical principles, he did not intellectually respect the epistemological position of enslaved Africans whose lives were the ultimate abolitionist weapon. The Wilberforce song, then, captured with uncanny precision the difference between will and force that separated the two campaigns by a distance greater than the Atlantic divide.

Where the enslaved developed their most profound rupture with the British campaign, however, was with respect to the arcane separation of slave trade abolition and emancipation. The enslaved could not accept the conceptual frameworks and strategy that situated the transatlantic slave trade and slavery in a sequential relationship, with the latter being a harder or more important obstacle to overcome. That is, they did not embrace the notion of stages of abolition, with the slave trade being first or foremost. The phased approach, real or imagined, confirmed for the enslaved that white abolitionists were dancing to a different domestic tune, and not to the Wilberforce song, which had undeniably an indigenous Caribbean rhythm.

Blackburn's assessment of British abolitionism reveals this point with clarity. He states that, notwithstanding the contributions of black participants like Equiano and Cugoano to the British platform, and to the movement in general, neither endorsed the political separation of slave trade abolition and emancipation in a way that Wilberforce's parliamentary presentation effectively achieved. He makes the point fully aware that the presence of these black supporters did provide an invaluable aura of authenticity to the British strategy. Close reading of Equiano's *Life*, published in 1789, and Cugoano's abolition tract, published in 1787, reveals, Blackburn concludes, that both advocates gave an 'impressive indictment of the commerce in humanity and the degradation of enslavement'.[41]

In general, black advocates within the British campaign did not endorse the racialist ideology of black dependency, symbolised by the iconic 'trademark' that showed a black male and female on their knees beseeching white compassion and affirmative action. This did not square with their own journey to freedom and use of an independent anti-slavery voice that entailed considerable personal enterprise, self-motivation and energetic interpersonal networking. As a consequence, Clare Midgley concludes, the 'black resister' was 'integrated into the British anti-slavery movement', and in other ways, 'remained very much an outsider'.[42]

The considerable influx of defeated French and Spanish slaveholders from St Domingue and Santo Domingo respectively opened up a large portal for detailed news of successful abolition under L'Ouverture. When, then, the British sent 60,000 soldiers into St Domingue to topple his regime and restore slavery, blacks in Jamaica especially took it as deeply personal as it is possible to imagine. With this act went out the dimmest flicker of hope among the enslaved that the British government could be abolitionist. Rather, they experienced a government that sought to put out the light that was leading them away from 200 years of darkness. News of L'Ouverture crushing of the British army confirmed what was long believed within enslaved communities that they had to look inward in order to move upward. While whites

---

[41] *Ibid.*, p. 141.
[42] Midgley, *Women Against Slavery*, p. 89.

in the Caribbean were burning Wilberforce in effigy, blacks were singing his song as a counter-discourse within Caribbean political economy.

Again, there was a minor white female strain within the British campaign that resonated with enslaved blacks. Helen Williams, for example, a keen abolitionist, celebrated the French Assembly for its abolitionist stance in 1794, and in so doing echoed the enslaved community's concern about the British movement. She wrote:

> I trust an English House of Commons will never persist in thinking, that what is morally wrong, can ever be politically right; that the virtue and the prosperity of a people are things at variance with each other; and that a country which abounds with such wealth, cannot afford to close one polluted channel, which is stained with the blood of our fellow-creatures.[43]

When the bill was eventually enacted, it was weakened by politically inspired compromises, gutted of its purest intent, and lacking the sharp, clinical edge of Toussaint's instrument. The enslaved community, more than any other, understood the social implications of its provisions. An inter-Caribbean slave trade, described as transfers, flourished in the aftermath of the abolition of the transatlantic slave trade as slave-owners and slave traders devised means, some legal and others not, to move the enslaved between colonies.

Families continued to be shattered as persons were placed on transfer lists and shipped out to other colonies. Slave ships captured on the high seas by British patrols spewed out 'liberated' Africans in the terrifying death hole that was Demerara. Jamaican enslavers, shocked by the stoppage out of Africa, began the process of driving domestic and skilled workers into field gangs, destabilizing the enslaved community's sense of itself as a relatively ordered place. There was some celebration, if only in order to show exuberance in the face of slave-owners' sense of their defeat. But it was not emancipation which was not a part of Wilberforce's agenda. The enslaved knew, finally, that the Wilberforce song was in fact a war song, and that it was time to reinvigorate their struggle and to 'tek force wid force'.

---

[43] *Ibid.*, p. 26.

The Ending of the British Slave Trade in 1807:
The Economic Context

DAVID RICHARDSON

Look around upon the miserable fate of almost all our unfortunate colour – super-added to ignorance, – see slavery, and the contempt of those very wretches who roll in affluence from our labours superadded to this woeful catalogue: Ignatius Sancho, 1772.[1]

"It's always best to do the humane thing, sir; that's been *my* experience". And the [slave] trader leaned back in his chair, and folded his arm, with an air of virtuous decision, apparently considering himself a second Wilberforce: Harriet Beecher Stowe, *Uncle Tom's Cabin*, 1852.[2]

Two hundred years on from Britain's abolition of its slave trade in 1807 debate over the causes of that remarkable event continues. Fundamental to the debate is the issue of the relative importance of economic factors in precipitating abolition. For over a century after 1807, abolition was principally seen as a victory for evangelically inspired humanitarianism, but the consensus built around this interpretation was broken when from the 1920s onward some historians claimed that economic factors were pivotal to explaining British abolitionism. Central to such claims were arguments that the British West Indian planter class was in decline from the 1760s onwards and fell victim to an emergent British industrial capitalism wedded to principles of free labour and free trade. Such arguments have been subjected to severe criticism. They still, however, attract support from some historians. Moreover, even among historians critical of the so-called decline thesis, there is an acceptance that explanations of British abolitionism need to take account of ideological and economic changes associated with the age of revolutions, including the British Industrial Revolution. The purpose of this paper is to explore how economic factors interacted with other factors in swaying parliament to outlaw the British slave trade in 1807.

1

There is an oft-told story that when George III and his prime minister, William Pitt the Younger, were driving out near Weymouth and encountered a pretentious equipage and outriders owned by a Jamaican planter, the king allegedly remarked

---

[1] *Letters of the late Ignatius Sancho, An African*, ed. Vincent Carretta (1998), p. 46.
[2] Harriet Beecher Stowe, *Uncle Tom's Cabin or, Life among the Lowly*, ed. Ann Douglas (1986), p. 47.

'Sugar, sugar, hey? All *that* sugar! How are the duties, hey Pitt, how are the duties?'[3] Though apocryphal, the story is commonly seen as emblematic of the wealth of absentee West Indian planters. As such, it is clearly consistent with Ignatius Sancho's comments, noted in the epigraph to this paper, on the 'affluence' of the 'wretches' who profited from slavery. It is equally consistent with claims that slave-based Caribbean sugar production nurtured British industrialization as well as with recent estimates of the wealth of Jamaica.[4] The timing, however, of the alleged remark of King George – probably around 1790 – and of that of Ignatius Sancho two decades earlier is intriguing, for, if some historians are to be believed, they occurred at a time when the standing of the West Indian planter class was in long-term terminal decline. According to the historian Lowell Ragatz, that decline began in the 1760s and, in tandem with economic changes in Britain, prompted a redefining of Anglo-Caribbean relations as a prelude to the abolition of British transatlantic slavery and West Indian sugar preference in the British market. Ragatz's interpretation informed the work of the West Indian scholar, Eric Williams, who, in his own seminal study, *Capitalism and Slavery*, attributed not only British industrialization to profits from slavery but also the success of British anti-slavery to shifts in the balance of power between a declining planter class and its allies and Britain's emergent industrial capitalists.[5] The 'decline thesis' thereafter became entrenched in West Indian historiography and while not without its critics remains for some an indispensable component of explanations of the ending of the British slave trade.[6] For scholars of this persuasion, it was economic change, not British humanitarianism, that determined the course of British anti-slavery.

At the heart of the decline thesis lie two key arguments. The first relates to the American Revolution, the second to the nature of slavery itself. According to Williams, the outbreak of the American Revolution was 'the first stage in the decline of the sugar colonies'; it provoked that 'growing feeling of disgust with the colonial system which Adam Smith was voicing and which rose to a veritable crescendo of denunciation at the height of the free trade era'.[7] Selwyn Carrington has recently echoed such remarks, arguing that close study of the British sugar industry endorses 'the decline theory of the British West Indies in the post-1775 period'.[8] Following a line of argument first developed by Ragatz and Williams, Carrington proceeded to catalogue a series of West Indian trade problems arising from American independence that, he argues, ultimately destroyed the viability of the British islands' sugar industry

---

[3] Richard Pares, *Merchants and Planters* (*Economic History Review*, Supplement 4, 1960), p. 38.

[4] The most famous is Eric Williams, *Capitalism and Slavery* (1944). A recent variant on the Williams thesis, emphasizing the impact of Africa and Africans on British industrialization, is to be found in Joseph E. Inikori, *Africans and the Industrial Revolution in England* (Cambridge, 2002). On the wealth of Jamaica at the time that Sancho was alive, see T.G. Burnard, '"Prodigious Riches": The Wealth of Jamaica before the American Revolution', *Economic History Review*, 2nd ser., LIV (2001), 506–24.

[5] L.J. Ragatz, *The Decline of the Planter Class in the British Caribbean 1763–1833* (New York, 1928); Williams, *Capitalism and Slavery*, chs 7–9.

[6] David Beck Ryden, 'Does Decline Make Sense? The West Indian Economy and the Abolition of the British Slave Trade', *Journal of Interdisciplinary History*, XXXI (2001), 347–74; Selwyn H.H. Carrington, *The Sugar Industry and the Abolition of the British Slave Trade, 1775–1810* (Gainesville, FL, 2002).

[7] Williams, *Capitalism and Slavery*, pp. 120–1.

[8] Carrington, *Sugar Industry*, p. xx.

by 1807. According to Carrington, the American war 'greatly reduced the amount of money invested in sugar production and laid the foundation for a general decline in economic growth'.[9] For Carrington's mentor, Williams, such problems were compounded by the removal through independence of a substantial proportion of the slaves in British America from British rule and by the rapid expansion after 1783 of British free trade in manufactures to the former 13 colonies. The first, he argues, made abolition of slavery easier than it would have been had the 13 colonies been English when the cotton gin was invented in the 1790s, and the second provided a glimpse of the trade possibilities outside the framework of the old empire and thus contributed to the success of Adam Smith's *Wealth of Nations* 'in undermining the mercantilist philosophy'. Provoking a radical reappraisal within industrializing Britain of the political economy of empire, American independence, in Williams's opinion, accelerated the destruction of the slave-based British planter class.[10]

Proponents of this argument also see decline as inherent in slavery itself. As with the other strand of the decline thesis, it is Adam Smith who provides the philosophical root of the argument. Smith asserted that the 'experience of all ages and nations ... demonstrates that the work done by slaves, though it appears to cost only their maintenance, is in the end, the dearest of any'.[11] He also observed that slaves were 'very seldom inventive', in part because should a slave 'propose any improvement of this kind, his master would be very apt to consider the proposal as the suggestion of laziness, and a desire to save his own labour at the master's expense'. The type of work, moreover, made no difference, for according to Smith, 'the manufactures carried on by slaves' were generally dearer than those of freemen.[12] Smith's views were not always adopted by his fellow political economists or contemporaries, but the idea that slave labour was inherently inefficient has become embedded in the decline thesis. For Ragatz, it was a 'fact' that slavery was 'ruinous as a form of labor' and 'must inevitably have come to an end through the operation of simple economic laws'.[13] Similarly, according to Williams, the greatest defect of slavery was that 'it quickly exhausts the soil', as rotation of crops and scientific farming 'were alien to slave societies'. For Williams, slavery was viable only where there was an abundance of land relative to labour, and even then survival of slave labour was a 'relay race',

---

[9] *Ibid.*, p. 61.

[10] This argument was first made by Thomas Clarkson, *An Essay on the Impolicy of the African Slave Trade* (1788), p. 34, which is cited at length in Williams, *Capitalism and Slavery*, p. 124. Not all proponents of the decline thesis slavishly follow Williams's line of argument, but even some of those sceptical of linking decline with American independence suggest that 'economic decline preceded abolition' (Ryden, 'Does Decline Make Sense?', p. 374). Christopher Brown has recently argued for a strong connexion between the American Revolution and the rise of the British anti-slavery movement but without linking this to economic conditions in the West Indies (Christopher Leslie Brown, *Moral Capital. Foundations of British Abolitionism* (Chapel Hill, NC, 2006)).

[11] Adam Smith, *The Wealth of Nations*, ed. E.R.A. Seligman (2 vols, 1925) I, 72, 345 (quotation). Smith went on to argue that '[a] person who can acquire no property, can have no other interest but to eat as much, and to labour as little as possible. Whatever work he does beyond what is sufficient to purchase his own maintenance can be squeezed out of him by violence only, and not be any interest of his own.'

[12] *Ibid.*, II, 177. Smith was not always so pessimistic about the lack of inventiveness among slaves; see Nathan Rosenberg, 'Adam Smith on the Division of Labour: Two Views or One?', *Economica*, XXXII (1965), 129–30.

[13] Ragatz, *Planter Class*, p. 238.

dependent on 'ever fresh conquests' of new lands to sustain it.[14] Such suggestions have been echoed by Carrington, who, citing approvingly an observation by Smith's contemporary, Arthur Young, that 'the culture of sugar by slaves was the dearest species of labour in the world', goes on to claim that by the late eighteenth century slavery as a labour system 'undoubtedly had run its course'.[15] Still others see planter pro-slavery arguments after 1787 as defending an 'increasingly anachronistic system of labour organisation'.[16] The inefficiency of slave labour, therefore, has become an indispensable axiom of the decline thesis, making inevitable the demise of slavery and the slave trade in the face of free labour.[17]

The decline thesis has attracted critics, among whom Seymour Drescher has perhaps been the sternest and most relentless. Conceding that British industrialization shifted the context within which British West Indian slavery came to be viewed by contemporaries,[18] Drescher nevertheless challenges suggestions that slave-based commerce became more marginal to British economic development before 1807.[19] There is some evidence that, as a source of revenue, customs duties on traded goods, of which sugar was one of the more important, tended to fall as a share of British government income before 1807.[20] But, in other respects, it appears that the trade performance of the West Indies remained strong through 1807. Indeed, British West Indian sugar exports expanded vigorously during the quarter century after 1783, thereby ensuring that the Caribbean share of British trade was sustained even in a period when the ratio of British overseas trade to total economic activity rose sharply.[21] If there was a crisis within the British planter class, therefore, it does not seem to have been mirrored in trade statistics. Neither does it seem to have been reflected in their demand for new Africans, the number and price of which continued at

---

[14] Williams, *Capitalism and Slavery*, p. 7. In this respect, Williams's argument mirrored what is sometimes seen as 'natural limits' claims regarding slavery. His arguments were anticipated by C.L.R. James, who, in another context, argued that on 'new land which was good . . . the slave *even though expensive* still gave good profits, and was often the only labour available' (emphasis added): *The Black Jacobins. Toussaint L'Ouverture and the San Domingo Revolution* (1980), p. 136n. The context of James' remark was the British intervention in 1793 in St Domingue.

[15] Carrington, *Sugar Industry*, pp. 218, 221. Earlier Carrington had claimed (p. 98) that owning slave labour 'was becoming a losing proposition' by this date.

[16] *The Abolitionist Struggle. Promoters of the Slave Trade*, ed. David Ryden (2003), p. x.

[17] Not all scholars working on slavery and the Caribbean assume that economic decline, the efficiency of slavery and abolition were inextricably connected; see Barry Higman, *Slave Population and Economy in Jamaica 1807–1834* (Cambridge, 1973), p. 4. Interestingly, there is no mention of the decline thesis in the context of the U.S. South, the historiography of which tracks or anticipates that on the British West Indies exactly, at least in terms of its origins (see Robert W. Fogel and Stanley L. Engerman, *Time on the Cross. The Economics of American Negro Slavery* (1974), ch. 1).

[18] One of the most outspoken critics of Williams, Seymour Drescher, observes, for example, that it was not accidental that 'abolition coincided with Britain's industrial revolution', though 'what the nature of that connection was has proven more elusive than Williams imagined it to be' (*Capitalism and Antislavery. British Mobilization in Comparative Perspective* (1986), p. 2).

[19] Most notably in Seymour Drescher, *Econocide. British Slavery in the Era of Abolition* (Pittsburgh, 1977).

[20] J.V. Beckett and Michael Turner, 'Taxation and Economic Growth in Eighteenth-Century England', *Economic History Review*, 2nd ser., XLIII (1990), 380–1. This did not reflect, however, an actual fall in customs revenues but rather growth of revenues from other sources, notably excise duties and income tax.

[21] Drescher, *Econocide*, p. 18. The overall ratio of trade to output rose from 9.4 per cent to 15.7 per cent in 1780–1801 (N.F.R. Crafts, *British Economic Growth during the Industrial Revolution* (Oxford, 1985), p. 131).

high levels through to 1807, nor in the profitability of sugar planting, which appears to have been as high on the eve of abolition as in the so-called 'silver age' of sugar in 1763–6.[22] In short, the importance of the West Indies to Britain and the financial well-being of British planters evinced little, if any, sign of slippage before the slave trade was outlawed in 1807.[23]

It is premature to claim that British West Indian slavery had run its economic course by the late eighteenth century. Recent assessments of competition between free and slave grown sugar in international markets after British slave emancipation reinforce this suggestion, as do comparisons between slave and free labour economies in the Americas, which suggest that per capita exports and incomes in the former were normally higher than in the latter between 1650 and 1850.[24] The most important evidence relating to the continuing resilience of slavery as an economic institution through 1807, however, is to be found in studies of slave labour productivity, the very issue on which Adam Smith pronounced so negatively in 1776. Smith's argument largely rested on the alleged indifference among slaves to incentives and their unresponsiveness to innovation. Such allegations flew in the face of claims by some ancient philosophers as well as some of Smith's contemporaries.[25] Equally importantly, they appear inconsistent with actual evidence relating to labour productivity in some slave societies. Moses Finley has suggested that a comparison of crop-seed ratios in first-century Italy and medieval England and France points 'away from the argument that inefficiency was an element in the decline of ancient slavery'.[26] Closer to the immediate period of our interest, the historian Barry Higman drew on demographic

---

[22] On slave price trends, see David Eltis and David Richardson, 'Prices of African Slaves Newly Arrived in the Americas, 1673–1865: New Evidence on Long-Run Trends and Regional Differentials', in *Slavery in the Development of the Americas. Essays in Honor of Stanley L. Engerman*, ed. David Eltis, Frank D. Lewis and Kenneth Sokoloff (Cambridge, 2004), pp. 181–218. On profitability, see John R. Ward, 'The Profitability of Sugar Planting in the British West Indies, 1650–1834', *Economic History Review*, 2nd ser., XXXI (1978), 197–213.

[23] For a similar conclusion in the context of U.S. slavery, see Fogel and Engerman, *Time of the Cross*, pp. 86–94.

[24] On the former, see Seymour Drescher, *The Mighty Experiment. Free Labor Versus Slavery in British Emancipation* (Oxford, 2002); on the latter, see David Eltis, Frank D. Lewis and David Richardson, 'Slave Prices, the African Slave Trade and Productivity in the Caribbean, 1674–1807', *Economic History Review*, 2nd ser., LVIII (2005), 673–700. For an extension of this argument to Brazil and Cuba see David Eltis, *Economic Growth and the Ending of the Transatlantic Slave Trade* (Oxford, 1987), p. 187, fig. 7.

[25] Writing in the fourth century B.C. Xenophon observed that slaves 'have no less need of something good to hope for than do free men – if anything, more, so that they may stay with you willingly', and similar sentiments were expressed by Columella, writing in the first century A.D. (Thomas Wiedemann, *Greek and Roman Slavery* (1981), pp. 133, 143). By contrast, Columella's contemporary, Pliny the Elder, thought chained slaves generated less profit than other forms of labour (*ibid.*, p. 136). For a discussion that goes beyond the question of the efficiency of slave labour and looks at how the ancients related slavery to progress, see David Brion Davis, *Slavery and Human Progress* (Oxford, 1984), pp. 24–7. Among the contemporaries of Smith who took a more optimistic view of the potential among slaves for improvements in productivity was the planter and author, Edward Long. Writing in 1774, just two years before Smith published his *Wealth of Nations*, Long noted in his *History of Jamaica* (3 vols.) I, ch. 3, that some gentlemen in the island had 'lately made use of the plough, and with great success', and went on to argue that were the plough to be more widely adopted, 'the Negroes, no doubt, would very cheerfully apply themselves to learn the art of handling and guiding it, upon being informed of its principal use, "the saving them a great deal of hard labour", and by continued practice they might become thoroughly expert in the management of it' (p. 452).

[26] Moses Finlay, *Ancient Slavery and Modern Ideology* (1980), p. 139.

and export data to argue that production per slave in Jamaica 'maintained a fairly consistent level between 1800 and 1834', even in the face of a falling slave population and the gross output of crops after slave imports were outlawed.[27] The picture of slavery's economic durability is further reinforced by studies of the antebellum United States South, which show a remarkable growth in labour productivity under slavery across most parts of the region in 1815–60.[28] Until recently, it was the story of what happened in the United States South which largely raised doubts about Smith's assertions about the superiority of free labour. But it is now clear that growth in total factor productivity in the Americas occurred during the lifetime of Adam Smith himself and in the context of plantation crops other than cotton. Thus productivity in rice-growing South Carolina rose by about 1.4 per cent a year between the 1720s and the American Revolution and it rose by similar proportions in the sugar-growing West Indies between 1700 and 1805. Much of this growth in the islands occurred in spurts, notably from 1793 onwards.[29] None of this is inconsistent with arguments that that the West Indies and other parts of the plantation Americas developed unbalanced and socially regressive economies under slavery, but on the evidence of productivity the British West Indian slave system plainly remained economically vibrant through 1807.[30] Moreover, Higman's findings, noted above, suggest that the high levels of productivity reached just prior to abolition were largely sustained in the generation after 1807.

Recent studies of the economic performance of the British West Indies, then, offer little if any support of terminal decline from 1763 or 1776 onwards. Publicly and privately, West Indian planters and their agents, as Ragatz and Carrington remind us, often voiced tales of woe about their economic fortunes in the late eighteenth century, but on the basis of our evidence this was largely rhetoric and conceivably a diversion to sustain public sympathy.[31] As Finley noted in another context, it is unlikely that 'the grumblers suffered in their purses'.[32] On the contrary, the generation of British Caribbean slaveholders after the American Revolution was probably just as wealthy as that noted by Sancho in 1772 or by George III around 1790. This did not escape the attention of other contemporaries. Echoing Sancho, the African-Briton, Quobna Ottobah Cugoano, drew attention in 1787 to 'the great and *opulent* banditti of slaveholders in the western part' and their 'virulent contradiction of facts' about

---

[27] Higman, *Slave Population*, p. 213.

[28] A.H. Conrad and J.R. Meyer, 'The Economics of Slavery in the Ante-Bellum South', *Journal of Political Economy*, LXVI (1958), pp. 95–130; Fogel and Engerman, *Time on the Cross*; R.W. Fogel, *Without Consent or Contract. The Rise and Fall of American Slavery* (New York, 1989).

[29] On South Carolina see David Eltis, Frank D. Lewis and David Richardson, 'Slave Prices, the African Slave Trade, and Productivity in Eighteenth-Century South Carolina: A Reassessment', *Journal of Economic History*, LXVI (2006), 1054–65; on the Caribbean, see Eltis, Lewis and Richardson, 'Caribbean Productivity'.

[30] Ironically, there are claims that British abolition was actually motivated by a crisis of over-production of sugar in the British islands in 1804–7, an argument that is consistent perhaps with the picture of productivity presented here but in other respects seems implausible.

[31] Movements of sugar exports and sugar prices, both of which tended to rise, suggest that planter revenues probably rose through 1807, even when one takes account of the higher costs associated with shipping sugar to market in wartime from 1793 to 1807.

[32] Finley, *Ancient Slavery*, p. 149.

the 'wicked traffic' in order to sustain their 'cursed avarice'.[33] Beliefs about planter wealth were also acknowledged by pro-slavery interests, one of whom admitted, in a comment remarkably reminiscent of that attributed to George III, that it was 'a natural conclusion to the minds of the Vulgar that the planters gain immense profits and can well bear great Taxes'.[34] Contrary to the assumptions of some historians, therefore, British abolitionism developed against a background of economic growth and prosperity, not stagnation, decline or crisis, in Britain's slave colonies, with slave-owners enjoying wealth and lifestyles unimaginable to the huge majority of Britons.[35]

Should a different interpretation of the economic condition and status of the British sugar islands at the end of the eighteenth century affect our interpretation of the relationship between economics and abolitionism? Fundamentally, probably not, for economics was bound to intrude into the debates over the slave trade and slavery, whatever the economic state of the sugar islands. A successful anti-slavery campaign would naturally involve a change in property rights; it would place a moral constraint on merchants' investment decisions; it would re-define the relationship between slave and slave owner; and for some it would pose a potent threat to the security and stability of the West Indian economy at a time when it provided an important source of income, employment, and tax revenues for Britain.[36] These were all issues in which a property-owning parliament charged with defence of the realm had an obvious and immediate interest. Recent research by historians that underlines the continuing value of the West Indies to Britain as well as rising slave-labour productivity only reinforces the importance of these issues to debates about slavery inside and outside parliament. Advocates for slavery emphasized the contribution of the slave trade and slavery to the British economy and treasury and the threat that abolition of the slave trade posed to this. They focussed on both the short-term instability as well as the risks to the long-term economic survival of the sugar islands from depriving plantation owners of access to fresh supplies of Africans. Abolitionists, by contrast, focussed on planter wealth and how the labour productivity that underpinned this hinged on a brutal, destructive, and shameful treatment of their enslaved Africans by planters. Such behaviour, it was assumed, was unlikely to change as long as planters had relatively easy access to cheap supplies of disposable African slaves.

For both pro- and anti-slavery sides, therefore, the demographic performance of Africans under West Indian slavery and the factors that shaped it assumed centre-stage in debates over the slave trade in 1788–1807. Accompanying actors in this debate were abolitionists, whose strategic and tactical decisions shaped the course of the British anti-slavery movement; the enslaved Africans themselves, whose character, humanity, and resistance to enslavement became issues for discussion; French revolutionaries and Napoleon Bonaparte, whose military ambitions, struggles with a rebellious St

[33] *Unchained Voices. An Anthology of Black Authors in the English Speaking World of the Eighteenth Century*, ed. Vincent Carretta (Lexington, KY, 1996), pp. 151–2, italics added.

[34] T.N.A. (P.R.O.), CO 137/89: 23 May 1792, cited in Carrington, *Sugar Industry*, p. 222.

[35] On the very high per capita wealth of Jamaican planters before 1776, see Burnard, 'Prodigious Riches'.

[36] For an example of such arguments, see *House of Commons Sessional Papers of the Eighteenth Century*, ed. Sheila Lambert (132 volumes, Wilmington, DE, 1975), LXXII, 101.

Domingue, and equivocations over the status of slavery in the French colonies created obstacles to and opportunities for the abolitionist cause at different junctures before 1808; government ministers, notably Prime Ministers Pitt and Grenville, who, in changing political circumstances, chose to take different official positions on ending the slave trade; and the largely un-enfranchised middle and working classes whose petitioning and 'popular Clamour ... so industriously excited' by Thomas Clarkson and others was seen by slavery advocates as a vital weapon in the abolitionists' arsenal.[37] In any interpretation of why parliament outlawed British slave carrying in 1807, shifts in national and international politics and how they affected perceptions of Britain's national interest must be seen to have played some part.

It remains the case, however, that the passage of the act abolishing the slave trade on 25 March 1807 was almost certainly inconceivable unless hard-headed parliamentarians were convinced that ending the slave trade would not do irreparable harm to the economic standing and future prospects of the British West Indies. This was recognized from the earliest days of the abolitionists' parliamentary campaign against the slave trade and war with France from 1793 only heightened this imperative.[38] In economic terms, it meant assuming that a change in or even a reversal of the long-run negative natural reproduction rate of slaves in the British West Indies was achievable, thereby largely removing the islands' dependence on slave imports. It also assumed that, with appropriate encouragement and intervention by the state, planters could and would reform their 'manners', provide incentives other than the whip for slaves, and throw off their reputation as a 'cruel and barbarous set of people'.[39] In effect, parliamentary interdiction of the British slave trade seems to have rested on a belief in the willingness and capacity of planters rationally to adjust to a changed slave supply regime and to reinvest some of their obvious wealth in measures intended to enhance slave reproduction and survival rates while sustaining existing levels of labour productivity. In retrospect, productivity seems largely to have been sustained through 1834, when slavery in the British islands was formally abolished, but slave populations continued to decline in most British colonies in 1807–34. Moreover, continuing and possibly increased slave restlessness produced three major slave revolts in Barbados in 1816, Demerara in 1823 and Jamaica in 1831. The 'mighty experiment' in politically induced slave amelioration implicit in the 1807 act thus failed.[40] The interesting questions centre on if and why parliament and parliamentarians ever thought that it could work.

Part of the answer probably lies in the former British colonies in mainland North America, where slave populations were largely self-reproducing before the Revolution and continued to increase rapidly even in the absence of sustained slave imports from

---

[37] For the last point see, Law Society Library, Chancery Lane, London Slave Trade miscellaneous papers, volume 3.

[38] As early as May 1789, William Wilberforce, when speaking against the slave trade, emphasized that he did not intend to appeal to the 'passions' of parliamentarians but to their 'cool and impartial reason' (*Cobbett's Parliamentary History of England. From the Norman Conquest, in 1066, to the Year 1803* (36 vols, 1806–20), VIII, 41–2).

[39] *Sessional Papers*, ed. Lambert, LXXI, 265. This was said in 1788 to be a 'stigma which has been thrown upon the whole body of Slave-holders'.

[40] The phrase 'mighty experiment' is, of course, from Drescher's book of the same title, which has influenced the thinking behind this paper.

Africa through to and beyond 1808. By comparison, negative net reproduction rates of 2 per cent or more were reported in some, if not all, the British West Indies before and after the American Revolution. Historians have tried with incomplete success to date to explain the contrast between mainland and island slave reproduction, most recently favouring explanations based on variations in crop and related plantation regimes.[41] The evidence available to parliament on slave reproduction variations, however, was different and seems to have been related to planter treatment of slaves, notably reports of misbehaviour towards slaves, of which there were many in parliamentary papers and other sources in 1787–1807. The same sources also documented that, notwithstanding such treatment, reproduction was sufficient by the early nineteenth century to sustain slave population numbers in Barbados, the oldest British plantation colony, and was close to achieving the same in Antigua. Neither imported significant numbers of slaves between 1783 and 1807.[42] Furthermore, for other colonies, there were numerous examples presented to parliament of slave owners who claimed to have successfully chosen to use ameliorative policies rather than slave imports to sustain and increase their labour force.[43] Parliamentarians sympathetic to abolitionism, therefore, did not have to look far by 1807 for signs that slave populations could increase through natural reproduction and, indeed, that reforms in planter attitudes and behaviour might contribute to this.

Were there any grounds, however, for believing that planters – that 'barbarous set of people' – were generally likely to respond positively to the ending of slave imports by seeking to increase their coerced labour force through encouraging natural reproduction? One obvious consideration was that for the most part planters were hardly likely to harm the material well-being or reproductive capacity of their slaves when their own financial and social standing hinged on Caribbean economic success and slave reproduction. Incentive mechanisms were, of course, a principal of Smithian economics and their influence was perhaps growing in the late eighteenth century. There are suggestions that there were the beginnings of a shift in attitudes respecting labour in Britain during the age of abolitionism. This, it is claimed, placed greater emphasis on wage incentives and the dignity of work, which in turn was tied to a consumer revolution, much of its inspired, ironically, by access to slave-produced goods.[44] This shifting perception of labour may help to explain the empathy of British industrial workers to the plight of the enslaved overseas as well as their willingness to participate in the mass petitioning that was such a feature of the British anti-slavery movement before and after 1807. Such changes in attitude related to free labour, however, and remained far from universally accepted in early nineteenth-century Britain. Was it, nevertheless, conceivable that those who voted to end the slave trade

---

[41] For a summary see Barry W. Higman, 'Economic and Social Development of the British West Indies, from Settlement to c.1850', in *The Cambridge History of the United States, Volume 1: The Colonial Era*, ed. Stanley L. Engerman and Robert E. Gallman (Cambridge, 1996), pp. 297–337.

[42] On slave imports into these and other colonies, see David Eltis, Stephen D. Behrendt, David Richardson and Herbert S. Klein, *The Atlantic Slave Trade. A Database on CD-Rom* (Cambridge, 1999).

[43] See, for example, *House of Lords Sessional Papers for 1792*, ed. F.W. Torrington (New York, 1975), pp. 398–9.

[44] For a review and discussion see David B. Davis, *Inhuman Bondage. The Rise and Fall of Slavery in the New World* (Oxford, 2006), pp. 246–7.

saw their action as both contributing to the removal of a stain on Britain's moral authority and simultaneously encouraging wealthy West Indian planters to improve the well-being of their slaves without directly threatening their existing property rights in slaves or the economic survival of the British West Indies? In other words, did the 1807 act represent an attempt to reconcile humanitarianism with sustainable economic efficiency and growth?

On this question, there were mixed indications of planters' capacity to reform before 1807. On the negative side, planters showed little obvious enthusiasm for changing their attitudes towards their slaves when faced with the possibility of an imminent curtailment of slave imports. They continued to argue that slaves were not ill-treated, that their workloads were no greater than those of the average English agricultural labourers, and that negative reproduction resulted from the constitution, character and behavioural patterns of the enslaved.[45] Typically, therefore, planters seem to have responded before 1807 to the threat of abolition by trying to stock up on slaves, with the result that prices of newly imported slaves in the British islands rose to unprecedented heights in 1788–92 and 1804–7, periods when abolitionist campaigning was at its peak.[46] Perhaps the consequence of panic buying on the part of planters – some of it fostered by generous credit provision – this outcome could be seen as indicative of an inability or unwillingness on the part of slaveholders to promote slave reproduction, at least in the short-term. Interestingly, it also anticipated what would happen in most British sugar colonies when abolition of the slave trade occurred in 1807.

Against this, however, there were signs before 1807 that, when linked to incentive mechanisms, parliamentary intervention in transatlantic slavery could foster adjustments by slave traffickers and slave owners sufficient to produce apparently more positive outcomes for the enslaved without at the same time diminishing levels of economic activity. One obvious example was parliamentary intervention in the slave trade itself in 1788–1807. Such intervention was prompted, among others things, by outrage at reported conditions on slave ships in the 1780s. It centred initially on regulation of the slave carrying-capacity of British ships and later on restrictions on participation in the slave trade. Measures affecting the former were first introduced in 1788 under the Dolben Act and later extended by legislation in 1799. Under the Dolben Act, the carrying capacity of ships was tied to a formula based on their tonnage; this formula was subsequently amended in 1799 to one based on the internal dimensions of ships, subject to the provision that the maximum number of enslaved Africans carried on board any ship be limited to 400. Significantly, the Dolben Act stipulated that all slave ships should carry at least one surgeon; established minimum

---

[45] See for example the suggestion that slaves were idle or indolent and that the labour they performed was 'slight, compared with any field labour in any part of Europe' (*Sessional Papers*, ed. Lambert, LXXI, 87). The former claim was difficult to reconcile with the obvious wealth of many planters and thus raised questions about the credibility of planter arguments. It was also directly contested by abolitionists: one to do so was John Newton, the former slave ship master (*The Journal of a Slave Trader, 1750–1754*, ed. Bernard Martin and Mark Spurrell (1962), pp. xii–xiii), who, among other things, argued that 'with equal advantages' Africans 'would be equal to ourselves in point of capacity' and were not 'naturally indolent'.

[46] On prices, see Eltis and Richardson, 'Prices'.

food and water requirements per slave per day in transit; and included financial incentives for shipmasters and surgeons to improve the survival rate of slaves.[47] Payment of the last was linked to the keeping of registers of slaves by surgeons, documents which subsequently became an important source of information to parliament about the operation of the slave trade. The Dolben Act and subsequent legislation thus established the principle of using parliamentary regulation and tax-based incentive mechanisms to try to ameliorate the condition of slaves in transit.[48] In doing so, it reflected a growing belief in British society in the efficacy of state intervention to tackle public health issues.[49]

Pro-slavery interests consistently lobbied against such intervention, arguing that it threatened the very existence of the slave trade, while Thomas Fowell Buxton later denounced the Dolben Act as 'a very feeble attempt . . . to abate the horrors of the Middle Passage – to admit a little more air into the suffocating and pestilent holds of the Slave-ship'.[50] Neither view appears to have matched reality. The British slave trade continued at historically high levels in 1789–1807, despite the outbreak of war with France in 1793, and it continued to generate rates of profit for British slave carriers that were close if not equal to those earned by earlier generations of traders.[51] At the same time, the indications are that slave mortality rates on British ships, while much higher than on most oceanic voyages, fell by about half between the pre- and post-Dolben periods, averaging about 5 per cent per voyage in 1793–1807. On many ships reported mortality levels were lower than 3 per cent, qualifying shipmasters and surgeons for bonus payments.[52] Historians remain unsure about the impact of the Dolben legislation on slave mortality on British ships, but parliament was subsequently regularly supplied with evidence of slave mortality patterns as well as the continuing buoyancy of the British slave trade. Such evidence could have done little to strengthen the credibility of gloomy planter and slave trader economic forecasting in the minds of uncommitted parliamentarians while it appeared consistent with suggestions that humanitarian-inspired intervention was compatible with sustained economic activity and efficiency. This message was only reinforced by the continuing high levels of British slave carrying in 1800–7, notwithstanding the even tighter regulation of such activity introduced in 1799.

By the last date, parliamentary regulation of the slave trade was accompanied by efforts by politicians to use incentives directly to encourage slave reproduction in the West Indies. Conscious of the demographic crisis underlying British West

[47] A set of penalties was also established for overloading of slaves and misreporting of mortality, with payments offered to informers. For a brief discussion of the legislation see Herbert S. Klein and Stanley Engerman, 'Slave Mortality on British Ships, 1791–1797', in *Liverpool, the African Slave Trade, and Abolition*, ed. Roger Anstey and P.E.H. Hair (Liverpool, 1976), p. 119.

[48] The historian Elie Halévy observed that Adam Smith remained 'the only authority' on political economy in late eighteenth century England, 'and he [was] little heeded' (cited in Maurice Dobb, *Theories of Value and Distribution since Adam Smith. Ideology and Economic Theory* (Cambridge, 1973), p. 65).

[49] Robin Haines and Ralph Shlomowitz, 'Explaining the Decline in Mortality in the Eighteenth Century British Slave Trade', *Economic History Review*, 2nd ser., LIII (2000), 262–83.

[50] *Substance of the Debate in the House of Commons on the 25th May 1823 on a Motion for the Mitigation and Gradual Abolition of Slavery throughout the British Dominions* (1823), p. 4.

[51] Roger Anstey, *The Atlantic Slave Trade and British Abolition 1760–1810* (1975), p. 47.

[52] Klein and Engerman, 'Slave Mortality'.

Indian slavery, parliament resolved in 1797 to urge colonial authorities to invest in schemes to encourage more stable unions among slaves and improvement of birth and survival rates of their offspring. These resolutions received an ostensibly positive response in some colonies. Responding to a resolution of the house of commons of 6 April 1797, the planter-dominated assembly of Grenada agreed in December 1797 to better protect and promote the natural increase of population of slaves. The preamble to the agreed measures linked them specifically to removing 'in a Course of Time, the Necessity of further Importation of slaves from Africa'.[53] Grenada was not alone. A similar measure passed in St Kitts linked improved slave reproduction to the 'the cause of Humanity' and to good economic sense. It noted that, while intervention might raise 'the current expenditure of estates', it would, if successful in raising slave reproduction and thereby rendering 'the Importation of African Negroes unnecessary', offer 'a full and ample compensation' for such expenditure.[54] In other colonies, efforts to promote slave reproduction focused on using differential customs duties to encourage the import of juvenile slaves. One such measure by Jamaica was seen to link positive reproduction with tangible economic benefits, noting that 'Negroes imported above a certain Age, are too deeply rooted in the savage Prejudices and the vicious and lazy Habits prevalent in Africa, ever to be civilized, or to become industrious and fruitful Labourers.'[55]

A cynical view might regard such statements and the measures they supported as window-dressing by planters under pressure and as having little long-term impact on the reproduction and survival rates of slaves in the British West Indies. Such an outcome is hardly surprising as long as slaves remained outside the discourse relating to their future. But in the context of the debate over the slave trade such interventions in slave demography deserve greater attention than they have usually been accorded. For one thing, they echo acknowledgments by some planters that creole – or Caribbean-born – slaves typically experienced greater longevity, were more productive, and were less prone to rebel than imported or African-born slaves.[56] The last was a not unimportant concern in the minds of both planters and British political leaders from the late 1780s onwards and was reinforced by the slave uprising in French St Domingue in 1791 following a decade of massive slave imports from Africa.[57]

---

[53] *Sessional Papers*, ed. Lambert CXXII, 70.

[54] *Ibid.*, p. 96.

[55] *Ibid.*, pp. 85–7.

[56] On higher productivity, see the evidence of Robert Thomas in 1788 who argued that creoles were 'generally industrious' but Africans were 'very indolent'. *Ibid.*, LXXI, 260.

[57] On concerns among planters pre-dating the St Domingue or Haitian slave revolt see Henry Huntington Library, San Marino, CA: Robert Hibbert letterbook, letter from Robert Hibbert, 20 May 1788: 'I presume the popular clamour respecting the Trade to Africa has ere this subsided and that we may expect supplies as usual. It is lucky that the Rumour of this intended Novelty which spread like Wild Fire amongst our own Negroes, and to which great additions were made, no less than that there was to be an Abolition of Slavery altogether, has had hitherto no very fatal effects, but our Alarms are not yet over, and whether the Idea was originally dictated by Malignity or Enthusiasm, certain it is that Nothing was ever more calculated to raise Commotions amongst a Set of People naturally peaceable and harmless, but who, if they knew their Power have our Lives and property entirely at their Mercy.' I owe this reference to David Eltis. A similar concern was expressed by Alexander Campbell of Grenada (*Sessional Papers*, ed.

Whether or not any of the planters' claims about the qualities of creole slaves were true – and the creole-led Barbados slave rebellion of 1816 subsequently challenged at least one of them – their distinctions between American- and African-born slaves provided a clear rationale linking improved slave reproduction to stable and sustainable economic performance in the British West Indies. Moreover, the language behind demographically-related interventions betrays a sense, at least ten years before 1807, that closure of the slave trade was likely if not certain, but that with appropriate and timely action by planters the outcome of such an event need not be catastrophic. On the contrary, actions to address the demographic deficit of the slave population were seen by some as having the potential to improve the quality of the labour force in the islands and thereby their economic performance. The resolutions by parliament to encourage slave reproduction – and planters' responses to them – may be considered, therefore, an important landmark linking humanitarianism to economic efficiency and stability. In this respect, they laid the foundation ideologically for the final push of abolitionists to end the slave trade in the national interest a decade later.[58]

Various factors, of course, combined to encourage parliament to abolish the British slave trade in 1807. Other studies in this collection focus on factors other than economic ones. But it is hardly likely that, in the middle of a prolonged war with Napoleonic France, parliamentarians would have abolished the slave trade if they believed that such a move would weaken Britain's economic and fiscal base. Security issues were high on the political agenda in 1793–1807, a factor that made Pitt's reluctance officially to embrace abolitionism a problem for the cause and Grenville's willingness to do so a perhaps key moment in determining the outcome in 1807.[59] National security also meant that the wealth generated by the West Indies became a primary element in the defensive armoury of pro-slavery interests against abolitionism. Such wealth, however, made planters vulnerable to charges of brutal and inhuman treatment of the enslaved and, in a world of changing economic discourse about the dignity of labour and incentives, became the backcloth for debates over ways to sustain a productive plantation-based slave society in the British West Indies independent of constant new supplies of slaves from the Africa. Such a possibility was more than just an abolitionists' dream by 1807. It already existed in Barbados, Britain's oldest and seemingly most stable slave plantation economy, and it was close to being realised in

[57] (continued) Lambert, LXXI, 164), who reported that 'Slaves begin to be a little turbulent, and express themselves, that the Parliament of Great Britian would make them if it was not for their masters. With these Ideas, the whole of the White inhabitants might be destroyed in a night or a day.' In his speech to the Commons in May 1823, Buxton noted how in response to the Dolben Act the pro-slavery duke of Chandos had reported in the House of Lords that 'his pockets were filled with letters from his correspondents in the West Indies' expressing fears that the Dolben Act would foment slave rebellion and the ruin of the sugar islands, outcomes that, Buxton observed wryly, failed to materialise (*Substance*, p. 5). Campbell and Chandos here were both anticipating what the historian David Davis has dubbed the 'nuclear retribution' fear among planters that advocacy of abolition stoked up the danger of slave rebellion (David B. Davis, *Challenging the Boundaries of Slavery* (Cambridge, MA, 2003), p. 81). For a discussion of the impact of slave rebellions on British abolitionism, see Gelien Matthews, *Caribbean Slave Revolts and the British Abolitionist Movement* (Baton Rouge, LA, 2006).

[58] On the exploitation by abolitionists, notably James Stephen, of the foreign slave trade of British traders to promote their cause in 1806–7, see Anstey, *British Abolition*, pp. 364–90.

[59] The decision to introduce the bill in the Lords, the embodiment of property-ownership in Britain, was also a key political decision.

some other colonies. Moreover, planters eager to throw off a reputation for brutality while retaining property rights in people showed some willingness to invest in mechanisms to encourage higher slave reproduction. Barbados proved, in retrospect, to be the exception rather than the rule, but together with developments in the southern United States was a useful ideological weapon in indicating that sustainable economic growth and prosperity were possible in slave societies without reliance on slave imports. When, therefore, in 1808 James Mill, the political economist and father of John Stuart Mill, bemoaned 'the great difficulty with which the salutary doctrines of political economy are propagated in this country', he was surely overlooking the contribution of economics to the successful outcome of the movement to abolish the British slave trade.[60]

2

The belief that parliamentary abolition of the British slave trade in 1807 was predicated on the decline of the British West Indian planter class and on an inefficient slave regime is no longer tenable. British West Indian planters were at least as wealthy in 1807 as when Ignatius Sancho commented on their opulence over three decades earlier. Their continuing personal wealth and their importance to British overseas trade and taxation makes parliament's actions in 1788–1807 against the slave trade – the life-blood of the British West Indies, according to pro-slavery arguments – all the more remarkable as a triumph of anti-slavery. Some historians have drawn attention to the extra-parliamentary activities and intra-parliamentary stratagems used by abolitionists to achieve their goals. In doing so, however, they have perhaps failed to emphasize sufficiently how ideas and values associated with emergent systems of political economy were or could be mobilized to weaken key elements of pro-slavery's defence of the slave trade by suggesting potential compatibilities between economics, self-interest and humanitarianism. As proponents of the decline theory appreciated, therefore, economics did matter to abolitionism. It mattered, however, not because abolitionists were facing pro-slavery interests in economic retreat but because they were able ideologically to reconcile defence of West Indian prosperity and of Britain's national interest with the more enlightened moral content of an emergent political economy and their own humanitarian beliefs.

---

[60] James Mill, *Edinburgh Review*, October 1808. Mill was writing in a context other than slavery, and may have been writing 'in a pessimistic mood' (Dobb, *Theories*, p. 65), but abolition of the slave trade would surely have been considered 'salutary' by Mill.

'Contrary to the Principles of Justice, Humanity and Sound Policy': The Slave Trade, Parliamentary Politics and the Abolition Act, 1807[*]

STEPHEN FARRELL

In June 1806, for the first time after nearly 20 years of campaigning inside and outside parliament, the Commons and the Lords united in declaring that the British slave trade was 'contrary to the principles of justice, humanity, and sound policy'.[1] When a bill was introduced early the following year, intended to give these joint resolutions legislative effect, it used exactly the same words at the beginning of its preamble (or initial justificatory statement). The formulation, which would resurface continually in parliamentary debates, was not new. Indeed, it had been used, in a slightly different order ('humanity, justice, and sound policy'), by William Pitt, the prime minister, on introducing his delaying motion on inquiry into the slave trade in May 1788, when the abolitionists were already being associated with the cause of 'justice and humanity'. The words 'justice, humanity and sound policy' were used again by Henry Dundas, the minister most strongly associated with those wishing to resist immediate abolition, in his twelfth resolution on the subject on 23 April 1792.[2] For Pitt, as for Dundas, the phrase encapsulated the evident conflict that arose between opposing the slave trade for genuinely sincere humanitarian and religious reasons (justice for Africa, as it were), and supporting it on the necessary ground of prudential 'sound policy'. By the latter they meant, not the modern sense of opting for a preferred course of action, but the importance of adhering to the generally unquestioned commercial and strategic requirements of national and imperial government as a whole.[3] The abolitionists naturally emphasized the immorality of the slave trade and its apologists took their stand on the viability of the existing trading system, but, with each side producing counter arguments that employed their opponents' own modes of discourse, the issues

[*] I am grateful to David Fisher, Clyve Jones, Michael McCahill, Roland Thorne and James Walvin for their advice and support; and to the owners of the various manuscripts cited for permission to quote from them.

[1] *C.J.*, LXI, 393; *L.J.*, XLV, 730.

[2] *Cobbett's Parliamentary History of England. From the Norman Conquest, in 1066, to the Year 1803* (36 vols, 1806–20), XXVII, 496; XXIX, 1216; James W. LoGerfo, 'Sir William Dolben and "The Cause of Humanity": The Passage of the Slave Trade Regulation Act of 1788', *Eighteenth-Century Studies*, VI (1973), 433–4.

[3] John Ehrman, *The Younger Pitt. The Years of Acclaim* (1969), pp. 387–402; Michael Fry, *The Dundas Despotism* (Edinburgh, 1992), pp. 200–1.

of 'justice and humanity' as against 'sound policy' were never really as separate as they might appear.[4]

Nevertheless, in examining the causes of the ultimate success of the abolition movement in Britain, historians long agreed that humanitarian motives had been paramount. Such was true whether, as by the extra-parliamentary activist Thomas Clarkson, the credit was given to a confluence of influential writers and campaigners,[5] or whether, as his later idolisers asserted, the glory was entirely owing to the cause's leading Commons advocate, William Wilberforce.[6] This comfortable consensus was shattered by the challenging and polemical 'decline thesis' propounded in 1944 by Eric Williams, who argued that British abolition was almost entirely induced by economic and geopolitical factors of domestic and colonial policy, with humanitarian ideas serving only as a cynical cover for self-interest.[7] Since later commentators have been able to demonstrate that by the early nineteenth century there was neither an actual nor a perceived long-term downturn in the prosperity of the West Indian colonies, attention has turned instead to hypotheses concerning the role of working and middle class opinion in the eventual attainment of abolition.[8] Yet the first great outburst of anti-slavery activity, including hundreds of petitions to parliament, occurred in the years 1788–92, when little was done to show for it, and the Abolition Act went through in 1807, when popular opinion was far more muted. Although no obvious correlation between direct public pressure and legislative success can therefore necessarily be deduced, what seems certain is that the long-term weight of public hostility to the slave trade, both within the dissenting and radical reform traditions and, perhaps critically, among those in the socially and religiously conservative mainstream, had a considerable impact on the abolition movement.[9]

As Howard Temperley has pointed out in relation to claims that abolition resulted from economic factors, it is necessary to show how such background causes 'were translated into political actions and finally into specific legislative acts'.[10] The trick for the abolitionists, cleverly exploiting favourable commercial and strategic arguments

---

[4] Jeff D. Bass, 'An Efficient Humanitarianism: The British Slave Trade Debates, 1791–1792', *Quarterly Journal of Speech*, LXXV (1989), 152–65; Seymour Drescher, 'People and Parliament: The Rhetoric of the British Slave Trade', *Journal of Interdisciplinary History*, XX (1990), 561–80.

[5] Thomas Clarkson, *The History of the Rise, Progress, and Accomplishment of the Abolition of the African Slave-Trade by the British Parliament* (2 vols, 1808), esp. I, 259–66, and the fold-out 'river-map'.

[6] See Sir Reginald Coupland, *Wilberforce* (1924) and *The British Anti-Slavery Movement* (1933).

[7] Eric Williams, *Capitalism and Slavery* (1944). See also Selwyn H. H. Carrington, *The Sugar Industry and the Abolition of the Slave Trade, 1775–1810* (Gainesville, 2002).

[8] Most notably in *Econocide. British Slavery in the Era of Abolition* (Pittsburgh, 1977) and *From Slavery to Freedom. Comparative Studies in the Rise and Fall of Atlantic Slavery* (New York, 1999) by Seymour Drescher, who, like other commentators, sees working class abolitionism as the key factor. One influential alternative is the class hegemony argument associated with David Brion Davis, *The Problem of Slavery in the Age of Revolution* (Ithaca, 1975), esp. pp. 403–53.

[9] James Walvin, 'The Impact of Slavery on British Radical Politics, 1787–1838', in *Comparative Perspectives on Slavery in New World Plantation Societies*, ed. Vera Rubin and Arthur Tuden (*Annals of the New York Academy of Sciences*, CCXCII, 1977), p. 348, and *idem*, 'The Propaganda of Anti-Slavery', ch. 2 in *Slavery and British Society, 1776–1846*, ed. James Walvin (1982), pp. 49–68. See also Nicholas Hudson, '"Britons Never Will be Slaves": National Myth, Conservatism, and the Beginnings of British Antislavery', *Eighteenth-Century Studies*, XXXIV (2001), 559–76.

[10] Howard Temperley, 'Capitalism, Slavery and Ideology', *Past and Present*, No. 75 (1977), 96.

in the Commons, was to square the circle between the two apparently irreconcilable approaches of humanitarianism and self-interest at the parliamentary level. According to the accepted interpretation of Roger Anstey, who provided the fullest account of the Westminster dimension of the abolition movement, this was achieved by the passage of the Foreign Slave Trade Act in May 1806.[11] This act undoubtedly set the scene for what was to follow, but one effect of Anstey's work was to underestimate the importance of the political mechanics of securing the general measure that followed on from it.[12] In contrast, this essay, covering the period between June 1806 and March 1807, will argue that the success of the Slave Trade Abolition Bill was far less certain, being subject to various parliamentary vicissitudes. Curiously enough, even the apparently unobjectionable wording of the preamble ('WHEREAS the *African* Slave Trade is contrary to the Principles of Justice, Humanity, and sound Policy') had to be defended from attack in the Lords and was later dropped during proceedings in the Commons.[13]

1

Pitt, who was an abolitionist by conviction but a politician by practice, died in January 1806, having failed to prohibit the slave trade.[14] When, not much more than a year later, the Abolition Bill was approved by an unexpectedly large majority in the Commons, 23 February 1807, Lady Bessborough commented that 'people say Mr. Pitt never could have been seriously anxious about it, since it was so easily carried the first time it was tried with any thing like a wish of success'.[15] Borne down by the physically heavy demands of running his wartime government, he undoubtedly neglected some of his earlier favourite projects of reform, including abolition.[16] But, apart from his success in forcing Sir William Dolben's Slave Trade Regulation Bill through the Lords in 1788, he was obstructed by vocal cabinet disagreements on this issue, as well as hampered by private royal disapproval.[17]

In any case, after the first effort had ended in the stalemate of an inquiry, the motions for abolition that Wilberforce introduced nearly every year in the Commons were lost there on almost every occasion; the second, in 1791, was defeated by

[11] Roger Anstey, 'A Re-Interpretation of the Abolition of the British Slave Trade, 1806–1807', *E.H.R.* LXXXVII (1972), 304–32, and *idem, The Atlantic Slave Trade and British Abolition, 1760–1810* (1975), pt. 3.

[12] Anstey, *Atlantic Slave Trade*, pp. 391–402, provides a slightly anti-climactic account of the final passage of the Abolition Act.

[13] House of Lords R.O., HL/PO/JO/10/8/115: printed bill, 6 Feb. 1807; *Cobbett's Parliamentary Debates* [hereafter *P.D.*] (41 vols, 1804–20), IX, 63–66.

[14] Almost unforgivably, in the view of William Hague, *William Pitt the Younger* (2004), p. 589.

[15] *Lord Granville Leveson Gower (First Earl Granville). Private Correspondence, 1781–1821*, ed. Castalia, Countess Granville (2 vols, 1916), II, 238.

[16] John Ehrman, *The Younger Pitt. The Consuming Struggle* (1996), pp. 425–35.

[17] LoGerfo, 'Sir William Dolben', pp. 448–9; Patrick Lipscomb, 'William Pitt and the Abolition Question: A Review of an Historical Controversy', *Proceedings of the Leeds Philosophical and Literary Society. Literary and Historical Section*, XII (1967), 87–128; G. M. Ditchfield, *George III. An Essay in Monarchy* (Basingstoke, 2002), pp. 136, 160.

Figure 1   Print of William Pitt the younger (1759-1806), prime minister and convinced abolitionist, by Richard Earlom, after the original by Gainsborough Dupont (WOA 147). (© Palace of Westminster.)

163 votes to 88, while those attempted in 1793, 1795–9 and 1805 failed by much narrower margins. In 1792, largely at the instigation of Dundas, the Commons passed a compromise motion, calling for the trade to be ended by 1796, but this proposal the Lords put off indefinitely, imitating the delaying tactics of its opponents in the lower House by insisting on conducting their own lengthy inquiry. By the mid-1790s, the effect of the French Revolution was to have suppressed abolitionist endeavours, although another palliative measure was gained in the form of William Smith's Slave Carrying Act in 1799 (its complement, Henry Thornton's Slave Trade Limitation Bill being thrown out by the Lords after a blunder over proxies). After the hiatus of Henry Addington's administration, during which Wilberforce was encouraged by the possibility of reaching a bilateral abolitionist position in the peace talks with France, in 1804 another Commons bill was thwarted in the Lords by being brought in too late in the session.[18] This was a dreary catalogue of lost opportunities, except insofar as it provided those parliamentarians sympathetic to abolition with plenty of time to learn from their mistakes.

One of these was Pitt's cousin and successor as prime minister, Lord Grenville, who, as leader of the Lords, had previously been active in the abolitionist cause.[19] His supporters, although numerically weak in the cabinet, dominated the lower echelons of the new government.[20] It was the opposition whigs who, gaining from the wholesale scramble for offices, formed the largest contingent in the Ministry of All the Talents, with their leader Charles James Fox, a committed abolitionist, becoming foreign secretary.[21] Fox, whose other main concern was to end the war with France, endangered his health by attending the abolition debates in June 1806 and told his nephew Lord Holland, during what proved to be his final illness, that the '[abolition of the] Slave Trade and Peace are two such glorious things, I can't give them up, even to you. If I can manage them, I will then retire.'[22] Abolition was, therefore, clearly a priority for the leading ministers, although they could not on this question command the support of their cabinet colleagues: Lord Sidmouth (Addington as was), whose faction represented the only other major grouping in the coalition; William Windham, who soon ceased to be even nominally a Grenvillite; or Earl Fitzwilliam, despite his old allegiance to Fox. If this was a weakness, it was balanced by the adherence, on the abolition issue at least, of Wilberforce, a natural tory who was nevertheless ready to place the distasteful art of parliamentary manoeuvring at the service of his moral crusade.[23] His fellow parliamentary 'Saints', members of the influential Clapham Sect of conservative evangelicals, could be counted on for support by the whigs, not least because their political values encapsulated the

---

[18] Anstey, *Atlantic Slave Trade*, pp. 273–82, 299–306, 321–6, 329–32, 340, 344–6.

[19] Peter Jupp, *Lord Grenville, 1759–1834* (Oxford, 1985), pp. 74–75, 355–6.

[20] James J. Sack, *Party Politics and Factionalism in the Age of Pitt and Liverpool* (Chicago, 1979), pp. 85–101.

[21] For the formation and course of the Talents ministry, see A. D. Harvey, *Britain in the Early Nineteenth Century* (1978), pp. 170–96.

[22] *Memorials and Correspondence of Charles James Fox*, ed. Lord John Russell (4 vols, 1857), IV, 469, 471.

[23] For good summaries of Wilberforce's role in the passage of the Abolition Act, see Robin Furneaux, *William Wilberforce* (1974), pp. 245–59, and John Pollock, *Wilberforce* (1977), pp. 199–214.

same hierarchical ideals of society.[24] The fact that they, plus a small number of sympathisers and known abolitionists, were no longer an isolated voice in parliament, but could now rely on less inhibited government influence, made their position much stronger.

By contrast, the West India interest in the Commons was demonstrably weaker, despite being the numerically larger of the two groups.[25] It comprised individuals who owned property in or traded with the Caribbean, as well as those connected with them, such as the representatives of the major slaving ports; these included the members for London, where, from the early 1780s, there was a central organization in the form of the planters' and merchants' committee.[26] Yet towards the turn of the century the interest was internally divided and increasingly on the defensive, particularly because its strength really derived, not so much from its political clout as such, as from the as yet unquestioned position of the West Indian sugar economy within Britain's commercial system.[27] Such an assumption could no longer be made by the time of the passage, in May 1806, of the Foreign Slave Trade Act, which was designed to prohibit British traders (whether in British or foreign ships) from carrying enslaved Africans to the colonies of other European powers or to newly conquered British possessions which might have to be restored at the end of the war. The abolitionists promoted this by using purely economic and geopolitical arguments, and deliberately concealed their real humanitarian motivations, while at the same time denying that the bill was a preliminary to further legislation. Not surprisingly, General Banastre Tarleton, who belonged to a family of West Indian merchants and sat for the major slave trading port of Liverpool, angrily denounced the bill in the Commons as introducing abolition by a 'sidewind'. Some of his colleagues, notably the planter Sir William Young, welcomed the measure, believing it to be beneficial to proprietors in the conquered territories, which in itself revealed signs of disagreement within the lobby.[28] But more significant, perhaps, was the psychological precedent which the Foreign Slave Trade Act provided as a precursor to possible total abolition, not least because it actually accounted for a half to two thirds of the total value of the slave trade.[29]

Symbolically enough, just before the planters' and merchants' sub-committee for opposing the abolition of the slave trade held its last meetings in June 1804 (it had not met since 1796), the Society for Effecting the Abolition of the Slave Trade, which had not held a formal gathering since 1797, had reconvened on 23 May 1804.[30]

---

[24] Ernest Marshall Howse, *Saints in Politics. The 'Clapham Sect' and the Growth of Freedom* (1952), pp. 10–27; Abraham D. Kriegel, 'A Convergence of Ethics: Saints and Whigs in British Antislavery', *Journal of British Studies*, XXVI (1987), 423–50.

[25] For an enumeration of 'West Indians' in the House, as well as of the abolitionists, see pp. 163–5 below.

[26] Lillian M. Penson, 'The London West India Interest in the Eighteenth Century', *E.H.R.*, XXXVI (1921), 373–92; James A. Rawley, *London, Metropolis of the Slave Trade* (Columbia, 2003), pp. 123–48; Anstey, *Atlantic Slave Trade*, pp. 286–91.

[27] Andrew J. O'Shaughnessy, 'The Formation of a Commercial Lobby: The West India Interest, British Colonial Policy and the American Revolution', *Historical Journal*, XL (1997), 71–95.

[28] *P.D.*, VI, 597–9, 805, 839, 917–19.

[29] Anstey, *Atlantic Slave Trade*, pp. 365–76.

[30] Institute of Commonwealth Studies Library, University of London, West India Committee Archives, M915/11; B.L., Add. MS 21256, f. 99.

The society, hereafter referred to as the London Committee to distinguish it from branches established elsewhere, had originated in 1787 under the notional chairmanship of Granville Sharp and brought together anti-slavery supporters from both dissenting and evangelical backgrounds to lobby parliament for the preliminary step of ending the slave trade. With its mostly quaker members providing invaluable business networks, the London Committee's circularization of anti-slavery publications and encouragement of hostile petitions made it central to the abolitionist movement.[31] Popular abolitionism faltered badly in the 1790s, when the war against revolutionary France, where radicalism had been erected into a system of government, made it almost impossible for reformers to voice similar ideas at home. Furthermore, the bloody independence struggle in St Domingue (Haiti), a former French colony, made the British governing classes fearful of such rebellions taking place in their own Caribbean possessions. However, when Napoleon reinstated slavery in the French islands and declared himself emperor, radicalism began to be rehabilitated in Britain and abolitionism came to form part of the patriotic yearnings of wartime Britain.[32] Clarkson, who now came out of retirement to begin campaigning and writing again, optimistically reported to two fellow members of the London Committee on 9 July 1805, that 'he had found the ardour of all the former friends of the Abolition with whom he had conversed to remain unabated and that wherever he had been all ranks of people were warm in the cause and desirous of lending their aid.'[33]

One of the most striking expressions of public opposition to the slave trade was the petition to the Lords in favour of the Foreign Slave Trade Bill, which was signed by the inhabitants of Manchester, a major provincial centre of abolitionist activity. It had been organized at short notice to counter one from 439 local merchants for the bill, which was brought up by Lord Westmorland, a staunch anti-abolitionist, on 13 May 1806. On presenting it, complete with 2,354 names attached, the following day, the earl of Derby stated that he 'had authority to say, that had there been a little more time, at least treble the number of signatures would have been obtained'.[34] To anticipate slightly, the general election later that year also offered a good opportunity for pressure to be brought to bear. In Yorkshire, where Wilberforce was joined by another abolitionist candidate in Walter Ramsden Fawkes, three quakers temporarily laid aside their habitual political self-effacement to issue an address in Wilberforce's favour, and Edward Baines of the *Leeds Mercury* explained that his newspaper's opposition to the return of Henry Lascelles, the younger son of the prominent slave-owner Lord Harewood, 'originated as much, perhaps more, in the Editor's detestation of the Slave Trade, and a dread of its supporters dominating in the Senate,

---

[31] Anstey, *Atlantic Slave Trade*, pp. 239–64; J. R. Oldfield, 'The London Committee and Mobilization of Public Opinion against the Slave Trade', *Historical Journal*, XXXV (1992), 331–43; David Turley, *The Culture of English Antislavery, 1780–1860* (1991), pp. 4–5, 17–31, 54–5, 63, 69; Judith Jennings, *The Business of Abolishing the British Slave Trade, 1783–1807* (1997).

[32] Robin Blackburn, *The Overthrow of Colonial Slavery, 1776–1848* (1988), pp. 146–9, 157–8, 295–9; Linda Colley, *Britons. Forging the Nation, 1707–1837* (New Haven, 1992), pp. 353–6, 358–9; Davis, *Problem of Slavery in the Age of Revolution*, pp. 117, 310–11, 423–7.

[33] Ellen Gibson Wilson, *Thomas Clarkson. A Biography* (1989), pp. 105–7; B.L., Add. MS 21256, f. 114.

[34] *Cowdroy's Manchester Gazette*, 10, 17 May, 7 June; House of Lords R.O., HL/PO/JO/10/8/106: MS petitions, 13, 14 May 1806; *L.J.*, XLV, 624, 628; Seymour Drescher, 'Whose Abolition? Popular Pressure and the Ending of the British Slave Trade', *Past and Present*, No. 143 (1994), 141–4.

as from any other Consideration'.[35] The slave trade was certainly one reason behind Lascelles's decision to withdraw before the election took place,[36] and the issue was raised in at least ten other constituencies, including Liverpool.[37] The result there, with Tarleton being forced to retire in favour of the literary whig William Roscoe, had a national impact, even though Roscoe's triumph had little to do with his abolitionist stance.[38]

2

By 1806, therefore, three essential initial preconditions for the final success of abolition had been met in terms of the commitment of ministers, the weakened state of the West India interest and the supportive role of public opinion. However, to understand the final ending of the slave trade, it is necessary to examine some of the crucial features of the internal parliamentary dynamics which eventually resulted in the Abolition Act. The first of these was undoubtedly the boldness with which ministers acted in the wake of the passage of the Foreign Slave Trade Act. In their enthusiasm, Fox and Grenville, like Wilberforce, were tempted to press immediately for a general measure, but there was every chance that the lateness of the session would allow the Lords to stifle such an initiative, as had been done at the instigation of Lord Eldon in 1804. Well aware of the risk of squandering the present favourable circumstances, the Saint and abolitionist guru James Stephen wrote (in an informative briefing paper) that there would be considerable opposition from the planters and merchants, as well as their conservative apologists, but concluded that if 'all the Members of the present very able and powerful Administration, can be brought to act together for that generous purpose ... it seems impossible to doubt their success'.[39] As he explained to Sidmouth, whose objections to anything other than gradual abolition he failed to overcome, Grenville in fact settled for a compromise, in which a broadly attractive resolution would be put to the Commons and then taken to the Lords for their concurrence, the Abolition Bill being held over until the new session.[40]

---

[35] 'Friends and the Slave Trade: A Yorkshire Election Declaration, 1806', *The Journal of the Friends' Historical Society*, XLVI (1954), 65–66; *Leeds Mercury*, 1, 8, 15 Nov. 1806.

[36] E. A. Smith, 'The Yorkshire Elections of 1806 and 1807: A Study in Electoral Management', *Northern History*, II (1967), 66–72.

[37] *The History of Parliament. The House of Commons, 1790–1820*, ed. R. G. Thorne (5 vols, 1986) [hereafter *H.P., 1790–1820*], I, 179; II, 215, 230, 298, 309; Michael Hinton, 'The General Elections of 1806 and 1807', University of Reading Ph.D., 1959, pp. 92–99; Drescher, 'Whose Abolition?', pp. 144–9.

[38] Ian Seller, 'William Roscoe, the Roscoe Circle and Radical Politics in Liverpool, 1787–1807', *Transactions of the Historic Society of Lancashire and Cheshire*, CXX (1968), 58–61; F. E. Sanderson, 'The Structure of Politics in Liverpool, 1780–1807', *ibid.*, CXXVII (1977), 76–9, 84–85; *The Horner Papers. Selections from the Letters and Miscellaneous Writings of Francis Horner, M.P., 1795–1817* ed. Kenneth Bourne and William Banks Taylor (Edinburgh, 1994), p. 435.

[39] B.L., Add. MS 59305A, ff. 59–66; H.M.C., *Fortescue MSS*, VIII, 146–7; Clarkson, *History*, II, 508–9, 566–7; R. I. and S. Wilberforce, *The Life of William Wilberforce* (5 vols, 1838) [hereafter *Life of Wilberforce*], III, 261–2, 268, 270.

[40] George Pellew, *The Life and Correspondence of the ... First Viscount Sidmouth* (3 vols, 1847), II, 427–30, 445–8; *The Correspondence of William Wilberforce*, ed. R. I. and S. Wilberforce (2 vols, 1840) [hereafter *Wilberforce Correspondence*], II, 87–88.

This resolution was the motion to declare the slave trade 'contrary to the principles of justice, humanity, and sound policy', and to commit the House to its abolition, that Fox introduced with a highly charged speech in the Commons on 10 June 1806. There was little substantive debate – his opponents mostly confined themselves to pointing out what they saw as the irrelevance of passing a resolution to which the Commons had effectively stood committed since 1792 – and Fox's call for unanimity was as good as answered when only 15 divided in the minority against it (to 114 in its support).[41] Employing the formal procedure of a conference, a rather theatrical means of communicating with the Lords, on the 13th the Commons requested the other House to agree with this resolution.[42] This they did on 24 June, after a debate, initiated by Grenville, during which the only major opposition came from Lord Hawkesbury, who followed his father Lord Liverpool in resisting abolition on practical grounds, Westmorland, who was forthright but ineffective, and Sidmouth, whose objection was deemed 'whimsical' by the succeeding speaker.[43] The session ended with ministers having made a dramatic demonstration of intent, which must have been apparent in parliament, while at the same time, using the less obvious sleight of hand of having effectively made the supposedly non-government question of general abolition (a matter of conscience) into just as much an issue of ministerial confidence as had been the earlier Foreign Slave Trade Act (a matter of purely commercial regulation).[44] The audacity of Fox and Grenville was to have shown not only that they had clear abolitionist majorities in the Commons, where votes in the past had frequently been fairly close, but also (of 43–18 and 41–21) in the Lords, which had not previously divided on the general question as such.[45] In the sense that it thereafter became almost unthinkable that an abolition measure would fail, the resolutions of June 1806 had irrevocably changed the terms of the debate. Judging from the speeches made, as well as the voting totals, it is apparent that by then most M.P.s and peers would have judged the issue as one of morality over economics.[46] Such was the impetus behind the parliamentary movement for abolition that it survived the summer recess and the general election, although Wilberforce was among those who knew there would be a struggle ahead and feared the damaging effect of Fox's death in September 1806.[47]

When the new parliament met in December 1806, Grenville, who had been distracted by the alternative idea of gradually eliminating the trade through a prohibitory tax on imports of enslaved Africans, proceeded with his original intention

[41] *P.D.*, VII, 580–603. See also the longer account in *Substance of the Debates on a Resolution for Abolishing the Slave Trade, which was moved in the House of Commons on the 10th June, 1806, and in the House of Lords on the 24th June, 1806* (1806).

[42] *C.J.*, LXI, 402–3; *L.J.*, XLV, 693.

[43] *P.D.*, VII, 801–9.

[44] E.g., 'It is understood, that, on opening of parliament [*sic*], a bill is to be brought in, *under the auspices of his majesty's ministers*, for the immediate and total abolition of the slave-trade': [John Gladstone], *Letters concerning the Abolition of the Slave-Trade and other West India Affairs. By Mercator* (1807), p. 2 (emphasis added).

[45] House of Lords R.O., HL/PO/JO/5/1/155: minute book, 16 May, 24 June 1806. Not '41–20' on the latter occasion, as erroneously stated in *PD*, VII, 809.

[46] Drescher, *Econocide*, pp. 214–23.

[47] *Life of Wilberforce*, III, 271; *Wilberforce Correspondence*, II, 92–94; Pollock, *Wilberforce*, pp. 204–5.

of putting it 'out of the power of our opponents again to defeat us by the disgraceful methods of delay'. This he did by presenting to the Lords, 'within the first days of meeting, a Bill simply abolishing the Trade, and declaring the being engaged in it a misdemeanour punishable at law'.[48] His strategy was again courageous, since it was unusual for bills, let alone major public bills, to begin in the Lords. It also displayed considerable resolve, as the upper House had traditionally taken a lead from the opponents of abolition, whether they were proprietors, senior judges, colonial governors, experienced military and naval officers, or the royal dukes.[49] At least he had the advantages that the Pittite opposition was in disarray, partly because George III had not yet come out openly against his ministers, and that the prince of Wales, a supporter of the administration, had apparently agreed not to join his brothers in attacking abolition.[50] Clarkson, who hoped to use his chest of African produce to lobby peers (as 'Many of the Lords are yet very ignorant of the Subject, and if we could get twenty or thirty to take the Trouble of seeing the different Articles, they might have very different Ideas of the subject from what they have'),[51] observed that 'The Princes (I do not mean of Wales) are canvassing against Us, and will do Us much Mischief. This Circumstance occasions Us to be very busy in trying to counteract their Efforts.'[52] In the same light, Wilberforce, one of whose supporters informed him of the need for a printed statement of the evidence for abolition, since 'People are shockingly indifferent on the subject, and very incredulous', wrote a pamphlet specifically in order to provide a summary of the case against the slave trade just before the main debate in the Lords.[53] He continued to bombard Grenville with anxious comments, for example on the Scottish representative peers or the need for papers to be laid, but far from this being disruptive interference, Wilberforce was in reality displaying a fine understanding of the perils and pitfalls of parliamentary management.[54]

There was much external assistance of this type, but the real credit for the success of the Abolition Bill in the Lords must be given to Grenville himself.[55] The prime minister, who fended off queries and conceded the production of official correspondence on 2 and 12 January 1807, negotiated privately with Westmorland on the timing of the second reading, and with the duke of Clarence (the chief royal opponent), who surprisingly promised not to divide the Lords if he saw the House

---

[48] H.M.C., *Fortescue MSS*, VIII, 169; *Life of Wilberforce*, III, 271–2, 286–7.

[49] *Failed Legislation, 1660–1800. Extracted from the Commons and Lords Journals*, ed. Julian Hoppit (1997), p. 13; Michael W. McCahill, *Order and Equipoise. The Peerage and the House of Lords, 1783–1806* (1978), pp. 57–60; Anstey, *Atlantic Slave Trade*, pp. 315–18.

[50] Stanley Ayling, *George the Third* (1972), pp. 438–9; *Life of Wilberforce*, III, 256–9.

[51] Library of the Religious Society of Friends, London, TEMP MS 128/14/41: Clarkson to Wilkinson, 21 Dec. 1806.

[52] St John's College Library, Cambridge, Clarkson MS 19: Clarkson to Taylor, 26 Jan. 1807. This and later references, for which I am indebted to Jonathan Harrison, the Special Collections Librarian, are given by permission of the Master and Fellows of St John's College, Cambridge.

[53] *Wilberforce Correspondence*, II, 105–6; *Life of Wilberforce*, III, 273–4, 288–9; W. Wilberforce, *A Letter on the Abolition of the Slave Trade; Addressed to the Freeholders and other Inhabitants of Yorkshire* (1807), pp. 2–3.

[54] B.L., Add. MS 58978, ff. 82, 86, 90, 92, 100, 103.

[55] Jupp, *Lord Grenville*, pp. 389–91; Lipscomb, 'Pitt and the Abolition Question', pp. 117–18; Michael W. McCahill, 'William, First Lord Grenville', in *Leaders in the Lords. Government Management and Party Organization in the Upper Chamber, 1765–1902*, ed. Richard W. Davis (Edinburgh, 2003), pp. 40–2.

THE RIGHT HON. LORD GRENVILLE.

Figure 2   Print of William Wyndham Grenville, 1st Baron Grenville (1759-1834), prime minister during the Talents ministry, 1806-7, by Samuel William Reynolds the elder, after the original by John Hoppner (WOA 398). (© Palace of Westminster.)

was against delay, about the hearing of counsel on behalf of petitioners against the bill.[56] Having made clear on 2 February that he would not permit any postponement, he gave over the 4th to the hearing of counsel, but refused the requests of such opponents as Eldon and Hawkesbury for further examination of witnesses, so allowing him to maintain momentum by moving the second reading of the bill the following day.[57] Drawing on his experience of previous occasions, Grenville had taken pains to summon abolitionist lords to attend or to furnish him with proxies. Among those he wrote to, Viscount Hereford apparently did not respond and the bishop of Peterborough was excused sick, but Derby, the bishop of London (having earlier sent in a precautionary proxy) and the archbishop of Canterbury were listed as present and voted in person for abolition; and Lords Carlisle, Leicester, Rivers and Willoughby de Broke had uncancelled proxies which must have been among those given in the bill's favour.[58] Attendance was a vital matter because, as Thornton, the evangelical member for Southwark and chairman of the Sierra Leone Company, wrote to Patty More on 4 February, 'The Slave Traders are very low in spirits, but we suspect them to be affecting to under estimate their own strength and are not without fear of a weak attendance of our friends in the H[ouse] of Lords.'[59]

In fact, 109 lords were present on 5 February to hear Grenville, ably seconded by other abolitionists in the debate, speak decisively for the bill on the sole ground of 'justice', and to witness the usual dissentients, Sidmouth among them, make almost no impression.[60] Having at the last moment expected over 70 supporters, Grenville was vindicated when 72 (and 28 proxies) voted for the second reading with 28 (and six proxies) against, a result usually attributed to the firm exercise of the natural ministerial vote.[61] The division list reveals, not that many former opponents of abolition divided in its favour, but rather that (compared with the division of 68–61 against Thornton's bill on 5 July 1799) the abolitionist vote had held up well, while that of the anti-abolitionists had halved.[62] Grenville had appealed to the Lords on the basis that 'the whole country' looked to their House to 'wipe away the stigma attached to its character in continuing this detestable traffic', and this attempt to place the debate beyond the confines of parliamentary discussion seems to have had an effect.[63] Indeed, it is plausible to argue that the peers' voting behaviour was very largely due to the conscious decision of many of them to bow to public pressure, especially

[56] *P.D.*, VIII, 257–9, 431–2; B.L., Add. MS 59305A, ff. 112, 128–9; Add. MS 58869, ff. 205, 207.

[57] *L.J.*, XLVI, 49, 51–2; *P.D.*, VIII, 601–2, 612–18.

[58] B.L., Add. MS 58964, ff. 33, 117; Add. MS 59305A, ff. 109, 112, 114, 135, 136; Add. MS 59305B, ff. 151, 152; *L.J.*, XLVI, 52 (attendance list); *The Times*, 10 Feb. 1807 (majority list); House of Lords R.O., HL/PO/JO/13/81: proxy book, 4, 5 Feb. 1807.

[59] Wigan Archives, Wigan Leisure and Culture Trust, D/DZ EHC 18 (M786): Henry Thornton letterbook, p. 190.

[60] *L.J.*, XLVI, 52; *P.D.*, VIII, 657–72; *Life of Wilberforce*, III, 292–4.

[61] *Life of Wilberforce*, III, 291–2; A. S. Turberville, *The House of Lords in the Age of Reform, 1784–1837* (1958), p. 143; David Large, 'The Decline of "the Party of the Crown" and the Rise of Parties in the House of Lords, 1783–1837', *E.H.R.*, LXXVIII (1963), 675.

[62] The list of the majority attached to Lambeth Palace Library MS 2104, Porteus Notebook, f. 85, is a cutting from *The Times*, 10 Feb. 1807 (and the same names are listed in that day's *Morning Chronicle*). For the 1799 division list, see *The Later Correspondence of George III*, ed. Arthur Aspinall (5 vols, Cambridge, 1962–70), III, 226–8.

[63] *P.D.*, VIII, 663.

given the long-term effect of the evidence presented in condemnation of the slave trade.[64] As Grenville commented to an absent supporter, 'the triumph obtained on that day is considered as so decisive as to any opposition in the House of Lords, that the opponents of the Bill have declared that they do not mean to give us any further trouble there'.[65] On 6 February 1807 Hawkesbury, who acknowledged that the bill would pass, nevertheless moved an amendment to alter the preamble so as to concede abolition on motives of expediency rather than of 'justice and humanity'. With Eldon remarking that the existing wording was the best means of encouraging international co-operation, Hawkesbury was only able to divide ten (including himself) against 33 for retaining it unchanged, and nothing but outbursts of vain indignation disrupted the remaining stages, which were completed without incident.[66]

Capitalizing on this victory, the Abolition Bill was brought to the Commons on 10 February 1807, when Lord Howick (Charles Grey), who had replaced Fox as foreign secretary and leader in the Commons, moved its first reading. The bill's opponents, principally the merchant and West India Dock Company chairman George Hibbert and the Liverpool member General Isaac Gascoyne, complained that public opinion was being given undue importance and urged that more time be provided for evidence to be heard against it. On 20 February counsel were called in to speak on their behalf, but, despite repeated pleas from the anti-abolitionists, the Commons negatived all attempts at making further inquiries. A field day was therefore expected on 23 February, when, the bill having technically had its formal second reading on the 20th, the actual question before the House would be on its committal.[67] Unlike on former occasions on which the Commons had had to pronounce on the issue of abolition, there were three major differences in the psychological effects that were brought to bear on members. First, the sizeable majority in the Lords made it impossible to rely on the previous assumption that any abolition motion in the lower House would have been stifled in the upper chamber. Second, coming so soon after the declaratory resolutions of June 1806 and the general election later that year, it was difficult to argue that the Commons, or for that matter the people, had not had the chance to give it their consideration. And third, members were not being asked to concur with a cross-party motion for preliminary investigation or further inquiry, but had now to decide on a quasi-ministerial measure which had formidable weight and momentum behind it.

3

The London Committee, which had always been involved in sophisticated lobbying of parliament, had passed resolutions as recently as 1805 for securing the attendance

---

[64] See Michael W. McCahill, *The House of Lords in the Age of George III, 1760–1811* (forthcoming), ch. 11. I am grateful to Dr McCahill for kindly letting me read several chapters of his manuscript prior to its publication.

[65] B.L., Add. MS 59305B, f. 157.

[66] *L.J.*, XLVI, 55–57; House of Lords R.O., HL/PO/JO/5/1/156: minute book, 6 Feb. 1807; *P.D.*, VIII, 677–83, 691–3, 701–3.

[67] Dale H. Porter, *The Abolition of the Slave Trade in England, 1784–1807* (Hamden, 1970), pp. 136–8; *C.J.*, LXII, 115, 149–50; *P.D.*, VIII, 717–22, 940–3.

and support of members, including one calling on the committee 'individually and collectively to make out as correct Lists as they can of Members of both Houses of Parliament friendly and hostile to the Abolition'.[68] It has long been known that, according to the committee's fair minute book, on 10 February 1807 the eight members in attendance at 18 Downing Street, 'proceeded to draw out Lists of the Members of the House of Commons known to be friendly to the Abolition of the Slave Trade and also of those known and supposed to be adverse to the measure'. An average of 11 members attended four further meetings, on the 11th, 13th, 17th and 20th, to examine and correct these lists, the entry for 13 February repeating that members were being divided into 'friendly' and 'adverse' categories.[69] In confirmation of this, Thornton's wife Mary Anne wrote to Hannah More on 21 February that the Abolition Bill

> will not be lost for want of pains, for a large party have hired a house in Downing Street and meet every day. Each has a list of members to whom he can have access for the purpose of recommending the subject and prevailing on them to attend. Among these John Thornton is among the most active.[70]

Like Henry's brother John Thornton, who attended two of the meetings, the quaker William Allen, who was at three of them, recorded in his diary on the 14th, that 'I have spent a great deal of time this week on the business of the Abolition of the Slave Trade, and have strong hopes that the measure will succeed.'[71]

None of the lists of members, of which several versions were presumably prepared, has previously come to light.[72] Yet it is almost certain that one of these versions is in fact the manuscript survey of the house of commons on the abolition of the slave trade which exists in the Holland House papers in the British Library (Add. MS 51917), an edition of which is printed as an appendix to this article.[73] This document actually has four headings ('Staunch Friends', 'Friendly', 'Doubtful' and 'Adverse'), but two of these match the categories mentioned in the society's minutes, and using terms which were relatively unusual (contemporary lists more often used 'for' and 'against'). Of the other two terms, 'Staunch Friends' clearly refers to those members who were known to be certain, while the 'Doubtful' section, evidently meaning those whose opinions or attendance were unknown rather than undecided, was obviously a useful additional heading to employ. Although initial preparation of the survey could have been begun at any time since the general election late the previous year, it seems reasonable to suppose that it must date from the time of the committee meetings in mid-February 1807; this particular version must have been written out after 21 January, since it includes John Alexander Bannerman, who

---

[68] B.L., Add. MS 21256, ff. 104, 108, 109.

[69] *Ibid.*, ff. 124–6.

[70] Henry Thornton letterbook, p. 192. This is quoted in Viscountess Knutsford, *Life and Letters of Zachary Macaulay* (1900), p. 268.

[71] B.L., Add. MS 21256, ff. 124–6; William Allen, *Life of William Allen, with Selections from his Correspondence* (3 vols, 1846–7), I, 84.

[72] Writing of such a survey prepared by the London Committee in December 1788, Anstey commented that, if extant, it 'would be invaluable': *Atlantic Slave Trade*, p. 270.

[73] This document has been known about for at least 20 years: *H.P., 1790–1820*, I, 186, 372.

was returned at a by-election that day, among the 'P's in the uninterrupted sequence of 'Doubtful' names, and was still being worked on when that of the Hon. William Assheton Harbord, who was returned on 7 February, was interlineated in the 'Adverse' section. It is not otherwise possible to tell how late on a version this is, but it can safely be supposed that the survey was at some point shown to Holland, an abolitionist and cabinet minister, which is why it survives among his papers.[74] Who gave the survey to Holland is a matter of speculation, but one candidate could be the young whig barrister and author Henry Brougham, who was currently cutting his teeth on the slave trade question.[75] As a member of the London Committee, he was present at all but one of the five meetings which dealt with the lists of members.[76] Wilberforce mentioned him as being 'useful to Lord Howick about Slave Trade' in the context of the decisive debate that month, and by March he had evidently made himself invaluable to Holland, who was hoping to bring him into parliament.[77] Whether or not Brougham took a leading part, it seems probable that this concerted lobbying campaign was a collective labour involving, among others, Thomas Babington M.P. (naturally a 'Staunch Friend'), Clarkson, B. M. and T. F. Forster, Zachary Macaulay and Wilberforce.[78]

The last, who only missed the first meeting, noted in his diary after the second, which was held on 11 February: 'An Abolition Committee. Looking at the list of the House of Commons. A terrific list of doubtfuls. Lord Grenville not confident on looking at Abolition list; yet I think we shall carry it too. Several West Indians with us. How popular Abolition is, just now!'[79] It was no doubt after scrutinizing the survey that Grenville reported to Smith, the unitarian who had been defeated for Norwich but was very active in the last stages of this campaign (and was himself optimistic after having attended the first meeting), that 'Still I fear we are not quite at the end of our labours for I see many symptoms of much opposition to it in the Ho[use] of Commons and I deeply regret your absence at such a time.'[80] The numbers of members in each section of the surviving survey indicate why Grenville was worried, since both the 'first' and 'last' counts (or totals calculated before and after the alterations to the survey, as explained in the Appendix) showed that the combined 'Staunch Friends' and 'Friendly' would divide only 234 and 241 (or somewhere in the range 210 to 265) compared to the combined 'Doubtful' and 'Adverse' totals of 379 and 386 (or somewhere in the range 354 to 411). Even if most of the 'Doubtful' members stayed away and the rest split evenly for and against abolition, the bill's backers feared they would have to face 85 'Adverse' members (on the 'first' count)

---

[74] For Holland's later views on emancipation, see V. E. Chancellor, 'Slave-Owner and Anti-Slaver: Henry Richard Vassall Fox, 3rd Lord Holland, 1800–1840', *Slavery and Abolition*, I (1980), 263–75.

[75] Chester W. New, *The Life of Henry Brougham to 1830* (Oxford, 1961), pp. 21–31.

[76] B.L., Add. MS 21256, ff. 124–6.

[77] *Life of Wilberforce*, III, 299; University College London Library Services, Special Collections, Brougham MSS: James to Henry Brougham sr, 20 Mar. 1807.

[78] B.L., Add. MS 21256, ff. 124–6.

[79] *Life of Wilberforce*, III, 295. The mention of 'doubtfuls' lends credence to the identification of the British Library survey as the same list.

[80] B.L., Add. MS 21256, f. 124; Add. 59305B, ff. 166, 170; Richard W. Davis, *Dissent in Politics, 1780–1830. The Political Life of William Smith, MP* (1971), pp. 105–19.

or 99 (on the 'last' count), the latter figure being only as high as the average that the abolitionists themselves had been able to muster in divisions between 1804 and 1806.[81] Using the 'last' count, the 'Staunch Friends' and 'Friendly' sections together represented 38 per cent of those listed, as against 16 per cent for those 'Adverse'. Assuming that each section attended in equal proportions, then if more than half of the 'Doubtful' members (46 per cent) voted against abolition, the bill would presumably have been defeated, which is surely what Wilberforce meant by referring to the 'terrific list of doubtfuls'.[82]

Undoubtedly, as they had agreed early the previous year, the committee members proceeded by discreet private application rather than by such high profile methods as holding public meetings, which were deemed counter-productive.[83] The assiduity of their lobbying can partly be judged by an analysis of the 51 actual and notional transfers of members between different sections of the survey (as described in the Appendix), an operation applied to 50 (or about eight per cent) of the individuals listed. A small and politically mixed set of four members were transferred from 'Friendly' to 'Doubtful',[84] as was Windham; his original inclusion as 'Friendly' was wishful thinking, but his placement as a 'Doubtful' was possibly a sign that he would be absent. The only other figure transformed into a 'doubtful' was Lord Huntly, who had initially been considered 'Adverse'. As might be expected, most of the transfers were from the 'Doubtful' section, no fewer than 13 of them, presumably on the basis of a personal indication to that effect, being moved to 'Adverse'. These changes were not without justification. Three such members voted against abolition: the Hon. Charles Herbert on 23 February, and Reginald Pole Carew (marked 'ag[ains]t') and Sir James Pulteney on 6 March; and another three had obvious West India connexions: Christopher Bethell Codrington (a descendant of the slave-owning benefactor of All Souls, Oxford), Sir Richard Gamon and Sir Arthur Leary Piggott ('adverse'), who, as attorney-general, had taken charge of the Foreign Slave Trade Bill the previous year.[85] Only one other member, Daniel Parker Coke (formerly 'Friendly'), became 'Adverse'.

More encouragingly for the abolitionists, five members were converted from 'Doubtful' into supporters, although one of these, Robert Holt Leigh, whose name was not apparently interlineated in the 'Friendly' section, may only have been entered as a 'Doubtful' in error before being crossed through. Lord Brooke was considered 'friendly', as was John Maitland *en route* to finishing among the 'Staunch Friends', while Henry Willoughby (annotated 'friendly if not Staunch') went straight to the latter section. Henry Arthur Herbert (once deemed 'Doubtful') proved himself a 'Staunch Friend' by fulfilling his County Kerry constituents' instructions to vote for abolition, as he informed the Commons on 27 February.[86] Although four members,

---

[81] Anstey, *Atlantic Slave Trade*, p. 299.

[82] *Life of Wilberforce*, III, 295.

[83] B.L., Add. MS 21256, ff. 116–17; Davis, *Problem of Slavery in the Age of Revolution*, pp. 446–7.

[84] Thomas Francis and William Henry Fremantle (jointly 'doubtful') were both junior ministers, Lord Lovaine was a Pittite, and the Hon. Charles William Wyndham ('Doubtful') was a former Portland whig.

[85] The others were Sir Charles Merrik Burrell ('adverse'), Patrick Duigenan, Anthony Hardolph Eyre, James Ferguson, Hugh Leycester, James Shaw and Mark Wood.

[86] *P.D.*, VIII, 1052.

about whom there must have been an element of ambiguity, were moved from 'Staunch Friends' to 'Friendly',[87] 22 were transferred the other way, presumably on assurances being given that they would attend as requested. Significantly, most of these seem to have been shifted in small groups, which would fit with the idea of one lobbyist having been entrusted with a short alphabetical sequence of names and then having had his corrections entered on the actual survey. Thus, the Baring brothers (Alexander, Henry and Thomas), who were all new members, Sir Robert Barclay, who was also in banking, and Joseph Foster Barham, who favoured abolition despite being a Jamaican planter, were together marked down as 'transfer[re]d to Staunch list', apparently at the same time that Thomas Richard Beaumont was likewise 'transfer[re]d'.[88] Again, Sir William Middleton, James Macdonald, Sir Charles Mordaunt and (the previously 'Doubtful') John Maitland were shifted as a group, although only Middleton's name was deleted from the 'Friendly' section, suggesting unfamiliarity with the procedure or perhaps understandable haste.[89] Displaying similar but suggestive irregularity, Sir Thomas Charles Bunbury ('certain') and John Staniforth were inserted among the 'Staunch Friends' without being crossed out in the 'Friendly' section, while the Hon. William Howard ('<u>certain</u>') and Lord William Russell ('<u>Staunch</u>') were probably intended to be so transferred, but were left in their original positions.

With memories of the embarrassing failures of favourable motions in 1796 and 1805, when key supporters had been absent, the abolitionists clearly made every effort to summon their friends.[90] Even Lord Muncaster (a 'Staunch Friend'), whose wife was not long dead, could not be excused, and it seems unlikely that Babington, unworldly to a fault though he was, would have cried off on the eve of the debate (the only evidence for which is an undated letter in the *Wilberforce Correspondence*).[91] Not every application met with success. Thomas Johnes (rightly, it appears, a 'Doubtful') replied from his Cardiganshire fastness of Hafod on 14 February 1807 to Howick, that 'I am very sorry I cannot give my concluding vote for the abolition of a trade that has been so disgraceful to us', but promised to attend parliament the following month in support of ministers.[92] Nevertheless, there was certainly a large attendance of members and public visitors on the 23rd. The quaker Hagger Lowe, a Southwark businessman, reported to his brother two days later that 'tho[ugh] I was at the Gallery door by 2 o[']clock in the afternoon yet it was so full I could not get a seat for several hours'. In fact, although the Speaker arrived at about 3 p.m., the large number of

---

[87] The brothers the Hon. Charles Lawrence and the Hon. Lawrence Dundas, with the Hon. William Frederick Elliot Eden, were moved as a group; the fourth so transferred was Sir Edward Knatchbull.

[88] A similar group is made up of Frederick William Grant, the Hon. Edward Harbord, the Hon. William Herbert and Samuel Horrocks, the last three all being annotated as transferred.

[89] A similar mixture of country gentlemen and businessmen – John Langston, Thomas Buckler Leth-bridge, Sir John Lubbock and Magens Dorien Magens (none of whose names were deleted) – were probably moved at the same time.

[90] Anstey, *Atlantic Slave Trade*, pp. 281–2, 345–6.

[91] *Life of Wilberforce*, III, 292–3, 299; *Wilberforce Correspondence*, II, 114–15.

[92] Durham University Library, Earl Grey MS, GRE/B37/1/10. Reproduced by permission of Durham University Library.

items of private business took so long to complete that the debate did not start until about 6 p.m.[93]

Howick, who, in common with almost all the abolitionist speakers that day, was a 'Staunch Friend', opened the debate nervously, with a long statement balancing the competing arguments of 'justice and humanity' with 'sound policy'. Even before he had finished, however, it was plain that what Wilberforce termed 'high principles of rectitude' would dominate the discussions, and weighty counter-arguments presented by Gascoyne and Hibbert (both 'Adverse') evidently had little effect amid the rush of anti-slavery orations. Some of the latter must have made a great impact: for example, the technically under age Lord Milton, who was in fact marked down as 'Adverse', because his father was the anti-abolitionist cabinet minister, Fitzwilliam; and the veteran soldier General Sir John Doyle, who was omitted from the survey, because his condemnation of slavery drew on his own experiences in South Carolina.[94] Of Roscoe's 'mild, quiet, unaffected, and sensible' contribution, in which he stated that it was 'the greatest happiness of my existence to lift up my voice' against 'this inhuman traffic' with 'the friends of justice and humanity', Richard Sharp (another 'Staunch Friend'), who was sitting beside him, told him that his vote, as the representative of Liverpool, 'was worth twenty'.[95] Sir Samuel Romilly, the solicitor-general, who was likewise assured that he had made 'a considerable impression on the House', pronounced a panegyric on Wilberforce that led to a remarkable ovation in the latter's favour. As the Foxite abolitionist John Courtenay pointed out in the chamber on the 27th, this had hurried on the division, in which 283 voted for the committal of the Abolition Bill, against only 16 in the minority. The majority of 267, Romilly observed, 'exceeded the expectations of the most sanguine'.[96] Clarkson, believing that 'our efforts were blessed by Providence', confided to a friend that 'I want words to express the joy I feel on the occasion.'[97]

Great as was this margin of victory, what surprised Lowe, who 'waited to hear the result of the division', at just after four in the morning, was that 'there must have been a great number that went away without Voting at all, for it was a very full House'.[98] Similarly, Clarkson commented that 'several of the old opponents of this righteous cause went away, unable to vote against it; while others of them staid [*sic*] in their places, and voted in its favour'.[99] Assuming that a 'full House' contained 342 on the floor of the chamber, then subtracting the 304 present for the division (including the Speaker and two tellers on each side), would mean that 38 had abstained or otherwise retired before the vote took place; adding in the 150 that could be fitted into the

[93] Warwickshire R.O., Lowe of Evington MS, CR2926/4; *C.J.*, LXII, 150–61.

[94] *Life of Wilberforce*, III, 296–9; E. A. Smith, *Lord Grey, 1764–1845* (Oxford, 1990), p. 117; *P.D.*, VIII, 940–95. See also, *Substance of the Debates on the Bill for Abolishing the Slave Trade, which was brought into the House of Lord, on the 2d January, 1807, and into the House of Commons on the 10th February, 1807* (1808).

[95] *Life of Wilberforce*, III, 299; *P.D.*, VIII, 962; Henry Roscoe, *The Life of William Roscoe* (2 vols, 1833), I, 376.

[96] *Memoirs of the Life of Sir Samuel Romilly, written by himself, with a Selection from his Correspondence*, ed. by his sons (3 vols, 1840), II, 187–8; *Life of Wilberforce*, III, 296–9; *P.D.*, VIII, 1049.

[97] St. John's College Library, Cambridge, Clarkson MS 19: Clarkson to Wadkin, 24 Feb. 1807.

[98] Warwickshire R.O., Lowe of Evington MS, CR2926/4.

[99] Clarkson, *History*, II, 575.

Figure 3 Print of William Wilberforce (1759–1833), M.P. for Yorkshire, the leading parliamentary campaigner for abolition of the slave trade, by F. and W. Holl, after the original by Thomas Lawrence (WOA 96). (© Palace of Westminster.)

side galleries, would give a more improbable total of 188 abstainers. The true figure probably lies somewhere in this range.[100] As Clarkson suggests (though he was wrong in implying that the majority stayed in their seats to vote), the most likely cause of abstentions was a dislike of dividing against the perceived strength of opinion in the House. Since the minority had to stay in the chamber and then wait while the 'ayes', who had gone into the lobby, were counted on re-entering the chamber, they must have been highly conspicuous as 'diehards'; just as much so, indeed, as the 18 in total who on 6 March divided in committee to delay abolition for five years.[101] Among those known to have avoided this designation, by leaving before the vote occurred, were Lord Castlereagh and George Rose, both 'Adverse' Pittites. Windham, who was 'hoarse', chose not to appear at all, but most of the Addingtonians, reserving their objections for the committee, voted with the majority, and it was perhaps with them in mind that Wilberforce recorded that there were 'several voting with us for the first time'.[102] According to Charles Abbot (neutral as Speaker, but otherwise 'Friendly'), Sidmouth's brother Hiley Addington certainly divided for the committal, and (despite its ambiguity) the relevant entry in Abbot's diary seems to imply that Sidmouth's close adviser Charles Bragge Bathurst, who also 'spoke but partially against it', did likewise.[103] Apart from those like Howick and Wilberforce who must have stayed for the division, the only named supporters of the majority were the tellers Romilly and Samuel Whitbread, both 'Staunch Friends'.[104]

Since, unknown to the compilers of the survey, only a maximum of 569 members (163 'Staunch Friends', 56 'Friendly', 255 'Doubtful' and 95 'Adverse') were possibly able to be present (as detailed in the Appendix), then (subtracting the combined 'Staunch Friends' and 'Friendly' totals from 283) at least 64, and probably many more, had to be drawn from the 'Doubtful' and 'Adverse' categories (remembering though, that the survey did not in fact cover all the sitting members). If (as admittedly seems very unlikely) each category provided members in proportion, then the breakdown of the 283 would have been: 81 'Staunch Friends', 28 'Friendly', and as many as 127 'Doubtful' and 47 'Adverse'. In any case, the outcome was not solely the result of abstentions, but of many of the members being unexpectedly won over to the cause.

4

Since no list of the 'glorious 283' exists, and the 'miserable 16' in the minority provide too small a sample for extensive analysis, historians of abolition have had no means of

---

[100] See *H.P., 1790–1820*, I, 333. Curiously, if indeed about 492 members were present on 23 Feb., this would be almost exactly the same number as voted on Brand's motion on 9 April, after the fall of the government.

[101] *C.J.*, LXII, 161; *British Parliamentary Lists, 1660–1800. A Register* ed. G. M. Ditchfield, David Hayton and Clyve Jones (1995), p. 101; *H.P., 1790–1820*, I, 186.

[102] B.L., Add. MS 52204A, f. 48; *The Journal of Elizabeth Lady Holland (1791–1811)*, ed. earl of Ilchester (2 vols, 1908), II, 205; *Life of Wilberforce*, III, 299.

[103] *The Diary and Correspondence of Charles Abbot, Lord Colchester, Speaker of the House of Commons, 1802–1817*, ed. Lord Colchester (3 vols, 1861), II, 92.

[104] *C.J.*, LXII, 161.

testing their hypotheses about the ending of the slave trade at the actual point of its extinction.[105] That gap is at least partially filled by the London Committee's survey of 621 members, who, in their final positions, comprise 173 'Staunch Friends', 61 'Friendly', 286 'Doubtful' and 101 'Adverse' (or respectively 27.9, 9.8, 46.1 and 16.3 per cent of the total). The survey provides valuable scope for investigation, despite being a record only of perceived and not of actual attitudes (and for that reason the following discussion covers all 621 members, even those who may have been absent). It would not, of course, in any case have been completely accurate; for example, it is known that the 'Staunch Friend' George Garland was privately hostile to abolition, believing the future of the West Indies was at stake, while the 'Adverse' William McDowall, a West Indian merchant, may have been neutered in his opposition to abolition by the fact that he was dependent on ministers' assistance in relieving him from debt.[106] Yet its general accuracy can be seen by a comparison with the lists of 76 (including two tellers and excluding the absent William Clive) in the majority and of 64 of the 72 (including two tellers) in the minority on the abolition motion on 15 March 1796.[107] Of the 62 members still in the House (ten per cent of those named on the survey), 28 of the 30 who voted for abolition in 1796 were listed as 'Staunch Friends' or 'Friendly' (the two others being the 'Doubtful' William Mills and Windham), and 24 of the 32 who voted against abolition in 1796 were listed as 'Doubtful' (eight) or 'Adverse' (16). Yet seven previously against abolition were now considered supporters (Sir John Anstruther, John Blackburne, Foster Barham, Sir John Frederick, John Langston and Lord Walpole, while the Hon. George Cranfield Berkeley was actually absent) and one was unlisted (James Dawkins, who in fact voted for delaying abolition on 6 March 1807).[108]

In the 11 years since 1796 the composition of the House had presumably altered in favour of abolition, and a generational change had clearly taken place since the first abolition initiatives in the late 1780s. Of the 184 members who, for whatever reason, were not returned again at the general election of 1806, perhaps 15 (including John Hudleston, Dolben and Smith) were prominent abolitionists, but maybe as many as 25 (including Charles Rose Ellis, Lascelles and Tarleton) were West Indians or others likely to have opposed the Abolition Bill.[109] Furthermore, at least 15 (by other counts, as many as 30) were Addingtonians, whose absence significantly weakened Sidmouth in his resistance to immediate abolition.[110] The election presumably influenced how the survey of members was compiled, particularly in the case of Frederick, now a 'Staunch Friend', whose return for Surrey was secured by the withdrawal of Henry Thornton's brother Samuel (who had already lost his seat at Hull), no doubt on the

[105] The terms are Wilberforce's: *Life of Wilberforce*, III, 298.

[106] *H.P., 1790–1820*, IV, 4–5, 492–3.

[107] *Voting Records of the British House of Commons, 1761–1820*, ed. Donald E. Ginter (5 vols, 1995), I, 9, 63; V, 391–4.

[108] Of course, the compilers may well have used the 1796 lists to assist them in drawing up the 1807 survey, and it is possible that Ferguson, Gamon, Pole Carew and Wood were transferred from 'Doubtful' to 'Adverse' for this reason.

[109] Of the six members who were wrongly included in the survey, having failed to get re-elected in 1806, one was included with the 'Staunch Friends' and one with those 'Adverse', the rest being considered 'Doubtful'.

[110] Anstey, *Atlantic Slave Trade*, pp. 391–2.

understanding that Frederick would vote for abolition.[111] In addition, while Sir Ralph Milbanke, like Henry Arthur Herbert, was a 'Staunch Friend' who was no doubt influenced by his County Durham constituents' instructions in favour of the bill,[112] it is at least open to speculation that constituency pressure at Berwick and Tewkesbury may have influenced the planters Alexander Tower ('Doubtful'), who admitted he owned slaves but claimed to favour abolition, and Bethell Codrington, who refused a request to vote for the bill, but did not (as far as is known) vote against it.[113]

However, the general election may not have been the decisive factor, despite the relatively high turnover of members.[114] Of the 621 members listed on the survey, 132 (or 21.3 per cent) were entirely new to the House. Unsurprisingly, 78 (59.1 per cent) of these were reckoned 'Doubtful', while the combined 'Staunch Friends' and 'Friendly' total came to 42 (31.9 per cent) as against 12 (9.1 per cent) 'Adverse'. Of the remaining 489, 202 (32.5 per cent) had first sat after 1 January 1801 (so including the Irish members added at the Union), and 287 (46.2 per cent) had sat, not necessarily continuously, since before that date. The recently elected members included a combined total of supporters of abolition amounting to 72 (35.6 per cent) with only 22 (10.9 per cent) 'Adverse', so repeating the pattern of the new members. However, among those who had first sat before the new century began, there were 120 supporters (41.8 per cent) and 67 opponents (23.3 per cent) of abolition, suggesting that both sides had more entrenched partisans among the older members. Yet the 'Adverse' were more dependent on the longer serving members, two thirds of them having begun their careers in the previous century, compared to only about half of the 'Staunch Friends' and 'Friendly' members.

If uncertainty about new members affected the composition of the survey, it was also apparent in the categorization of those members sitting for Welsh, Scottish and Irish seats.[115] As many as 19 of the 24 Welsh, 23 of the 44 Scottish and 64 of the 96 Irish were entered as 'Doubtful' or, in other words, two thirds of the members returned from constituencies in these countries were so described, with the other 58 being divided into 43 (26.2 per cent) for and 15 (9.1 per cent) against abolition. The members from Ireland, with 26 (or 27.1 per cent) 'Staunch Friends' and 'Friendly' against only six (or 6.3 per cent) 'Adverse', were more impressively abolitionist than their counterparts in Wales and Scotland, which would fit with the contemporary perception of them as generally favourable to the cause.[116] Also affected by lack of knowledge were the members from the large number of small English boroughs (those with fewer than 500 electors)[117] and the universities: these accounted for 262 (42.2 per cent) of those listed, and 110 of them (42 per cent) were classed as 'Doubtful'. Although 98 (37.5 per cent) of the rest were counted as abolitionists, these represented only two fifths of the total of 234 'Staunch Friends'

[111] *H.P., 1790–1820*, III, 833; V, 377.

[112] *P.D.*, VIII, 1050.

[113] *H.P., 1790–1820*, III, 202; V, 503.

[114] See *ibid.*, I, 281.

[115] Who would not all have been Welsh, Scottish and Irish themselves.

[116] Clarkson, *History*, II, 490, 499–500; Frank J. Klingberg, *The Anti-Slavery Movement in England. A Study in English Humanitarianism* (New Haven, 1926), pp. 118, 125–6; *H.P., 1790–1820*, III, 219.

[117] For a list of these boroughs, see *H.P., 1790–1820*, I, 358–63.

and 'Friendly', whereas the 54 (20.6 per cent) 'Adverse' members sitting for pocket or rotten boroughs actually provided just over half of the 101 members on that section of the survey. The position was reversed for the 117 members representing medium (over 500 electors) and large boroughs (over 1,000 electors), of whom 56 (47.9 per cent) were considered favourable to abolition, or nearly a quarter of all those so classed. Of the 20 (17.1 per cent) 'Adverse' from this category of borough, seven were from the slave ports of Bristol (Bragge Bathurst), Lancaster (John Dent and John Fenton Cawthorne), Liverpool (Gascoyne), London (Sir William Curtis, Sir Charles Price and James Shaw), and several others sat for other ports. Insofar as the medium and large English boroughs were, if only to a limited degree, the most democratic element in the electoral franchise as a whole, these figures give credence to the claim that public opinion played an important part in persuading members to support abolition. The same could be said for the survey's 78 English county members, who were also in some cases potentially dependent on popular election, since the statistics are almost exactly the same as for the medium and large boroughs: 37 (47.5 per cent) were 'Staunch Friends' or 'Friendly' and 12 (15.4 per cent) were 'Adverse'.

These calculations have been made on objective data, but other statistics are necessarily more subjective. Judging from the biographies in the *History of Parliament*, and specifically on the minority list for the division on the Hon. Thomas Brand's censure motion against the Grenville ministry's successors in office on 9 April 1807,[118] it is possible to classify 378 members (60.9 per cent) as certain or likely government supporters, 160 (25.8 per cent) as certain or likely backers of the Pittite rump in opposition, and 83 (13.4 per cent) as of unclear or non-existent political allegiance.[119] Apart from the 158 (41.8 per cent) 'Doubtful', the government supporters were made up of 172 abolitionists (45.5 per cent) and only 48 anti-abolitionists (12.7 per cent), which indicates how significant the ministerial sponsorship of abolition really was in practice. By contrast, apart from the 81 (50.6 per cent) 'Doubtful', only 39 of the opposition were abolitionists (24.4 per cent) and 40 were anti-abolitionists (25.0 per cent). With the exception of Windham, the three other cabinet ministers in the Commons (Howick, Lord Henry Petty and Thomas Grenville, the prime minister's brother) were all classed as 'Staunch Friends', as were 18 out of 37 junior ministers, four more being deemed 'Friendly'.[120] Most of these were Foxite whigs, but a few were Grenvillites, two of whom (the brothers Thomas Francis and William Henry Fremantle) were later reckoned 'Doubtful', as was William Elliot, the Irish secretary. Although two Addingtonians (Nathaniel Bond and William Wickham) were considered to be abolitionists, Hiley Addington and Bragge Bathurst were among the eight 'Adverse' junior ministers, who also included the prime minister's nephew Lord Temple, whose attitude, like that of the Fremantles, probably reflected that of his father, the marquess of Buckingham; and Piggott, whose connexion with the West India interest apparently overrode his otherwise impeccable Foxite pedigree. None of the five genuine Saints – Babington, Charles Grant, Henry and

---

[118] *Voting Records*, ed. Ginter, I, 18, 75; V, 552–8.

[119] Rather different figures are given in *H.P., 1790–1820*, I, 185; and Harvey, *Britain in the Early Nineteenth Century*, p. 203.

[120] See the ministerial list in *Later Correspondence of George III*, ed. Aspinall, IV, pp. xlvi–xlviii, l–li (to which has been added the king's household and members of the Irish treasury board).

Robert Thornton, and Wilberforce – were in government, but of the leading group of about 20 abolitionists, the Hon. Henry Erskine, Howick and Petty did hold office. Apart from their evangelical fervour, which they shared with John Kingston, Spencer Perceval and Walter Spencer Stanhope, what bound the Saints together was their membership of the London Committee, which also extended to James Martin, Matthew Montagu, Muncaster and William Morton Pitt. As well as the veteran Sir Philip Francis and the new member Stephen Lushington, this abolitionist group could count on Barclay, Isaac Hawkins Browne, Fawkes, William Plumer and Roscoe. Of all of these, only Spencer Stanhope and Browne were listed as 'Friendly' rather than 'Staunch Friends'.[121]

Almost as difficult to quantify as party allegiance is the occupational structure of the members on the survey. However, counting the overwhelming majority of 484 members (77.9 per cent) with a landed and professional background together, as distinct from the 137 (22.1 per cent) with clear commercial concerns (including, for the moment, West Indian ones), makes for an interesting comparison. Leaving aside the 234 (52.6 per cent) landed and professional members who were 'Doubtful', there were 179 (37.0 per cent) supporters of abolition, amounting to three quarters of all the 'Staunch Friends' and 'Friendly' members, as against 71 (11.4 per cent) 'Adverse', or over two thirds of all the opponents of abolition. This picture was not, however, reversed for the commercial members, 52 (38.0 per cent) of whom were 'Doubtful'. Among them, there were 30 (21.9 per cent) who were 'Adverse' to abolition, being nearly a third of this section of the survey, but there were also 55 (40.1 per cent) who were supporters of abolition, providing nearly a quarter of all the 'Staunch Friends' and 'Friendly' members. Taking out the 22 West Indians, the extent of support for abolition among the commercial members is even more marked: 54 (46.1 per cent) of the remaining 115 were supporters of abolition, and only 18 (15.7 per cent) were among its opponents. Three of the Saints (Grant and the Thorntons) and five other leading abolitionists (Barclay, Francis, Kingston, Martin and Roscoe) were among the businessmen pressing for abolition, and even two of the West Indian members (Foster Barham and Sharp, whose partner Samuel Boddington was omitted from the survey) were 'Staunch Friends'.[122]

Of the other 20 of the 22 members who have been identified as having significant West Indian interests,[123] eight were classified as 'Doubtful', which in itself suggests that the survey was perhaps less reliable for the opponents than for the supporters of abolition, and 12 as 'Adverse' (accounting for about an eighth of the 101 'Adverse' members altogether). They were about equally divided between planters and merchants, a handful having interests in both respects, though two of the former (William Beckford, who probably had not taken his seat, and Young, who was appointed to office) were absent in February 1807. Of the remaining 18, eight did

---

[121] Howse, *Saints in Politics*, p. 58; *H.P., 1790–1820*, I, 296; B.L., Add. MS 21256, ff. 111–12.

[122] Other abolitionists with looser West India connexions were Abbot, Thomas Creevey, Charles Long, Lushington, Abraham Robarts and John William Ward.

[123] This count differs slightly from that in the best analysis of the West India interest, namely B. W. Higman, 'The West India "Interest" in Parliament, 1807–1833', *Historical Studies*, XIII (1967–9), 1–19, esp. p. 3. See also, Gerrit P. Judd, *Members of Parliament, 1734–1832* (New Haven, 1955), pp. 67–9, 93–4; *H.P., 1790–1820*, I, 290, 325–6.

not figure in the lists of the minorities against the committal on 23 February and for delaying the implementation of abolition for five years on 6 March (with overlaps, these lists contain 29 names in all).[124] Three of these missing eight were admittedly 'Doubtful' (Evan Baillie, John Irving and Tower), but five were supposedly 'Adverse' (Bethell Codrington, William Dickinson, McDowall, William Manning and Clement Tudway). The six West Indians who voted in the main division against the Abolition Bill were the 'Doubtful' members Anthony Browne, Richard Erle Drax Grosvenor (unless it was his brother Thomas Grosvenor) and Thomas Hughan, and the 'Adverse' ones Hibbert, the Hon. Edward Lascelles (Henry's brother and Harewood's heir) and Thomas William Plummer. In addition to the tellers, Dent and Gascoyne, the other known voters were: Captain Edward Leveson Gower, who was not named on the survey; Scrope Bernard, another of Buckingham's members, the Hon. John Cust (unless this was in fact Thomas Grimston Estcourt), and Colonel Thomas Stanley, all of whom were 'Doubtful'; and the 'Adverse' Captain Charles Herbert, whose wife was Windham's niece, Sir George Nugent, Buckingham's nephew, Temple, another renegade Grenvillite, and Sir Charles Morice Pole, an Addingtonian.[125] Pole was a teller for his own amendment on 6 March, when he was joined by his fellow Addingtonians: Charles Adams,[126] Hiley Addington, Bragge Bathurst, Estcourt, Davies Giddy, Osborne Markham, Pole Carew and Pulteney (only Adams and Giddy being 'Doubtful' rather than 'Adverse'). Browne, Gascoyne, Hibbert and Hughan again divided against abolition on this occasion, when Temple had apparently paired off.[127] Unless it was his brother Henry (a 'Doubtful' West Indian), the 'Mr Dawkins' who joined them in the minority was probably the unlisted James, the heir to a large Jamaican estate. The other four in the second division were three other West Indians (the 'Doubtful' Henry Swann, with John Fuller and Sir David Wedderburn, both 'Adverse'), and a lone 'Adverse' Pittite, Sir Henry Paulet St John Mildmay.

5

Following the division on 23 February 1807, the Abolition Bill was considered safe, and Grenville and Howick were emboldened to strengthen its contents by the inclusion of penal and other extensive clauses, about which they had hitherto been unsure.[128] The result of the vote had been surprising in that, as John Allen wrote in

---

[124] The lists are in Speaker Abbot's diary for 6 March: T.N.A. [P.R.O.], PRO 30/9/34, f. 147v. The first gives 14 of the 16 in the minority, plus two tellers; the second gives all 17 in the minority, plus the one teller. See also, *Voting Records*, ed. Ginter, I, 18, 75; V, 550–1.

[125] Windham attended the House 'for the first time for a long while', as he put it, on 27 Feb.: *The Diary of the Right Hon. William Windham, 1784 to 1810*, ed. Mrs Henry Baring (1866), p. 468. So he cannot have been one of the two unknown M.P.s in the minority on the 23rd, despite Wilberforce's later statement to this effect: *Life of Wilberforce*, V, 140.

[126] This name, which could be rendered as 'Chuch Daws', is illegible, but the capital 'D' is a copy of the initial 'A' of Addington immediately above it in Abbot's original, strongly suggesting that Charles Adams (and not Windham) is who is meant. Adams was also a teller with Temple for the anti-abolitionist delaying motion on 10 Mar.: *C.J.*, LXII, 226.

[127] *H.P.*, 1790–1820, V, 355.

[128] B.L., Add. MS 58947, f. 48; Add. MS 58978, ff. 110–12; Add. MS 58998, ff. 145–8; Add. MS 59305B, ff. 166–70, 178.

his diary, 'the friends of the Slave Trade had previously made unusual exertions to procure votes against the Bill'.[129] After a hesitant start, in mid-January it was reported that the agent for Jamaica, Edmund Pusey Lyon, believed that 'the whole West India Interests are at length Unanimous on this subject', and rightly predicted that the general meeting of planters and merchants, who had previously been preoccupied with the Caribbean economic depression, would on the 21st agree measures 'with a View to the taking every step, that can be desired, for opposing the Bill.' On that day (when the M.P.s Dickinson, Fuller and Gascoyne were added to it), the standing committee was given full powers to act on behalf of the West India interest and a hostile petition to the Lords was approved. The following month, the standing committee's petition and a slew of others against abolition, Lyon's among them, were presented to the Commons, but the disunity of the anti-abolition members there was only too apparent.[130] Hibbert admitted this, when he asked in the chamber, 'who ever heard of them as combined into a political phalanx or squad, displaying, in this or in the other house, a compact and regular front in critical moments of the battle[?]'[131] However, Hibbert, not least by vainly raising the issue of compensation, was in the vanguard of a West Indian fight back during subsequent debates, their case resting almost entirely on that of national interest.[132]

On 27 February 1807, Hughan, reacting against the abolitionist rhetoric of the 23rd, Anthony Browne, who had been unable to catch the Speaker's eye on that occasion, and Fuller, the only planter to figure prominently in the debates (although he had been silent or absent on the 23rd),[133] all strongly opposed the principle of the bill. Yet, even though Windham now openly washed his hands of the measure (as he did again on 16 March), the West Indians' position was eroded by the planter Foster Barham's statement in favour of the bill (albeit accompanied by compensation) and other abolitionist contributions. On 6 March Pole's amendment to delay abolition till 1812 received Addingtonian support, as has been seen, but it also drew forth other interventions in favour of the bill, including one from Henry Thornton's Southwark colleague Sir Thomas Turton, a rare example of someone reckoned 'Doubtful' speaking in this sense.[134] The amendments adding the extra clauses to the bill, providing almost all its detail, were reported to the House on 9 March, when the date by which the last slave trade voyages had to be completed was altered from 1 January to 1 March 1808. The date the bill would otherwise come into force remained 1 May 1807, not 1 January 1808, as is often wrongly stated (perhaps in confusion with the situation in the United States, where the slave trade was abolished from the beginning of the new year).[135] Under pressure from the West India interest, but in the face of private protests from Smith (although not Wilberforce), Howick

---

[129] B.L., Add. MS 52204A, ff. 48–9.

[130] B.L., Add. MS 38416, f. 317; West India Committee Archives, M915/3, minute book, 1805–22, ff. 112–21, 131–6; *C.J.*, LXII, 123–4, 129, 143, 148; *P.D.*, VIII, 829–38; Alan M. Rees, 'Pitt and the Achievement of Abolition', *Journal of Negro History*, XXXIX (1954), 177–82.

[131] *P.D.*, VIII, 981.

[132] Davis, *Problem of Slavery in the Age of Revolution*, pp. 117–18.

[133] *Wilberforce Correspondence*, II, 117.

[134] *P.D.*, VIII, 1040–53; IX, 59–62.

[135] *C.J.*, LXII, 219–23; *Parliamentary Papers* (1807), I, 41–56.

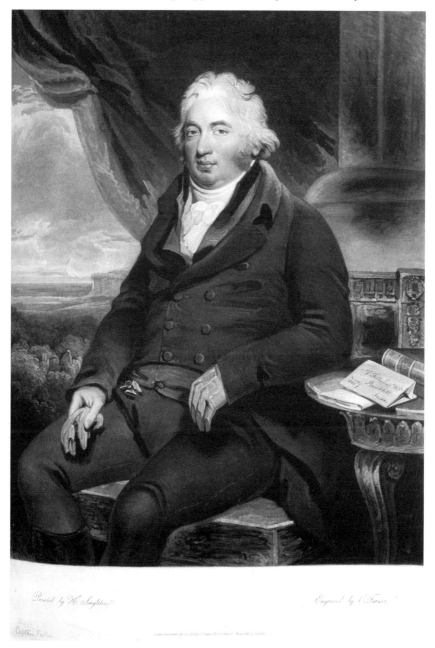

Figure 4   Print of John Fuller (1757–1834), M.P. for Sussex, West Indian planter and opponent of slave trade abolition, by and published by Charles Turner, after Henry Singleton, mezzotint, published 18 July 1808. 19 5/8 in. x 14 1/8 in. (500 mm x 359 mm) paper size. Bequeathed by Frederick Leverton Harris, 1927 (NPG D14588). (© National Portrait Gallery, London.)

conceded that the preamble would be altered to exclude the phrase 'contrary to the principles of justice, humanity, and sound policy', as these words were considered likely to be unintentionally inflammatory in the Caribbean.[136] To offset coverage of this concession as a capitulation, the abolitionists had a corrective paragraph inserted in sympathetic newspapers.[137] Hibbert, who on 12 March initiated the debate on West Indian commercial distress (the relief of which, by altering the sugar duties, has been seen as a form of compensation for abolition), again led the resistance to the Abolition Bill's third reading on 16 March, but there was evidently no appetite for another futile division. The following day, after a debate embarrassing to all parties, (the 'Friendly') Earl Percy's foolhardy attempt to emancipate the future children of enslaved Africans – on the undeniable reasoning that if the trade was 'contrary to the principles of justice, humanity, and sound policy', then so was the institution of slavery itself – was met by the House being counted out.[138]

Despite the fact that Grenville was on the point of leaving office over the issue of catholic relief, which created considerable unease among the abolitionists, he secured the Lords' approval of the bill's amendments on 23 March, when, according to the clerk assistant Henry Cowper's annotations on the reprinted draft of the bill, the omission of words from the preamble was 'obj[ecte]d to' but 'after debate ag[ree]d to'. The incoming ministers had, in fact, given assurances that they would not disrupt the bill's passage, and even the discovery of a drafting error, which meant that the bill had to be hurriedly sent back to the Commons, did not prevent its being given royal assent, by commission, on 25 March.[139] The large body of West India planters and merchants, who had spent the previous two days preparing hostile submissions to the Lords and the king, had run out of time.[140] Their jubilant opponents on the London Committee met on the 25th to resolve

> that the warmest thanks of the Society are justly due to W. Wilberforce Esq. and the other Members of the Legislature to whose virtuous and active exertions it is under Providence indebted for having effected the first great object of its Institution in obtaining an Act of Parliament for the Abolition of the Slave Trade.

The committee also wrote to its supporters asking them to endeavour 'to promote the observance of the Act', and at the ensuing general election Clarkson suggested that candidates should not be supported if they declined to pledge themselves against calling for the reversal of the new law (as both Gascoyne and Tarleton did in defeating Roscoe in Liverpool).[141] On 26 March Howick, now back in opposition, told the Commons that the Abolition Act had been carried by himself and other ministers

---

[136] B.L., Add. MS 59305B, ff. 176; Davis, *Dissent in Politics*, pp. 117–19; *Life of Wilberforce*, III, 300–1; *P.D.*, IX, 63–66. The deletions can be seen on the act (see cat. no. 26).

[137] B.L., Add. MS 21256, f. 129; *The Times*, 13 Mar. 1807.

[138] *P.D.*, IX, 85–101, 114–40, 142–6.

[139] *Ibid.*, IX, 146–7, 168–70; House of Lords R.O., HL/PO/JO/10/8/119: printed bill, 18 Mar. 1807; *L.J.*, XLVI, 119–20, 123, 128–31, 134, 137; *C.J.*, LXII, 281, 284–5, 290; *Wilberforce Correspondence*, II, 118–19; *Life of Wilberforce*, III, 301–2; Clarkson, *History*, II, 577–9; Furneaux, *William Wilberforce*, p. 255.

[140] West India Committee Archives, M915/3, minute book, 1805–22, ff. 153–71.

[141] B.L., Add. MS 21256, ff. 129–30; St John's College Library, Cambridge, Clarkson MS 26: Clarkson to Wadkin, 1 May 1807; *H.P.*, *1790–1820*, II, 230.

only in their personal capacity, a statement which, although strictly true, was possibly also motivated by a wish to place the act above merely factional politics, so making it harder for the abolitionists' opponents to rush the incoming ministers into promoting its repeal.[142] This ploy did not prevent the act being cherished, then and later, as the one shining achievement of the short lived Talents ministry.[143]

If the abolitionists had been concerned to strengthen the bill in order to make it as politically irreversible as possible, the final legislation was not totally effective in prohibiting the slave trade. For instance, the payment of 'head money' for Africans liberated at sea created a secondary market in slaves and the regulation of transferring them between the Caribbean colonies also developed into a major abuse.[144] Although 'soldier-slaves' already serving in West India regiments were given their freedom under that year's Mutiny Act, at least 300 enslaved Africans, captured on foreign slavers up until the end of the war, were conscripted into the British armed forces under the terms of the Abolition Act.[145] In addition, not only was the effective re-enslavement of Africans tolerated in the free settlement of Sierre Leona, which now became a crown colony, but illegal British involvement in slave trading certainly continued, so that even after Brougham had secured in 1811 an act to make it a felony, no conviction was obtained until 1817, at least according to William Garrow's then boast in the Commons to that effect.[146] The abolitionists were not unaware of the act's weaknesses, and shortly after its passage they gathered to form the African Institution, which, under the chairmanship of the king's abolitionist nephew, the duke of Gloucester, served as a new vehicle for continuing anti-slavery activity.[147] It was another 30 years before slavery and apprenticeship were ended in the British West Indian colonies, but the abolition of the slave trade, not least in its economic effects, was an important contributing factor to that eventual reform.

6

In the Commons on 23 February 1807, Fawkes, Wilberforce's colleague as member for Yorkshire, said that he rose 'to perform a solemn but voluntary pledge made to my constituents, that I would mark, with my express reprobation, a traffic, the most unjust and execrable'.[148] This was just one manifestation of the effectiveness of public opinion in bringing the slave trade to the point of abolition, a crucial

---

[142] P.D., IX, 279.

[143] A. D. Harvey, 'The Ministry of All the Talents: The Whigs in Office, February 1806 to March 1807', Historical Journal, XV (1972), 627, 629–30.

[144] See Michael Jordan, The Great Abolition Sham. The True Story of the End of the British Slave Trade (Stroud, 2005), pp. 141–56.

[145] Roger Norman Buckley, Slaves in Red Coats. The British West India Regiments, 1795–1815 (New Haven, 1979), pp. viii, 20–42, 80–1, 130–3.

[146] Michael J. Turner, 'The Limits of Abolition: Government, Saints and the "Africa Question", c. 1780–1830', E.H.R., CXII (1997), 319–57; David Eltis, 'The British Trans-Atlantic Slave Trade after 1807', Maritime History, IV (1974), 1–11; H.P., 1790–1820, III, 267; IV, 7.

[147] Morning Chronicle, 18 Apr. 1807; Howard Temperley, 'Anti-slavery', ch. 2 in Pressure from Without in Early Victorian England, ed. Patricia Hollis (1974), pp. 27–51.

[148] P.D., VIII, 963.

factor emphasized by the correlation between members representing medium and large English boroughs and those considered to be abolitionists. But popular pressure would not have succeeded had not the collective forces of capitalism, for whatever economic motives, left the West India interest isolated, so that it is significant that so many of the commercial men in the Commons were described as favourable to abolition.[149] As Hibbert maintained in the same debate, not without a hint of reproach, the sectional interest to which he belonged

> felt their intimate connection with the mother country; they could trace all the profit of their labours into every channel where it might benefit the British capitalist, manufacturer, and landholder; they have looked upon the merchant, the banker, the manufacturer, the landholder, the soldier, and the seaman in this house as their representatives.[150]

But once the previously unquestioned predominance of this economic justification for the slave trade had given way, members and peers could for the first time act upon the latent humanitarianism of the abolitionist cause. It, nevertheless, still required ministers to give the lead, and the strong association between government supporters and those perceived to be 'Staunch Friends' and 'Friendly' to abolition must have been important.[151] Replying to Grenville's summons to attend the Lords, the duke of Montrose, a former minister under Pitt, confessed on 30 January that

> On the Slave Trade, I have had more difficulty than on any question I ever considered, & fear I am not quite convinced as a Politician ... I don[']t know that had I been in a responsible office, I could have prevailed upon myself to have originated the question; but called upon to give my voice in Parliament, for or against the Trade, I cannot continue so abominable a practice, by a positive vote of mine; so must put an end to the Trade in this Country.[152]

Montrose, in recognition perhaps of the strength of the abolition cause, appears to have absented himself from the crucial vote in the Lords, as did (having paired) the Pittite loyalist the Hon. Richard Ryder (a 'Staunch Friend') during the equivalent debate in the Commons. Perhaps conscious that 'a *sudden* and complete revolution' had indeed taken place in popular opinion, Ryder afterwards recorded that

> Nobody expected this great question would have been carried with so high a hand. I cannot but rejoice at it; but unless one is to suppose that a *sudden* and complete revolution has taken place in the public mind without any new assigned or assignable cause upon this subject, and that not confined to one but extended to both Houses of Parliament, it is to one who holds my opinion both disgusting

---

[149] See Seymour Drescher, 'Capitalism and Abolition: Values and Forces in Britain, 1783–1814', ch. 9 in *Liverpool, the African Slave Trade, and Abolition* ed. Roger Anstey and P. E. H. Hair (*Historic Society of Lancashire and Cheshire Occasional Series*, II, enlarged edn, 1989), pp. 167–95, esp. pp. 187–91.

[150] *P.D.*, VIII, 981.

[151] Ehrman, *The Consuming Struggle*, p. 434; Frank J. Klingberg, *Anti-Slavery Movement*, pp. 129–30.

[152] B.L., Add. MS 59305B, f. 147.

and alarming to observe that the present Administration can do so much more than Pitt could accomplish in the plenitude of his power.

Emphasizing the significance of the ministerial contribution to abolition, the 'Staunch Friend' of abolition as of Pitt, George Canning, whose future record on advancing the cause of 'justice and humanity' with relation to ending colonial slavery itself would be just as much tempered by considerations of 'sound policy', commented that the abolition of the slave trade 'shows what a Government *can* do if it pleases'.[153]

[153] *Later Correspondence of George III*, ed. Aspinall, IV, 517; Anstey, *Atlantic Slave Trade*, pp. 398–400; Wendy Hinde, *George Canning* (Oxford, 1989), pp. 152, 343–4.

Survey of the House of Commons on the Abolition of the Slave Trade, February 1807

Source: The manuscript survey is held by the British Library in Add. MS 51917, an unbound and unfoliated volume of the Holland House papers. I am grateful to the staff of the department of Manuscripts for their assistance in the preparation of this edition of the survey.

Identification: The original manuscript has no title or endorsement other than the headings of the four sections: 'Staunch Friends', 'Friendly', '<u>Doubtful</u>' and '<u>Adverse</u>' (hereafter SF, F, D and A, respectively). Its identification as a list of the members of the 1806 parliament relating to abolition was established during preparation of the 1790–1820 section of the *History of Parliament*, in which its compilation was attributed to Lord Holland: *The House of Commons, 1790–1820*, ed. R. G. Thorne (5 vols, 1986), I, 186, 372. It now seems likely that the survey, possibly the only extant example, was one of the versions created by the Society for Effecting the Abolition of the Slave Trade (or London Committee) in February 1807, prior to the debate on the committal of the Slave Trade Abolition Bill in the Commons that month. For a discussion of the probable construction, dating and provenance of the survey, see above (pp. 154–5).

Physical description: The survey was compiled on three large sheets of paper (approx. 39.3 cm by 32 cm), each of which was folded in half (creating a 'side' of approx. 19.65 cm by 32 cm). The three folded sheets – now separate from each other – were originally bound together one to the next (not interleaved), through the three holes on the left hand edge of each folded sheet (as the two loose threads in the top sheet still demonstrate). Except for the fourth (which only carries annotations), the 12 'pages' so formed each contain one or two columns of names of M.P.s. The names, which are in roughly alphabetical order within each section, are divided into: SF (three pages, five columns), F (two, three), D (four, eight) and A (two, three). Apart from blotches and other marks, the document displays great uniformity of style and, despite its forbidding appearance, was evidently compiled in a very methodical manner.

Neither of the two (or more) hands has been identified. The neatness and regularity of the columns of names (ignoring subsequent changes) strongly suggests that they were first written out by a clerk employed for the purpose, presumably copying from an earlier version of this survey. The subsequent deletions, transfers, additions, interlineations, corrections and other alterations, which are generally in a darker ink and a less legible hand, were probably the work of at least one other person. The long list of names added at the end of the D section (filling in the rest of those accidentally omitted earlier in that section) is in a hand which resembles that of most of the other alterations, although it seems impossible to be sure of this.

Editorial conventions: The document is reproduced in its existing pagination; the page numbers given are not in the original, but are added in square brackets for ease of reference. However, because of the size and complexity of the text, pages with two columns have been divided, so that the columns are printed on separate pages here, the columns being described as the left hand or right hand (or only) column on any given page. The altered and annotated columns of names appear as in the original, with insertions entered interlineally or alongside each column; the annotations on page 4 are reproduced next to the names to which they refer in the left hand column on page 5. Whether or not they were transfers or unexplained afterthoughts, names which are evidently later additions (most of which are unlikely to have been in the first clerk's hand) have been rendered in italics. In the case of unambiguous transfers, in which names were deleted and re-entered in another section, notes in square brackets indicate where a name has been transferred from (e.g. [from D]) and to (e.g. [to SF]) within the survey. Names lined out (on being transferred to another section) have been reproduced as such. (Insertions of names which were not transferred from other sections or deletions of names which were not entered in other sections are referenced in the endnotes.) Occasional crossings out, as with other significant annotations, are either reproduced or pointed out in the endnotes, but minor corrections of spelling or the insertion of full first names are not usually noticed; no attempt has been made to reproduce minor inconsistencies, such as the variable use of stops and superscripted final letters in abbreviations. Apart from 'Hon.' (for 'Honourable') and 'Rt. Hon.' (for 'Right Honourable'), all abbreviated titles are expanded within square brackets.

The members: The members of the house of commons returned at the general election in October-November 1806 were eligible to sit in the third parliament of the United Kingdom of Great Britain and Ireland, which met for the first time on 15 December 1806 and was dissolved on 29 April 1807. One consistent feature of the layout in the original manuscript is that the title and/or initials of each member appear neatly down the left hand side of each column of names, with the surnames mostly being regularly indented using a feint horizontal line. For example, the SF section begins:

Willm. ____ Adam
Visc^t. _____ Althorp
Geo _____ Anson
W. L _____ Antonie
A _____ Atherley
Sir J _____ Aubery . . .

This pattern has not been replicated here because its effect would in any case have been lost by the editorial convention adopted of expanding the full names within square brackets (except in cases where greater clarity is obtained by confining such information to an endnote). The expanded form given is generally in line with *The History of Parliament on CD-ROM* (Cambridge, 1998): 'Members of the 1806 Parliament' (which, although giving a correct count of 680 members for that parliament, omits Sir John Anstruther [F] and Thomas Whitmore [F]). All the members can be identified by consulting the biographical volumes of the *History of Parliament. The House of Commons, 1790–1820*, which is the unstated source for most of the information given here and in the endnotes. Unless otherwise recorded in an endnote (attached to the final position of a member's name), members sat for the whole parliament (but re-elections resulting from the change of government in March are ignored). Viscounts FitzHarris and Palmerston, who were involved in a double return of four members for Horsham, were not technically members of this parliament.

Omissions: The survey correctly omits Viscount Garlies, who became the 8th earl of Galloway, 13 November, and Charles Lennox, who succeeded as the 4th duke of Richmond, 29 December 1806, as well as Sir Stephen Lushington and James Simmons, who died on 12 and 22 January 1807, respectively. Rightly, the lists exclude John Metge, who resigned his seat in January, and the Hon. William Cornwallis and Henry Bromley, who vacated theirs on 5 January and 5 February, respectively (exact dates of leaving the Commons, as in the endnotes, are supplied from T.N.A. (P.R.O.), E197/1, pp. 120, 155). While no mention is made of Benjamin Gaskell and James Mingay, who lost their seats on petition on 4 February, also omitted was the Hon. Henry Grey Bennet, who was not unseated until 24 April. In addition to those marked as absent (for whom, see below), diplomatic office in Vienna no doubt accounted for the exclusion of Robert Adair, as did military service abroad for Lord Burghersh, assistant adjutant-general for Sicily and Egypt, and the naval officers Sir Home Riggs Popham (soon afterwards court martialled) and the Hon. Robert Stopford, but the unnoticed Captain Edward Leveson Gower R.N., a prisoner of war released on parole, in fact attended to vote against abolition on 23 February 1807. Both the Hon. Robert Clive and Sir Henry Watkin Dashwood were probably too ill to attend, and the habitually inactive Lord Robert Edward Henry Somerset, a serving officer, and Lord John Thynne, a courtier, also fail to appear on the survey. The fact that they were new members may explain why Sir John Doyle (who spoke for abolition in the key debate) and George Simson were overlooked, but no such rationalization can be given for the omission of William Johnstone Hope, Ralph John Lambton, William Mellish and William Ord. Of the two members named James Buller, probably the one who represented West Looe was omitted (another is in the SF section); most likely Thomas Tyrwhitt, who sat for Plymouth, was forgotten in confusion with the two Amersham members called Thomas (Drake) Tyrwhitt Drake (one appears in each of the D and A sections).

Apart from a handful of members who joined the Commons after the general election (for whom, see below), almost all of those returned at by-elections or seated by the House in the interim were ignored by the compilers of the survey. Twenty three of them were potentially able to take their seats before 23 February 1807: Sir John Fleming Leicester (10 January), Robert Ward (10 January), James Cornwallis (12 January), Richard Henry Alexander Bennet (14 January), John Fownes Luttrell (14 January), Henry Conyngham Montgomery (15 January), Sir Arthur Wellesley

(15 January), the Hon. Thomas Brand (16 January), Samuel Boddington (17 January), Love Parry Jones (20 January), William Shipley (21 January), Charles Cockerell (24 January), William Conyngham Plunket (26 January), Henry Watkin Williams Wynn (26 January), Baron Lecale (27 January), Michael Symes (27 January), Viscount Hamilton (31 January), Samuel Elias Sawbridge (2 February), John Trevanion Purnell Bettesworth Trevanion (4 February), Walter Jones (4 February), William Gordon (17 February), the Hon. Richard Neville (19 February) and James Dawkins (23 February). (Nine others subsequently became members before the dissolution: Sir Jacob Henry Astley (4 March), James Adams (9 March), William Brownlow (13 March), the Hon. Chapple Norton (16 March), Sir John Borlase Warren (27 March), James Craig (31 March), Henry Smith (2 April), Sir Vicary Gibbs (18 April) and the Hon. Henry Wellesley (20 April).)

Of the 680 members who sat in the 1806 parliament (there were no more than 658 at any one time), a total of 59 were therefore, with varying degrees of justification, excluded from the survey.

Alphabetical inconsistencies: Only a handful of members who entered the Commons after the meeting of parliament are included in the survey, and interestingly they are among the few who were placed out of the normal roughly alphabetical sequence. Lord Binning [D], who was returned at a by-election for Cockermouth, 17 January, and John Alexander Bannerman [D], who was returned at a by-election for Bletchingley, 21 January 1807, were included together among those with names beginning with 'P' in the D section; the fact that the former, but not the latter, was clearly interlineated, seems to be inconsistent. More to be expected, perhaps, is that the Hon. William Assheton Harbord [A], who was returned for Plympton Erle, 7 February, was interlineated among the 'H's in the A section. Charles Callis Western [SF] and Thomas Creevey [SF], who were both seated for their constituencies by the House following election petitions, 4 February, were included together (but not by interlineation) within the 'G's, perhaps implying that the writer had reached this point in the survey when he learnt this news.

That an attempt was made to adhere to the alphabetical sequences is shown by the fact that when Henry Arthur Herbert was transferred from D to SF, his name was added first at the end of that section, and then deleted so that it could be placed with the other 'H's. Likewise the Hon. Charles Herbert and Hugh Leycester were transferred from D to the end of the A section, and then moved to their respective alphabetical placings. Apart from the Hon. Charles William Wyndham, whose name (perhaps because he was not returned to the Commons till 29 January) was placed among the 'L's in the F section before being transferred to D, the only other anomaly was the inclusion of the double-barrelled William Sturges Bourne [SF] with the 'S's (the usual alphabetical rule evidently being to follow the last part of double-barrelled surnames or the peerage title).

The sole exception to the generally alphabetical approach, was the presumably accidental omission of the 'L'-'P' part of the D section, with the sequence jumping from the letter 'J' to the letter 'P' (the 'K's having to be inserted to the left), half way down the right hand column on page 8. It is possible that the transcriber may have been jolted off track by the surname Jones Parry: Love Parry Jones, whose return for Horsham was confirmed by the House, 20 January, changed his surname from Jones to Jones Parry on 14 February 1807, and, although he was not entered on this survey, his name may have triggered the error in the sequence. The 'L'-'P' names were included on page 10, following the 'Y's, with the right hand column being almost entirely in the hand of a different person.

Insertions and deletions: In counting the number of insertions for the purposes of the calculations below, the following have been ignored: the 31 members added at the end (page 10, right hand column) of the D section (including Sir Charles Morgan, whose name was subsequently deleted); and the eight members (John Irving, Thomas Johnes, Gilbert Jones, Sir John Dashwood King, Robert Knight, the Hon. George Knox, the Hon. Thomas Knox and John Kynaston Powell) added on the fault line (page 8, right hand column) in the D section. As already mentioned, the interlineations of Lord Binning [D] and the Hon. William Assheton Harbord [A] related to their delayed entry to the Commons that session. However, the other 13 interlineated names, unless they were afterthoughts or errors, may indicate a possible change of opinion on the part of the member: William Cavendish [SF], the Hon. William Elliot [SF], William Kenrick [F], Robert Shapland Carew [D], Richard Augustus Tucker Steward [D], the Hon. Montgomery Granville John Stewart [D], Charles William Taylor [D], Sir Richard Williames Vaughan [D], James Henry Leigh [D], James Martin Lloyd [D], John Markham [A], the Hon. Edward Richard Stewart [A] and Clement Tudway [A].

Apart from a handful of other instances, almost all the deleted names were so lined out on being unambiguously transferred to a different section. Only six members were deleted without any very obvious explanation (unless they were simply absent): Richard Bateman Robson [D], the Hon. Alexander Hope [D], the Hon. Charles Hope [D], Sir Charles Morgan [D], the Hon. William Brodrick [A] and George Johnstone [A].

Unadjusted totals: Altogether (including all changes and deletions), there are 676 names on the survey (177 in SF, 88 in F, 307 in D and 104 in A). A 'first count', ignoring inserted but including deleted names (and disregarding the fact that several names are duplicated), would have given a highly inaccurate breakdown (calculated simply by subtracting the 63 insertions from the total number of names) of 152 in SF, 82 in F, 294 in D and 85 in A. A 'last count', taking notice of transfers by including inserted and discounting deleted names (but again disregarding the fact that several names are duplicated) would have given a slightly more accurate breakdown (calculated simply by subtracting the 49 deletions from the total number of names) of 170 in SF, 71 in F, 287 in D and 99 in A. (This compares with Roland Thorne's count of 172 in SF, 69 in F, 100 in A and the rest in D: *H.P., 1790–1820*, I, 186.) It will be seen that, during the process of making the transfers, the sections would have oscillated in the ranges of 145–177 for SF, 65–88 for F, 274–307 for D and 80–104 for A (and the numbers given as contemporaneous totals do in each case, except arguably for the error in the A section, fall within these ranges). For the relevance of these totals, see above (pp. 155–6).

Errors and sample size: The survey was probably originally constructed from an unreliable source, perhaps a newspaper or other contemporary publication. The compilers quite possibly used *The Royal Kalendar for 1807* (published in London in 1807), pp. 37–88, which also helpfully gave details of members' town and country addresses. Support for this conjecture is given by the fact that it lists, as member for Boroughbridge, one 'Henry Hawkins', a mistake (for Henry Dawkins) which is reproduced in the D section of the survey. Other errors of spelling and identification (inconsistent initials and the like), which do not seem to have derived from *The Royal Kalendar* but may have resulted from relying on other out of date lists (possibly including previous handwritten surveys on the slave trade), could have been introduced through ignorance (e.g. 'Sir C. J. Hippisly' for Sir John Coxe Hippisley [D]) or miscopying (e.g. 'Lord C. H. Somersall' for Lord Charles Henry Somerset [D]). The larger proportion of minor inaccuracies in the D and A sections may have been owing to the abolitionists' relative unfamiliarity with the names of their opponents.

Following *The Royal Kalendar*, one supposes, the compilers wrongly included the following six men, who were not in fact returned at the general election of 1806: George Cumming [SF] (whose name was at some point deleted), George William Gunning [D], Ponsonby Tottenham [D], Edmund Turnor junior [D], George Wood [D] and Hans Sloane [A]. Their names are given in {} in the actual list below. Moreover, since 49 of the 676 names are duplicates (including, in the case of four members, triplicates), the actual number of individuals listed is, in fact, only 621. This figure, which includes M.P.s who were not necessarily present for the abolition debates (see below), is the sample used as the basis for the analysis of the survey as the perceived state of the Commons on the abolition of the slave trade, for which, see above (pp. 161–5).

Actual and notional transfers: There were 46 straightforward transfers of members' names from one section to another, including the nine cases where the original entry of each name was not actually deleted from its place in the F section. These 46 transfers involved 45 members, John Maitland being the only member transferred twice; the other three members whose names appear three times overall (twice in the same section in each case) complete the total of 49 duplicates.

Several annotations to the survey confirm the transfer of the member to a different section, but in five cases annotations indicating a different section of the list are not connected with an actual transfer. It is convenient to process these five names as if they had, in fact, been physically transferred: the Hon. William Howard [F] 'certain' [to SF]; Lord William Russell [F] 'Staunch' [to SF]; Lord Brooke [D] 'friendly' [to F]; Sir Arthur Leary Piggott [D] 'adverse' [to A]; and (the only one of these names actually lined out) the marquess of Huntly [A] 'doubtful' [to D]. This brings the total number of transfers up to 51. For an analysis of them, see above (pp. 156–7).

Adjusted totals: From the total of 621 members, it is necessary to make several reductions in order to reach a realistic state of the Commons on the eve of abolition, not least by deducting the six inexplicably lined out members (for whom, see above). As well as the aged John Bullock [F], who was 'out of town', annotations indicate that the young Viscount Royston [F], who never took his seat, was 'in Russia', and that the Irish secretary William Elliot [D] was in 'Ireland'. Vice-admiral the Hon. George Cranfield Berkeley [SF], whose name was marked 'absent' and subsequently lined out, and his fellow officers Sir Samuel Hood [D] and Eliab Harvey [A], who were both 'at Sea', were almost certainly not present during the session.

Viscount Acheson [D] lost his County Armagh seat on succeeding to an Irish peerage, 14 February 1807 (though Sir Lawrence Parsons [A] did not lose his King's County seat in the same way till 20 April, and the duke of Buccleuch's heir Lord Dalkeith [D] and the duke of Gordon's heir Lord Huntly [A] were not promoted to the Lords till 11 April). Frederick William Trench [D] vacated his seat, 15 December 1806, as did Sir William Pierce Ashe A'Court [D] and Sir John Lethbridge [D] the following month (but Lord Spencer Stanley Chichester [D] did not resign until 5 March, nor did Sir Robert Barclay [SF] until 24 April 1807). The Saltash members Arthur Champernowne [D] and Matthew Russell [D] were unseated on petition, 19 February, as was the Chippenham member Charles Brooke, 23 February, while George Holme Sumner [D], who had been elected for Guildford, suffered the same fate, presumably without having played any part in proceedings, on 16 March. Unlike three members who were temporarily out of the House (Josias Du Pré Porcher [D] in mid-January, William Henry Fremantle [D] in mid-February and Viscount Stopford [A] in mid-April), the brothers Edward and Thomas William Coke [both SF] missed the division on the committal by effectively having to swap their Derby and Norfolk seats in late February. By that time the West Indian planter Sir William Young [A], who had been appointed governor of Tobago earlier that month, was probably no longer in the House.

Their political biographies suggest that John Foster [SF] and David Latouche [SF] (probably not alone among the Irish members), as well as William Garrow [D], Viscount Jocelyn [D] (a minor) and William Beckford [A] failed to attend that session. In common with other military men, the following seem also to have been on active service, mostly abroad: the Hon. Edward Charles Cocks [SF], Lord William Fitzroy [SF], Baron Blayney [D], Henry Frederick Campbell [D], the Hon. Galbraith Lowry Cole [D], Robert Honyman [D], Lord Proby [D], James Athol Wood [D] and Alexander Mackenzie Fraser [D]. Thomas Johnes [D] stayed home for no apparent reason: Durham University Library, Earl Grey MS, GRE/B37/1/10. But ill health, not always their own, was the excuse pleaded for the absence of George Skene [SF], Edmund Bastard [F], William Lewis Hughes [F], William Honywood [D], Godfrey Wentworth Wentworth [D] and the Hon. William Monson [D]. Moreover, Richard Wharton [SF], William Hussey [F], Sir Robert Williams [D], Charles Shaw Lefevre [D] and Sir Robert Peel [A] were all on the official sick list, while George Garland [SF] had leave of the House to attend to urgent private business: *C.J.*, LXII, 62, 93, 101, 104, 126, 127. Finally, Charles Gregan Craufurd [D] and Lord Newark [D] are known to have paired off.

A realistic count, which includes the 51 straightforward and notional transfers, takes account of duplicates and adjustments, and incorporates all insertions as well as subtracting the six unexplained deletions, would have given a breakdown of the remaining 569 members as 163 in SF, 56 in F, 255 in D and 95 in A, for a discussion of which, see above (p. 160).

[page 1]

Staunch Friends[1]

[left hand column]

Will[ia]m Adam[2]
[John Charles Spencer] Visc[oun]t Althorp
Geo[rge] Anson
W[illiam] L[ee] Antonie
A[rthur] Atherley
Sir J[ohn] Aubery [i.e., Aubrey][3]
T[homas] Babington
[4]
                    H[enry] Baring [from F]
J[ohn] Baker   *T[homas] Baring* [from F]
W[illiam] Baker   *A[lexander] Baring* [from F]
                    J[oseph] F[oster] Barham [from F]
H[enr]y Bank[e]s
S[i]r Rob[ert] Barclay [from F][5]
Geo[rge] Barclay
Ja[me]s Barnett
M[ichael] H[icks] Beach
~~Hon. G[eorge] C[ranfield] Berkeley absent~~[6]
R[ober]t M[yddelton] Biddulph
E[dward] W[ilbraham] Bootle   *T[homas] R[ichard] Beaumont* [from F]
Hon. E[dward] Bouverie
I[saac] H[awkins] Browne
E[dward] Buller
Ja[me]s Buller[7]
John Buller
Geo[rge] Byng
        Sir [Thomas] C[harles] Bunbury [from F][8]
J[ohn] Calcraft
N[icolson] Calvert
Rt. Hon. G[eorge] Canning[9]
Lord G[eorge Augustus] H[enry] Cavendish
G[eorge] H[enry] C[ompton] Cavendish
        W[illiam] Cavendish[10]
Hon. [Edward] C[harles] Cocks
Edw[ar]d Coke[11]
T[homas] W[illiam] Coke[12]
N[icholas] W[illiam] R[idley] Colbourne [i.e., Colborne]
H[arvey] C[hristian] Combe
Rt. Hon. I[saac] Corry

[page 1, right hand column, SF continued]

J[ohn] Courtenay

Hon. E[dward] S[pencer] Cowper

J[oseph] Cripps

{~~G[eorge] Cuming [i.e., Cumming]~~}[13]

J[ohn] C[hristian] Curwen

R[ichard] Dawson

W[illiam] J[oseph] Denison

C[harles] Dundas[14]

~~Hon. C[harles] L[awrence] Dundas~~ [to F]

~~Hon. L[awrence] Dundas~~ [to F]

[Hugh Fortescue] Visc[oun]t Ebrington

~~Hon. E. W. [i.e., William Frederick Elliot] Eden~~ [to F]

Hon. G[ilbert] Elliott [i.e., Elliot Murray Kynynmound]

Hon. W[illiam] Elliot [i.e., Eliot][15]

Hon. H[enry] Erskine

[George Henry Fitzroy] Earl [of] Euston

J[ohn] Fane

W[alter Ramsden] Fawkes

R[obert] Ferguson

Ronald~~son~~ [Craufurd] Ferguson

Rt. Hon. J[ames] Fitzgerald

Lord R[obert] S[tephen] Fitzgerald

Rt. Hon. R[ichard] Fitzpatrick

Lord W[illiam] Fitzroy

Lord C[harles] Fitzroy

H[on.] A[ndrew] Foley

Tho[mas] Foley

[William Pleydell Bouverie] Visc[oun]t Folkestone

Rt. Hon. J[ohn] Foster

Sir P[hilip] Francis

Sir J[ohn] Frederick

G[eorge] Garland

C[harles Callis] Western[16]

T[homas] Creevey[17]

Sir J[ames] Graham[18]

Col[onel] F[rancis] W[illiam] Grant [from F]

[page 2, left hand column, SF continued]

Charles Grant
Rt. Hon. H[enry] Grattan
P[ascoe] Grenfell
Rt. Hon. T[homas] Grenville
Lord A[rchibald] Hamilton
Hon. E[dward] Harbord [from F]
[Charles Winn Allanson] Lord Headley
Hon. W[illiam] Herbert [from F]   H. A. Herbert [from D]¹⁹
B[enjamin] Hobhouse
F[rancis] Horner
[Charles Grey] Visc[oun]t Howick
W[illiam] Huskisson
[Samuel] Horrocks [from F]
W[illiam] Jacob
J[ohn] Jeffery
J[oseph] Jekyll
J[ervoise] C[larke] Jervoise
T[homas] Kempe [i.e., Kemp]
John Kingston
~~Sir E[dward] Knatchbull~~ [to F]
Hon. W[illiam] Lambe [i.e., Lamb]
D[avid] Latouche
R[obert] Latouche
Sir W[illiam] Lemon
Sir T. W. [i.e., Henry Thomas] Liddell
J. [i.e., George] Longman
S[tephen] Lushington
²⁰
                                                          Langstone [from F]²¹
Hon. W[illiam] B[eauchamp] Lygon   *Lethbridge* [from F]²²
Hon. W. H. Lyttleton²³   *Lubbock* [from F]
                                                          Magens [from F]
W[illiam] A[lexander] Maddox [i.e., Madocks]
[Philip Henry Stanhope] Visc[oun]t Mahon
[James Maitland] Visc[oun]t Maitland
H[enr]y Martin
Ja[me]s Martin   *Sir W. Middleton* [from F]²⁴
R[ichar]d Martyn [i.e., Martin]   *J. Macdonald* [from F]
Hon. W[illiam] Maule   *Sir C. Mordaunt* [from F]
Sir R[alph] Milbanke
J[ohn] Maitland [from F, previously D]²⁵

[page 2, right hand column, SF continued]

Sir W[illiam Mordaunt] Milner
R[obert] P[emberton] Milnes
M[atthew] Montague [i.e., Montagu]
P[eter] Moore
[George Howard] Visc[oun]t Morpeth
Edw[ar]d Morris
[John Pennington] Lord Muncaster
E[dward] M[iller] Munday [i.e., Mundy]
Rt. Hon. Sir [Simon] J[ohn] Newport
[Charles Augustus Bennet] Lord Ossulston
H[enr]y Peirse
Hon. S[pencer] Percival [i.e., Perceval]
Lord H[enry] Petty
W[illiam] M[orton] Pitt
W[illiam] Plumer
Hon. G[eorge] Ponsonby
Hon. F[rederick Cavendish] Ponsonby
[Henry George Herbert] Lord Porchester
F[rancis] Pym
A[braham] Robarts
Sir S[amuel] Romilly
W[illiam] Roscoe
Hon. R[ichard] Ryder
R[ichard] Sharp
R[obert] Shaw
J[ohn] Simeon
G[eorge] Skeene [i.e., Skene]
G[eorge] Smith
J[ohn] Smith
S[amuel] Smith
Rt. Hon. J[ohn] Smyth
Lord R[obert] Spencer
[Edward Smith Stanley] Lord Stanley
[John] Staniforth [from F][26]

[page 3, only column, SF continued]

W[illiam] S[turges] Bourne
W[illiam] Taylor
H[enry] Thornton
R[obert] Thornton
Rt. Hon. G[eorge] Tierney
Lord J[ohn] Towns[h]end
J[ohn] E. Tremaine [i.e., Hearle Tremayne]
W[illiam] Suffnell [i.e., Tufnell]
N[icholas] Vansittart
Hon[ourabl]e G[eorge] Walpole
Hon. J[ohn] W[illiam] Ward
J[ohn] Wharton
R[ichard] Wharton
S[amuel] Whitbread[27]
Sir R[obert] Wigram
R[obert] Wigram
W[illiam] Wilberforce
R[ichard] Wilson
[Henry] A[rthur] Herbert[28]
H[enry] Willoughby [from D]

170 [written over 168 or 169]

[page 4]²⁹   [page 5]

                                                              Friendly³⁰

                                      [left hand column]³¹

                                      Rt. Hon. C[harles] Abbott [i.e., Abbot]
                                      Sir J[ohn] Anstruther
                                      M[ervyn] Archdall
                                      ~~Sir R[obert] Barclay~~ [to SF]
transfer[re]d to   ~~J[oseph] F[oster] Barham~~ [to SF]
Staunch list   ~~Henry Baring~~ [to SF]
                                      ~~Tho[ma]s Baring~~ [to SF]
                                      ~~A[lexander] Baring~~ [to SF]
                                      Edw. [i.e., Edmund] Bastard
                                      J[ohn] P[ollexfen] Bastard
transfer[re]d   ~~T[homas] R[ichard] Beaumont~~ [to SF]
                                      J[ohn] Blackburn[e]
                                      W[illiam] Bagwell
                                      Rt. Hon. N[athaniel] Bond
                                      Hon. A[ugustus] C[avendish] Bradshaw
                                      C[harles] J[ohn] Brandling
                                      Ja[me]s Brogden
                                      Rt. Hon. D[enis] Browne
                                      Visc[oun]t Barnard [i.e., Bernard]³²
            Friendly³³   J[ohn] B. [*sic*] Bullock (out of town)³⁴
                                      Sir C. Bunbury certain [to SF]³⁵
Honble C. L. Dundas [from SF]   J[ohn] Calvert
_____ *L. Dundas* [from SF]   Lord J. Campbell³⁶
Honble E. W. Eden [from SF]   ~~D[aniel] P[arker] Coke~~ adverse [to A]
                                      D[enis] B[owes] Daly
                                      Ja[me]s Daly
                                      F[rancis] F[errand] Foljambe
                                      Sir M[artin] B[rowne] F[f]olkes³⁷
                                      ~~T[homas] F[rancis] Fremantle~~) doubtful
                                      ~~W[illiam Henry] Fremantle~~   ) [to D]³⁸
                                      T[homas] S[herlock] Gooch
                                      Ja[me]s Graham³⁹
                                      ~~F[rancis] W[illiam] Grant~~ [to SF]

[page 5, right hand column, F continued]

~~Hon[ourabl]e E[dward] Harbord~~ transfer[re]d [to SF]
Sir J[ohn] Henderson
~~Hon[oura]ble W[illiam] Herbert~~ transf[erre]d [to SF]
~~S[amuel] Horrocks~~ trans[ferre]d [to SF]
H[enry Thomas] Howard
Hon. W[illiam] Howard <u>certain</u>[40]
W[illiam] L[ewis] Hughes
                    Sir E[dward] Knatchbull [from SF]
W[illiam] Hussey
[William Edwardes] Lord Kensington
      W[illiam] Kenrick[41]
[John] Langston [to SF][42]
R[obert] H[olt] Lee [i.e., Leigh] [from D][43]
J[ohn] Lemon
Doubtful[44] ~~[Hon.] C[harles William] Wyndham~~ [to D]
Rt. Hon. C[harles] Long
W. [i.e., Thomas Buckler] Lethbridge [to SF][45]
~~[George Percy] Lord Lovaine~~ [to D]
Sir J[ohn] Lubbock [to SF][46]
Sir E[dward] Lyttleton [i.e., Littleton]
Hon. J[ohn] Mead[e]
~~Sir W[illiam] Middleton~~ [to SF]
C[harles] Moore[47]
M[agens] D[orrien] Magens [to SF][48]
Ja[me]s Macdonald [to SF][49]
      J[ohn] Maitland [from D, to SF][50]
Sir C[harles] Mordaunt [to SF][51]
Sir J[ohn] Nicholl
G[erard] N[oel] Noel
W[illiam] Northey
H[enry Brooke] Parnell
[Hugh Percy] Earl Percy
Hon. W[illiam] W[ellesley] Pole
Hon. V[ere] Paulett [i.e., Poulett]
J[ohn] Pytches
[Philip Yorke] Visc[oun]t Royston in Russia[52]

[page 6, only column, F continued]

Lord W[illiam] Russell <u>Staunch</u>[53]
Sir R[obert] Salisbury [i.e., Salusbury]
Rt. Hon. Sir W[illiam] Scott
H[enry] Shelley
R[ichard] B[rinsley] Sherridan [i.e., Sheridan]
W[alter] S[pencer] Stanhope
Rt. Hon. T[homas] Steele
J[ohn] Staniforth [to SF][54]
C[harles] M[anners] Sutton
G[eorge Granville] V[enables] Vernon
[Horatio Walpole] Lord Walpole
T[homas] Whitmore
Rt. Hon[oura]ble W[illiam] Wickham
~~Rt. Hon[oura]ble W[illiam] Windham~~ [to D]
W. [i.e., John] Woolmore
C[harles] W[atkin] W[illiams] Wynne [i.e., Wynn]

<u>72</u>

[page 7]

<u>Doubtful</u>[55]

[left hand column]

Hon[oura]ble G[eorge] Abercrombie [i.e., Abercromby]

[Archibald Acheson] Visc[oun]t Acheson[56]

Cha[rle]s Adams

Sir W[illiam] P[ierce] A[she] A'Court[57]

Hon[oura]ble C[ropley] Ashley

W[alter] Bagenell [i.e., Bagenal]

Evan Bail[l]ie

G[eorge] Bail[l]ie

Sir C[harles] W[arwick] Bamp[f]ylde

H[ugh] Barlow

S[nowdon] Barne

J[ohn Maxwell] Barry

R[ichard] Benyon

Tho[ma]s Bernard

Scrope Bernard

A[lbemarle] Bertie

C[alverley] Berwicke[58]

[Andrew Thomas Blayney] Lord Bla[y]ney

Tho[ma]s [Cherburgh] Bligh

H[enry] Bonham

Hon. B[artholomew] Bouverie

Hon. D[uncombe] P[leydell] Bouverie

[Henry Boyle] Visc[oun]t Boyle

Hon. C[ourtenay] Boyle

R[obert] H[aldane] Bradshaw

Ja[me]s Brodie

Hon. [*sic*] [Henry] V[aughan] Brooke

[Henry Richard Greville] <u>Lord Brooke friendly</u>[59]

Anth[on]y Browne

P[atrick] C[raufurd] Bruce

adverse[60] ~~Sir C[harles Merrik] Burrell~~ [to A]

Hon. F[rancis] N[athaniel] Burton

Hon. C[harles Harward] Buttler [i.e., Butler]

[page 7, right hand column, D continued]

Hon. J[ames Wandesford] Butler
J[ohn] Campbell
A[rchibald] Campbell
G[eorge] Campbell
H[enry] F[rederick] Campbell
Geo[rge] Canning[61]
    R[obert] S[hapland] Carew[62]
~~Hon. [sic] R[eginald] P[ole] Carew~~ ag[ains]t[63] [to A]
W[illiam] R[alph] Cartwright
Hon[oura]ble H[enry] Caulfield [i.e., Caulfeild]
Arthur Champernowne[64]
C[harles] Chaplin
C[harles Bagot] Chester
Lord S[pencer] S[tanley] Chichester[65]
T[homas] Cholmondel[e]y
Hon[oura]ble [Henry] J[ohn] Clements
W[illiam] H[enry] Clynton [i.e., Clinton]
~~C[hristopher Bethell] Codrington~~ [to A]
J[ohn] Caldclough [i.e., Colclough]
Hon. G[albraith] L[owry] Cole
E[dward] S*inge* Cooper
Sir G[eorge] ~~A.~~ Corn[e]wall[66]
J[ohn] Coates [i.e., Cotes]
Sir J[ohn] G[eers] Cotterell
S[tapleton] Cotton
C[harles Gregan] Crawford [i.e., Craufurd]
Hon[oura]ble R[obert] Curzon
Hon. J[ohn] Cust
[Charles William Henry Montagu Scott] Earl [of] Dalkeith[67]
R[alph] A[llen] Daniell
J[ohn] De Ponthieu
Hon. H[enry] A[ugustus] Dillon [Lee]
S. F. [i.e., Dugdale Stratford] Dugdale
~~D[octo]r [Patrick] Duigenan~~ [to A]
C[harles] Edmonstone
Rt. Hon. W[illiam] Elliott [i.e., Elliot] Ireland[68]
R[ichard] Ellison
Hon. C[harles] F. Elphinstone [i.e., Elphinstone Fleeming]
~~A[nthony] H[ardolph] Eyre~~ [to A]
F[rederick] J[ohn] Falkiner

[page 8, left hand column, D continued]

H[enry] Fawcette [i.e., Fawcett]

R[obert] N. [*sic*] Fellowes

W[illiam] H[enry] Fellowes

~~Ja[me]s Ferguson~~ [to A]

Sir T[homas] Featherstone [i.e., Fetherston]

Hon. E[dward] Finch

Rt. Hon. M[aurice] Fitzgerald

W[illiam] Fitzhugh

[George John Forbes] Visc[oun]t Forbes

W[illiam] Frankland

      two Freemantles [from F][69]

Arthur French

Tho[ma]s Fydell

H[enry] Fynes

~~Sir R[ichard] Gamon~~ [to A]

W[illiam] Garrow

D[avies] Giddy

D[aniel] Giles

T[homas] Goddard

T[homas] Godfrey

Hon. [*sic*] W[illiam] Gore[70]

Lord [Granville Leveson] Gower[71]

Tho[ma]s Graham

R[obert] Greenhill[72]

Hon. J[ames] W[alter] Grimstone [i.e., Grimston]

R[ichard] E[rle] D[rax] Grosvenor

T[homas] Grosvenor

{G[eorge] W[illiam] Gunning}[73]

H*ans* Hamilton

Sir H[ew Hamilton] D[alrymple] Hamilton

John Hammett [i.e., Hammet]

H[enry] Hawkins [i.e., Dawkins][74]

Sir G[ilbert] Heathcote

A[nthony] Henderson

~~Hon. Charles Herbert~~ [to A][75]

~~Hon. [*sic*] [Henry] A[rthur] Herbert~~ [to SF][76]

P[eter] Heron[77]

Sir G[eorge Fitzgerald] Hill

[page 8, right hand column, D continued][78]

Hon. W[illiam] Hill
Sir C. J. [i.e., John Coxe] Hippisl[e]y
J[ohn] Hodson
A[rthur Howe] Holdsworth
R[obert] Honeyman [i.e., Honyman]
W[illiam] Honeywood [i.e., Honywood][79]
Sir S[amuel] Hood at Sea[80]
~~Hon. [Alexander] Hope~~
~~Hon. C[harles] Hope~~
H[umphrey] Haworth [i.e., Howorth]
T[homas] Hughan
W[illiam] H[oare] Hume
R[obert] Hurst
Hon. C[hristopher] H[ely] Hutchinson
J[ohn] Jackson
D[enham] Jephson

Sir J[ohn] D[ashwood] King [81]

T[homas] Johnes
[Robert Jocelyn] Visc[oun]t Jocelyn

R[obert] Knight

G[ilbert] Jones[82] J[ohn] Irving

[Hon.] G[eorge] Knox
[Hon.] T[homas] Knox
P. K. Kynaston [Powell][84]

Sir W[illiam] Paxton
Hon. C[harles] A[nderson] Pelham[83]
Hon. J. A[nderson] Pelham[85]
Hon. ~~H.~~ J[osceline] Percy[86]
J[ohn] Perring
R. M. Phillips [i.e., Philipps][87]
Sir A[rthur Leary] Piggott <u>adverse</u>[88]
J[osias] D[u Pré] Porcher[89]
[Thomas Hamilton] *Lord Binning*[90]
[John Alexander] Bannerman[91]
G[eorge] Porter
E[dward] B[erkeley] Portman
R[ichard] Power
W[illiam] S[tephen] Poyntz
R[ichard] Price
[Archibald John Primrose] Lord Primrose
Hon. F. A. Pretty [i.e., Prittie][92]
[John Proby] Lord Proby
~~Sir J[ames] M[urray] Pult[e]ney~~ [to A]
Hon. W[indham Henry] Quin
J[onathan] Raine
Hon. J[ohn] Ramsay

[page 9, left hand column, D continued]

R[ichard] Ramsbottom
[George Augustus Henry Anne Parkyns] Lord Rancliff[e]
Sir M[atthew] W[hite] Ridley
Hon. F[rederick John] Robinson
J[ohn] Robinson
~~R[ichard] B[ateman] Robson~~[93]
G[ustavus] H[ume] Rochfort
M[atthew] Russell[94]
J[ohn] Rutherford [i.e., Rutherfurd]
E[dward] S[outhwell] Ruthven
[Sir] H[enry] Strac*h*ey[95]
F[rancis] Savage
N[athaniel] Saxon
R[ichard] P[hilip] S[c]udamore
Lord R[obert] Seymour
A[rthur] Shakespear[e]
~~Ja[me]s Shaw~~ [to A]
R[alph] Sheldon
T[imothy] Shell[e]y
Hon. J[ohn] Simpson
Joshua Smith
W[illiam] Smythe [i.e., Smyth][96]
N[athaniel] Sneyd
Lord A[rthur John Henry] Somerset
Lord C[harles] H[enry] Somersall [i.e., Somerset]
Sir M[arcus] Somerville
Lord F[rancis] A[lmeric] Spencer
T[homas] Stanl[e]y
R[obert] Steele
S[amuel] Stephen[s]
G[abriel] T[ucker] Stuart [i.e., Steward]
     R[ichard] A[ugustus Tucker] Stuart [i.e., Steward][97]
Sir J[ames] Stuart [i.e., Stewart]
Ja[me]s Stuart [i.e., Stewart]
Hon. M[ontgomery Granville John] Stuart [i.e., Stewart][98]
A[ndrew] Strahan
J[oseph] H[olden] Strutt
Lord W[illiam] Stuart

[page 9, right hand column, D continued]

J[ames] A[rchibald] W. Stuart [i.e., Stuart Wortley]
G[eorge] H[olme] Sumner[99]
H[enry] Swan[n]
T[homas] P[owell] Symonds
       C[harles] W[illiam] Taylor[100]
M[ichael] A[ngelo] Taylor
[John Henry Upton] Lord Templetown
T[homas] Thistlethwaite [i.e., Thistlethwayte]
T[homas] Thoroton
Lord G[eorge] Thynne
W[illiam] Tighe
Ja[me]s Topping
{P[onsonby] Tottenham}[101]
A[lexander] Tower
Hon. W[illiam] A[ugustus] Towns[h]end
F[rederick] W[illiam] Trench[102]
{E[dmund] Turner [i.e., Turnor] jun[ior]}[103]
Sir T[homas] Turton
T[homas] D[rake] Tyr*w*hitt [Drake][104]
Sir F[rederick] F[letcher] Vane
G[eorge] Vansittart
Hon. J[ohn] Vaughan
Sir R[obert] W[illiames] Vaughan[105]
Col[onel Charles] Vereker
R[ichard] Vyse
G[odfrey Wentworth] Wentworth
F[rancis] J[ohn] Wildair [i.e., Wilder][106]
W[alter] Wilkins
Owen Williams
Sir R[obert] Williams
R[obert] Williams
~~H[enry] Willoughby~~ [to SF][107]
W[illiam] Wingfield   <u>Friendly</u>
{G[eorge] Wood}[108]   if not
J[ames] A[thol] Wood   <u>Staunch</u>[109]
~~M[ark] Wood~~ [to A]
T[homas] Wood
J[ohn] A[tkyns] Wright

[page 10, left hand column, D continued]

H[enry] P[enruddocke] Wyndham
T[homas] Wyndham
Sir W[atkin] W[illiams] Wynne [i.e., Wynn]
Hon. Sir Jf S. Yorke[110]   *C. Wyndham* [from F][111]
Rt. Hon. C[harles Philip] Yorke   *Lord Lovaine* [from F]
Dr Lawrence [i.e., Laurence][112]   *Rt. H[on]. W. Windham* [from F][113]
J[ohn] Leach
C[harles] S[haw] Lefevre
C[harles] Leigh
~~R[obert] H[olt] Leigh~~ [to F]
J[ames] H[enry] Leigh[114]
J[ohn] Leland
C[harles] P[owell] Leslie
Sir J[ohn] Lethbridge[115]
~~H[ugh] Leycester~~ [to A][116]
[Cornelius O'Callaghan] Lord Lismore
Sir E[dward] P[ryce] Lloyd
J[ames] M[artin] Lloyd[117]
W[illiam] E[liott] Lockhart
W[illiam] Loftus
R[ichard Godolphin] Long
M[ountifort] Longfield
E[dward] L[oveden] Loveden
Ja[me]s Lowther
John Lowther
[Alexander] F. Mackenzie [i.e., Mackenzie Fraser]
Hon. G. [i.e., James Archibald] S[tuart Wortley] Mackenzie
Sir [i.e., John] R[andoll] Mackenzie[118]
J[ohn] McMahon
E[dmond] A[lexander] McNoughton [i.e., Macnaghten]
Hon. S[tephen] Mahon
~~John Maitland~~ friendly [to F, then SF]
Lord C[harles Henry] S[omerset] Manners   )[119]
Lord R[obert William] Manners   )
Rob[ert] Manners   )

[page 10, right hand column, D continued]

(Russell Manners[120]
(Sir W[illiam] Manners
[Charles Marsham] Lord Marsham
    Hon. M[ontague James] Mathew[121]
    - [William] Maxwell
    E[dward] May
    [Richard Philipps] Lord Milford
    Sir T[homas] Miller
    C[harles] Mills Doubtful[122]
    Hon. E[dward] Monckton
    W[illiam] Mills
    Hon. W[illiam] Monson
    Sir J[ames] Montgomery
    Lord H[enry Seymour] Mo[o]re
    ~~*Sir C[harles] Morgan*~~[123]
    R[obert] Morris
    Sir T[homas] Mostyn
    Sir O[swald] Moseley [i.e., Mosley]
    Sir P[atrick] Murray
    Hon. F[rancis] Ne[e]dham
    [Charles Herbert Pierrepont] L[or]d Newark
    [Thomas Wynn] L[or]d Newborough
    Sir E[dward] Obryen [i.e., O'Brien]
    J[ames] Ocallaghan [i.e., O'Callaghan]
    W[illiam] Odell
    H[enry] M[eade] Ogle
    C[harles] O[']Hara
    Hon. [John] R. B. Oneill [i.e., Bruce Richard O'Neill]
    Sir A[rthur] Paget
    [Henry William Paget] L[or]d Paget
    Hon. C[harles] Paget
    Sir L[awrence] Palk[124]
    J[ohn] Palmer
    W[alter] Palk

[page 11]

<u>Adverse</u>[125]

[left hand column]

Rt. Hon. [John] H[iley] Addington
W[illiam] Adams
M[iles] P[eter] Andrews
Rt. Hon. [Charles Bragge] Bathurst
W[illiam] Beckford
Lord G[eorge] T[homas] Beresford
H. [i.e., John Claudius] Beresford
~~Hon. W[illiam] Broderick [i.e., Brodrick]~~[126]
Cha[rle]s Brooke[127]
Tho[ma]s Brooke
[Charles Bruce Brudenell Bruce] Lord Bruce
Sir C[harles Merrik] Burrell [from D]
Fran[ci]s Burton
Sir John Callander
[Robert Stewart] Visc[oun]t Castlereagh
J[ohn] F[enton] Cawthorne
([Edward Clive] Visc[oun]t Clive[128]
(W[illia]m Clive
[Thomas Cochrane] Lord Cochrane
          R[eginald] P[ole] Carew [from D]
Bryan Cooke
          C[hristopher Bethell] Codrington [from D]
Sir W[illiam] Curtis
          D[aniel] P[arker] Coke [from F]
D[avies] Davenport
John Dent
L. Desborough [i.e., Edward Disbrowe]
W[illiam] Dickinson
T[homas] T[yrwhitt] Drake[129]
          D[octo]r [Patrick] Duigenan [from D]
Hon. D. Saunders [i.e., Robert Saunders Dundas]
Rt. Hon. W[illiam] Dundas
T[homas] G[rimston] Estcourt
T[homas] Everett
          Col[onel Anthony Hardolph] Eyre [from D]
F[rancis] Fane
H[enry] Fane
Hon. N[ewton] Fellowes
C[ecil] Forrester [i.e., Forester]

[page 11, right hand column, A continued]

     J[ames] Ferguson [from D]
John Fuller
I[saac] Gascoigne [i.e., Gascoyne]
Rt. Hon. Sir W[illiam] Grant
     Sir R[ichard] Gamon [from D]
B[enjamin] Hall
     Hon. C[harles] Herbert [from D][130]
Eliab Harvey (at Sea)[131]
Sir C[hristopher] Hawkins
[John Henniker Major] Lord Henniker
Geo[rge] Hibbert
[George John Montagu] Visc[oun]t Hinchin[g]brooke
[Joshua Vanneck] Lord Huntingfield
     Hon. W[illiam] A[ssheton] Harbord[132]
~~[George Gordon] Marquis [of] Huntley [i.e., Huntly]~~ doubtful[133]
C[harles] Jenkinson
H[enry] Joddrell [i.e., Jodrell]
~~Geo[rge] Johnstone~~[134]
H[ylton] Jolliffe
G[eorge] A[nthony] L[egh] Keck
W[hitshed] Keene
R[obert] Ladbrooke [i.e., Ladbroke]
Hon. E[dward] Lascelles
H[ugh] Leicester [i.e., Leycester] [from D][135]
W[illia]m MacDowal [i.e., McDowall]
Sir H[oratio] Mann
W[illiam] Manning
O[sborne] Markham[136]
Adm[iral John] Markham[137]
Sir T[homas] T[heophilus] Metcalf[e]
Sir H[enry] P[aulet St John] Mildmay
[Charles William Wentworth Fitzwilliam] Visc[oun]t Milton
Sir H[arry] Neale
Geo[rge] Nugent
Rt. Hon. [Sir] E[van] Nepean
Hon. [Thomas] C[ranley] Onslow
~~Lord~~ J[ohn] Osborne [i.e., Osborn]
Sir L[awrence] Parsons[138]
John Pattisson [i.e., Patteson]

[page 12, only column, A continued]

Sir R[obert] Peele [i.e., Peel]
Hon. E[dmund] Phipps
Sir C[harles Morice] Pole
         Sir J[ames] M[urray] Pult[e]ney [from D][139]
W[illiam] Praed
Sir C[harles] Price
T[homas] W[illiam] Plummer
Rt. Hon. G[eorge] Rose
G[eorge] H[enry] Rose
Sir C[harles Lockhart] Ross
{H[ans] Sloane}[140]
        J[ames] Shaw [from D]
T[homas] A[ssheton] Smith
Hon. C[harles] W[illiam] Stewart
[Hon. Edward Richard] Stewart[141]
[James George Stopford] Visc[oun]t Stopford[142]
Earl Temple[143]
G[eorge] W[hite] Thomas
[William Henry Cavendish Scott Bentinck] Marquis [of] Ti[t]chfield
Sir D[avid] Wedderburn
    C[lement] Tudway[144]
[Francis Charles Seymour Conway] Earl [of] Yarmouth
Sir W[illiam] Young[145]   —— 101 [written over 92][146]
~~Hon. C[harles] Herbert~~[147]
    ~~*H[ugh] Leycester*~~[148]
    M[ark] Wood [from D]

NOTES

[1] The heading appears in the middle of the top of the page above the two columns.

[2] The following seven M.P.s in this column are annotated with a large 'T': William Adam, Viscount Althorp, Thomas Babington, Sir Robert Barclay, James Barnett, Michael Hicks Beach, Robert Myddelton Biddulph, and either William Baker or Henry Bankes (the 'T' having been overwritten by the word 'Barham').

[3] The name is marked with a tick to its left.

[4] As two lines below, the line space here is introduced only in order to fit in the name entered to the right.

[5] Vacated his seat, 24 Apr. 1807.

[6] Vice-Admiral Berkeley was commander-in-chief on the North American station.

[7] Probably James Buller of Downes House, Crediton, Devon, who was member for Exeter.

[8] Inserted, but not deleted from the F section.

[9] His less well known cousin and namesake appears in the D section.

[10] Inserted, but not transferred from elsewhere.

[11] He vacated his seat for Derby, 19 Feb., and was elected for Norfolk, 4 Mar. 1807.

[12] He was unseated as member for Norfolk, 19 Feb., but was elected for Derby, 26 Feb. 1807.

[13] No longer in the Commons (and deleted with a double line), although he returned to it in 1818.

[14] The name is marked with a tick to its left.

[15] Not to be mistaken for the Rt. Hon. William Elliot [D].

[16] Out of sequence (but not apparently interlineated, nor transferred from elsewhere), having been seated for Maldon, 4 Feb. 1807.

[17] Out of sequence (but not apparently interlineated, nor transferred from elsewhere), having been seated for Thetford, 4 Feb. 1807.

[18] Not to be confused with James Graham [F].

[19] H[enry] A[rthur] Herbert: also entered, but lined through, near the end of this section.

[20] As two lines below, the line space here is introduced only in order to fit in the name entered to the right.

[21] For clarity, the four names inserted here, none of which were deleted from the F section, can be expanded as:

[John] Langstone [i.e., Langston] [from F]
[Thomas Buckler] Lethbridge [from F]
[Sir John] Lubbock [from F]
[Magens Dorrien] Magens [from F].

[22] Presumably Thomas Buckler Lethbridge, rather than his father Sir John Lethbridge [D], who had left the House.

[23] Hon. W[illiam] H[enry] Lyttleton [i.e., Lyttelton].

[24] For clarity, the three names inserted here, of which only Middleton's was deleted from the F section, can be expanded as:

Sir W[illiam] Middleton [from F]
J[ames] Macdonald [from F]
Sir C[harles] Mordaunt [from F].

[25] The only member to be transferred twice: the name was previously in D, where it was lined through, and was then inserted in F, although it was not deleted from that section on being transferred to SF.

[26] His name was not deleted from the F section.

[27] An unidentified squiggle, perhaps a question mark, has been added against this name.

[28] Also entered earlier in this section, having been transferred from D.

[29] The annotations here were written on the right hand side of page 4 facing the names in the left hand column on page 5.

[30] The heading appears in the middle of the top of the page above the two columns (which is why it appears off to the right here).

[31] Displayed here with a large left hand margin in order to provide space for the names entered to the left of the column, which are actually on page 4.

[32] [James Bernard] Visc[oun]t Barnard [i.e., Bernard].

[33] This does not refer to John Bullock, but is the heading for the three names inserted below. For clarity, they can be expanded as:

Hon[oura]ble C[harles] L[awrence] Dundas [from SF]

____ *[Hon.] L[awrence] Dundas* [from SF]

Hon[oura]ble E. W. [i.e., William Frederick Elliot] Eden [from SF].

[34] The 75 year old Father of the House was very inactive politically by this time.

[35] I.e., Sir [Thomas] C[harles] Bunbury certain [to SF]: not deleted here, but nevertheless transferred to SF.

[36] Lord J[ohn Douglas Edward Henry] Campbell.

[37] The surname is preceded by the word 'Fawkes', which was overwritten as 'Folkes' and then crossed out. There is some blotting and smudging at the bottom of this column.

[38] Names bracketed together and both transferred to D.

[39] Not to be confused with Sir James Graham [SF].

[40] But not transferred to SF (but counted as a notional transfer).

[41] Inserted, but not transferred from elsewhere.

[42] Not deleted, but transferred to SF.

[43] From the regularity of the line spacing, this does not appear to have been inserted, but his name is counted as a transfer for statistical purposes.

[44] The word 'Doubtful' is written in the margin to the left of the name, which is out of sequence.

[45] Not deleted, but transferred to SF.

[46] Not deleted, but transferred to SF.

[47] Elected for Heytesbury, 27 Jan. 1807.

[48] Not deleted, but transferred to SF.

[49] Not deleted, but transferred to SF.

[50] Not deleted, but transferred to SF, having been transferred from D.

[51] Not deleted, but transferred to SF.

[52] The 21 year old, an adventurous traveller, was lost at sea the following year.

[53] The word 'Staunch' added here is clearly attached to Lord William Russell (whose name was not, however, transferred to the SF section, but is counted as a notional transfer), and is not the heading of this part of the, in fact 'Friendly', section of the survey. *H.P., 1790–1820*, erroneously made 'Staunch Friends' out of Sir Robert Salusbury, Henry Shelley, Walter Spencer Stanhope, Thomas Steele, Charles Manners Sutton, Lord Walpole and Thomas Whitmore.

[54] Not deleted, but transferred to SF.

[55] The heading appears in the middle of the top of the page above the two columns.

[56] He succeeded as 2nd earl of Gosford, 14 Feb. 1807.

[57] Vacated his seat in January 1807.

[58] The 'r' is deleted in the original.

[59] Not transferred to the F section (but counted as a notional transfer).

[60] The word 'adverse' is actually written at the bottom right hand side of the previous page (page 6).

[61] Not to be confused with the famous George Canning [SF].

[62] Inserted, but not transferred from elsewhere.

[63] This is entered slightly above the name, as if (but not actually) referring to Robert Shapland Carew.

[64] Unseated on petition, 19 Feb. 1807.

[65] Vacated his seat, 5 Mar. 1807.

[66] The 'A' is deleted in the original.

[67] Summoned to the Lords in his father's barony as Lord Tynedale, 11 Apr. 1807.

[68] He was chief secretary to the lord lieutenant of Ireland.

[69] *Thomas Francis Fremantle* [from F] and *William Henry Fremantle* [from F], who (having also been elected for Harwich) was seated for Saltash, 19 Feb. 1807.

[70] 'Gower' has been overwritten 'Gore'.

[71] Lord Gower was no longer a member, so this was probably a mistake for his half-brother.

[72] The surname has a dotted line beneath it.

[73] No longer in the Commons, although he returned to it in 1812.

[74] Member for Boroughbridge.

[75] Entered twice in the A section: once at the end, where the name was deleted, and then in its alphabetical position.

[76] Entered twice in the SF section: once at the end, where the name was deleted, and then in its alphabetical position.

[77] The initial given is perhaps not, in fact, a 'P'.

[78] Displayed here with a large left hand margin in order to provide space for the names entered to the left of the column.

[79] 'Honeywood' has been written over 'Honeyman'.

[80] Rear-Admiral Hood was on a secret mission abroad.

[81] There is no apparent line gap here in the original.

[82] The alphabetical sequence jumps here, with Thomas Johnes being inserted two lines above, John Irving being added to the right, and a few surnames beginning with a 'K' entered to the left (none of them having been transferred from elsewhere); the missing 'L'-'P' names are given at the end, after the 'P'-'Y' part of this section.

[83] Corrected from 'Hon. A.'

[84] I.e., *John Kynaston Powell.*

[85] Hon. J. [i.e., George] A[nderson] Pelham.

[86] The 'H' is deleted in the original.

[87] R[ichard] M[ansel] Phillips [i.e., Philipps].

[88] Piggott, the attorney-general, was not transferred to the A list (but is counted as a notional transfer).

[89] He resigned his seat for Bletchingley, 9 Jan., and was elected for Dundalk, 20 Jan. 1807.

[90] Inserted out of sequence (but not transferred from elsewhere), having been elected for Cockermouth, 17 Jan. 1807.

[91] Out of sequence (but not apparently interlineated, nor transferred from elsewhere), having been elected for Bletchingley, 21 Jan. 1807.

[92] Hon. F[rancis] A[ldborough] Pretty [i.e., Prittie].

[93] Deleted, but not transferred elsewhere.

[94] Unseated on petition, 19 Feb. 1807.

95 The 'h' has been inserted above the surname.

96 Apparently changed from 'Smith'.

97 Inserted, but not transferred from elsewhere; the second initial may not, in fact, be an 'A'.

98 Inserted, but not transferred from elsewhere.

99 Unseated on petition, 16 Mar. 1807.

100 Inserted, but not transferred from elsewhere, with a dotted line beneath the surname.

101 No longer in the Commons.

102 Vacated his seat, 15 Dec. 1806.

103 No longer in the Commons.

104 Presumably one of the members for Amersham; the 'w' has been inserted above the surname.

105 Inserted, but not transferred from elsewhere.

106 Seated for Horsham, 20 Jan. 1807, although he had also been returned for Arundel at the general election.

107 Presumably, since his name was transferred to SF, the words below refer to him.

108 No longer in the Commons.

109 These words, which are enclosed within the roughly horizontal line shown above and a curving line falling from left to right across the page (not depicted here) presumably refer to Henry Willoughby.

110 Hon. Sir Jf [i.e., Joseph] S[ydney] Yorke.

111 For clarity, Wyndham (who was elected for Sussex, 29 Jan.) and the other two names inserted here, none of which were deleted from the F section, can be expanded as:

[Hon.] C[harles William] Wyndham [from F]

[George Percy] Lord Lovaine [from F]

Rt. H[on.] W[illiam] Windham [from F].

112 D[octo]r [French] Lawrence [i.e., Laurence].

113 He was unseated as member for Norfolk, 19 Feb. 1807, but chose to sit for New Romney, where he had also been elected.

114 Inserted, but not transferred from elsewhere.

115 He vacated his seat in Jan. 1807.

116 Entered twice in the A section: once at the end, where the name was deleted, and then in its alphabetical position.

117 Inserted, but not transferred from elsewhere.

118 The 'Sir' is an error.

119 Bracketed together.

120 Bracketed together.

121 From here to the end of this column has been written in a different hand, indented to the right.

122 It is not clear if this refers to Charles Mills or Hon. Edward Monckton, but the word has been smudged out, perhaps because it was noticed that it was, in any case, already in the D section.

123 Deleted, but not transferred elsewhere.

124 The initial has been corrected from 'R'.

125 The heading appears in the middle of the top of the page above the two columns.

126 Deleted, but not transferred elsewhere.

127 Unseated on petition, 23 Feb. 1807.

128 Bracketed together.

129 Presumably one of the members for Amersham.

130 Also entered, but lined through, near the end of this section.

131 Rear-Admiral Harvey was on service in the West Indies.

132 Inserted out of sequence (but not transferred from elsewhere), having been elected for Plympton Erle, 7 Feb. 1807.

133 Deleted, but not transferred to the D section (and counted as a notional transfer); he was summoned to the Lords in his father's barony as Lord Gordon, 11 Apr. 1807.

134 Deleted, but not transferred elsewhere.

135 Also entered, but lined through, near the end of this section.

136 Appointed commissioner of barracks, which disqualified him from parliament, in late Mar. 1807.

137 Inserted, but not transferred from elsewhere.

138 He succeeded as 2nd earl of Rosse, 20 Apr. 1807.

139 He had actually dropped the 'Murray' on changing his surname to Pulteney.

140 No longer in the Commons.

141 Inserted, but not transferred from elsewhere.

142 Transferred from Great Bedwyn to Marlborough in Apr. 1807, after being appointed to office.

143 [Richard Plantagenet Temple Nugent Brydges Chandos Grenville] Earl Temple.

144 Inserted, but not transferred from elsewhere.

145 Appointed governor of Tobago, which disqualified him from parliament, in early Feb. 1807.

146 Below to the left there is a column of numbers: '37/36/34'. If 34 was a mistake for 24, the number of names as counted in the third column of the A section, this would mean that a running total of 97 was at some point arrived at during the composition of this section (107 being impossible).

147 Also entered earlier in this section, having been transferred from D.

148 Also entered earlier in this section, having been transferred from D.

Packaging Liberty and Marketing the Gift of Freedom: 1807 and the Legacy of Clarkson's Chest

MARCUS WOOD

How slavery should now best be remembered through the display of art and material objects is an almost impossible problem to solve. The following discussion tries to get close to three things. Firstly, I want to think about why the most successful images and objects developed by the abolition movement were made the way they were. Secondly, I want to think about the visual rhetoric of this propaganda and how well it has travelled, in other words to speculate on why some of it has remained within popular cultural currency up to this day. And thirdly, I want to think about the visual archive we are left with now – what do art objects, or indeed any objects, have the potential to tell us about the memory of slavery, and which ones have the most narrative power? When it comes to slavery, art and cultural display, we are dealing with some terrible aesthetic and moral conflicts. Should the torture implements, and restraints, used on slave bodies, or paintings and prints showing slave abuse, be put on display at all – do not these things simply invite sadomasochistic fantasy, and sentimental self-identification?[1] (Fig. 6, see catalogue no. 16.) Can, and indeed should, aesthetically beautiful work be produced about mass human trauma perpetrated on the scale of the slave trade? (Fig. 1.) Was this work made primarily by white artists, intellectuals and propagandists for an exclusively white audience, and as such can it ever truly speak for the experience of the slave, rather than for a free-white fantasy of that experience?

Bearing in mind these questions it is important to think about why Britain has decided to pour significantly large resources into a set of exhibitions and events commemorating the two hundredth anniversary of the passage of a piece of compromised and well overdue legislation. These shows celebrate the passing of a law by a series of white senior statesmen and politicians, and the 1807 Abolition Act is still generally seen as a phenomenal achievement expressive of superior British morality and religious devotion. It is, however, crucial to ensure that the extended and colossal amorality of Britain's centuries-long involvement in, and final domination of, the Atlantic slave trade does not become buried beneath a mountain of self-congratulation and biographical self aggrandizement, albeit cleverly dressed up with the sack cloth of sentiment and the ashes of nostalgia. That Britain finally abolished the slave trade was a good thing, that it constituted a moral triumph for the nation is far less certain. One thing the passage of the Abolition Act could never do was to make any form

---

[1] This question is most fully explored in Marcus Wood, *Slavery, Empathy and Pornography* (Oxford, 2003).

Figure 1 'Slave Ship (Slavers Throwing Overboard the Dead and Dying, Typhoon Coming On)', 1840, by Joseph Mallord William Turner (1775–1851), oil on canvas, 90.8×122.6 cm, Museum of Fine Arts, Boston, H. L. Pierce Fund (99.22). (© Museum of Fine Arts, Boston.)

of reparation to the millions of Africans who had already been sacrificed to the voracious needs of British, and European, imperial expansion in the Caribbean and the Americas. Another thing that this act could not, and never can, do is wash the traumatic inheritance of slavery from our collective national memory. A national moral failing of such incalculable proportions cannot disappear with the passing of an act, and so it will continue to burrow away into the cultural fat of our collective repression, and to reappear in various metamorphosed forms, some attractive, some terribly ugly.

Repression and narrative disguise surrounded the memory of slavery from the moment Britain decided it had attained the moral high ground, with the stroke of a pen in 1807. The propagandas generated by the abolition campaign, and the visual propagandas in particular, had an agenda that tended to keep the slave at a discreet and abstracted distance, and to personalize, sanctify and celebrate the white male leaders of abolition. The myth of the abolition moment is motivated by the desire to erase and re-inscribe. Within this dynamic there is a constant pressure for sin, guilt and evil to vanish, in order that they might be instantly overwritten by British pathos, avuncular concern and moral enlightenment. The latter qualities were symbolically enshrined within the bodies and biographies/hagiographies of a set of canonized leaders of abolition, Granville Sharp, Thomas Clarkson and William Wilberforce being the most prominent names. This exhibition is both a testimony to how these figureheads retain their grip on the official memory of slavery, and an interrogation of what that memory might now mean.[2] The Clapham sect abolitionists were not lightly nicknamed 'the Saints', but how long they retain their halos is up for debate. The British cultural memory of slavery is consequently not an innocent thing, and the 1807 abolition moment must in part be remembered as a device cleverly constructed to police a particularly ghastly part of national memory. We must consequently look at everything that is put on display around this bicentenary with open, curious and even suspicious eyes.

Anti-Slavery Propaganda – Why Was it so Successful, and Why Does it Remain So?

The imagery generated around the British drive to abolish the slave trade from 1787 to 1807 was initially part of what would now be termed a national, then international, 'consciousness-raising' campaign.[3] British slave trade abolition has a good claim to be the first mass propaganda campaign to draw on the full resources of leisure industries in the industrial age. As such the whole range of visual materials initiated by the London Committee had one primary goal: to make English people of all ages, both sexes, literate and non-literate, think about the suffering of Africans during the course of their enslavement in Africa, and their subsequent transportation on the middle passage.

---

[2] For the continued cult of memory around the 'big three' abolitionists, see the following exhibits: portrait of Granville Sharp by George Dance (cat. no. 14); portrait of Thomas Clarkson by von Breda (cat. no. 15); Clarkson's chest (cat. no. 22); portrait of William Wilberforce by George Richmond (cat. no. 23); and Wilberforce election token (cat. no. 28)

[3] By far the best account of the propagandistic and agitational aspects of English slave trade abolition is J. R. Oldfield, *Popular Politics and British Anti-Slavery. The Mobilisation of Public Opinion Against the Slave Trade, 1787–1807* (Manchester, 1995). See also Marcus Wood, 'Free Publishing and British Abolition Propaganda, 1780–1838', in *Free Print and Non-Commercial Publishing Since 1700*, ed. James Raven (Aldershot, 2000), pp. 67–93.

The aim was simple and focussed, and partly as a result of the visual propaganda generated, British involvement in the transportation of African slaves became officially illegal precisely two centuries ago. An incalculable number of people in Britain, France and America, had first begun to think about, indeed to believe that they had seen the slave trade in action, by looking at some of the most powerful and durable visual propaganda ever developed around a site of traumatic abuse.[4]

But if the facts appear simple, and the link between visual propaganda and its political goal straightforward, the publicity which the abolitionists generated was anything but transparent. Much of this material carried visual imagery, and yet it frequently broke down established formal barriers between the arts, dissolved established categories of high and low art, and even challenged long established rules around public and private space, and what constituted male and female performative domains. The committee was centred in London but rapidly developed a remarkably effective and widespread set of linked societies throughout the big cities of the north and the provinces. The London Committee drew on traditional forms of publicity but would ally them to new distribution methods.[5] So for example the prominent late Augustan poet William Cowper was asked to write popular ballads which could then be mass produced in handbill form, illustrated with woodcuts or etchings, and sent out as a free mail-shot, distributed in taverns and market places, or delivered door to door. Pamphlets by Sharp, Clarkson and leading American quaker abolitionists, most significantly Anthony Benezet, were also sent out as free publications, and translated into other European languages. Sentimental oil paintings were commissioned by young rising stars of the art world, and their work then produced in fine mezzotint editions for the connoisseur's market, or more generally distributed as etchings. George Morland's famous 1790 abolition diptych *African Hospitality* and *The Slave Trade* is probably the most celebrated and successful example of this practice. The new technologies which allowed wood-engravings to be set on a level in a single form with metal type, and printed on a flat bed press with a single pull, allowed for illustrated broadsides to be produced in vast quantities and again circulated free. The most spectacular example of this type of publication, and an image which from its publication in 1789 gained almost instant celebrity in England, France and the East Coast of North America, was the famous *Plan of the Slave Ship Brookes* (see catalogue no. 4). This image has remained in constant circulation, re-circulation and re-invention from the moment of its creation by the London Committee, until the present. It remains the most widely known image that purports to describe the horror of the middle passage, and maintains an authority as the final statement concerning the inhuman conditions of the slave trade. It is, however, in representational terms completely unreal, a bizarre idealised fantasy of how a slave ship might most efficiently be packed with a human cargo without breaking the spatial rules laid down by a

[4] For abolition's relation to the popular visual arts in England see Oldfield, *Popular Politics*, pp. 155–83; Marcus Wood, *Blind Memory. Slavery And Visual Representation in England and North America, 1789–1865* (Manchester, 2000); Hugh Honour, *The Image of the Black in Western Art from the American Revolution to World War I* (Cambridge, Mass., 1989); Jean Fagan Yellin, *Women and Sisters* (New Haven, 1989).

[5] Oldfield, *Popular Politics*, pp. 96–123; Seymour Drescher, 'Whose Abolition? Popular Pressure and the Ending of the British Slave Trade', *Past and Present*, No. 143 (1994), 136–66.

new piece of legislation usually known as Dolben's Act.[6] Detached, abstract, formally enticing, diagrammatically precise, it is an image which invites a viewer to fill in its emotional blankness. And yet this image also denies the African body any cultural or creative autonomy. In this sense the *Plan* is a deeply compromised artefact which presents the slave through a vision of absolute disempowerment and non-entity. At one narrative level the image functions as a slave dealer's utopia, and so forces the viewer, albeit ironically, to share their fantasy of slavery with that of an idealized slave captain trying to fill his ship as efficiently as possible.

The plan was rapidly adapted within popular culture in a manner that broke down the formal division between two and three dimensional art, and different reproductive media. Within months of its production the print had been developed into three-dimensional models by both Wilberforce and in revolutionary Paris where the French radical revolutionary and abolitionist the comte de Mirabeau had a model with miniature three-dimensional figures constructed.[7] Wilberforce's model (see catalogue no. 5) was produced in the form of a scale reproduction of a ship based on the original dimensions of the print, and the two dimensional engravings of the slave bodies were then pasted down onto the slave decks. In a sense it put the stark two dimensionality of the original, suddenly in a 'real' space. It is all the more chilling to remember that while the ship was shown and passed around the house of commons, or fingered by politicians as Wilberforce sought to win them over to the cause in his private chambers, the actual ship, the Brookes, continued to float across the waters of the Atlantic filled with slave cargoes.[8]

The new industrial methods of ceramic production pioneered by the one-legged quaker, Josiah Wedgwood, were also centrally exploited in the cause. Wedgwood was not only a keen abolitionist, and technically a revolutionary potter, but a man with extraordinary entrepreneurial flair. When he came to think about abolition publicity methods he had already exploited his royal connexions and commissions in England and Russia to sell product line dinner services. He had also demonstrated how effectively advertising could move between different art forms and encouraged the foremost painters to use his most spectacular ceramics as props in their portraits of aristocrats. Refined and impressive vases jostled for pride of place with the black slave children and dogs, who formed part of the exotic background paraphernalia of late eighteenth century portraiture[9] (Fig. 2). When he produced the famed jasper and porcelain cameo version of the abolition seal (developed from a design and the motto 'Am I not a Man and a Brother?' originally thought up by the London Committee), he manufactured a powerful political icon in a form which allowed it to cross over into the fashion accessory business. Women could wear the striking cameo in various forms about their bodies, as a hair pin, a broach, worked into a charm bracelet, and gentlemen had them set into cane tops, cuff links and snuff boxes. The abolition seal

---

[6] Wood, *Blind Memory*, pp. 16–30.

[7] *Ibid.*, pp. 27–9.

[8] For a meditation on the irony of this situation see Marcus Wood, *High Tar Babies. Race, Hatred, Slavery, Love* (Manchester, 2001), pp. 86–88.

[9] For Wedgwood and abolition, see Adam Hochschild, *Bury the Chains. The British Struggle to Abolish Slavery* (2005), pp. 128–9, 133–4, 259, 326; for blacks in eighteenth-century portraiture, see David Dabydeen, *Hogarth's Blacks* (Manchester, 1987).

Figure 2 Designed by the Society for Effecting the Abolition of the Slave Trade (the London Committee), and made by Josiah Wedgwood, 'Abolition Seal', jasperware, 1788 (private collection).

became a stamp of fashionability and political sensitivity. Tasteful, but not in your face, it moved around between classes, sexes and social factions, a protean form sliding in and out of politics and fashion. The imagery of abolition was then phenomenally successful within its own terms, and gave white audiences, then and perhaps now, exactly what they wanted to see: passive and abused slave bodies hanging in a cultural space that invited white empathetic projection.

Expanding Thomas Clarkson's Chest and the Dangers of the Cult of Personality

In March 2006 I received an official letter from the house of commons inviting me to write about the current slavery exhibition and informing me that a centre-piece of the show would be a travelling chest belonging to the legendary abolitionist Thomas Clarkson. The more I have looked at, and looked into, this chest the more it appears an object which is capable of condensing the entire inherited history of British involvement in the slave trade, and the haunted questions of the abolitionist's motives. I consequently want to stick with the chest, and Clarkson's fluctuating historical fortunes, for together they provide strangely nuanced and unendingly complex ways of getting into the highly problematic nature of any object, work of art, or indeed individual philanthropic life, which claims to tell the story of slavery and abolition. I am going to spend the rest of this discussion meditating on the meanings of this chest, which emerges as a sort of abolition 'Pandora's box'.

To return to my letter, it said: 'We are particularly excited to have secured Clarkson's chest for display, this is the first time it will have been lent by the Wisbech and Fenland Museum, and it will be central to the exhibition.' This seems enthusiastically innocent enough, and shows the chest as a museological possession moving from one marginal location to a more central one because of the pressure of the anniversary. Yet viewed from a certain angle what we have here might be seen to have a specific political agenda rooted in the aggrandisement of a white abolition patriarchy, and related to recent turf wars over the abolition pantheon. If one abolitionist is to be made the centre of attention, as Clarkson is in this show, then other abolitionists are going to be sidelined, and beyond this what happens to the slave presence? If one object, the chest belonging to Clarkson, is to be made central, then other objects are going to be marginalized, and some even left out altogether. This confident and delighted gesture of taking Clarkson's chest into the centre might be constructed as a perpetuation of the hagiography of a saintly abolitionist. Viewed this way the chest is a holy relic, or even a religious fetish, and its inclusion in the show can be seen as part of a longstanding power struggle between the two figureheads of the first wave of British abolition, namely Wilberforce and Clarkson. Certainly any account of the British drive to abolish the slave trade which omitted Clarkson would be a case of *Hamlet* without the prince, but maybe it is necessary to step further back and to ask exactly what such a relic means, and how it should be read in this show? Above all it is necessary to consider how this chest might speak for, and to, the memory and experience of slaves who endured the middle passage?

Surely the primary message of this chest does not relate to the slave body but to the body, the legendarily indefatigable body, of Clarkson the 'workhorse' of the abolition movement. This chest is then highly symbolic and raises a set of central questions about visual culture's role in fixing and changing the shifting constructions of the 1807 act. The inherited history of the chest within the performance culture of abolition and its fascinating position, suspended between trade advertisement, travelling museum exhibit, *aide mémoire* and proto-PowerPoint presentation, imbue it with a unique cultural vivacity and ambiguity.

The Abolition Jubilee and the Hagiographic Pantheon

After a rather lack-lustre start the processes of celebration set off by the 1807 act rapidly assumed hagiographic proportions.[10] By the middle of the nineteenth century Victorian children, when they were taught about the history of slavery, were primarily taught about the history of its abolition. The year 1807 became a blinding moment of national Pauline conversion, abolition was our road to Damascus, and Wilberforce and Clarkson latter day St Pauls. Slavery became primarily the story of the 'heroes of abolition', a litany headed by Wilberforce and followed by Granville Sharp, Clarkson and Thomas Fowell Buxton. The mass publications of the missionary societies endlessly repeated the lives and acts of the fathers of abolition without remission until the end of the nineteenth century.

What is not so commonly noted, particularly with regard to the circulation and transmission of popular imagery, is the longevity of this myth. The history of British involvement in the slave trade and slavery continued to consist of the history of its triumphant abolition. As the First World War moved into full swing a copy of C.D. Michael's best-selling children's classic *The Slave and his Champions* (1891) was given by 'Mama and Dada to Doris with love on her fourteenth Birthday June 24 1915' (Fig. 3). The book had an attractive coloured cover printed in gold black and red over a soft blue background. The cover nicely shows how the history of slavery had been completely distilled into the history of the abolition campaign. The cover displays an embossed and gilded head of Wilberforce in a roundel, and below this a dramatic scene showing Granville Sharp accosting the owner of the slave Jonathan Strong. The book has six pages at the start entitled 'Slavery Past' mainly devoted to describing the African slave trade. The rest of the text consists of heavily illustrated biographical chapters on each 'champion' of the slave. The myth of the abolition moment is perfectly formulated: slavery disappears and is obliterated by a refulgent British freedom which, in its turn, is the divine gift of the great philanthropists. The chapter on Clarkson ends by making sure that the entire African continent understands its perpetual debt: 'in the distant future descendents of those whose ransom was the labour of his life will hear of Thomas Clarkson and will learn something of what he did for them. . . who will not envy him the grateful love that will make his memory sacred to the multitudes of Africa'.[11] This book was to remain in print, and slavery was to remain enshrined within the memory of its abolition, until after the Second

---

[10] Seymour Drescher, *Econocide. British Slavery in the Era of Abolition* (Pittsburgh, 1977); and *idem*, 'Whose Abolition?', pp. 136–66.

[11] C. D. Michael, *The Slave and his Champions* (1915), p. 75.

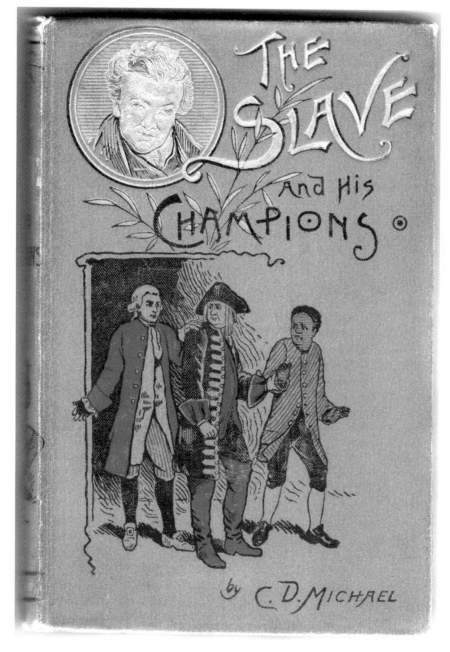

Figure 3   Anonymous, cover art for C.D. Michael, *The Slave and his Champions* (S.W. Partridge, 1915). (Collection of the author.)

World War. It should, however, be noted that from the beginning of his interest in abolition Clarkson was also interested in the long-term fate of the African continent and in its potential to become a central nexus within Britain's trade empire, once slavery was abolished. And Clarkson's chest is an object which quite literally embodies this ambitious proto-Victorian vision, this desire to own and run Africa as a vast trading post for the christian mercantilists of the British empire.

It was really not until the landmark publication of Eric Williams's brilliant *Capitalism and Slavery* that a counter thesis emerged that was capable of shaking up public opinion. Williams was an angry and principled black Marxist historian who blew the lid off the historiographical orthodoxies, and moral complacency, which had been set up around the British narrative of its role in slavery and the slave trade. Much of the detail of Williams's argument has now been countered, and some discredited, and this essay is not the place to go into the legacy his book generated.[12] What is certain is that the ideas he put forward relating to abolition as a moral smoke screen for a series of cold blooded policy changes within nineteenth century British imperial policy, meant that it was no longer possible to see abolition simply as a space enabling Wilberforce and Clarkson to manufacture a great moral victory. Williams also saw that British attention was moving beyond the limited economic concerns of the doomed sugar islands of the Caribbean and was looking to bigger imperial game with the exploitation of the Indian sub continent and central Africa. It is worth asking where Clarkson's chest stands in relation to these sea changes of imperial vision for it is both an elegy over the horrors of the Atlantic slave trade, and simultaneously a clarion call to the next generation of missionary politicians who were to expand into Africa. In this sense the chest is a semiotic time bomb, for while it draws a moral line beneath the horrors of slavery it simultaneously opens up the propagandistic avenues which would enable and publicize what would become, within half a century of the abolition of slavery in the British Caribbean, the obscenely labelled 'scramble for Africa'.

Puffing out Clarkson's Chest: How do you Visualise the Heroes of Abolition, and whose Image Lasts?

A lot of the legacy of the 1807 act has been taken up with debates over who should be celebrated, who should have pride of place within the white abolition pantheon, and this exhibition, as it circles in fascinating ways around the developing legacies of Sharp, Clarkson and Wilberforce contributes to this ongoing cultural narrative. From a very early date battles, and not very seemly or morally elevated battles, raged over whether it should be Wilberforce or Clarkson who took the real honours. This might well be a debate to which the dead slaves, the survivors of the middle passage, and indeed their descendants, might not bring that much enthusiastic interest. The black legacy might be a radically different one which might consider the biographical myths of Wilberforce and Clarkson a rather marginal affair.

---

[12] For a furious and detailed attempt to counter Williams, see G. R. Mellor, *British Imperial Trusteeship, 1783–1850* (1951), a book which ironically demonstrates how the Victorian narrative of abolition was still solidly in place up to the early 1950s.

Looking at the current privileged position of Clarkson's chest it is important to remember that he has moved very much centre stage in studies of the art and literatures of abolition during the last decade or so. Things are moving fast, yet as recently as 1995 J. R. Oldfield devoted a chapter to Clarkson in his beautifully researched *Popular Politics and British Anti-Slavery* which opened with the assertion: 'Yet today Clarkson remains a sadly neglected figure eclipsed by his friend and co-worker William Wilberforce.' The chapter is devoted to placing Clarkson firmly back at the centre of British abolition, 1788–1807. The current exhibition continues this drive and gives rightful place to Clarkson's varied and striking work on the front lines of abolition fact finding. His series of best-selling publications (dwarfing those of Wilberforce), his radical sympathies and his support of the French revolution are set up on one side. Clarkson conducted unending dirty hands research in the major slave ports of London, Bristol and Liverpool. He carried the work out over a protracted period, travelling vast distances, and he was prepared to go into precarious territory much in the manner of a contemporary undercover journalist in a war zone. He seems to have developed what now appears a born journalist's instinctive nose for blood, and an increasingly brilliant ability to get reluctant witnesses to tell him their deepest secrets in direct yet deeply moving language. Oldfield alludes to another perspective which testifies to Clarkson's obsessiveness, seriousness and tactlessness.

This negative testimony inevitably feeds back, or leads back, into the vicious attack which Wilberforce's sons made on Clarkson in their absurdly adulatory 1838 *Life of William Wilberforce*. Yet by the mid-1990s a general consensus was emerging that Clarkson was the 'true hero' of abolition. And so during this period Anti-Slavery International, although with Lord Wilberforce still overseeing its list of members, moved into new premises in South London named Thomas Clarkson House. And one year after the publication of Oldfield's book official recognition came most categorically when Clarkson was allowed an engraved tablet in Westminster Abbey alongside the legendary great and good of British public and creative life. Wilberforce had of course long been most visibly enshrined within the abbey. The event of Clarkson's inclusion was intimately related to the popular visual imagery of abolition, and made a big splash in the media. I have not the space to go in detail through the re-arrangement of his legacy, and Wilberforce's, which the event generated. It is, however, important to take a single example which raises a series of questions about how easily the suffering and horror of slavery can be overlaid by the narratives attached to leaders of the abolition movement. It is also relevant that this example leads us again to re-evaluate the meaning and function of Clarkson's chest.

Under the banner headline 'The Man who Broke their Chains', and beneath a slightly enlarged reproduction of the upper part of the renowned *Plan of the Slave Ship Brookes*, copies of which Clarkson had carried out to Paris in the momentous year of 1789, there was a long celebratory article in that bastion of tory-middle-Englandism, *The Daily Telegraph*[13] (Fig. 4). The whole thing is set up as a sort of historico-moral prize-fight, between the two deceased 'moral giants' of

---

[13] Isabel Wolff, 'The Man who Broke their Chains', *Daily Telegraph*, 14 Sept. 1996, *Telegraph Weekend* (supplement), pp. 1, 15.

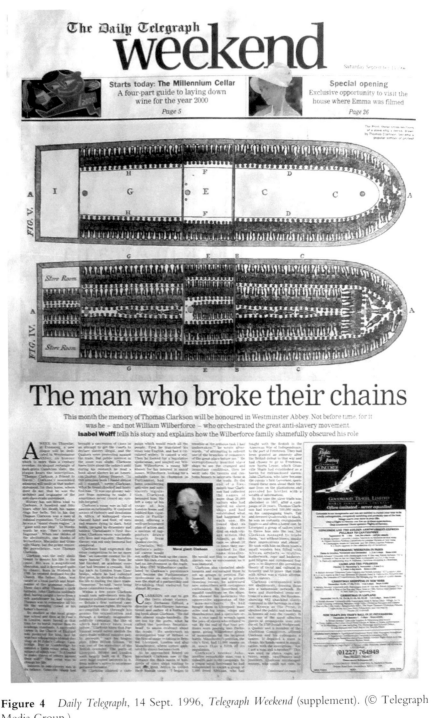

Figure 4 *Daily Telegraph*, 14 Sept. 1996, *Telegraph Weekend* (supplement). (© Telegraph Media Group.)

abolition. Poor Wilberforce after centuries of being in sole possession of the moral high ground is now on a slippery slope. The sub-title informs the reader: 'This month the memory of Thomas Clarkson will be honoured in Westminster Abbey. Not before time, for it was he – and not William Wilberforce – who orchestrated the great anti-slavery movement. Isabel Wolff tells his story and explains how the Wilberforce family shamefully obscured his role.' In these crucial words, the words most readers never penetrate beyond, the slaves are not named, but remain as an anonymous collective, an abstraction referred to tangentially in the single pronoun 'their'. The slaves are, however, clearly pictured lying in orderly engraved rows, just as the London Committee had wanted the British public to see, and then re-imagine them, in 1789. Clarkson is figured as the colossus, the titan who 'broke' their chains, but ironically in this image their chains are very much still intact. Indeed the whole visual arrangement of this front page reveals more than the editors might have thought. While the excised cross sections of the slave ship hang across the top of the layout, and dominate, Clarkson appears centrally in colour in a portrait, an early nineteenth century oil painting, which carries the stark caption 'Moral Giant, Clarkson' (Fig. 5). Clarkson in peruke and lace cravat gazes vaguely off to his right and looks towards – Concorde! which is set in a vertically extended rectangle for 'Goodwood Travel'. One might speculate on what the 'Moral Giant' and quaker would have thought of this supersonic machine heading out across the Atlantic on an ironically luxurious and rapid version of a new Anglo-American middle passage.

The main text of the article goes on in a manner that is equally fascinating in terms of how it reveals the survival of nineteenth century strategies for ensuring that the slave body and experience are closed down, and even silenced, by the biographical myth of a single 'giant' abolitionist. The piece opens with some dramatic scene setting for the ceremony of the unveiling: 'At Evensong a new plaque will be dedicated in Westminster Abbey . . . an elegant rectangle of dark green cumbrian slate, the plaque bears the inscription "Thomas Clarkson a friend to Slaves".' And so the history of Britain and Atlantic slavery is spectacularly reduced to a battle of the Titans to see who really deserves to be named the slave's friend. And yet this battle was a long established one, and the terms seem strangely familiar. To the Victorians Clarkson was: 'the Unwearied Friend of Afric's Injured Race', and one may ask how far forward the memory of slavery has really come in the last 200 years or so?

To return, in this context, to the travelling chest of Clarkson, does its status exist in relation to an imposed memory of slavery which in its turn continues to operate exclusively through the history of abolition? Surely the chest functions at one primary level as another symbolic gesture in the battle to put Clarkson back centre stage. And while Wilberforce is marginalized by this gesture, the slaves are simply left beyond the cultural pale. We need to ask, what exactly is the semiotic weight of such an item, and how does it stand in relation to the abolition reliquaries already set up in other countries to celebrate other emancipation moments. The grand semiotic cousins of this object are surely other abolition fetish objects, for example the 'Emancipation Inkwell' which Lincoln used when signing the first Emancipation Declaration, an item now proudly displayed in The Lincoln Museum, or the bejewelled and pearl encrusted quill pen in Petropolis with which Queen Isabella signed Brazil's Golden

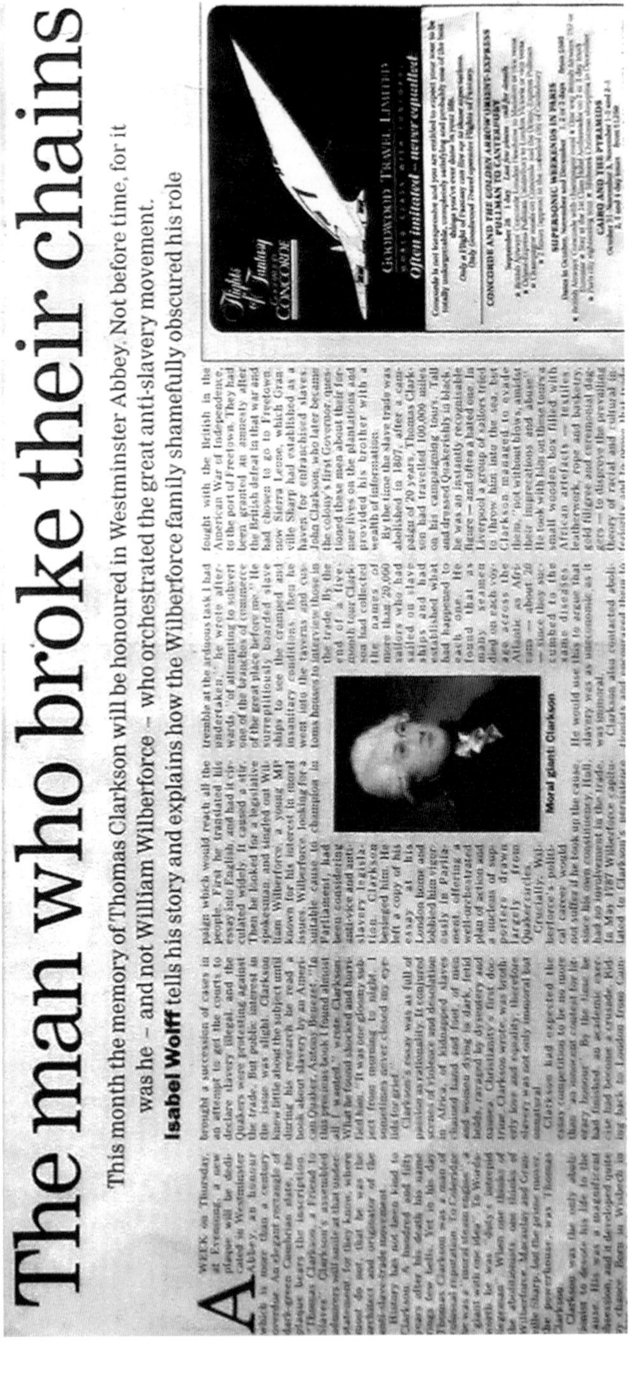

Figure 5   *Daily Telegraph*, 14 Sept. 1996, *Telegraph weekend* (supplement), detail. (© Telegraph Media Group.)

Law of 1888.[14] Surely the inclusion of these personal relics of abolitionists carries the implicit message that the descendants of slaves are still supposed to feel devotion, joy and gratitude for the industry and generosity of their benefactors. There is a further sense that we can get physically closer to these 'moral giants' by developing a devoted relationship with material objects they owned and touched.

Perhaps the most worrying inference is that the continued cult of Clarkson ensures that his enormous moral weight is still seen to be operating within an evangelical equation which simultaneously wipes out sin and memory. The worship of Clarkson takes us back to a world where the amount of moral good achieved by the 1807 Abolition Act precisely counters the total amount of evil generated by the slave trade. This moment of moral exchange, or fusion, whereby the gift of freedom wipes out the evil of slavery, is a sinister but most effective equation, which can actually efface the past. Within this essentially millenarian, or jubilatory narrative the climax of abolition enables the transformative vision at the heart of the visual archive celebrating the emancipation moment.[15] The imposition of a tumultuous moment of freedom upon the passive slave body, together with a concomitant worshiping of the body of the apotheosized abolitionist, or his personified extensions (Liberty, Britannia, Justice) obliterates the past, and all memory of suffering, abuse and horror.

Objectifying Memory and Effacing the Past: The Power of Objects to Replace History

I wished the [privy] council to see more of my African productions and manu-factures, that they might really know what Africa was capable of affording instead of the Slave-trade, and that they might make a proper estimate of the genius and talents of the natives. The samples which I had collected had been obtained by great labour, and at no inconsiderable expense: for whenever I had notice that a vessel had arrived immediately from that continent, I never hesitated to go ... even as far as Bristol, if I could pick up but a single new article.

    Clarkson, *History*, II, 13.

When it comes to the memory of slavery, the cult of personality and the power of objects, Clarkson provides a fascinating nexus in terms of what he did, how he did it and how he might be constructed now. The renowned display chest, the contents of which Clarkson amassed at his own personal expense, was used in a variety of contexts to publicize abolition from a series of didactic perspectives, and it rightly holds centre stage in the current exhibition. The chest and its contents create a charged and contradictory cultural space which throw up a series of unanswered, and maybe unanswerable, questions about what the abolitionists thought they were doing, and about how they should be remembered now.

The chest itself is a perfectly plain rectangle of polished hard wood measuring 28, by 76 by $35\frac{1}{2}$ centimetres. (See catalogue no. 22.) It has two unembellished strong brass

---

[14] For the history and reception of the 'Emancipation Inkwell' see http://www.thelincolnmuseum.org/new/publications/1843.html.

[15] The thesis is superbly set out in Clarkson, *The History of the Rise, Progress, and Accomplishment of the Abolition of the African Slave-Trade by the British Parliament* (2 vols, 1808), I, 5–23.

carrying handles. When closed this object has a certain monumental simplicity and is always going to carry intimations of mortality. Given its proportions, its starkness, its lack of ornament, it is not unlike a miniature pauper's coffin, the sort of object in which the remains of a bastard baby might have been laid to rest. Yet inside the box has a highly elaborate, even warren-like structure. It was divided into four levels by trays. Each tray was a different depth and subdivided by thin wooden partitions into a series of compartments, many of the smaller ones covered by individual tight-fitting lids. Looking at the object today it carries a myriad of associations. Full of surprises it is a sort of conjuror's box of tricks, holding a lot more than it seems it could. Clarkson may well have seen the box as a sort of majestic symbolic hold-all encompassing the entire development of the abolition movement. His *History* of the abolition of the slave trade was published in America under the significantly reconstituted general title, 'The Cabinet of Freedom', suggesting a profound metaphorical connexion between his great book and the object he toured with.[16] Yet filled with its little covered boxes, each containing a different hidden treasure, it relates both to the gentleman's cabinet of curiosities, and at a more instinctive level to the curious child's delight in forming and organizing collections of just about anything. At this level it shares something of the same aesthetic appeal as the intense boxed displays developed by the pioneering American conceptual artist Joseph Cornell. The simple box, containing so many carefully stowed objects, is also reminiscent of the seaman's chest, the object synonymous with the nomadic existence of the mariner, constantly packing and unpacking his worldly goods. Given its intricate internal structure, and its timber construction, the chest might even carry a more universal message relating to maritime metaphorics. Viewed this way it is reminiscent of a merchant ship, loaded in its different decks with different international trade goods. In this sense it carries ironic echoes of the slave ship itself, echoes which become all the more potent if one considers exactly what Clarkson put into this container, and how the various objects related to each other and spoke through him to an audience.

So when and what did Clarkson put in this box and why did he do it? Initially the chest was an elaborate visual aid used to illustrate a certain theory of trade economics. Pro-slavery arguments had focussed on the exclusive profitability of the slave-trade with Africa and laid stress on the fact that this 'human traffic' was Africa's only significant export market. Clarkson's box was filled with samples of manufactured goods, agricultural materials and even art objects which were intended to display the full range of trade markets which Africa supported and which could be developed within Europe. The box in this sense was intended to demonstrate that slavery was not an inevitable or even necessary aspect of future European mercantile expansion within Africa. Clarkson was following the general practice of the London Committee in using a typically up to date and cutting edge visual aid. His box is a both a moveable lecture kit, and a beautifully choreographed travelling salesman's sample case.

The long eighteenth century was a period when burgeoning international trade markets, and increased spending power among the nascent middling classes in Britain, lead to the sudden influx of increasingly diverse materials into everyday English life.

---

[16] (New York, 1836). I am grateful to Stephen Farrell for passing this reference on to me.

Hardwoods from India, Africa and the Americas began to appear in a variety of decorative domestic contexts in Britain. New types of exotic flowers and plants were starting to appear in English gardens, and so a market for new types of seeds developed. Exotic objects from the expanding empire were brought back as gifts, collected and kept in cabinets. Sample books, catalogues, the travelling salesman, phenomena now so familiar, were beginning to develop around the increased production and consumption of foreign goods. Certain types of furniture were manufactured as exotic display items; as table tops and other flat surfaces showed off a full range of exotic woods and veneers, or marbles and semi precious stones, they were permanent domestic inventories of colonial produce. Clarkson's chest, taken around lecture halls and public forums throughout the land, related very directly to these developing markets and spaces of material exchange. At a certain level Clarkson was acting as abolition's travelling salesman. That the collection of samples he used was constructed with great attention to detail, and with the intention of showing the variety of produce across different African regions, comes out in the detailed lists of materials and sources which Clarkson laid out in his *History*:

> In my attempts to add to my collection of specimens of African produce, I was favoured with a sample of gum ruber astringens [*sic*], of cotton from the Gambia, of indigo and musk, of long pepper, of black pepper from Whidah, of mahogany from Calabar, and of cloths of different colours, made by the natives, which, while they gave other proofs of the quality of their own cotton, gave proofs also, of the variety of their dyes.[17]

Mobile, condensed, constantly developing and evolving, and full of magical and mysterious little objects, Clarkson's chest was the perfect display item for the man selling abolition to a sceptical market. The most spectacular success of the chest's content in winning a convert came very early on and involved the biggest game of all, in the form of William Wilberforce. After an abortive first meeting with the young M.P. for Hull, Clarkson, shy and awed by the slightly older man's spectacular political position, had failed even to raise the question of abolition. His second attempt involved setting up a fashionable dinner party at the house of the lanky Bennet Langton, a wealthy and deeply committed member of the tightly knit quaker abolition community. It was at the dinner that Clarkson brought out his samples of African produce, which acted as a sort of intellectual aperitif to the main arguments about the horror of slave transportation. Wilberforce, who had already been sounded out by his friend the prime minister, Pitt, agreed to become the parliamentary spearhead of the London Committee.

The fine copper engraved portrait of Clarkson, adapted from a painting by A. E. Chalon, is fascinating from the perspective of this legendary meeting.[18] Clarkson is shown seated in a simple chair, his posture is not relaxed but tense, as if braced for action and ready to stand, or even spring, up; he grips the chair arms, while his right hand holds a quill pen. To the top right of Clarkson's head

---

[17] Clarkson, *History*, I, 373.

[18] For the original oil painting see *Transatlantic Slavery. Against Human Dignity*, ed. Anthony Tibbles (1994), p. 88.

is a marble bust of Sharp standing on a mantle piece, while further along and
half out of the picture frame is a bust of Wilberforce. The entire bottom right
of the engraving is taken up with the elaborate display of Clarkson's chest and
its contents. The chest stands open, and like some sort of rectangular cornucopia
its contents of brightly striped textiles, knives, musical instruments, grains, seeds
and pods, spills out over the carpet, and over one of the labelled and minutely
sectioned shelves which has been removed from the chest. Compositionally Wilberforce, Clarkson and the chest are powerfully conjoined. Wilberforce forces his
way into the scene, and a diagonal runs down from Wilberforce's gaze, through
Clarkson's heart, and on to the chest. There could hardly be a more powerful
statement of cause and effect, or of the power of material objects to effect political
change.

Clarkson's chest was not, however, simply a collection of substances and objects
celebrating the growth potential and creativity of the African continent. At a certain
stage of its development Clarkson added an appalling and non-African section to its
contents. It was not only African produce that Clarkson brought in the slave ports, he
recounts a revelatory experience during a research expedition in Liverpool. Clarkson
saw a shop window display of various tools used in slave restraint and torture. He
then bought the objects and proceeded to have them engraved, the engraving was
reproduced with a detailed description first in the illustrated pamphlet (see Fig. 6
below) *An Accurate Account of that Horrible and Inhuman Traffic the Slave Trade ... with
a Description of the Iron Instruments used in this Abominable Traffic* and then subsequently
repeated in reworked form in the *History*:

> There were specimens of articles in Liverpool, which I entirely overlooked at
> Bristol, and which I believe I should have overlooked here, also, had it not been
> for seeing them at a window in a shop; I mean those of different iron instruments
> used in this cruel traffic. I bought a pair of the iron hand-cuffs with which the
> men-slaves are confined. The right-hand wrist of one, and the left of another, are
> almost brought into contact by these, and fastened together, as the figure A in the
> annexed plate represents, by a little bolt with a small padlock at the end of it. I
> bought also a pair of shackles for the legs. These are represented by the figure B.
> the right ancle [*sic*] of one man is fastened to the left of another, as the reader will
> observe, by similar means. I bought these, not because it was difficult to conceive
> how the unhappy victims of this execrable trade were confined, but to show the
> fact that they were so ... I bought also a thumb-screw at this shop. The thumbs
> are put into this instrument through the two circular holes at the top of it. By
> turning a key, a bar rises up by means of a screw from C to D, and the pressure
> upon them becomes painful. By turning it further you may make the blood start
> from the ends of them. By taking the key away, as at E, you leave the tortured
> person in agony, without any means of extricating himself, or of being extricated
> by others. This screw, as I was then informed, was applied by way of punishment,
> in case of obstinacy in the slaves, or for any other reputed offence, at the discretion
> of the captain. At the same place I bought another instrument which I saw. It was
> called a speculum oris. The dotted lines in the figure on the right hand of the
> screw, represent it when shut, the black lines when open. It is opened, as at G H,

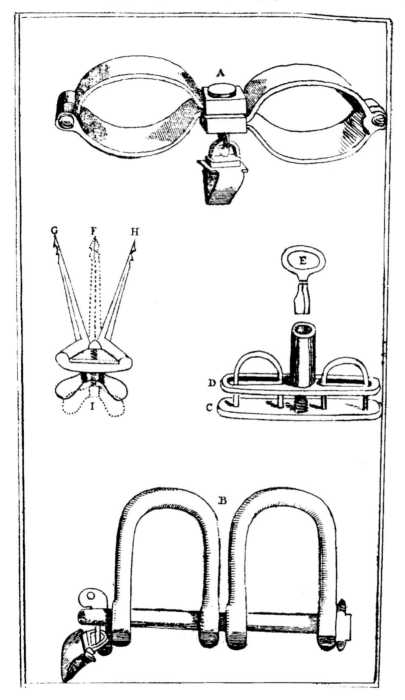

Figure 6 Anonymous, copper engraving, 'The Iron Instruments used in this Abominable Traffic', from Thomas Clarkson, *An Accurate Account of that Horrible and Inhuman Traffic the Slave Trade* (2nd edn, John Fairburn *jr*, n.d.). (Collection of the author.)

by a screw below with a knob at the end of it. This instrument is known among surgeons, having been invented to assist them in wrenching open the mouth as in the case of a locked jaw. But it had got into use in this trade. On asking the seller of the instruments on what occasion it was used there, he replied, that the slaves were frequently so sulky, as to shut their mouths against all sustenance, and this with a determination to die; and that it was necessary their mouths should be forced open to throw in nutriment, that they who had purchased them might incur no loss by their death.[19]

The language has the objective quality of descriptive scientific prose, yet simultaneously invites the reader in, and encourages us imaginatively to try on, and to try out, the different objects; there is consequently a disturbing combination of coldness and intimacy, which is quite Sadeian in its effects. Clarkson also kept hold of the objects themselves and included them in his chest when he went before the privy council committee for the first set of hearings on the slave trade. Consequently the objects exist at a variety of levels of representation, as two dimensional engravings circulated among a readership, but also as objects of gruesome fascination, to be held, fingered and fantasised in the hands of Britain's leading parliamentarians.

The composite metaphorics of the chest become even more densely fascinating, not to say contradictory, when it is noted that when Clarkson took his case to the privy council he had added to these torture implements a large piece of rope, tied with a specially enlarged monkey's fist knot at the end[20] (see catalogue no. 22). This item related to the abuse, not of slaves, but of British sailors, and Clarkson explained that it was this type of rope whip which was often the cause of death by flogging. As such the whole assemblage now established a relationship between African trade, the British seamen and the slave cargoes they took from Africa to the Americas. The same sea chests which would have been stowed below decks with the sailors and their hammocks on the way out, had to be moved along with the sailors and their hammocks for the journey from Africa to the Caribbean. During the middle passage the lower decks were fitted out with shelves and filled with slaves, consequently the common sailors had to vacate their former quarters on the slave decks and had to sleep on the open deck, gaining what rest and shelter they could. The movements of the bodies of slaves and sailors, the spaces they shared, and the sufferings they shared, forge powerful traumatic links between them.

It is now forgotten that a good deal of the force of Clarkson's anti-slave trade propaganda was directed towards uncovering the suffering of white sailors during the middle passage. Abolitionists were attempting to dislodge a series of well-formed and almost mythic pro-slavery arguments anchored in the celebration of British naval excellence and the centrality of the slave trade to the achievement and continuance of that prowess. The lynch pin of this position was the theory that the slave trade was the 'nursery of British seamanship'. In other words the argument that the trusty tars aboard the navy's 'men-of-war', who fought so dexterously against the French and Dutch in order to protect and expand British foreign territories, had been thoroughly and

---

[19] Clarkson, *History*, I, 375–7.
[20] Hochschild, *Bury the Chains*, pp. 127, 154–5.

efficiently trained up as merchant seamen in the slave trade. Much of the testimony of trauma in Clarkson's famous 'Abstract' of the evidence presented to the house of commons in the first anti-slave trade hearings concerned the excessive abuse of white sailors. The practice aboard the 'Guinea traders' was shown as chaotic, abusive, sadistic and fundamentally inefficient. There were numerous accounts of sailors mercilessly flogged to death for trivial or non-existent offences by out-of-control captains. Clarkson and the abolitionists were making a pragmatic argument which had a strategic position within their overall offensive, but this part of the evidence is now difficult for audiences to deal with. Recent history, not to mention fiction, dealing with the middle passage has tended, quite rightly, to accentuate black suffering. Yet what should be done with the traumatic experiences and memories of white sailors, who while they were punished and murdered might also have contributed to slave abuse and torture? Clarkson's knotted flogging rope is a difficult icon to deal with, but in some ways it symbolizes the world of levelling brutality on board the slavers, where human values were reduced to the consideration of profit margins, and where black slaves and white sailors alike were seen as merchandise. Under the despotism of a bad captain the human rights of the sailors were not substantially greater than those of the slaves. The absolute authority of the captain and his officers meant that the sailor's bodies, while on the ship also existed outside the protection of the law.

How this now helps us to come to understand the legacy of the middle passage is not clear, but surely it takes us into an important memorial space. The manner in which Clarkson's chest forces the experiences of slaves and sailors into proximity is a powerful reminder of the limitations of other contemporary approaches to the comparison of these two levels of experience. If, for example, one considers the print *Abolition of the Slave Trade* (see catalogue no. 16) this comes over strongly. The etching is finally impossible to read. It pornographically and comically exploits the sufferings of a young slave woman, while presenting the sailors as both callous, satirically distanced and confusingly somewhat sympathetic in their take on the torture they both observe and contribute to. What we do not get, however, is a sense that the sailors may be as terrified and brutalised as their victim. The objects in Clarkson's chest silently comment upon this dilemma.

So where does the public exhibition of Clarkson's chest within the symbolic home of British democracy leave us 200 years after the passage of the Abolition Act? Surely it is the very multivalent nature of the chest and its contents that constitute its unique value as a memory tool. Clarkson's chest, embedded, warts and all, at the heart of this exhibition, is a magnificent thing, a troubling thing and finally a terribly important thing. The whole crazy, contradictory and compromised legacy of the middle passage might be seen to be embodied within it. This chest and its contents are a physical embodiment of the ambiguities at the heart of British abolition, its publicity strategies and its continuing legacy. As such the chest provides an open space for meditating upon the evolving relationship of Britain with its difficult slavery history.

The Black Presence in England and Wales after the Abolition Act, 1807–1930[*]

CAROLINE BRESSEY

1. *Black Historical Geographies*

The black people who oversaw the 'era of abolition' were diverse and the majority probably lived their lives as ordinary members of the working class. This essay aims to give an overview of some of the people who were a part of the continuous black presence in England and Wales during the 'era of abolition', throughout the long nineteenth century and into the last century. The essay ends with the formation of the League of Coloured People in 1930. The League sought to fight increasingly overt racism in Britain, realized especially through the entrenchment of the colour bar which impacted upon the lives of black people from the Edwardian era until well beyond the *Windrush* era.

As Kathy Chater has illustrated in her paper for this volume, the ethnic origins of black people was not regularly recorded in official documents in Britain during the era of slavery. This pattern continued into the nineteenth century, and included the national census when it was introduced, and thus it is equally difficult to determine how large the black population in Britain was during this period. However, it seems that many historians have taken this absence of statistics of the black presence to mean an absence of black people themselves. Kenneth Little acknowledged that if the evidence of late nineteenth-century commentators was to be believed then by the 1870s the black man or woman had virtually disappeared except for crossing sweepers and an occasional black bishop.[1] Peter Ackroyd's London biography confirmed this as their presence was accorded only ten lines (although this amounts to a paragraph which is ten lines longer than many other publications). The final sentence of that paragraph tells us that, in the nineteenth century black people 'rarely appear in novels or narratives, except as occasional grotesques, and their general fate seems to have been one of settlement among the urban poor'.[2]

As Jan Marsh's recent exhibition of black figures in visual culture between 1800 and 1900 illustrated, there are other mediums which can give us alternative references

---

[*] I would like to thank my friends and colleagues for their comments and discussions which have stimulated and supported my research into this period and the editors for their comments. I also thank the Economic and Social Research Council for the Research Fellowship which has enabled me to research and write this paper.

[1] Kenneth Little, *Negroes in Britain. A Study of English Race Relations in English Society* (1972), p. 212.

[2] Peter Ackroyd, *London. The Biography* (2000), p. 714.

to the black presence. These include images such as 'Victorian "crowd scenes" which characteristically include at least one black figure, in conscious tribute to urban diversity'.[3] More ordinary characters have been revealed in studies such as Ian Duffield's research taken from the archive offices of New South Wales and Australia, among which he found 195 black men and six women, including Charlotte Claydon. An unmarried single parent, Claydon stole £6 in Bethnal Green and arrived in Sydney in 1837.[4] In my own research I have used institutions with photographic archives as a means of accessing the archives of black people which led me to investigate the black presence in prisons, hospitals and children's homes. Others like Duffield have found similar records fruitful as occasionally the colour of a man or woman's skin is included in a description which accompanies their details. From such archives we know that William Cross Wasdon, a 'man of colour' who was a hawker in Exeter came into contact with the law for 'playing an unlawful game with 3 Thimbles and a Ball' when he was aged 19 in August 1823.[5]

However, the numbers of the nineteenth century's black working classes who avoided contact with the state because of poverty, illness or crime, are difficult to estimate and very difficult to calculate. They are to be found, as Chater has pointed out, in wills, baptism and other Church records, and newspapers. From such sources the presence of John Day in St Sidwells, Devon comes to light. A 'man of colour', he was a shopkeeper and known in his local neighbourhood as a waiter at dinner and evening parties. We only know about him because the *Western Times* reported his death in 1837.[6] We know one young man was educated at the Gloucester British School in 1845, but his presence is highlighted because he was teased and had tricks played on him. Action was taken, offering rewards to boys who would give information on those who stole from the African boy or were otherwise cruel to him. What happened to him beyond his school days, or even this young man's name is, as yet, unknown.

How such ordinary black people responded to the news of the eventual abolition of the British slave trade and slavery is also difficult to access. Did any communities of black people meet to discuss the publication of Mary Prince's autobiography (*The History of Mary Prince, a West Indian Slave*) in 1831? Did they celebrate the abolition of colonial slavery in 1833, only to be disappointed by the degrading policy of 'apprenticeships' which followed, or disgusted by the compensation of £20 million which was paid to slave owners as part of the abolition process, while not a penny was given to those who had been enslaved?

There are few published reflections on issues of race and racism during the abolition era or the abolition movement by black people themselves until the establishment of the anti-race and anti-imperial movements in the 1880s. Among these is Merriman-Labor's vision of *Britons Through Negro Spectacles* in 1909. Although it was taken to

---

[3] Jan Marsh, 'The Black Presence in British Art 1800–1900: Introduction and Overview', in *Black Victorians. Black People in British Art 1800–1900*, ed. Jan Marsh (Aldershot, 2005). pp. 12–22. The exhibition was held in the Manchester Art Gallery (October 2005–January 2006) and the Birmingham Museum and Art Gallery (January–April 2006).

[4] Ian Duffield, 'Skilled Workers or Marginalised Poor? The African Population of the United Kingdom, 1812–1852', *Immigrants and Minorities*, XII (1993), 49–87.

[5] Black and Asian Studies Association, *Newsletter*, 45, Apr. 2006, p. 22.

[6] *Ibid.*, 31, Sept. 2001, p. 23.

be a comical collection of observations, it perhaps still gives us some insight into the reflections of a black man at the time – along with the restraints racism placed on such reflections. In the book's preface Merriman-Labor prefaced his opinions with the self deprecating statement: 'Considering my racial connection, and the flippant character of literature which, at the present time, finds ready circulation among the general public, I am of opinion that the world would be better prepared to hear me if I come in the guise of a jester.'[7] Merriman-Labor's claim that there were not many more than 100 black people living in London seems an underestimate now, given the work of researchers such as Stephen Bourne, Hakim Adi and Jeffrey Green. Green has introduced us to the diverse membership of the black community in the early part of the century with his work on *Black Edwardians*, along with Stephen Bourne's work on black entertainers who worked in British theatre and film.[8] Also beginning in Edwardian Britain, but carrying on into the 1960s, Adi has concentrated on recovering the experience of West Africans in Britain, particularly the influence on British social and political life of West African students, and the students' own politics and political organizations.[9]

Marika Sherwood has brought to light many aspects of black history in the British Isles which demand greater attention. She has published a number of papers and books focusing on the biographies of many black men and women, including political activists from the twentieth century such as Claudia Jones, the communist founder of Carnival in London and editor of the *West Indian Gazette*, and Pastor Daniels Ekarte who started the African Churches Mission in Liverpool in 1931.[10]

2. *Significant Members of the Black Presence*

There are characters from this period who were well known to their peers and through the work of those researchers above and others such as Peter Fryer, have become better known to us. The radical political activist William Cuffay, the nurse and businesswoman Mary Seacole, and the musician and composer Samuel Coleridge-Taylor are particularly pertinent.

Although Cuffay faced racist commentary in the press, the Chartist movement of which he was a dedicated part, welcomed his leadership on matters of principle far broader than ideologies of race or colour. Other members of the black presence were forced to challenge more directly. One was William Craft, who challenged the racist views of the anthropologist James Hunt from the floor of a debate held in 1863. Craft, an African-American who had fled slavery with his wife and settled in London, was one of a number of men and women who escaped enslavement and spent time living and lecturing against slavery in England. Among those recovered

---

[7] A.B.C. Merriman-Labor, *Britons Through Negro Spectacles* (1909).

[8] Jeffrey Green, *Black Edwardians. Black People in Britain, 1901–1914*, (1988); Stephen Bourne, *Black in the British Frame. The Black Experience in British Film and Television* (2001) and *Sophisticated Lady. A Celebration of Adelaide Hall* (2001).

[9] Hakim Adi, *West Africans in Britain, 1900–1960. Nationalism, Pan-Africanism and Communism* (1998).

[10] Marika Sherwood, *Pastor Daniels Ekarte and the African Churches Mission* (1994) and *Claudia Jones. A life in Exile* (1999).

among the black presence in Northamptonshire include John Anderson, who lived in Corby between 1861 and 1862.[11] Yet, these men and women came to Britain at a time when there were numerous attacks on Southern American slavery in the media. But Christine Bolt has argued that this sensibility really reflected part of a general hostility towards American institutions that masqueraded as a respectable concern for the 'American Negro', rather than a genuine concern for black people in America.[12]

3. *The Era of Abolition*

In this context it is always important to remember that the Act of Abolition in 1807 legally ended British involvement in the slave trade,[13] but that the battle for the abolition of slavery itself continued until 1833, then onto 1865 and the abolition of slavery in the United States which became a focus of the post 1833 abolition movement.[14] Black men and women had been an important part of the abolition campaign, and would remain so, but they also remained part of radical working-class political formations with which the abolition campaign had intersected.

Cuffay's local leadership within the radical Chartist movement was cut short when he was accused of being a member of the Post Ulterior Committee that had supposedly hatched a plan to blow-up London.[15] At his trial Cuffay drew strongly on the principles of equality for his defence and objected to being tried by a middle-class jury. In his final speech Cuffay denied the court's right to sentence him, and 'demand[ed] a fair trial by my peers according to the principles of the Magna Carta'.[16] He further added that a government supported by organized espionage was a disgrace to 'this great and boasted free country'.[17]

In the preface to *Running a Thousand Miles for Freedom* William Craft similarly evoked the principles of the American constitution to justify the escape of himself and his wife from enslavement.

> Having heard while we were slaves that 'God made one blood of all nations of men,' and that also the American Declaration of Independence says, that 'We hold these truths to be self-evident, that all men are created equal; that they are endowed by their Creator with certain inalienable rights; that among these are life, liberty and the pursuit of happiness; ... we felt perfectly justified in undertaking

---

[11] For more information on the Northamptonshire Black History Project and to gain access to their database of the black presence in the area, see their website, http://www.northants-black-history.org.uk/index.asp.

[12] Christine Bolt, *Victorian Attitudes to Race* (1971).

[13] There is mounting evidence that this was not the case, and that a number of British companies continued to profit and involve themselves directly and indirectly with the trade in enslaved people well into the 1860s and even the 1880s. Marika Sherwood is due to publish a book on this subject in 2007.

[14] Although the abolition of slavery in the United States was seen as a great success, slavery continued elsewhere, for example, it was not abolished in Brazil until 1888.

[15] Peter Fryer, *Staying Power. The History of Black People in Britain* (1984), pp. 237–46.

[16] *Ibid.*, p. 242.

[17] *Ibid.*, p. 407.

the dangerous and exciting task of 'running a thousand miles' in order to obtain those rights which are so vividly set forth in the Declaration.[18]

By the late 1850s and 1860s, there was also a growing hostility towards black people in Britain, supported by the derogatory theories of race which were particularly popular with James Hunt and his supporters. Hunt delivered a paper 'On the Physical and Mental Characteristics of the Negro', at the annual conference of the British Association in Newcastle in August 1863, but William Craft was there to challenge him. When William and Ellen Craft arrived in England they undertook numerous lecture tours. They were popular on the lecture circuit (and lived in Hammersmith, west London for some time[19]), thus when Craft rose to challenge Hunt he was not unknown and *The Times* reported that the audience 'loudly expressed assent or dissent from views of each speaker and the discussion assumed quite a political turn'.[20]

Craft began his response by stating that although he was 'not of pure African descent he was black enough' to respond.[21] He was critical of Hunt's argument that 'negroes were not erect', something Craft thought could also be said about agricultural labourers in southern parts of the United Kingdom, a point that was met by cries of 'hear, hear' from the audience.[22] He also pointed out that the position he was forced to occupy in the United States gave him no chance to prove what he was capable of. To further illustrate his point he used the example of Sarah Davies. She was an orphan who had been a slave at the court of Dahomey in West Africa. Craft felt:

> [h]e might refer to the instance of the little girl brought to this country by Captain Forbes. This child was presented to the Queen, who had her carefully educated. When she grew up she mingled in good society, and interested everyone by her proficiency in music, and recently she had been married to a commercial gentleman of colour at Lagos.[23]

Craft ended by saying that he was sorry that scientific and learned men were wasting time discussing a subject which did not benefit mankind, and completed his defence with a poem by Cowper. He spoke with great fluency and modesty, and at the end of his contribution was loudly applauded.[24] Yet Hunt was able to dismiss Craft's points as vague general assumptions as compared to the scientific facts he had presented.[25] Hunt's response was not only scathing but mocking too. He ended by demanding that scientific evidence, such as that which he believed he had presented to the

---

[18] William Craft, 'Running a Thousand Miles for Freedom', p. 486, in *I Was Born a Slave. An Anthology of Classic Slave Narratives, vol. two, 1849–1866,* ed. Yuval Taylor (Edinburgh, 1999), pp. 484–531.

[19] Yuval Taylor, Introduction, *I was Born a Slave,* ed. Taylor pp. xv–xxxviii.

[20] *The Times,* 31 Aug. 1863, p. 7.

[21] James Hunt (Discussion), 'On the Physical and Mental Characteristics of the Negro', *The Anthropological Review,* III (1863), 388.

[22] *The Times,* 31 Aug. 1863, p. 7.

[23] Hunt (Discussion), p. 389. To find out more about the life of Sarah Forbes Bonetta see, Caroline Bressey, 'Of Africa's Brightest Ornaments: A Short Biography of Sarah Forbes Bonetta', *Social and Cultural Geography,* VI (2005), 253–66.

[24] *The Times,* 31 Aug. 1863, p. 7.

[25] Hunt (Discussion), p. 389.

conference, 'should be met by scientific argument and not poetical clap-trap, or by gratuitous and worthless assumptions'.[26]

Carter Black also believed that 'philanthropy' should not have been brought into the discussion, and until Craft could 'rail away the seal which nature had impressed on the physical character of the Negro' he would be unable to argue the equality of the 'negro' and the European.[27] These comments show how easy it was for scientists to dismiss the claims for equality made by black people and it gives us some idea how difficult it would be for black people to challenge successfully the ideas of scientific racists.

Nevertheless, it is still difficult to make broad assumptions about the Victorians' attitudes to race. According to *The Times* Craft had many supporters in the audience, and in the same year as Craft took the floor in Newcastle, Sarah Remond, a black American woman and a United States passport holder, was denied a visa to visit Paris from London. She declared that she expected such treatment from America but not Americans under 'English influences'. The British press strongly supported her position, and the United States ambassador in London felt so vilified that he threatened to return to America.[28] Remond's comment implies that she did not expect to find colour racism in Britain in operation as it was in America; this was a belief that Mary Seacole had held when she arrived in London in 1848.[29] When Seacole's offer of her nursing services for soldiers in the Crimea was turned down by the British government '[d]oubts and suspicions arose in [her] heart for the first time ... Was it possible that American prejudices against colour had some root here [in Britain]?'[30]

4. *The Colour Line*

Ida B. Wells was another African-American who visited Britain, first in 1893 and then again in 1894 to bring the continuing racist treatment of black people in the United States to the attention of the British public. Here she was given a degree of support by the British press that surpassed all her expectations, but she also commented on the 'colour' racism that was on the rise in British politics when she was in Britain.

During her stay in London Wells made two trips to the house of commons. On her first visit she was shocked by the forced segregation of women in the House, and wrote to the Chicago paper *Inter-Ocean* commenting on the gendered division of the public gallery. She was also well aware of the racial debates occurring within British politics and commented on the case of Dadabhai Naoroji who was the first Indian to be elected to the house of commons. Political celebrity came to Naoroji's political campaign unexpectedly and almost overnight, when the prime minister, Lord

[26] *Ibid.*, p. 391

[27] *Ibid.*, p. 390

[28] *The Black Abolitionist Papers*, ed. C. Peter Ripley *et al.* (5 vols, Chapel Hill, 1985–1992) I, 469–73.

[29] Mary Seacole, *Wonderful Adventures of Mrs Seacole in Many Lands* (1857).

[30] Ziggi Alexander and Audrey Dewjee, 'Mary Seacole', *History Today*, XXXI (1981), 45.

Salisbury, declared in a speech that 'however great the progress of mankind has been, and however far we have advanced in overcoming prejudice, I doubt if we have yet got to the point of view where a British constituency would elect a black man'.[31]

Salisbury's opponents rallied to Naoroji's side and the National Liberal Club gave a banquet in his honour to mark their opposition to and disapproval of Lord Salisbury's intolerant language.[32] The *Newcastle Leader* pointed out that the majority of British subjects were in fact black men, and that to condemn a man only because of his colour reminded the public of the 'very worst days' of slavery.[33] Perhaps, as Wells put it, the English public were reluctant to draw a colour line, for Naoroji was elected Liberal M.P. for Central Finsbury in 1892. He also held an affinity with black people oppressed in America, and was one of the first to join the Anti-Lynching Committee when it was formed in London following Ida B. Wells' successful tour in 1894, and his financial support for the Pan-African conference held in London in July 1900 marks one of the earliest recorded illustrations of Afro-Asian solidarity in Britain.

If Naoroji's election proved that 'the colour line' was one that could still be broken in mainstream politics, prejudice against 'aliens' was becoming far more entrenched. The Conservatives retained a dominance in office between 1895 and 1905, and they brought a spirit of imperialism into politics. This despite having Sir Mancherjee Merwanjee Bhownaggree – the second Indian man to serve in the house of commons – who was returned to parliament as their representative for Bethnal Green for ten years following his first success in 1895.

As some of the politics above has illustrated London was certainly a cosmopolitan city. The presence of African and West Indian children in the Barnardo's rescue homes established in the 1870s are testament to this. These young people along with French, German, Italian, Greek and Spanish children reflected the cosmopolitan make-up of the capital. In 1887 Dr Barnardo reported that in the institutions Youth's Labour House, 'no fewer than *fourteen* languages and dialects' were spoken among the young people who were there at that time.[34] But this diversity was attracting the attention, probably unwanted by many, of parliament. The Royal Commission on Alien Immigration reported in 1903, and in 1905 the Aliens Act placed immigration restrictions on the statute book for the first time in 80 years.[35]

The Aliens Act was not directed at Africans or West Indians, but primarily at poor Jewish immigrants. The movement towards this atmosphere of anti-alienism is often associated with British attitudes towards foreign and imperial affairs which became increasingly jingoistic. In turn this is often seen to have been fuelled by the so called scramble for Africa which resulted in all but two small areas of Africa being divided amongst the European powers between 1870 and 1914, and increasing working class conservatism.[36]

---

[31] Peter Fryer, *Staying Power; Crusade for Justice. The Autobiography of Ida B. Wells* (Chicago and London, 1984), p. 262.

[32] Alfreda Duster, *Crusade for Justice* (Chicago, 1972).

[33] Quoted in Rozina Visram, *Asians in Britain. 400 Years of History* (2002), p. 133.

[34] *Night and Day*, June 1887, p. 3, original emphasis.

[35] Stephen Inwood, *A History of London* (1998).

[36] David Thompson, *England in the Nineteenth Century. From Waterloo to the First World War* (1951).

However, Marc Brodie's recent research on *The Politics of the Poor* in East London, has called into question many of these assumptions of the working class, the Jews and the Irish. The *Jewish Chronicle* challenged the idea of Jewishness itself in a changing political environment when in November 1885 it argued that: 'Surprise or no surprise, Jews actually do support Radicals; wonder or no wonder, Jews are often Tory. The fact is that Jews have become so thoroughly English that they regard their responsibility as voters entirely as Englishmen.'[37]

Brodie illustrates that the Jewish vote was not only important to those who voted, but to the political landscape of the East End. Although the Liberals considered themselves to be the 'natural' Jewish party, it seems many Jews who did have the vote tended to vote Conservative. He also has a number of examples of Jewish candidates being defeated in wards which included significant Jewish votes. Alongside this Brodie argues that a 'detailed case could be made ... that without the Jewish vote St George's [-in-the-East] would have been won by the Liberals in every election from 1892 to 1910, a result which would turn much of the assumed political impact of anti-alienism in the East End completely on its head'.[38] This is an exciting prospect.

The need to interrogate the Jewish and Irish working-class experience and disentangle them from prejudice about these communities, is matched by a similar one for the black presence. How did black men vote? Did they also regard their responsibility as voters entirely as Englishmen? Brodie argues that the role of women in households where men voted was important, discussing politics with their fellow workers, then continuing political discussions at home. How did black women, whether in black or 'mixed' households, influence the political landscape? This is one of many avenues yet to be researched. However, as the presence of the *Jewish Chronicle* testifies, there were Jewish men and women who identified with a Jewish community, albeit a diverse one, and this was also the case with black men and women.

If our understanding of the scramble for Africa on the politics of working people is undergoing a rethink, we know the dramatic colonization of Africa did create a political focus for black and Asian people. In July 1899 Booker T. Washington, an African-American who fought for the rights of black people, wrote to the *Colored American* from London. In it he declared that outside Africa there was no better place to study Africa than in London, and, in some respects, London was better than Africa itself. This was largely due to the fact that Britain controlled the 'most valuable part of the Dark Continent', and because it gave space to those who contested Britain's place in Africa and its treatment of Africans.

In his report Washington included a letter he had received from Sylvester Williams regarding a conference he was attempting to organize in London the following year. His initial outline presented various speakers talking to subjects that united Africans and those of African decent, with themes which included 'organised plunder versus human progress has made our race its battlefield' and 'Europe's atonement for her blood guiltiness to Africa is the loud cry of current history'. Williams had hoped that Washington himself would speak on 'The industrial emancipation of our people

---

[37] Quoted by Marc Brodie, *The Politics of the Poor. East End Politics* (Oxford, 2004), p. 185.
[38] *Ibid.*, p. 188.

in the light of current history' although in the end he was unable to attend. The conference Williams was putting together was the first Pan-African conference to be held and it represented a shift in radical politics of race.

5. *The First Pan-African Conference, London, 1900*

The Pan-African Conference was held over three days in Westminster Town Hall on the 23 July 1900. The *Colored American Magazine* heralded the conference as the mark of a new era for black people throughout the world.[39] As Immanuel Geiss has stated, the conference was a major turning point in the history of Pan-Africanism, being the first time 'Pan-African' as a term appeared and assumed organizational form.[40] Out of almost 40 people who attended this historic meeting at least five were women.[41] Anna Jones, Anna J. Cooper (who read a paper on 'The Negro Problem in America'), Miss Barrier and Miss Ada Harris were all American; Mrs J. F. Loudin was also American but had settled in London with her husband J. Loudin, who had been the leader of the Fisk Jubilee Singers when they had toured Europe. Mrs Jane Rose Roberts, the elderly widow of Liberia's first president was also present. During the conference it was agreed that the permanent establishment of the Pan-African Association would take place.

The *Colored American Magazine* considered the most striking paper given at the conference to be 'The Necessary Concord to be Established between Native Races and European Colonists', by Benito Sylvain. In this paper Sylvain argued that the metropolis of the British Empire had been rightly chosen for the meeting place of the conference, as this took the debate to the heart of the British people who: '[O]f all civilizing powers, were responsible for the anti-liberal reaction which had characterized the Colonial policy for the last fifteen years. The British government had tolerated the most frightful deeds of colonizing companies.'[42] Out of the conference came the (short lived) *Pan-African* which was first published in October 1901 and edited by Williams. Just over a decade later Duse Mohamed Ali began his editorship of the monthly *African Times & Orient Review*, a monthly journal which was 'devoted to the interests of the coloured races of the world'. Published in London, Ali's first editorial responded to the Universal Race Congress which had been held in London in 1911 and which had demonstrated to him the need for a Pan-Oriental/Pan-African journal in the seat of the British empire.

The need for co-operation was becoming ever important for those involved in radical politics, as the experiences of many black workers, particularly seafarers, continued to decline. The year before Ali founded his paper, the Committee on Distressed Colonial and Indian Subjects reported. The main focus of the committee was the position of black and Asian seamen who were finding it increasingly difficult

---

[39] S. Hamedoe, 'The First Pan-African Conference of the World', *The Colored American Magazine*, IV (1900), 223–31.

[40] Immanuel Geiss, *The Pan-African Movement* (1974).

[41] *Ibid.*, p. 182.

[42] Hamedoe, 'The First Pan-African Conference of the World', p. 226.

to find continuous employment, either at sea or on land. One witness believed that as many as three in five of these marginalized poor were in fact seafarers. Among the others were students and those who, brought to England as servants, had left bad treatment at the hands of their colonial masters stepping into the shadows of networks left by their eighteenth century ancestors.[43]

6. *The Race Riots, 1917 and 1919*

The impact of the First World War on the black experience in Britain again highlights the pressures that were increasingly placed upon black workers, both as workers and men and women living in particular communities. Those who immigrated to Britain to work during the war were welcomed by many, such as the *Empire News* which argued that 'we need black labour now, we need it badly. We want every hand we can get, every ounce of muscle, every effort, and we cannot afford to quibble about the colour of the skin.' But although black workers might be acceptable, black husbands, lovers and neighbours were not. 'The war has forced the colour problem into prominence. Where we formerly saw one black in a large city we now see hundreds; where we formerly saw one woman married to a black, or living with him, we now see scores. Such marriages should not be allowed.'[44]

In 1917 a landlord who rented out property in Canning Town, in London's East End was taken to court by a family he was trying to force out of his property. The mother told the magistrate that it was because her daughter was married to a black man. The magistrate stated that the family had a right to stay.[45] Also reported in an article on 'the black man's rights' was the appearance of Mrs Beard, summoned to court for assaulting Mrs Lynch, 'a half-caste' woman. In this case the magistrate also defended the equal rights of black people as British subjects, but these examples give a hint of the prejudices and violence that black people faced in everyday life during and between the wars.

One of the most extreme cases of this violence came during the race riots of 1919 which exploded in Cardiff and Liverpool. The race riots which took place in Cardiff in 1919 resulted in the murders of at least three men, an Irishman, John Donovan (who was shot), an 'Arab' and an 'unidentified negro' (who died from 'wounds, chiefly to the head') which were part of violence that, as reported by the *Western Mail*, resulted in 15 people being injured, shots being fired in the streets of Cardiff, as well as the homes of Arab and black seamen being besieged and ransacked by mobs.[46] Similar riots in Nottingham, Liverpool and London marked one of the lowest ebbs in race relations in twentieth-century Britain. During the riots in Liverpool Charles Wootten was murdered. Wootten, a West Indian ship's fireman, was chased into the Mersey by a Liverpool crowd of over 200 people. The mob stoned him until he sank beneath the waters, and despite police presence on the bank, nobody was arrested for

---

[43] Fryer, *Staying Power*, p. 295.

[44] 'The Black Invasion', *Empire News*, 12 Aug. 1917.

[45] *Stratford Express* (Borough of East Ham and West Ham and Stratford), 14 July 1917.

[46] *Western Mail* (Cardiff), 13 June 1919.

this murder. This was, according to Marika Sherwood's research, the first recorded lynching in England or Wales.[47]

In her book on the complex relations between workers and ideologies of racial difference which were manipulated in these and other riots, Laura Tabili relays a request for help which appeared in a letter written to the India Office by Mrs Mary Fazel in September 1925. Her husband, and the father of her three children, had disembarked in Cardiff and registered by the local authorities as an alien, who ignored his status as a British subject and his certificate of nationality. Fazel Mohamed was one of thousands who were caught up in what Tabili calls 'the most notorious instance of ongoing state involvement in racial subordination', the coloured alien seamen order.[48] As in the eighteenth and nineteenth centuries, black men and their families organized to fight against their discrimination by the highest levels of government. As their protests took shape, the order was broadened to reach beyond its original focus of 'Arab' seamen, to disparate groups of workers who were defined by their vulnerable position in the labour market coupled with 'racial characteristics'. These state imposed ideas of racial difference were eventually cemented into a special certificate of nationality and identity in 1932. A 'second-class passport for black workers only' that would come to be applied throughout the empire, it marks a significant moment in the legal discrimination against black people in Britain.[49]

7. *The Colour Bar*

The increasing discrimination facing black people was reflected by Eric Walrond. Born in Georgetown, British Guiana, in 1898 Walrond is considered by some as one of the most important, if one of the least known, authors of the Harlem renaissance during the 1920s and 1930s. He was aware that when he wrote about Britain it was with 'an adoring eye' for 'the Negro in the British overseas colonies ... sees England through a romantic and illusive veil'. But his essays on Britain still contain vital accounts of racial prejudice during the 1930s.[50] Walrond argued that the discrimination against black people in Britain, which came to be known as the colour bar, existed in geographical spaces as well as social and cultural exchanges. Despite what he described as a large presence of black people in Cardiff, Liverpool, Tyneside and London (who were part of mixed communities), black people were not allowed in certain districts. It was in the north of England that Walrond believed the colour bar was most deeply entrenched. Here high unemployment among black and white men resulted in severe competition for jobs which, as in early periods, resulted in racial violence. Black men were increasingly vulnerable due to their lack of organization as well as the blatant racism they faced from white employers.

---

[47] Marika Sherwood, 'Lynching in Britain,' *History Today*, XLIX (1999), 21–3.

[48] Laura Tabili, *We Ask for British Justice. Workers and Racial Difference in Late Imperial Britain* (Ithaca, NY, 1994), p. 114.

[49] *Ibid.*, p. 116.

[50] Eric Walrond, 'The Negro in London, from *Black Man*, March 1936', in Black and Asian Studies Association *Newsletter*, April 2006, pp. 26–7.

The situation in London was very different, with the reality of black life, complex, varied and unpredictable. As Walrond pointed out, it was possible for a black man to book a suite at the Park Lane Hotel, although the African-American singer and political activist Paul Robeson was barred from the Savoy, and the Mills Brothers (an African-American jazz group) were refused entry to 40 hotels. Those who came to study at university faced little or no prejudice, he claimed, but they were not encouraged to stay in England, and for those who worked as clerks or artisans there were few employment opportunities.[51]

For those who worked at the West India Docks in London's East End, it was a similar situation to the north of England, where black men, who were workers and fathers, found there were sometimes few options open to them beyond the dole. It was indeed a paradox that London, the capital of an empire which contained more black people than any other, the city to which many men and women fled as fugitives from slavery, should be so extremely bad at what Walrond called interracial relations.[52]

8. *The League of Coloured Peoples*

It was in response to increasingly oppressive social and cultural geographies of racism like these that The League of Coloured Peoples was founded at a meeting held at the Central Y.M.C.A., Tottenham Court Road, London in March 1931. Its president was Dr Harold Moody, who was born in Kingston, Jamaica, in 1882. He came to London in 1904 to study medicine at King's College, but the racial prejudice he faced as a student and then as a qualified doctor meant that, along with his successful medical practice in Peckham, south London, he remained committed to the campaign for the rights of black people, and served as the League's president until his death in 1947.

As was stated in the first volume of its journal, the *Keys*, the League's aims were to highlight the problems, but also success, of black people within the British empire, to challenge racial discrimination and fight for equality. This included, in 1935, an investigation into the coloured alien seamen order, and its intervention on behalf of the men affected by the operation of the British Shipping Assistance Act was probably one of their best pieces of work.[53]

However, the League of Coloured Peoples was also aware that it could not ignore the claims of black people who were part of other nations and empires. The persecution of the Jews in Germany, and the apathy with which the news was received by the rest of the world appalled them. Later they commented on the colour bar laws that were practised in Paris during the Second World War, when in 1940, although theatres were reopened, black and Jewish artists were banned from performing on stage.[54]

---

[51] For more information on African students see Adi, *West Africans in Britain*.

[52] Walrond, 'The Negro in London', p. 27.

[53] *Keys*, III, no. 1, July-Sept. 1935, pp. 3, 4; Oct.-Dec. 1935, pp. 16–18.

[54] See *Keys*, I, no. 1, July 1933, p. 1–2; *Letter no. 10*, July 1940, pp. 69–70; *Letter no. 11*, Aug. 1940, p. 13.

Little is known in England of the legal disabilities under which the African labours in South Africa. The tragic plight of the aboriginal in Australia is a closed book to many at present. The recent persecution of the Jews in Germany, and the apathy with which the news was received by the rest of the world was appalling ... On our very doorsteps in Cardiff, Liverpool, London and elsewhere our brothers and sisters are daily meeting with racial discrimination in their search for work. Many served the Empire in the last war but that is of no avail now ... Hotels, restaurants, and lodging houses refuse us with impunity.[55]

Within Britain the League of Coloured Peoples was concerned with the racial discrimination which people faced on a day to day basis, at work, at home, and in the media. Cardiff, Liverpool and London were often highlighted as places where hotels, restaurants, and lodging houses routinely refused entry to black people. Although it is now closely associated with encouraging the employment of especially black women, the racist attitudes of the medical profession were often brought to the attention of the League. In 1933, a woman who applied to 25 hospitals found herself refused by every one on the grounds of the colour of her skin. The Overseas Nursing Association, which had first heard of the woman's case, told the League of Coloured Peoples that they had applied to 18 hospitals in London and throughout the country and all had said that would not take coloured probationers.[56]

The lives of black children, and the future of the community, were also of great importance to the League of Coloured Peoples, and there were often outings and social events arranged for young people. But the League's primary concern was for the social problems that seemed to face many of these young people. In 1938 Nancie Hare wrote a long piece on this, and painted a bleak picture of their lives among the working class in London and Cardiff. In these two cities many black people were forced to live in slums, where a large part of the housing stock was poorly built or in bad repair.[57]

During the War, the *Keys* was suspended, and replaced with monthly *Letters* which were published under 'the hum of hostile planes and the boom of friendly guns'.[58] These *Letters* continued to consider the issues of race and racism black people faced, as well as the experiences of black people who were living through the London blitz. Those who kept London going included men such as 'Buzz' Barton. He was a well known Jamaican boxer who had made his mark in England, and during the war became a first aid worker in London. The participation of the black population in proportion to its numbers was said to be considerable, a contribution which the League hoped would not be forgotten, one of many of their hopes which is yet to be realised.[59] Among them was the demand for self-government for all colonial peoples, and that economic, educational, legal and political rights should be enjoyed equally by all men and women whatever their colour. Moreover it declared that all racial

[55] See *Keys*, I, no. 1, July 1933, p. 2.

[56] See *ibid.*, II, no. 1, pp. 13, 17.

[57] See *ibid.*, V, July–Sept. 1937, pp. 11–12, 25.

[58] See *Letter no 7*, Apr. 1940, p. 3; *Letter no 14*, Nov. 1940, pp. 25, 31.

[59] *Letter no 15*, Dec. 1940, pp. 67–88.

discrimination in employment, restaurants, hotels and other public places should be made illegal and that the breaking of such laws would be punished.

★

The year 1807 marked a hard won moment for black people and their supporters. It was hardly the end, or even very far from the beginning of the end, of the struggle for black peoples' rights both in England and Wales and the empire at large. Britain continued to exploit black people, through enslavement and colonialism. The extent to which Britons remained directly or indirectly involved with the continuation of slavery requires further research. How black people in Britain fitted into these complex relations throughout the nineteenth century is an important part of any such research. As with the Jewish and Irish experience the black experience requires far greater attention and it is essential that it is included in all aspects of British history (work by authors such as Catherine Hall illustrate why it is impossible to consider empire fully without this dimension). Why the experience of black people themselves (not just what colonial administrators thought of them) is still routinely ignored in many aspects of historical research begs another question. Until some of these questions begin to be answered we will have little idea of how black people lived their everyday lives, or the real extent to which race and racism played a part in the governing of Britons, whatever the colour of their skin.

The Development of the Anti-Slavery
Movement after 1807

MIKE KAYE

From the first meeting of the 12 men of the London Committee in May 1787 to the actual abolition of the slave trade throughout the British colonies in March 1807, took just under 20 years. In this relatively short period of time, a campaign developed into a mass movement that not only managed to challenge traditional assumptions about the slave trade, but also convinced many people that they had an obligation to end it.

The campaign between 1787 and 1807 successfully engaged the support of different sections of society including both radicals and conservatives as well as members of the political *élite* and working class people. Ordinary members of the public voiced their opposition to the slave trade through a variety of mechanisms, including public meetings, petitions and consumer boycotts of slave produced goods. The strength of public opinion slowly began to have an impact in parliament as did the escalating human costs of maintaining the slave system, especially after the Haitian slave revolt in 1791.[1]

The achievements of the movement to abolish the transatlantic slave trade were unparalleled at the time and even today there are only a limited number of campaigns which could claim to have had the same impact. The dynamic relationship between the campaign, public opinion and parliament was instrumental to its success and this inter-relationship can be seen in other campaigning initiatives to combat slavery over the following two centuries.

1. *The Campaign against Slavery Itself*

After the passage of the 1807 act the abolitionists needed to confront slavery head on, but instead the anti-slavery movement lost momentum. Many considered that their work was now done and argued that slavery would die a natural death now that the trade had been stopped. Some wanted to ameliorate the conditions in which slaves were held, but did not favour total abolition. Others were reluctant to do anything which might damage the British economy or involve attacking the vested interests of absentee landowners.

Nevertheless, after 1807 abolitionists managed to mobilize hundreds of thousands of people to sign petitions calling for an end to the foreign slave trade. At the Congress of Vienna in 1815, the British government pressed rival European powers to sign

[1] See Seymour Drescher's essay 'Public Opinion and Parliament in the Abolition of the British Slave Trade' in this publication for a more detailed discussion of the impact of public opinion.

treaties which prohibited the slave trade, but France, Spain and Portugal distrusted Britain's motives and wanted time to supply their colonies with slaves. In the end only a declaration stating that the slave trade was 'repugnant to the principles of humanity and universal morality' was agreed. The international slave trade was not made illegal and no time frame was set for its abolition.[2]

In 1823 a new generation of abolitionists joined older colleagues to form the London Society for Mitigating and Gradually Abolishing the State of Slavery throughout the British Dominions. The name reflected the cautious and conservative line the new group was taking.

Enslaved Africans and their descendants were not interested in a gradualist approach. In 1816 a slave rebellion in Barbados led to the destruction of a quarter of the country's sugar crop. Some 120 enslaved Africans died in the fighting or after being captured and a further 144 were tried and executed.[3] Another large rebellion took place in Guyana in 1823 involving some 9,000 slaves. Around 250 slaves were killed as the revolt was put down and a young white missionary, John Smith, was made a scapegoat for the rebellion. Smith was sentenced to be hanged and died in prison before King George IV pardoned him.

Once again the actions taken by enslaved Africans to free themselves would prove crucial to the direction of the abolitionist movement in Britain. Smith was seen as a persecuted martyr by many in Britain and this had the effect of bringing the Church of England deeper into the anti-slavery movement. Thomas Clarkson was one of only three anglicans who founded the London Committee in 1787, but when he took to the road again in 1823 to mobilize support for the cause he received support not only from quakers, but also from the Church of England, the Scottish clergy and the Bible and Church Missionary Societies. Clarkson travelled over 10,000 miles during two trips which lasted a total of 13 months. By 1824, the new Society had 230 branches,[4] but, as Clarkson recognized, the Society's gradualist approach was at odds with its grass roots support base which wanted immediate abolition and a renewal of the boycott of sugar produced by enslaved Africans which had been supported by some 300,000 people in 1791.[5]

Elizabeth Heyrick was one of those more radical voices who did much to maintain and revitalize the anti-slavery movement. She criticized the mainstream anti-slavery figures for their 'slow, cautious, accommodating measures'. She openly sympathized with slave insurrections; campaigned for a sugar boycott which included the shops that sold slave produced goods; and helped inspire the establishment of up of 70 women's anti-slavery societies. These women's committees were generally more radical than their male equivalents. They called for slaves to be freed immediately and reworked the Wedgwood design with the slogan 'Am I not a Woman and a Sister'.[6]

In the early 1830s the abolitionist movement once again revived, revitalized by the rejection of gradualism, the growth of a broader reform movement and by the

[2] Suzanne Miers, *Slavery in the Twentieth Century* (Walnut Creek, 2003), p. 14.

[3] See Michael Craton, *Testing the Chains. Resistance to Slavery in the British West Indies* (Ithaca, 1982), pp. 254–66.

[4] Ellen Gibson Wilson, *Thomas Clarkson* (1989), p. 161.

[5] Adam Hochschild, *Bury the Chains* (Boston, 2005), p. 261.

[6] *Ibid.*, p. 324–5.

slave rebellions in the Caribbean. New publications, notably the *Anti-Slavery Reporter* and Mary Prince's account of her experiences as a West Indian slave, also helped to raise awareness.[7] The decision by radical abolitionists to form the Agency Anti-slavery Committee and pay lecturers to tour the country was also very effective in mobilizing public support. The number of local branches increased dramatically to 1,300 and calls for the 'entire Abolition of Colonial Slavery' from the Anti-Slavery Society resulted in 5,484 petitions being sent to parliament between October 1830 and April 1831.[8]

The passage of the parliamentary Reform Act in 1832 gave the campaign greater power as it expanded the electorate and allowed abolitionists to make their votes count during the December 1832 elections. Because of the act half of the plantation owning M.P.s lost their seats and this had a major impact on the composition of parliament. Events in Jamaica in 1831–2 also forced the pro-slavery lobby to re-consider its position.

In 1831, Samuel Sharpe, a respected baptist deacon, triggered a rebellion of thousands of enslaved Africans by reportedly telling them that they had been freed and that they should stop work and claim their freedom. This quickly escalated into a violent revolt in which more than 200 people were killed and property worth £1,132,440 was destroyed.

It took British troops more than two weeks to regain control, after which they executed a further 312 rebels.[9] Before his own execution Sharpe said 'I would rather die upon yonder gallows than live in slavery.' His owners were paid £16 10s. in compensation for the loss of their property.[10]

This was a pyrrhic victory for slave owners. The Jamaican insurrection warned the British government that it might soon be fighting a full scale war to try and prevent the loss of one of its colonies, as had befallen the French in Haiti. Lord Howick, the parliamentary under-secretary at the colonial office, wrote in 1832 that 'Emancipation alone will effectively avert the danger.'[11]

This was one of the reasons for the passage of an act in 1833 which abolished slavery throughout the British colonies on 1 August 1834.[12] This act ensured that people could no longer be bought, sold or owned in British colonies. However, the act had two clauses which made it a bitter pill to swallow. First, the West India lobby, realizing that abolition was inevitable, had successfully lobbied for plantation owners to be compensated for their 'lost property'. Slave owners received £20 million, approximately 40 per cent of the national budget at that time, while the Africans who had been enslaved got nothing.[13]

---

[7] The *Anti-Slavery Reporter* was first published by the Anti-Slavery Society in 1825. *The History of Mary Prince. A West Indian Slave* was also first published by the Anti-Slavery Society in 1831.

[8] Wilson, *Thomas Clarkson*, p. 164.

[9] See Craton, *Testing the Chains*, pp. 291–321.

[10] Hochschild, *Bury the Chains*, p. 343.

[11] *Ibid.*, p. 344.

[12] The act abolished slavery in the British Caribbean colonies, Bermuda, Canada, Mauritius and Cape Colony, but not in India or other Eastern possessions or the British trading posts on the West African coast, which were not crown colonies. See Miers, *Slavery in the Twentieth Century*, p. 5.

[13] *Ibid.*, p. 347.

Second, slaves would become 'apprentices' in 1834 and the majority would be forced to work until 1840 before they would be free. This system was essentially slavery by another name. Only widespread strikes and demonstrations in the Caribbean and campaigning in Britain, where over half a million people signed petitions on this issue,[14] brought the apprenticeship system to an end on 1 August 1838.

Although free, former slaves were still left in an unenviable situation. Unlike slave owners, former slaves received no financial compensation, nor were they given access to land. As a result, some were left without jobs and had no option but to work for their former masters for a pittance, but now they had new expenses including having to pay rent and taxes.

The year 1838 did not however mark the end of slavery internationally. Millions remained enslaved in the other European colonies and even in 1860 there were over six million slaves in the United States, Brazil and Cuba alone.[15] In order to campaign for the abolition of slavery around the world the British and Foreign Anti-Slavery Society (currently known as Anti-Slavery International) was established in 1839.[16] As the second half of the nineteenth century progressed more countries took steps to outlaw slavery. Laws to abolish slavery were passed in the French colonies (1848), the United States of America (1865), Cuba (1886) and Brazil (1888). However, the formal abolition of slavery did not prevent people from being forced to work against their will in conditions which were not dissimilar to those faced by enslaved Africans on the plantations of the Caribbean.

2. *Manifestations of Slavery in the Nineteenth and Twentieth Centuries*

Even as the slow process of freeing slaves took place around the world, slave owners were making provisions to ensure that they would continue to have a ready supply of labour that they could exploit for little or no pay. Draconian labour legislation left former slaves with no room for collective bargaining. For example, in British Honduras, being insolent, disobedient or absent without leave could be punished with three months hard labour.[17] Many former slaves were reduced to little more than serfdom and were forced to provide free labour to the landlords in exchange for land to live on. Others became indebted to plantation shops that sold goods at inflated prices and then had to work as bonded labourers for the landlord until the debt was paid off. These types of labour exploitation were so severe that years later they would be categorized by the United Nations as practices similar to slavery.

Despite these mechanisms which allowed for the continuing exploitation of former slaves, some plantation owners had already started looking abroad for a new supply

---

[14] Wilson, *Thomas Clarkson*, p. 161.

[15] James Walvin, *Black Ivory* (1992), p. 322.

[16] Anti-Slavery International's name has changed several times during its history and is summarized as follows: the British and Foreign Anti-Slavery Society (1839–1909); the Anti-Slavery and Aborigines Protection Society (1909–47); the Anti-Slavery Society (1947–56); the Anti-Slavery Society for the Protection of Human Rights (1956–90); Anti-Slavery International for the Protection of Human Rights (1990–95); and finally Anti-Slavery International (1995–present).

[17] Hochschild, *Bury the Chains*, p. 359.

of labour which could replace slaves. In 1836, the former M.P. John Gladstone, a plantation owner in Guyana and the father of the future British prime minister, William Gladstone, wrote that he had doubts as to 'how far our Negro apprentices in the West Indies may be induced to continue their services in the plantations after the apprenticeship expires in 1840. We are therefore most desirous to obtain and introduce labourers from other quarters.'[18] In 1837, Gladstone's desires were satisfied when he was given official clearance to import so-called 'coolie' labour from India on five-year fixed contracts.[19] The Indian workers were often deceived or coerced by agents into signing these contracts and often ended up working for little more than food and shelter. The British and Foreign Anti-Slavery Society investigated the situation in Guyana and found that labourers were forced to work against their will and subjected to floggings. Mortality rates on the plantations were very high due to the harshness of the work and the poor living conditions.

The use of coolie labour was not confined to Guyana and took place in Mauritius, Jamaica, Trinidad and St Lucia. Furthermore, the British also recruited around 47,000 indentured Chinese labourers to work in gold mines in South Africa where they suffered long hours, bad working conditions and virtual imprisonment in compounds.[20]

The Anti-Slavery Society campaigned on the issue of coolie labour after it was formed in 1839 for nearly 80 years. Gradually it built up pressure on the British government to address the problem, leading first to an official investigation which confirmed the findings of the Anti-Slavery Society and then to improvements in working conditions and the prohibition of the legal export of labourers to foreign colonies. However it was only in the twentieth century that real progress was made when the Liberals highlighted the exploitation of Chinese labourers in South Africa as part of their electoral campaign in 1906. The public reacted strongly against what they considered a slave labour system and it was a factor in the Liberal election victory. As a result, the recruitment of Chinese coolies was stopped in 1907,[21] but the government prevaricated on the wider question of coolie labour. The government set up a committee under Lord Sanderson to undertake a full investigation into the use of Indian labourers in 1909 and it found that abuses and exploitation were endemic in the system. However, it was not until after the First World War that the use of coolie labour was finally ended and by then over half a million Indians had become indentured labourers in British colonies, notably Guyana, Trinidad and Jamaica.[22] In the case of indentured labour, anti-slavery sentiment was effectively harnessed to put pressure on parliament, eventually resulting in the abolition of the coolie system.

[18] Tom Stevens, 'Trafficking Coolie Labour', *The Reporter* (Jan. 2002), p. 13.

[19] The term 'coolie' comes from *Kuli,* an indigenous tribe in Gujarat, who were used for cheap labour. The word was subsequently applied to both Indian and Chinese indentured labourers. *Ibid.*

[20] Many of those held in slavery, both in the past and present, have been involved in resistance and campaigning against slavery. For example, in the case of Chinese indentured labourers, one historian documented that there was a serious uprising on roughly one out of every 11 boats leaving China with coolie labourers.

[21] Miers, *Slavery in the Twentieth Century,* p. 50.

[22] Walvin, *Black Ivory,* p. 327.

Paradoxically, combating slavery was also manipulated and even used as a justification for colonial expansion. Nowhere was this done with greater effect than in the Congo, which was annexed by King Leopold II of Belgium under the guise of opposing slavery and promoting development. In 1876, King Leopold II sponsored a conference of explorers and geographers in Brussels. Leopold said that he hoped the conference would open up routes into the Congo basin and set up bases in the interior which would be used as a means of abolishing the 'Arab' slave trade, which primarily affected East and Central Africans who were transported across the Indian Ocean and to the Persian Gulf.[23]

Leopold's humanitarian facade masked colonial ambitions and facilitated the establishment of an independently administered territory in the Congo. He won the support of the United States and other European powers and, in May 1885, he established the Congo Free State (equivalent to today's Democratic Republic of Congo) and made himself the absolute ruler of one thirteenth of Africa. He then declared all 'vacant land' property of the state and began to set up a slave labour system to exploit the Congo's resources. This system was enforced by an army, the *Force Publique*, which grew to a force of 19,000 men. The bulk of the army were Africans who were either forcibly conscripted or bought from local chiefs, including the notorious Zanzibar-based slave trader, Tippu Tipp.[24]

The Congolese were also forced to work as porters and to collect ivory and rubber. Wives, elders or village chiefs were kidnapped to ensure that men carried out the required work. Those abducted would sometimes be released if quotas of rubber were delivered, but many died in the stockades, were prostituted or used as forced labourers themselves. Brutal punishments such as floggings with the *chicotte* whip or hangings were carried out for the slightest 'offence'. As the rubber boom gained momentum in the 1890s, so too did the brutality of the slave labour system. Local rebellions, of which there were many, were violently suppressed by the *Force Publique* which pillaged whole villages, forced their inhabitants into slavery and used scorched earth tactics. Those who refused to collect rubber, did not provide soldiers with food or were suspected of supporting the rebels, were killed outright.

The severing of limbs was a systematic policy in the Congo with soldiers rewarded for the number of hands they collected. One *Force Publique* officer recorded how he cut off the heads of 100 villagers when they refused to provide supplies to his troops. William Sheppard, a black missionary, documented how a chief had shown him 81 severed hands which he was taking to a state official to prove that they had punished villagers who had not complied with demands that they collect rubber.

In July 1890, George Washington Williams, a black pastor who was working in the Congo, began to investigate and document cases involving slavery. Hundreds of Europeans had seen what Williams saw, but he was the first person to denounce what he called 'crimes against humanity'. Williams drew the public's attention to slavery

---

[23] This trade in which Africans were transported across the Sahara to East Africa and sold on to destinations in Saudi Arabia, Yemen and Oman pre-dated the transatlantic slave trade and continued late into the 19th century when there was still a demand for some 7,000 slaves a year. See *ibid.*, p. 312.

[24] Leopold redeemed thousands of people from their Swahili Arab masters in Eastern Congo only to use them as forced labourers or conscript them into the *Force Publique*. See Miers, *Slavery in the Twentieth Century*, p. 40, and Adam Hochschild, *King Leopold's Ghost* (New York, 1998), p. 130.

in the Congo by an open letter to King Leopold. This letter was later published as a pamphlet and distributed widely in Europe and the United States. Williams stated:

> Your Majesty's Government is engaged in the slave-trade, wholesale and retail. It buys and sells and steals slaves. Your Majesty's Government gives £3 per head for able-bodied slaves for military service ... The labour force at the stations of your Majesty's Government in the Upper River is composed of slaves of all ages and both sexes.[25]

Though Williams died in 1891, other witnesses to the Congo atrocities started to take up the issue. John and Alice Harris went to the Congo as missionaries in 1898, but they soon began to document the human rights violations by taking photographs and recording testimonies. Alice Harris's photographs became an irrefutable source of evidence that grave human rights violations were taking place and a powerful tool for mobilizing the general public in Britain and elsewhere.

At around the same time a shipping clerk named Edmund Dene Morel began to realize that workers in the Congo were forced labourers, since they were not being paid and virtually no goods were being sent to Congo for trading purposes. In 1901, Morel left his job and dedicated himself to exposing slavery in the Congo. As a journalist working in London, Morel was pivotal in broadcasting the truth about the Congo to a mass audience, and in involving M.P.s and humanitarian groups like the British and Foreign Anti-Slavery Society. He wrote hundreds of articles for newspapers, reporting how porters were chained by the neck and how prisoners were worked to death and executed. Leopold banned him from the Congo, but insiders leaked information to Morel, including official documents, which showed that hostage taking and payments for forced conscription were official policies.

In 1903, this campaigning bore fruit when the house of commons unanimously passed a resolution calling for the Congolese to be 'governed with humanity'. The foreign office then ordered its consul, Roger Casement, to go into the interior and report back on the situation. Casement had been sending reports about human rights violations in the Congo to London for the previous two years and immediately undertook a three-and-a-half-month investigative trip in which he documented abductions, amputations, floggings and the destruction of villages. Alice Harris's photos were submitted along with the report to the British government. Casement's report was published in 1904 and generated great public interest for its portrayal of a state run on slavery.

Morel and Casement then formed the Congo Reform Association to take the campaign forward. On 23 March 1904, the Congo Reform Association met for the first time in Liverpool and attracted over 1,000 people. By 1905, more than 60 mass meetings had adopted resolutions condemning Leopold's rule as a revival of the African slave trade and calling on the United Kingdom government to take action.[26] Morel also organized local groups in Britain and supported the establishment of the American Congo Reform Association in 1904. In this he was greatly assisted by Alice and

---

[25] Hochschild, *King Leopold's Ghost,* p. 110.

[26] *Ibid.,* p. 214.

Figure 1 A Congolese man contemplates the severed foot and hand of his five-year-old daughter, Boali, May 1904. (By permission of Anti-slavery International.)

John Harris who spoke at more than 800 events in Europe and the United States, using their photographs and displaying *chicottes* and shackles to drive home the realities of slavery in the Congo. Congo Reform Association groups were also formed in Germany, France, Norway and Switzerland.

Leopold paid lobbyists to counter the negative publicity and growing international pressure. He also set up a commission of inquiry that was modelled on the 1896 Commission for the Protection of the Natives, which had proved effective in diffusing concern about reports of slavery in the Congo at that time. However, when the new commission published its report in November 1905, it included detailed personal testimonies that supported the allegations of slavery and atrocities made by Williams, Morel and Casement. The fact that Leopold's handpicked judges had issued a damning indictment of his regime, left the king internationally isolated.

Realizing that he would not be able to resist this pressure, Leopold began to negotiate with the Belgian government. In March 1908, the government agreed to buy the Congo for some 205 million francs. Of this money 50 million was earmarked to compensate the king for 'his great sacrifices made for the Congo' and was to be paid for out of the profits extracted from the Congo.[27] The purchase of the Congo had to be paid for and the fact that the Congo was still a hugely profitable colony meant that the 'Belgian solution' did not automatically end the slave labour system. The Congo Reform Association continued its campaign and in 1909 crowds of 3,000 and 5,000 attended meetings in Plymouth and Liverpool respectively. Morel's book sold 25,000 copies a week when it first appeared, demonstrating the strength of public feeling. Responding to international pressure, the Belgian government announced reforms for the Congo, which were to be completed by 1912.

In 1912, Alice and John Harris, now joint secretaries of the merged Anti-Slavery and Aborigines Protection Society, visited the Congo to investigate the situation and reported an 'immense improvement'. On 16 June 1913, the Congo Reform Association held its final meeting and Morel declared the campaign over. He noted: 'The wounds of the Congo will take generations to heal. But . . . the atrocities have disappeared . . . The revenues are no longer supplied by forced or slave labour.'[28]

While forced labour did later resurface in the Belgian Congo, the campaign effectively engaged the public and parliament in Britain and contributed to ending the Congo Free State (1885–1908) and the systematic enslavement of the Congolese people. King Leopold is thought to have made the equivalent of $1.1 billion from the exploitation of the Congo and its people.[29] The human cost is difficult to calculate as deaths were generally not recorded, but a recent study concludes that between 1880 and 1920 the population of Congo was reduced by at least a half. As the 1924 census puts the population of the Congo at 10 million, this means that roughly 10 million Congolese were worked to death, killed, starved or died from disease in this period.[30] Unlike Leopold, the Congolese were not compensated for their 'sacrifices'.

[27] *Ibid.*, p. 259.

[28] *Ibid.*, p. 273.

[29] As estimated by the Belgian academic, Jules Marchal. Quoted in Hochschild, *King Leopold's Ghost*, p. 277.

[30] This estimate by the academic Jan Vansina reaches the same conclusion as estimates made by Congo officials in 1919 and 1920. *Ibid.*, p. 233.

A strikingly similar pattern of slavery was taking place during this period in the Amazon of South America. This time the man behind it, Julio César Arana, was a local rubber baron who made no pretence at having humanitarian motives. Arana used money and hired gunmen to acquire some 12,000 square miles of land along the Putumayo river. The Putumayo was demilitarized because it marked the disputed border between Colombia and Peru and this allowed Arana to use his 1,500 armed vigilantes to take complete control of the area.[31]

Arana used methods similar to King Leopold to ensure the highest yields of rubber and profits. The indigenous inhabitants of the Amazon (which included Bora, Huitoto and Andoke Indians) became slave labourers. Local section chiefs often worked for commission instead of a salary, which encouraged them to use ever more extreme measures to increase rubber production, including punishments such as flogging, chaining and holding women hostage to ensure rubber quotas were met. One section chief killed 150 men, women and children in order to set an example and promised to 'exterminate every Indian who doesn't obey my orders about the rubber that I require them to bring in'.[32]

In 1907, a young engineer from the United States, Walter Hardenburg, stumbled upon the rubber slaves in the Putumayo and decided to try and do something to stop this use of slave labour. Hardenburg's description of the conditions in the Amazon echo those which George Williams used to denounce slavery in the Congo: '[They] are forced to work day and night at the extraction of rubber, without the slightest remuneration except the food necessary to keep them alive ... They are robbed of the crops ... they are sold wholesale and retail ... [and] are flogged inhumanely until their bones are laid bare, and great raw sores cover them.'[33]

By May 1909, Hardenburg had collected 18 sworn testimonies which documented the atrocities that were being committed in the Amazon. That same year he travelled to Britain, where Arana's company, the Peruvian Amazon Company, was registered, to try and make the facts known. Even in London Hardenburg found it difficult to publicise what was happening, as newspapers doubted his story and were wary of being sued for libel. However, in August 1909, Hardenburg delivered the dossier to John Harris at the Anti-Slavery and Aborigines Protection Society. Through Harris's contacts the truth about slave labour in the Putumayo finally came into public domain and obtained significant press coverage.

This resulted in foreign office and public pressure being brought to bear on the Peruvian Amazon Company. It responded by setting up a commission to investigate Hardenburg's allegations, but the foreign secretary, Sir Edward Grey, insisted that Roger Casement, the consul-general in Rio de Janeiro, accompany the commission when it started its work in October 1910. Casement, fresh from denouncing slavery in the Congo, ensured that there would be no cover up. His preliminary report, submitted to London in January 1911, fully supported Hardenburg's charges. The foreign office then increased its pressure on the Peruvian government to address the

---

[31] Richard Collier, *The River that God Forgot* (1968), pp. 54–8.

[32] *Ibid.*, p. 159.

[33] W.E. Hardenburg, *The Putumayo, the Devil's Paradise*, quoted in M. Racela, 'The Putumayo Rubber Atrocities', *The Reporter* (July 2000), p. 13.

situation and lobbied Washington to do the same. Grey informed the Washington embassy in June 1911 that the quantities of rubber being shipped down the Putumayo at that time 'can only have been rendered possible by a continuance of the old system of forced labour'.[34]

The Peruvian authorities did issue 237 arrest warrants against those involved in abuses in the Putumayo, but when Casement travelled back to the region later that year to assess the progress made, he found that only nine men had actually been arrested and that corrupt officials had assisted many to escape. Consequently, the foreign office decided to publish Casement's report in 1912. The report included an estimate that Arana's company had earned one and half million pounds from rubber shipments in a 12-year period and that 30,000 indigenous people had died during this time.[35]

The report's findings provoked international outrage and demands for action. In response to this, the British government set up a select committee to investigate the activities of the Peruvian Amazon Company and seized its records. Over the next five months, the committee took evidence from many witnesses including Roger Casement, Walter Hardenburg, John Harris and Arana himself. In March 1913, the high court granted a compulsory winding up of the Peruvian Amazon Company in a case brought by the Anti-Slavery and Aborigines Protection Society along with a shareholder of the company. The select committee also issued its report to the house of commons in which it concluded that 'Señor Arana, together with other partners . . . had knowledge of and was responsible for the atrocities perpetrated by his agents and employees in the Putumayo.' These atrocities reduced the local indigenous population from 50,000 to less than 10,000.[36]

Hardenburg's commitment and the support of the Anti-Slavery and Aborigines Protection Society helped bring the issue of slavery in the Putumayo region to public attention and mobilize the support of parliament and the British government in seeking to end this practice. While Arana and the other company directors were never prosecuted, many of his overseers were caught and tried in South America. Peru subsequently ceded the Putumayo territory, including land claimed by Arana, to Colombia.[37]

Even as these campaigns were helping to end the use of slavery in the Congo and the Amazon, the use of mandatory public works, deceptive and coercive contract labour, conscription, vagrancy laws and other forced labour mechanisms were continuing in European colonies. The Brussels Act of 1890, under the prompting of King Leopold, declared that the best way of tackling slavery was to establish colonial administrations, trading companies and build infrastructure for trade routes (rail, road, communications, etc.).[38] This provided a perfect justification for colonial conquest and the exploitation of the local population. The colonial governments needed cheap labour for their public building programmes and private businesses and argued that these were necessary for the development of the countries concerned.

---

[34] Collier, *The River that God Forgot*, p. 236.

[35] *Ibid.*, pp. 235–6.

[36] *Ibid.*, pp. 299 and 230.

[37] *Ibid.*, pp. 300–1.

[38] Miers, *Slavery in the Twentieth Century*, p. 21.

Figure 2   Sir Roger Casement who denounced slavery in both the Congo and the Amazon. (By permission of Anti-Slavery International.)

The indentured labour system used by the British to ensure access to hundreds of thousands of Indian and Chinese workers was not unique. Between 1876 and 1915, the Portuguese used a similar system to transport some 97,000 Angolans to work on cocoa plantations on the islands of São Tome and Principe. In theory these were contract labourers who chose to undertake this work, but all Africans in Portuguese colonies were obliged by law to work and so in practice most Angolans were forced to sign contracts against their will. Some were even abducted and taken to the coast in shackles before being transported to the islands.[39]

Some colonial governments also passed laws which gave them the 'right' to demand forced labour. The French introduced universal conscription into their colonies in west and equatorial Africa in 1919. Those conscripted were rarely assigned any military duties and most spent three years in labour brigades working for private contractors. These conscripts received minimal pay and many died due to bad treatment and working conditions. In one project alone, the French conscripted 127,000 equatorial Africans to work on the construction of a railway between 1921 and 1934. The official death toll during this time was over 14,000, but recent estimates put the figure at over 20,000.[40] Vagrancy laws were also used in colonies and elsewhere to obtain forced labour under the guise of a judicial process. For example, in the 1920s, Portuguese officials sentenced vagrants, debt-defaulters, and 'troublemakers' to work in São Tome and Principe.

In the Congo, conscription and forced labour resurfaced under Belgian rule and the forced labour system used in Congolese mines after 1918 was not dissimilar to that which took place under Leopold's regime. The Belgian government, along with other colonial administrations, also compelled farmers to grow cash crops which they then had to sell to the government at set prices. Those who refused or did not take sufficient care of their crops were punished with imprisonment, flogging or fines.

In Kenya, the British proposed a law which would force all men who had not been paid a salary for three months in the last year to work 60 days on public works (for minimal pay) and an additional 24 days on communal works (unpaid). This plan was only dropped in 1921 following a wave of protests in Britain, but Kenyan men were still obliged to provide 24 days of paid communal service a year.

The Belgian, British, French and Portuguese governments all, to a greater or lesser extent, introduced laws and systems which allowed them to extract forced labour from the local populations without buying or selling the individuals. Leopold's subjugation of the Congo also showed that millions of people could be effectively reduced to slavery without formally being owned.

In the aftermath of the horrors of World War I, there was a commitment amongst world leaders to establish a new global order in which such conflicts would not be repeated and a belief that universal and lasting peace could only be achieved if it was based on social justice. This belief was reflected in the mandates of the League of Nations and the International Labour Organization which were set up in 1919 as part of the peace conference in Paris. At this time chattel slavery still had not been

---

[39] For more information on this and the other references to the use of forced labour by the colonial powers in this section see *ibid.*, pp. 48–9 and 135–41.

[40] *Ibid.*, p. 135–6.

universally abolished and other slavery-like practices were coming to public attention. The challenge for these organizations, and later the United Nations, was to define what constituted slavery in the twentieth century and to persuade governments to eradicate slavery in practice.

In 1924, the League of Nations set up the Temporary Slavery Commission to review the situation of slavery 'in all its forms' around the world. This mandate allowed the commission to look at the vestiges of chattel slavery as well as long established practices that were similar to slavery, including forced labour, debt bondage and servile marriage. The results of the commission's work led to the drafting of the *Slavery Convention, 1926,* which defines slavery as 'the status or condition of a person over whom any or all of the powers attaching to the right of ownership are attached'. This was the first international standard against slavery and the slave trade and it called on governments to abolish slavery 'in all its forms'. The 1926 convention also set some limits on the use of forced or compulsory labour, but it referred this controversial issue to the International Labour Organization to consider in detail.

In 1930, the International Labour Organization presented its *Forced Labour Convention* (No. 29), which defines forced labour as 'all work or service which is exacted from any person under the menace of any penalty and for which the said person has not offered himself voluntarily'. The convention tried to tackle the exploitative practices used in the European colonies and elsewhere. It prohibited forced labour for private purposes; limited public work to minor communal services and normal civic duties; and restricted compulsory military service to work of a purely military nature. It also outlawed forced prison labour when the work was done for private companies. This was a problem in many countries at that time, including the United States, South Africa and India.[41]

World War II also had a major impact in terms of attitudes to slavery. There was shock at the way millions of people had been subjected to slavery practices in Nazi labour camps, as 'comfort women' and as forced labourers when captured as prisoners of war. One of the consequences of this was that freedom from slavery and servitude was enshrined in Article 4 of the *Universal Declaration of Human Rights, 1948.* However, it was clear that much more needed to be done to make this ideal a reality. For example, in 1951 the British government estimated that there were approximately 50,000 slaves in Saudi Arabia and thought the numbers were increasing.[42] There was also concern that the other forms of slavery, which had been identified 30 years earlier by the Temporary Slavery Commission, were not being adequately addressed.

The *United Nations Supplementary Convention on the Abolition of Slavery, the Slave Trade and Institutions and Practices Similar to Slavery, 1956,* tried to remedy these problems. This convention specifically states that debt bondage, serfdom, forced marriage and the delivery of a child to another person for the exploitation of that child, are all slavery-like practices and requires that they be criminalized and abolished as soon as possible.

[41] *Ibid.*, p. 147.

[42] Slavery was only finally abolished in Saudi Arabia in 1962, Oman in 1970 and Mauritania in 1980. See Mike Dottridge, 'Slavery in Saudi Arabia', *The Reporter* (Apr. 2001), p. 13.

Even while the international community took action against these long established slavery-like practices, other forms of slavery were becoming more prevalent, particularly the use of forced labour in gulags. To appreciate the scale of this problem it is worth highlighting the case of slave labour in the Soviet Union which reached its height in the early 1950s. Recently compiled research estimates that the total number of people who were used as forced labourers in the Soviet Union between 1929 and 1953 (including those who passed through the gulags, prisoners of war and those exiled to work in remote villages) totals just under 29 million.[43] Millions more people were used as forced labourers in the People's Republic of China, Cambodia and in many other countries during the second half of the twentieth century.

The enslavement of millions of people in this way provided the impetus for framing an international standard which would focus on stopping authoritarian regimes from using forced labour for economic advancement or as a means of punishing dissidents, criminals and any other groups considered enemies of the state by the authorities. The International Labour Organization's *Abolition of Forced Labour Convention, 1958* (No. 105) aimed to do this by prohibiting forced labour as an institution of political repression, economic advancement or labour discipline.

By the beginning of the twenty-first century, two new standards had been developed which identified and prohibited slavery-like practices. The first of these, the International Labour Organization's *Convention on the Worst Forms of Child Labour, 1999* (No. 182) requires governments to take immediate measures to prohibit and eliminate all forms of slavery, such as the sale and trafficking of children, debt bondage and serfdom and forced or compulsory labour, including forced recruitment of children for use in armed conflict.

The second standard, *The United Nations Protocol to Prevent, Suppress and Punish Trafficking in Persons, Especially Women and Children, 2000*, focuses on the transportation of people through violence, coercion or deception for the purposes of exploitation. This protocol requires governments to pass legislation which prohibits and punishes trafficking for both sexual and labour exploitation.

Collectively these standards provide us with internationally agreed definitions of practices which are considered modern forms of slavery.[44] Despite the development of these internationally agreed standards many governments have failed to take practical steps to implement their provisions and millions of people around the world today continue to be subjected to contemporary forms of slavery.

3. Slavery in the Twenty-first Century

In 2005, the International Labour Organization produced a minimum estimate of the number of forced labourers in the world today and found that at least 12.3 million individuals are forced to work against their will under the threat of some

---

[43] Anne Applebaum, *Gulag. A History of the Soviet Camps* (2003), p. 517.

[44] For a detailed review of standards and mechanisms relating to slavery see David Weissbrodt and Anti-Slavery International, *Abolishing Slavery and its Contemporary Forms* (Geneva, 2002).

form of punishment.[45] Those subjected to forced labour can be found in Europe, the Americas, Asia, the Middle East and Africa. The main contemporary forms of slavery in the world today fall into the following categories, which all include a forced labour component.

Debt bondage (also referred to as bonded labour) occurs when an individual offers their labour in exchange for a loan, but then loses all control over their conditions of work and the amount they are paid. Their debt is often inflated through excessive interest rate charges and can be passed on to other family members. This practice affects millions of people in south Asia, particularly in India, Pakistan and Nepal. Serfdom is also a problem in this region. For example, research carried out in Pakistan by the Pakistan Institute for Labour Education and Research estimated that millions of people were forced to provide unpaid labour for their landlord on their farm or in their house – a practice known as *beggar*. The continued existence of debt bondage and serfdom in the sub-continent partly explains why the Asia and the Pacific region accounts for so many of the world's forced labourers – nearly 9.5 million out of the 12.3 million total estimated by the International Labour Organization. However, these problems are not confined to Asia. In Latin America, debt bondage has been documented in countries like Bolivia, Brazil, Paraguay and Peru. Debt bondage is also a mechanism by which traffickers seek to control migrant workers and force them to work in conditions they did not agree to.

The unconditional worst forms of child labour are defined in *International Labour Organization Convention No. 182* as slavery, trafficking, debt bondage and other forms of forced labour; forced recruitment for use in armed conflict; prostitution, pornography and other illicit activities. These practices affect millions of children all over the world. For example, the forced recruitment of children for use in armed conflicts alone takes place in Burma (Myanmar), Burundi, Colombia, Côte d'Ivoire, Democratic Republic of the Congo, Nepal, Philippines, Somalia, Sri Lanka, Sudan and Uganda.[46] The International Labour Organization forced labour report estimates that between 40 and 50 per cent of the total number of forced labourers are children. However, the report stresses that it is a minimum estimate and a previous International Labour Organization publication, which focused exclusively on child labour, found that there were 8.4 million children in the unconditional worst forms of child labour.[47]

The International Labour Organization estimates that at any one time there are some 2.5 million people in the world who have been trafficked into forced labour and draws attention to the fact that 32 per cent of those trafficked are used exclusively for labour exploitation (e.g. domestic work, agricultural work, catering, packing and processing, etc.). The International Labour Organization stresses that 'in all countries and regions migrant workers, particularly irregular migrants, are at particular risk of

---

[45] International Labour Office, *A Global Alliance against Forced Labour* (Geneva, 2005). Unless otherwise stated statistics in this section are taken from this report.

[46] United Nations Secretary-General, *Report of the Secretary-General to the General Assembly Security Council on Children in Armed Conflict* (Geneva, 9 Feb. 2005).

[47] International Labour Office, *A Future Without Child Labour* (Geneva, 2002).

coercive recruitment and employment practices'.[48] Trafficking for sexual exploitation almost exclusively affects women and girls (98 per cent), but trafficking for labour exploitation also affects women more than men (56 per cent being women and girls).

While it is individuals and not states who are responsible for almost 80 per cent of forced labour cases around the world today, some governments are still directly responsible for the exaction of forced labour. The most well known international case is that of Burma where the military compels sections of the civilian population to undertake a variety of work, including construction projects and road repairs. The government of North Korea routinely exacts forced labour from those held in detention centres and labour camps and the Chinese government imposes Re-education through Labour on those detained for drug addiction, theft and prostitution. The Re-education through Labour is an administrative system that lacks judicial process and can lead to up to three years' detention. Some 260,000 people were detained in China under this system at the beginning of 2004.[49]

In some countries people are compelled to perform work for others simply because of their caste or ethnic group. For example, in Niger, research carried out by the non-governmental organization Timidria found that the majority of the 11,000 people interviewed could identify individuals by name as their masters and were expected to work for them without pay. Over 80 per cent of respondents said their master took key decisions in their lives, such as who they would marry and whether their children went to school. The allocation of labour on the basis of caste is a significant problem in south Asia. *Dalits* are assigned tasks and occupations which are deemed ritually polluting by other caste communities (e.g. the removal of human and animal waste, sweeping, disposal of dead animals, leatherwork, etc.). Refusal to perform such tasks leads to physical abuse and social boycott.

4. The Role of Parliament in Challenging Slavery Today

With millions of people still held in slavery around the world it is clear that parliament still has an important role to play in combating slavery in the twenty-first century. Indeed in recent years parliament has engaged with international slavery issues and been closely involved in the development of the policy relating to trafficking and the use of forced labour in the United Kingdom. Since 2001, there have been dozens of debates and parliamentary questions tabled on trafficking in both houses of parliament. An early day motion (E.D.M.) tabled by Tony Coleman on trafficking of women into the United Kingdom drew attention to the problem and called for increased penalties for those responsible (E.D.M. no. 536, tabled on 6 December 2001). The early day motion received the support of 188 M.P.s – only 40 of 2,163 early day motions tabled in that parliamentary session had more support.

The establishment in 2001 of a broad coalition of organizations to campaign on the need for legislation to prohibit trafficking and for the government to fund support

---

[48] International Labour Office, *A Global Alliance Against Forced Labour*, p. 18. For more on the relationship between migration and trafficking see Mike Kaye, *The Migration-Trafficking Nexus* (2003).

[49] International Labour Office, *A Global Alliance Against Forced Labour*, p. 27.

services for trafficked people did much to generate parliamentary interest in the issue. This campaign helped to stimulate hundreds of newspaper, television and radio reports on trafficking, as well as mobilize members of the public to take up these concerns with their M.P.s and with the government directly.[50]

Parliamentary and public pressure led to the government giving greater priority to trafficking. This was reflected in the decision to provide government funding to a non-governmental organization to provide specialized support and assistance to women trafficked into prostitution in the United Kingdom from March 2003 and in the fact that three separate pieces of primary legislation were approved between 2002 and 2004 to criminalize trafficking of people for all forms of exploitation.

During the passage of this legislation, the government proved responsive to concerns raised by non-governmental organizations and backbench M.P.s. Neil Gerrard tabled amendments to the proposed legislation in both 2003 and 2004 to highlighted weaknesses in the definitions of offences for trafficking for both sexual and labour exploitation. This led the government to review and amend the wording of the definitions to meet these concerns.

Parliament has continued to consider the issue of trafficking in 2005–6, particularly in relation to the protection and support of trafficked people. This is seen in the fact that more than 100 M.P.s supported Sandra Gidley's early day motion which called on the government to sign and ratify the Council of Europe Convention on Trafficking (E.D.M. no. 452, tabled on 29 June 2005) and by the Joint Committee on Human Rights' decision to undertake an inquiry into the human rights of people trafficked into the United Kingdom in 2006.

Foreign policy concerns relating to a variety of slavery practices are also regularly addressed in parliament. For example, recent early day motions have gained substantial support on diverse slavery issues, including bonded labour (E.D.M. no. 81, tabled by Eddie McGrady on 12 December 2000), slavery in cocoa production (E.D.M. no. 1440, tabled by Oona King on 13 June 2002) and contemporary forms of slavery (E.D.M. no. 681, tabled by David Drew on 17 January 2002) – the last of which attracted the support of 232 M.P.s.[51]

There is also scope for parliament to address issues which go to the root causes of slavery, like discrimination and poverty. Those subjected to forced labour are frequently from minority or marginalized groups. For example, slavery in Sudan affects different ethnic or religious groups. Bonded labour in India, Nepal and Pakistan disproportionately affects *dalits* and those who are considered to be of 'low' caste, *adivasis* (indigenous people) or people from other minority groups (including religious minorities). Similarly, caste or ethnic status underpins the use of forced labour in Niger and Mauritania, while in Paraguay, Bolivia and Peru it is indigenous peoples who are mainly affected by debt bondage. These same groups are also among the

[50] As part of Anti-Slavery International's campaign more than 15,000 people either signed petitions or wrote to their local M.P.s urging action to criminalize trafficking and provide protection and assistance to the victims. This figure does not include the thousands of people who undertook campaigning activity in response to calls from other N.G.O.s who were involved in the coalition.

[51] There have also been regular debates on country specific or general aspects of slavery. See for example, the international trafficking of women (15 Sept. 2004), the struggle against slavery (14 Oct. 2004) and slavery (7 July 2005).

Figure 3 Bonded labourers at work in a quarry in India. (By permission of Georgina Cranston and Anti-Slavery International.)

most impoverished sections of society in their respective countries. Those in extreme poverty are more likely to be subjected to slavery-like practices and those that are subjected to contemporary forms of slavery are unlikely to break out of a cycle of poverty and coerced labour.

Parliament therefore has a role in reviewing the relevant national policies and those of inter-governmental organizations to which the United Kingdom contributes funding in order to consider whether their poverty reduction strategy papers and long term development targets like the millennium development goals adequately take account of slavery issues.

In 2006, the *United Nations Supplementary Convention on the Abolition of Slavery, the Slave Trade and Institutions and Practices Similar to Slavery* had its fiftieth anniversary. Although this is one of the basic international standards which prohibits slavery practices, there are still more than 70 countries that have not ratified it. This, along with the continued existence of millions of forced labourers around the world, highlights the importance of sustaining the dynamic relationship between campaigning, public opinion and parliament which has proved effective in challenging and eliminating various manifestations of slavery over the last 200 years.[52]

The anti-slavery movement today continues to draw inspiration form the 1807 campaign both in terms of its effectiveness in mobilizing public opinion for political change, as well as from the advocacy techniques it pioneered and which have become the framework for successful human rights campaigns today.

[52] For more information on contemporary forms of slavery see Anti-Slavery International's website at www.antislavery.org or for information on how to support current campaigns go to: http://www.antislavery.org/2007/.

Exhibition Catalogue

Edited by Melanie Unwin

Introduction

The British Slave Trade: Abolition, Parliament and People is the latest in a series of parliamentary exhibitions open to the public in Westminster Hall. It seeks to explain why the abolition of the slave trade was a momentous issue in the moral and economic life of the country. As well as examining the role of key abolitionists and their endeavours to raise support for their cause, it demonstrates how parliament investigated the business of the slave trade and slavery. The focus of the exhibition is on the 30-year period leading up to the enactment of the bill for the abolition of the slave trade in 1807, the passing of that act was itself only a starting point in the campaign to abolish slavery; however the subsequent campaign, with its many vicissitudes, falls outside the remit of this exhibition. This catalogue documents the exhibits and provides a short explanation of their relevance to the subject. A bibliography is appended for those wishing to investigate the subject further.

Exhibitions in Westminster Hall are intended to support parliament's objective of promoting public knowledge and understanding of its role. This exhibition demonstrates how the legislative process was directly affected by the swirling (often conflicting) currents of popular opinion and commercial interests. There are striking resonances with parliament today. Evidence presented to parliamentary committees plays a key role; mass publications sway the mood of parliament; and pressure groups intensively lobby the various players. The exhibition includes two petitions submitted to parliament from the people of Manchester. The submitting of petitions is an example of a method of communicating with parliament which is still open to the public and actively used.

To engage young people, particularly those who are soon to be voters, in the work of parliament is an important imperative of the Parliamentary Education Service. Their appointment of Rommi Smith as writer-in-residence to the exhibition has been a new and exciting departure for parliamentary exhibitions. Her work will provide a unique opportunity for those pupils directly involved with the residency, but will also provide teaching resources which will be available to schools across the country.

Given the emotive and complex subject matter, no exhibition can fully capture all the nuances of the debate. So our exhibition is accompanied by a number of other events to explore these. A series of seminars has been organised in partnership with the History of Parliament Trust at the Institute of Historical Research. The *On the Road to Abolition* project has been undertaken in partnership with the National Gallery, National Portrait Gallery, Tate Britain and Westminster City Council and Archives. The project includes a map, website and downloadable audio tour (www.westminster.gov.uk/abolition) of the sites around Westminster which relate to the slave trade and black history in the area.

The online resource developed by the Parliamentary Archives, *Parliament and the British Slave Trade 1600-1807* (www.parliament.uk/slavetrade) allows some of the exhibition exhibits to be explored in more detail, but also draws extensively on the vast range of archival material which documents parliament's relationship with this issue. Designed as an interactive resource the website provides a reference point for visitors to the exhibition as well as those unable to come to London. The exhibition's writer-in-residence has been actively involved in the development of the website, which has provided another outlet for her work.

We hope that the website and this publication will provide a lasting legacy for the exhibition, allowing the material drawn together during this bicentenary year to be widely available in the future. This will provide the impetus for greater research into, and understanding of, the subject of Britain's involvement with the slave trade.

Acknowledgements

I am very grateful to Stephen Farrell and James Walvin for their invaluable work, support and help during the last two years. Machel Bogues joined the exhibition curatorial team a year ago and has brought an important perspective to the project for which I am also grateful. The Project Board members have provided significant input during the life of this project and have helped steer it safely to its culmination. The Advisory Board are owed a debt of thanks for their help and suggestions and sound guidance. I am personally very grateful to Baroness Young for her support and advice. The exhibition designers, Metaphor, graphic designers, Public Works Office, and audio scriptwriter, Jerome Vincent and Pier Productions have all made the exhibition an exciting and informative space.

I and the project team have benefited from the help of many individuals and organisations too numerous to name but who include: Paul Seaward, David Natzler, S. I. Martin, Philip Mould, Philip Attwood, Arthur Torrington, Tony Tibbles (for putting us on track at a very early stage and continued support), Madge Dresser, Cath Brookes, Peter Linge, Eithne Nightingale, Diane Hedditch and Dawn Hatch, Victor Launert, Mike McCann, Steve Cleary, Simon Roberton of Prudence Cuming Associates, Graham Howard and the organisations: Liverpool Maritime Museum, Burntwood School, Victoria and Albert Museum, Rendezvous of Victory, Manchester Local Family History Society and The Religious Society of Friends, to whom we are very grateful.

All the lenders to the exhibition are due thanks for their support. The staff and trustees of the Wisbech and Fenland Museum particularly have been very generous in lending us Thomas Clarkson's African Box, an important part of their collections especially in this bicentenary year. We are also grateful to Julia Park for her conservation services and advice on handling this unique item.

Anti-Slavery International have significantly contributed to this exhibition by curating the final section as well as lending objects from their own collection and providing representation on our Advisory Board for which we are grateful.

Our thanks go to all the authors of essays in the volume not only for their support of this project but for adherence to deadlines with good humour. I am particularly grateful to Marcus Wood whose unique insights into this subject have been a welcome intervention to the occasionally prosaic world of project management.

Finally, I must thank my colleagues in the curatorial office of the Palace of Westminster, whose help and support has made my involvement in this project possible, and Kelly Allnutt for her invaluable help over the last few months.

Melanie Unwin
January 2007

Curatorial team

Machel Bogues
Victoria and Albert Museum

Dr Stephen Farrell
History of Parliament

Professor James Walvin
Consultant Curator

Melanie Unwin
Deputy Curator, Palace of Westminster

Project Board

Dr John Benger (chair)
Jessica Bridges Palmer (press officer)
Tim Jarvis, Clerks Department
Jill Pay, Assistant Serjeant at Arms
David Prior, Assistant Clerk of the Records, Parliamentary Archives
Melanie Unwin, Exhibition Project Manager
Eliot Wilson, Clerks Department

Advisory Board

Exhibition Writer in Residence

1 *Slave on deck in chains*

British School
c.1820
Oil on board
260 mm height × 205 mm width
National Maritime Museum ZBA2428

Although painted after the abolition of the British slave trade, this oil sketch shows a young African boy, captive and bound with brass manacles and neck collar, on the deck of a ship, the sea being visible in the background to the right of the boy's elbow. The artist has captured the young African's misery and dejection as he is imprisoned, separated from friends and family, and transported across an ocean he may never before have seen to an unknown destination and to a life of enslavement. Slave traders had no interest in keeping together families or even people from the same region. Indeed, it was probably to their advantage to split up people who spoke the same language or who knew each other. Isolated and disorientated captives would be less able to organise resistance or escape from captivity while held in the British coastal forts in Africa, where they were incarcerated in dungeons until traded with slave ship captains, or on board.

We do not know this boy's name but the artist has depicted him as an individual who is lost in his own thoughts and emotions. The artist's sympathetic depiction enables the viewer to come to an understanding of those millions of people who were traded and enslaved as real people, unique individuals who actually existed, and not as an unknown faceless mass. For the abolitionist movement, conveying the realities of this trade in human beings to the inhabitants of Britain, who would see none of its distant horrors, set as they were in Africa and the Americas, was the hardest challenge.

2 Grocer's token

Obverse *M Lambe & Son Tea-Dealers & Grocers Bath 1794*
Reverse *Teas Coffee Spices & Sugar*
1794
Copper penny
29 mm diameter
National Maritime Museum ZBA2804

Tokens were used by eighteenth-century merchants as a promotional tool. They were produced to advertise a particular shop and may have been exchanged for goods or discount. Tokens were often of a standardised design, which could be personalised for a particular shop or merchant. This example has on the obverse an image of India House, the headquarters of the East India Company, in Leadenhall Street, London. The obverse includes a depiction of a camel and lists the goods available at M. Lambe and Sons, 'teas, coffee, spices and sugar', all exotic imported goods available for purchase by the people of Bath. Britain was by the 1700s a nation of consumers, drawing in goods from around the world via its maritime trade and naval power. An almost global network of mercantile trading was established by Britain, supported by the monarchy and parliament. The East India Company, established in 1600 by Elizabeth I, marked a beginning of state-sponsored overseas trade. By the late eighteenth century all the people of Britain, not purely the rich and middle class, could consume goods from overseas. In 1784 tea duties were reduced leading to a price war between merchants, and the price of tea fell. The more popular tea, and indeed coffee and chocolate became, so the demand for sugar grew. Sugar made these drinks palatable and the profitable sugar trade made it economically essential both to powerful individuals and to the country. The abolition of the slave trade and of slavery had a powerful opponent in the form of financial profit.

3 Guinea coin

17th century
Gold
25 mm diameter
Private Lender

This coin is called a 'guinea' because it was made from gold traded in Guinea, the 'Gold Coast', in West Africa. (Ships used in the slave trade, 'guinea ships' or 'guineamen' were also named after this coast.) The guinea coin was first struck by the Royal Mint to celebrate the founding of the Royal Adventurers trading into Africa. The guinea, equivalent to 21 shillings (in pre-decimal currency, one pound = 20 shillings), was so important that it became an established monetary unit in Britain. Guineas struck between 1664 and 1668 have a small elephant beneath the king's head, those struck between 1674 and 1684 have an elephant and castle.

The British Royal African Company was established in 1672 by royal charter under Charles II. In return for building and maintaining 17 forts on the African coast, the Royal African Company was awarded the monopoly on trading in captured Africans with the British colonies in the Caribbean and North America (the Americas). This charter was established solely for business profit for the British. It shows how the British were formally implicated in tolerating, and promoting, trading in human beings as an acceptable form of commerce.

The 23 shareholders in the Royal African Company included the king's brother, James, duke of York (subsequently James II). The forts were a combination of fortified settlement for the white population in charge of its business and prison for the Africans incarcerated, prior to being shipped to the Americas. They were fortified as a protection against attack either from Africans or, more dangerously due to their greater weaponry, from other European traders. By 1680 the Company was capturing, imprisoning and exporting an average of 5,000 Africans a year to the Americas. In the Americas the Africans were sold into slavery.

Other British merchants complained at their exclusion from such a profitable trade and the Royal African Company's monopoly was ended by the British government in 1698, thereby opening this 'trade' in human beings to all British traders.

4 The Slave Ship *Brookes* of Liverpool

Published by J Robertson, Edinburgh
1791
Wood engraving and letterpress
445 mm height × 296 mm width (bottom margin)
National Maritime Museum ZBA2721

In 1787 the Society for Effecting the Abolition of the Slave Trade was formed. Though a national organisation, it was the work of its London Committee which was to steer the campaign to eventual success. The London Committee was made up of a group of men, predominately associated with modern business and with a good understanding of the rapidly expanding consumer society that had emerged in the eighteenth century. It was their exploitation of marketing techniques, enabling the atrocities of the slave trade to be communicated to a mass audience, which was central to the abolition campaign's success. In 1788 they published speeches from the debate on Sir William Dolben's Slave Limitation (or Middle Passage) Bill, which rationed (by tonnage) the number of captive Africans that could be carried on a slave ship. The passing of this act offered opportunities for further publicity. Thomas Clarkson, a London Committee member, developed a plan of the *Brookes* slave ship produced by the Plymouth abolitionists into the detailed illustration we see here. The *Brookes* was allowed a maximum of 454 people. The plan shows bird's-eye views of the cargo decks, together with cross-sections. It graphically illustrates the amount of space allocated to each person. This plan was sent to every member of the house of commons and house of lords by the London Committee, who were lobbying for further debate on the slave trade. The black abolitionist Olaudah Equiano wrote to the Plymouth Committee:

> Having seen a plate representing the form in which Negroes are stowed on board the Guinea ships, which you are pleased to send to … Clarkson, a worthy friend of mine, I was filled with love and gratitude towards you for your humane interference on behalf of my oppressed countrymen. (*Olaudah Equiano, The Interesting Narrative and Other Writings* ed. Vincent Carretta [2003], p. 347.)

The plan was also distributed widely around the country where it had an immediate impact. It was accompanied by text which gave a graphic account of the conditions endured by prisoners on board the slave ships.

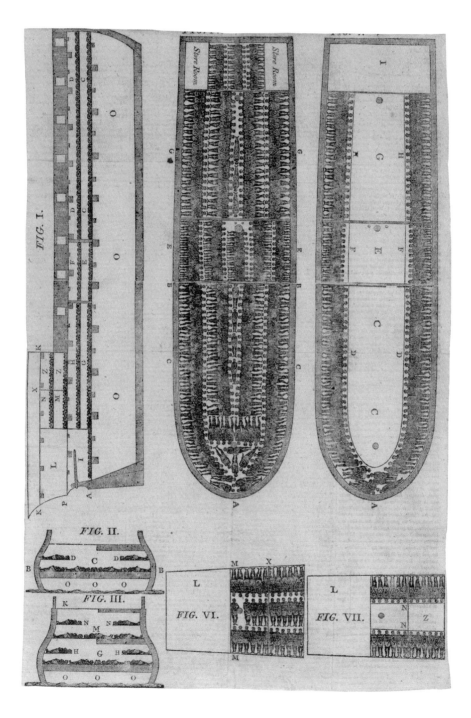

5 Model of the *Brookes*

Reproduction
Wood, brass, paint and paper
365 mm length × 92 mm height × 95 mm width

The original of this model is in the Wilberforce Museum in Hull. Wilberforce was
M.P. for Hull, his home town, from 1780-4, before becoming M.P. for Yorkshire.
Wilberforce was not formally involved with the campaign for abolition of the slave
trade until he was asked by his close friend, the newly elected prime minister, William
Pitt, to become the parliamentary spokesman for the campaign in 1787. The London
Committee made occasional contact with Wilberforce from October 1787, mainly
to ask him to raise the issue of abolition in debates, but it was not until 1791 that he
formally joined the Committee and became their spokesman in the house of commons.
After the circulation of the *Brookes* plan (see Catalogue No. 4), Wilberforce arranged
to have this model of the *Brookes* built, with the plan incorporated in it. As the lid
of the model shows, it was sent to Wilberforce at the house of commons, where he
would presumably have used it to support his arguments on the cruelty of the trade.

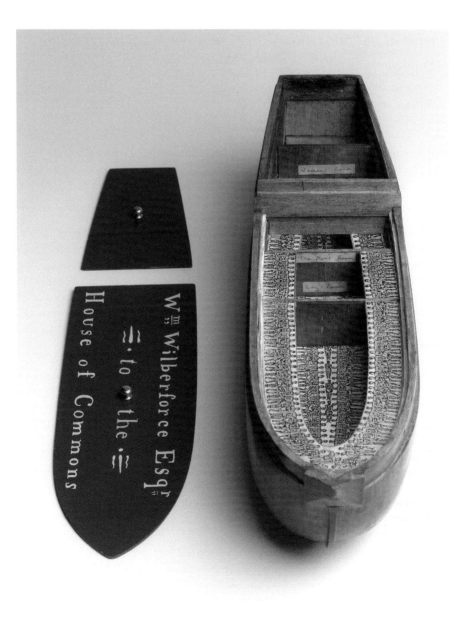

6 *An Account of the Ships that have arrived from the Coast of Africa in any of the British West India Islands between the Period of the 5th January 1791 and the 5th January 1796*

Delivered to the House of Lords from the Commissioners of the Customs on 24 June 1799

Paper and ink

560 mm height × 776 mm width (folded)

Parliamentary Archives HL/PO/JO/10/7/1105

This summary of the voyages of slave ships travelling between Africa and the British West Indies over a five-year period was laid before the house of lords on 24 June 1799 and ordered to be printed. Consequently the information it held would have been widely available.

The summary gives the name of each slave ship which sailed, the tonnage of the ship, the number of mariners (crew) aboard and an account of the 'Number of Slaves taken on board on the Coast of Africa' and the 'Number of slaves that arrived in the West Indies'. The numbers are further split into 'Grown Slaves, Males and Females' and 'Slaves under 4ft 4ins, Males and Females'. When captive Africans were loaded on the slave ships, their height determined whether they were considered as children or as adults. Anyone over the height of 4 feet 4 inches (132 cm) was considered an adult, regardless of age.

The page illustrated here is for the year 1792. The total number of captive Africans to arrive in the West Indies is given as 26,669, compared with a total of 31,553 who left Africa, meaning that 4,884 Africans (15.5%) died on board slave ships during these voyages.

The majority of deaths resulted from of malnutrition, sickness and disease, arising from the overcrowded and insanitary conditions and lack of medical attention, though some were the result of injuries from punishment beatings or violence during uprisings on board and, of course, suicides. Olaudah Equiano described the experience of being transported on board a slave ship:

> I was soon put down under the decks, and there I received such a salutation in my nostrils as I had never experienced in my life; so that with the loathsomeness of the stench, and crying together, I became so sick and low that I was not able to eat, nor had I the least desire to taste anything. (*Olaudah Equiano*, ed. Carretta, p. 56.) (see Catalogue No. 18 note★)

of the Ships that have arrived from the L

ish West India Islands between the per

& the Amount of the Tonnage and the Number of Mar

of the Slaves shipped on board each Ship on the Coas

ved in any of the said Islands.

	Number of Slaves taken on Board on the coast of Africa				Number of Slaves that arrived in the West Indies			
	Grown Slaves		Slaves und. 4.4		Grown Slaves		Slaves und. 4.4	
iners	Males	Females	Males	Females	Males	Females	Males	Females
23	179	41	24	9	168	39	24	9
8	140	83	28	28	112	72	20	14
19	198	152	27	42	137	103	18	28
9	168	36	16	9	164	35	16	9
20	154	63	31	21	148	60	31	20
17	98	53	45	26	92	52	41	26
11	114	45	31	19	114	45	30	18
20	141	116	12	15	132	113	11	14
13	79	32	6	5	76	31	6	5
13	100	68	6	12	93	63	5	11
13	142	131	23	12	94	106	10	12
16	93	44	16	6	88	39	12	6
22	218	77	30	21	214	77	36	19
11	61	54	10	6	61	52	18	5
24	212	112	64	75	139	81	43	55
30	124	34	55	24	122	33	53	23
15	82	35	17	15	76	34	17	15
17	108	79	44	36	89	50	43	32
23	188	99	11	12	182	96	10	12
21	235	111	36	31	221	104	54	31
8	48	10	2	1	47	10	2	1
15	95	53	24	27	89	51	23	26
8	3	2	49	26	3	2	49	25

7 Yoke

West Africa
19th century
Wood and metal
2310 mm length
Anti-Slavery International

Yokes were used to secure captive Africans together whilst moving them on foot. The 'Y' was fixed around a prisoner's neck and the other end was bound to the next yoke. The resulting line of prisoners is called a coffle. Prisoners were captured in a number of ways. The privy council committee inquiry of 1788-9 heard evidence from Isaac Parker, a witness put forward by Thomas Clarkson, who had been a member of armed raiding parties which, accompanied by an African trader Dick Ebro, had travelled up river from the coast and captured unsuspecting Africans. The British slavers brought with them a variety of goods made in British factories, as well as alcohol and guns, to trade with local leaders for their prisoners. As the trade became sophisticated and the demand for Africans grew, networks of traders became more widespread.

This is how Equiano described his own kidnapping:

> One day, when all our people were gone out to their works as usual, and only I and my dear sister were left to mind the house, two men and a woman got over our walls, and in a moment seized us both; and, without giving us time to cry out or make resistance, they stopped our mouths, tied our hands, and ran off with us into the nearest wood. (*Olaudah Equiano* ed. Carretta, p. 47.) (See Catalogue No. 18 note*)

Local African leaders and entrepreneurs became embroiled in the trade under pressure from the British and other Europeans, who forced them to trade for goods, including guns, which they desired. Africans were essential for the success of the slave trade, not only as captives for enslavement, but also as dealers and traders. However they worked within a trading structure established by the Europeans for profit. As Ottobah Cugoano explained:

> I must own, to the shame of my own countrymen, that I was first kid-napped and betrayed by some of my own complexion, who were the first cause of my exile and slavery; but if there were no buyers there would be no sellers. (Quobna Ottobah Cugoano, *Thoughts and Sentiments on the Evil of Slavery and other Writings* ed. Vincent Carretta [1999], p. 16.)

8 Slave ownership bracelet and key

Engraved *S. Bosanquet Layton 1746*
1746
Steel
80 mm diameter
National Maritime Museum ZBA2474

Unlike most manacles, this 'bracelet' was not designed for restraint but more likely to identify either the 'owner' of the enslaved wearer or their plantation, in this case 'S. Bosanquet Layton'. Branding was quite widespread in the British West Indies, though by no means universal. Most enslaved Africans would not have been marked with the name of their 'owners'. This 'bracelet', which was locked on to the recipient, would seem to indicate that there was only a temporary need for such a form of identification. Though it was not common practice, it may be that Bosanquet Layton felt it necessary to 'tag' individuals when they were leaving the plantation, possibly to deliver a letter (see Catalogue No. 9). Wearing this 'bracelet' would not only identify the wearer's 'ownership', but would also clearly indicate that he or she was on official business and was not a runaway.

Many slaves did run away when given the opportunity; however, life as a runaway was not easy. Not only would a runaway be leaving family and friends at the plantation, an experience they would already have suffered during their original capture in Africa, but also abandoning the security of a shelter and the ready availability of food. The option of where to run was limited; return to Africa was impossible, so the alternative was a permanent existence avoiding recapture. The physical punishment suffered by a captured runaway was the main deterrent available to plantation owners so they were severe. Whippings, mutilations, facial brandings and the cutting off of ears were all common, and legal, penalties.

9 Slave-carried letter

Kingston, Jamaica
30 June 1785
375 mm height × 236 mm width, 16 pp
National Maritime Museum MGS/19

This letter was carried by 'Scipio', an enslaved African, who was from the Blue Mountain Estate (plantation), to Kingston. The letter gives a report on the overall condition of the estate. It includes an account of food shortages amongst the enslaved workers as the result of a hurricane:

> I am exceedingly sorry to acquaint you that the negroes are absolutely in greater want of Provisions now than they have been at any time since the Hurricane. It is something very extraordinary And a cruel disappointment to them the Plantane trees not bearing as yet.

The letter is signed William Sutherland, probably the estate manager and has three enclosures which list the names, condition (able, poorly, elderly etc.) and jobs of the 458 enslaved Africans on the Blue Mountain Estate on 1 January 1785 together with details of the stock and land. It also includes a monthly breakdown of the numbers of 'negroes' and mules that had died.

Enslaved Africans were not physically imprisoned on the plantations and were regularly sent off their owner's property as part of their work, such as delivering messages. Once off the plantation, a messenger could undertake more than their master's official business. Domestic news could be passed on, allowing family and friendship ties to be maintained between a number of plantations. Also, communications were maintained with communities of runaways and maroons, including the planning of revolts and uprisings.

The mountain ranges of Jamaica were where maroon communities developed. The maroons were a mixture of free black people, mulattos (people of mixed race) and fugitives, who did not want to live under the control of the British governor of Jamaica. The mountainous regions contained both land suitable for coffee production and areas of inaccessible forest and mountains, which the maroons made their own and which proved impossible for the plantation owners and British authorities to penetrate.

Gentlemen

I send herewith a List of the Negroes & Stock And a State of the Cane Pieces Taken the 1st day of January last. And I have endeavoured to make a short State of matters as on the last day of every month agreeable to the Instructions sent me. — I did not well know what to say on that head where the Instructions desire that a monthly Account of the Provisions growing & on hand may likewise be rendered. — In this Parish the Negroes never keep any Provisions on hand, nor is there ever any Guinea Corn Planted for them And except after a disaster such as happened on the 30th of July they always have Plenty of Provisions in their grounds.

I likewise send herewith an Acct. of all the Rum delivered from Blue Mountain Estate this Crop.

I am exceedingly sorry to acquaint you that the Negroes are absolutely in greater want of Provisions now than they have been at any time since the Hurricane. — It is something very extraordinary And a cruel disappointment to them the Plantane trees not bearing as yet. — They all trusted and depended upon having plenty of Plantanes before this time. — I never expected to be under the necessity of acquainting

10 Conch shell

Shell
155 mm length
Courtesy of Mary Healey

The conch shell or 'abeng', was blown like a horn as a signal between enslaved Africans, runaways and maroons in the West Indies. In 1789 it was reported to parliament that throughout the West Indies it was unlawful for slave owners to allow 'Slaves to assemble together, and beat their Military Drums, empty Casks, and great Gourds, or blow their Horns or Shells'. (James Walvin, *Black Ivory. Slavery in the British Empire* [Oxford, 2001], p. 141.)

The fight against British slavery was not just being fought by abolitionists in Britain, but by the enslaved themselves, who took any opportunity offered to them to resist their imprisonment and forced labour. Individual acts could include anything from merely working slowly, to extreme acts such as poisoning the meals served to the plantation owners. But group acts of revolt and rebellion required communication over distances. Drums and horns were traditional forms of communication in Africa and the enslaved Africans continued to use them in the West Indies.

The abeng was also one of the primary forms of communication for the maroons of Jamaica. The maroon communities were established between 1655–1738, in five major towns (Accompong, Trelawny Town, Moore Town, Scots Hall, Nanny Town), in Jamaica's remote mountain regions. The maroons were in constant conflict with the British army who tried to ensure their recapture and prevent further slaves finding refuge. Despite taking on the might of the British army, the maroons were never defeated and the British were forced to sign a peace treaty with the maroons guaranteeing them their continued freedom and rights to the land they had already cultivated. In exchange the maroons agreed to return any future runaways to the plantations.

An abeng was once famously used in the Haitian slave rebellion to warn against impending attack. Consequently an abeng frequently appears in memorials and statues which commemorate slavery and the resistance of the enslaved when fighting for their freedom.

11 *Ignatius Sancho*

Francesco Bartolozzi, after Thomas Gainsborough
Published 1802
Stipple engraving
179 mm height × 119 mm width (paper size)
National Portrait Gallery NPG D23441 (Given by Henry Witte Martin, 1861-10-19)

In 1773 Ignatius Sancho (1729-80) bought a shop at No. 19 Charles Street, thereby establishing himself in the Westminster landscape and entitling him, by way of property ownership, to the vote. Sancho was a remarkable man: a published author and composer, a prolific letter writer, a man of taste and sensibility, whose friends included the author and parson Laurence Sterne, the politician Charles James Fox (for whom Sancho voted in the 1780 election) and the artist Thomas Gainsborough, who painted his portrait. Sancho was an accepted and respected member of London intellectual and artistic society. These were substantial achievements for someone born, not only into slavery, but actually on a slave ship. Orphaned shortly after birth, he was brought to England as a baby and 'given' to three sisters as a 'pet'. He was noticed by the duke of Montagu, who encouraged him to learn to read. Sancho worked as a servant for the Montagu family until 1771.

The majority of the black population in London, which numbered in the thousands by the late eighteenth century, were poor, often being servants or entertainers either in theatres or on the streets. Despite their numbers, black figures still attracted attention and sometimes abuse. Sancho, recording an evening out with his family, recalled:

> We went by water – had a coach home – were gazed at – followed, &c. &c. – but not much abused. (*The Letters of Ignatius Sancho* ed. Paul Edwards and Polly Rewt [Edinburgh, 1994], p. 104.)

However, some, like Ignatius Sancho, Ottobah Cugoano and Olaudah Equiano, were well-known figures who, as independent men, moved in polite society and used their position in society to promote abolition and to speak out against the injustices of slavery. Sancho's own life illustrated that Africans were equal in every way to the Europeans who enslaved them, and undermined the argument that Africans were mentally and culturally inferior.

In 1782, two years after his death, the *Letters of Ignatius Sancho, an African, to Which are Prefixed Memoirs of his Life* was published. This volume, which included many letters expressing his opposition to slavery and the slave trade, was an important influence in the fight for abolition.

Ignatius Sancho.

Published as the Act directs, July 2d 1781, by I. Nichols Red Lion Passage, Fleet Street.

12 *William Murray, 1st Earl of Mansfield*

Jean Baptiste van Loo

c.1737-38

Oil on canvas

749 mm height × 622 mm width

National Portrait Gallery NPG 474

William Murray, 1st earl of Mansfield (1705-93), was from 1756 the lord chief justice of king's bench, which was the highest jurisdiction of common law in the country. Scottish by birth, he had been educated at Westminster School and Christ Church, Oxford. At the time this portrait was painted, he was establishing a successful legal practice in London and had close connexions with the house of commons. Van Loo was a very fashionable French portraitist who worked in London between 1737 and 1742. In selecting van Loo for his portrait, Mansfield was inviting attention to himself as an important and notable lawyer.

Mansfield's involvement with the slave trade as lord chief justice was wide ranging. He had personal investments in plantation land in Virginia. His court heard a number of cases which discussed the issue of the legality of slavery in England. Mansfield was an establishment figure and had no intention of declaring all enslaved Africans in Britain free. However, he did prevent a number of individuals, such as James Somerset, from being forcibly returned to slave colonies by their former 'owners'. Mansfield's resistance to ruling slavery illegal in Britain (as opposed to the British colonies) infuriated the humanitarian and abolitionist Granville Sharp, who persistently brought cases to Mansfield's court in the hope that this would force Mansfield to make a definitive ruling. Mansfield's position was typical of many, in that, whilst they believed in personal liberty, they did not wish either to constrain a very profitable economic trade, or to take responsibility for what happened outside Britain in Africa or the colonies and the law upheld this position.

Mansfield had a further connexion with the slave trade. Mansfield's nephew had had an illegitimate daughter with a black woman. The daughter, Dido Elizabeth Belle (c.1763–1804), was taken in by Mansfield and brought up with two of Mansfield's other great-nieces who lived permanently at his home, Kenwood House, Hampstead. It would not have been unusual for Dido to have been taken into Mansfield's household as a servant. Black servants were a fashionable status symbol. Dido, however, was not treated purely as a servant, but more like a member of the family. Yet Mansfield did not grant Dido her freedom during his lifetime, though he did so in his will.

13 *Interior of Westminster Hall*

J Bluck after A C Pugin and T Rowlandson

Published in *The Microcosm of London* (R. Ackermann, 3 vols, 1808-10)

1809

Coloured aquatint

254 mm height × 204 mm width

Palace of Westminster WOA 544

Westminster Hall was the site of the law courts from 1178 until the 1820s. In 1739 the architect William Kent (1685-1748) designed the screen which was erected to separate off the courts from the rest of the Hall when they were sitting. The court behind the left-hand side of the screen was the king's bench (the court of chancery was on the right). Here Lord Mansfield presided over some of the most important cases which brought the injustice of the slave trade and slavery to the attention of the British public.

An early case that was to prove significant to the abolitionist movement was the Somerset case, heard in 1772. James Somerset, an enslaved African, had been brought to England in 1769 by his 'owner'. Somerset had run away and was living independently when he was recaptured and put on board a ship destined for the Americas. The case was brought on the ground that Somerset's former 'owner' had no right to force Somerset to return to the Americas because it was the constitutional right of every man in England to have the liberty of his person. Mansfield eventually ruled that Somerset should be set free as he had been unlawfully imprisoned and no one, including his 'owner' had the right to force him to return to the Americas. However Mansfield was careful not to suggest that enslaved Africans in Britain were automatically free. Despite this, the case was considered a substantial victory, and the black community in London, many of whom had attended the trial, celebrated in style. As reported in the *Public Advertiser* newspaper of 27 June 1772:

> On Monday nearly 200 Blacks, with their Ladies, had an Entertainment at a Public House in Westminster, to celebrate the Triumph which their Brother Somerset had obtained over Mr Stuart his Master. Lord Mansfield's Health was echoed round the Room; and the Evening was concluded with a Ball. The Tickets for Admittance to the black Assembly were 5s each. (Approximately equivalent to £25 today)

WESTMINSTER HALL.

14 *Granville Sharp*

George Dance
1794
Pencil on paper
248 mm height × 184 mm width
National Portrait Gallery NPG 1158

Granville Sharp first became personally aware of the situation of enslaved Africans in London in 1765. Jonathan Strong, a black man, horribly injured as a result of a beating by his 'owner', who had left him for dead, was found on the doorstep of Granville's brother's surgery. The Sharps cared for Strong during his recovery and subsequently found him a job. When in 1767 Strong was recaptured by his former 'owner', he appealed to Granville Sharp for help, which Sharp despite having no previous experience of the law, gave. This led to Sharp's long involvement with cases trying to secure freedom for enslaved black people in Britain and the abolitionist movement. The Somerset case (see Catalogue No. 13) was the most notable of these trials. Sharp had close contact with the black abolitionists, who counted him among their friends and used him to take forward cases that came to their attention.

After the Somerset case, the next notable triumph for the abolitionists and Sharp was the *Zong* trial. The slave ship *Zong* had left the African coast in 1781, under Captain Luke Collingwood, full of African prisoners. Conditions on board ship were particularly bad, with sickness threatening the lives of most of the African captives and crew, and water running short. Collingwood decided to throw 133 of the Africans overboard in order to ensure that he arrived with enough living Africans to make a profit. He could also then claim against the ship's insurance for the Africans he had drowned. The case came to court in London as an insurance dispute. The insurance company lost its case since Collingwood was deemed to have taken action necessary to save the ship; murder was not a charge that could be brought as the law viewed the Africans as no different from other forms of property, like horses or cattle. Equiano, reading of the case in the newspaper, brought it to Sharp's attention. Sharp persuaded the insurance company to appeal, though he could only do this on the grounds that the ship had not been in danger and that Collingwood's action had been the result of his mismanagement of the voyage. The request for an appeal was heard in front of Lord Mansfield in Westminster Hall in 1783, when Sharp was in court to hear Mansfield grant a new trial. A new court case was not however heard, partially due to Collingwood's death. However the case once again brought the inhumanity of the slave trade to the public's attention.

15 *Thomas Clarkson*

Carl Frederik von Breda

1788

Oil on canvas

908 mm height × 705 mm width

National Portrait Gallery NPG 235 (Bequeathed by Henry Crabb Robinson, 1867)

Thomas Clarkson (1760-1846) was one of the driving forces behind the campaign for abolition. This portrait, painted in 1788, shows Clarkson at the beginning of a seven year period of campaigning which turned anti-slavery sentiments from the passion of a few into a mass public movement for abolition.

Born in Wisbech, Cambridgeshire, Clarkson was at Cambridge University preparing to become a clergyman when he entered the 1785 annual essay competition, the title set being 'Is it lawful to enslave the unconsenting?' Clarkson won the competition and in researching his essay learnt about and was horrified by the Atlantic slave trade. Riding home from a public reading of his essay in London he was resting at Wadesmill, Hertfordshire, when:

> a thought came into my mind, that if the contents of the Essay were true, it was time some person should see these calamities to their end. (Thomas Clarkson, *The History of the Rise, Progress and Accomplishment of the Abolition of the African Slave-Trade by the British Parliament* [2 vols, 1808], I, 210.)

Within a year Clarkson had given up entering the Church and had decided to devote himself full-time to abolition. In 1787 Clarkson was one of the original 12 members of the London Committee along with Granville Sharp, Philip Sansom, and the quakers William Dillwyn, Samuel Hoare, George Harrison, John Lloyd, Joseph Woods, James Phillips, Richard Phillips, John Barton and Joseph Hooper. As the only Committee member without business commitments, Clarkson undertook the work of researching the trade for evidence that could be laid before parliament, and promoting the cause for abolition nationwide. He travelled to all the major ports as well as cities and towns around Britain. Clarkson rode over 35,000 miles during the next seven years. As well as giving public lectures and collecting evidence, Clarkson continued to write pamphlets which the London Committee published in great numbers, such as *An Essay on the Impolicy of the African Slave Trade* (1788) which he is holding in this portrait. Clarkson's research was to prove crucial to Wilberforce's work in the house of commons. Clarkson provided Wilberforce, and the privy council and house of commons committees (see Catalogue Nos 20 and 21), with evidence of the horror and degradation the slave trade inflicted on its African captives. He also provided evidence of the brutalisation and deaths of mariners involved in the trade and proof that there were profitable opportunities to trade in commodities, and not in people, with Africa.

16 *The Abolition of the Slave Trade*

Sub-titled *Or the Inhumanity of Dealers in human flesh exemplified in the Cruel treatment of a Young Negro Girl of 15 for her Virgin Modesty*

Isaac Cruikshank (1756-1811)
Published by S W Fores, No 3 Piccadilly
10 April 1792
Hand-coloured etching
335 mm height × 240 mm width
National Maritime Museum ZBA2503

On the 2 April 1792 Wilberforce described to the house of commons the brutal whipping of a captive African woman being transported on a slave ship, who had died five days later. The M.P.s in the Commons called for Wilberforce to name the culprit, to which he replied 'Captain Kimber'.

This image shows the African woman suspended by the ankle. The sailor who is hauling on the rope is saying *Dam me if I like it I have a good mind to let go*, the other two sailors are commenting *M Eyes Jack our girles at Wapping are never flogged for their modesty*, and *By G-d that's too bad if he had taken her to bed to him it would be well enough, Split me I'm almost sick of the Black Business.* Kimber flogged the woman because she refused to dance when ordered to (and Cruikshank is also suggesting she refused Kimber sexual favours). Forced dancing was used as a form of exercise to keep captive Africans healthy during the long voyage to the Americas, most of which was spent locked below deck in the overcrowded conditions exemplified by the *Brookes* plan (see Catalogue No. 4).

The last two decades of the eighteenth century saw a huge proliferation of print selling, especially in London. Political prints were particularly popular and new printing techniques made them relatively quick and cheap to produce. This print was published only five days after Wilberforce had made the event newsworthy with his Commons speech. It both draws attention to a brutal act, and comments on it via the sailors' remarks, which indicate a sympathetic position. It also serves to highlight Clarkson's argument that the trade dehumanised those who worked in it as well as the victims of it. However, the print also has sexual and pornographic overtones. The faceless female victim is deprived of her identity though her body is completely exposed to Kimber, the sailors, and the viewer.

Kimber was consequently tried for the murder, but was acquitted on the ground that the woman had died of disease, not of her injuries. Evidence given in the court case indicated she was suffering from venereal disease, ironically something she would have caught as a result of sexual attack by her captors.

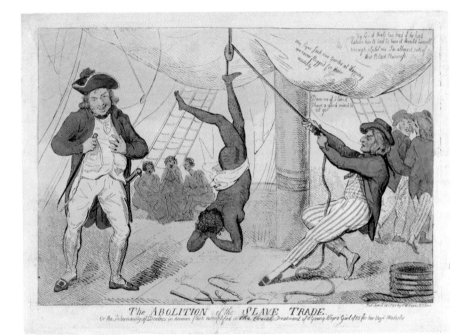

17 ANTI-SACCHARRITES, - or - JOHN BULL and his Family leaving off the use of SUGAR

Sub-titled *To the Masters & Mistresses of Families in Great Britain, this Noble Example of Œconomy, is respectfully submitted*

James Gillray (1756-1815)

Published by H. Humphrey, No 18 Old Bond Street

27 March 1792

Coloured engraving

316 mm height × 407 mm width (sight size)

Palace of Westminster WOA 5198

In 1791 William Fox published his *Address to the People of Great Britain, on the Propriety of Abstaining from West Indian Sugar and Rum*. Its publication, which ran to 15 impressions, with over 70,000 copies printed and distributed within four months, inspired 'anti-saccharism' – a national sugar boycott which, like the petitioning campaigns, kept the abolition campaign newsworthy and popular. Fox's publication was not in fact an abolitionist tract, but was inspired by an unexpected shortage of West Indian sugar, caused by the St Domingue revolution and the consequent termination of that French island's sugar exports (see Catalogue No. 19). Clarkson realised what an opportunity the boycott presented to the abolitionist campaign and, suggesting that every person who gave up sugar was also a potential signatory for a petition, recommended his local contacts to support and promote the boycott.

Gillray's cartoon satirises the royal family's involvement with the boycott. The king and queen (George III and Queen Charlotte) are at the tea table with their six daughters. The king, tasting his sugar-free tea, pronounces *O delicious! delicious!* for his sulky and dismayed daughters' benefit. The queen encourages them *O my dear Creatures, do but taste it! You can't think how nice it is without Sugar:- and then consider how much Work you'll save the poor Blackeemoors by leaving off the use of it! – and above all, remember how much expence it will save your poor Papa! – O its charming cooling Drink!* The Queen's apparent enthusiasm reflects the central role that women had in the boycott. Responsibility for the running of the domestic arrangements and the provision of food and drink meant that women had the power mandatorily to introduce the boycott to their households. The mention of the 'expence' of the sugar is Gillray's reference to the known meanness of the king and queen. Those rich enough to do so, could buy East Indian sugar produced outside the slave system, thereby supporting the boycott but not giving up their sweet tea. The fundamental irony of Gillray's cartoon is that George III was opposed to abolition, so his boycotting of sugar was purely for financial purposes.

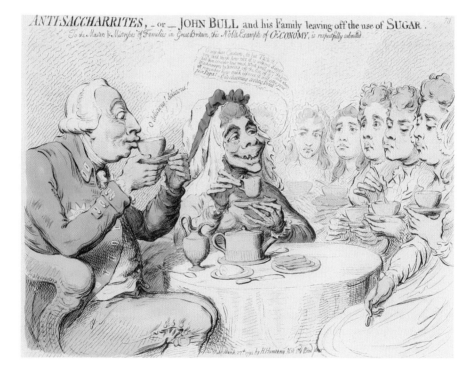

18 *The Interesting Narrative of the life of Olaudah Equiano, or Gustavus Vassa, the African. Written by himself*

1st edition, 2 volumes, London
1789
178 mm × 114 mm × 24 mm (binding Volume I) 181 mm × 114 mm × 22 mm (binding Volume II)
Private Collection

Olaudah Equiano (1745-97) was an active abolitionist. His book gives an account of his life in Africa, his kidnapping, and subsequent sale for transportation to Barbados and consequent enslavement.* It continues to track his life through freedom, and re-enslavement, travelling to England and his adventures as a free man. Equiano was a leading member of the black community. He helped enslaved Africans to gain and maintain their freedom and worked with Granville Sharp on the legal cases involving Africans. His publication of his autobiography was central to his campaigning for the abolition of slavery and the trade. Equiano, as his portrait in the frontispiece of his autobiography illustrates, was a member of fashionable society; and, as such, he was able to use his contacts to finance its publication. Equiano secured 600 subscribers, including white abolitionists, M.P.s, royalty, clergymen, businessmen and many members of the aristocracy. One of the businessmen was William, Ignatius Sancho's son. Equiano knew that the names of subscribers gave the book status and would have chosen his approaches carefully. On the publication of his autobiography, Equiano made a national tour to promote the book. He also advertised its publication in local newspapers.

After the frontispiece, Equiano opens his book with an address:

> To the Lords Spiritual and Temporal, and the Commons of the Parliament of Great Britain ... the chief design [of the *Narrative* being] to excite in your august assemblies a sense of compassion for the miseries which the Slave Trade has entailed on my unfortunate countrymen.

No doubt Equiano understood that, for all that his entire book would do to raise awareness of the miseries of the slave trade in the general population, it was parliament that had to be convinced.

His book ran to nine British editions during his lifetime and continued to be reprinted after his death, including in Dutch, German and Russian translations.

---

* There is now some dispute over the authenticity of some of Equiano's autobiography, as there is evidence of his having been born in the Americas and not in Africa. If this is the case, his account of being kidnapped and transported on a slave ship as a young man is not his own, though he would have undoubtedly heard similar accounts from other enslaved workers who had experienced them at first hand.

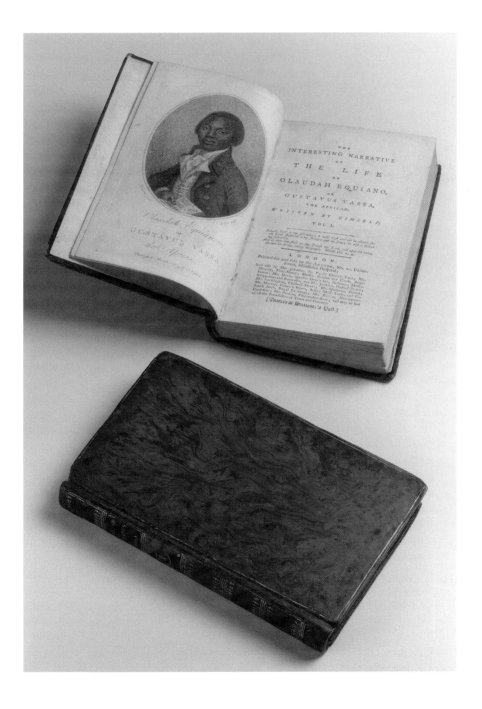

19 *Toussaint-L'Ouverture*

Francois Bonneville, after unknown artist
Published early 19th century
Mixed-method engraving,
216 mm height × 133 mm width (plate size) 298 height × 210 mm width (paper size)
National Portrait Gallery NPG D8212

François-Dominique Toussaint L'Ouverture (c.1743-1803) was born in St Domingue, a French West Indian colony. His father, an Arrada from the Dahomey Coast in Africa, had been captured and brought to the West Indies where he had been enslaved. Toussaint was born into slavery and whilst denied of his freedom had not known a life before enslavement. This is perhaps partially why he progressed on the plantation, learning to read and write, and earning his own freedom in 1777.

When news of the French Revolution (1789) reached St Domingue, the announcement by the National Assembly in France that all men were free and equal was not embraced by the colony's governor or plantation owners. They were unwilling to extend the *Declaration of the Rights of Man* to their enslaved workers or the rest of the black population. Unsurprisingly, widespread and violent revolts and uprisings were instigated, initially by the mulattos and maroons and then by the enslaved population. Toussaint, uncertain at first and rejecting the violence that was caused, nevertheless emerged as a leader in 1791. Over the next 13 years, armed struggle continued between the black and white populations of the island, the French, the Spanish and the British, all of whom wanted to seize the colony. In 1793 the British attempted to take the colony so as to reintroduce slavery, fearful that their own enslaved workers would follow the example of the St Domingue black population if the revolt were not put down. They were eventually forced out in 1797. Many thousands of British soldiers died of disease during the partial occupation, causing the British abolitionist campaign much damage as parliament debated the cost both in terms of lives and financially. In 1804, the year after Toussaint had died in a French prison, St Domingue was declared independent as the state of Haiti, the first black republic in the Americas.

Bonneville del. et Sculp.

TOUSSAINT LOUVERTURE

Général en Chef à St. Domingue.

A Paris chez l'Auteur rue St. Jacques N. 195.

20 *Report of the Lords of the Committee of Council appointed for the Consideration of all Matters relating to Trade and Foreign Plantations, 1789*

Printed 1789
Paper
377 mm height × 235 mm width (binding, closed)
Parliamentary Archives HL/PO/JO/10/5/133/1

In February 1788 the prime minister, William Pitt, commissioned a report by the privy council committee for trade and plantations (perhaps best thought of as a precursor of the modern department of trade and industry) on the slave trade and the effects of slavery in Africa and the West Indies.

The committee of the privy council gained its evidence by interviewing witnesses who could give first-hand accounts of the trade. Thomas Clarkson appeared before the committee himself to give evidence about the produce available in Africa which would be of use to British industry, if traded. This was the result of research he had undertaken and the samples he had collected in his African Box (see Catalogue No. 22). The committee heard that:

> he had never been in Africa, but had made a Tour last Year through England, in the View of collecting Information on the Subject of the Trade to Africa; and in this Tour had passed Two Months at Liverpool, and Two at Bristol, and in those Places had collected Specimens of the Productions of Africa. (Part I)

The Committee ordered some of Clarkson's specimens to be sent to experts for comment as to their suitability for use in British manufacturing. Mr Hilton, a representative of the cotton spinners and manufacturers of Manchester, replied:

> I am very happy in transmitting your Lordships a very favourable Report … The Sample of Cotton from Senegal is very good and fine, as your Lordships will see by the Specimen inclosed [*sic*], which is spun after the Rate of One hundred and forty Hanks, Twist Cotton Yarn, to the Pound, and it is thought superior in Quality to *any* of the Brazil Cotton, and *nearly equal* to the East India. (*Ibid.*)

The final report of the privy council committee, which ran to nearly 900 pages, was completed in March 1789 and was laid before the house of commons on 25 April 1789. This copy of the report is the one that was laid before the house of lords on the same day.

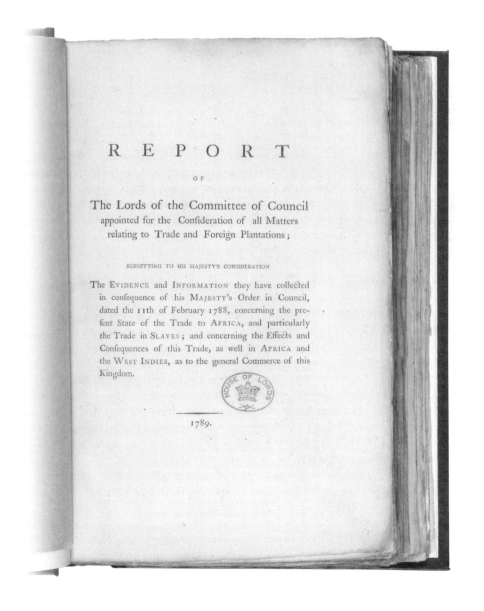

R E P O R T

OF

The Lords of the Committee of Council
appointed for the Confideration of all Matters
relating to Trade and Foreign Plantations;

SUBMITTING TO HIS MAJESTY'S CONSIDERATION

The EVIDENCE and INFORMATION they have collected
in confequence of his MAJESTY's Order in Council,
dated the 11th of February 1788, concerning the pre-
fent State of the Trade to AFRICA, and particularly
the Trade in SLAVES; and concerning the Effects and
Confequences of this Trade, as well in AFRICA and
the WEST INDIES, as to the general Commerce of this
Kingdom.

1789.

21 *Minutes of the evidence taken before the Select Committee, appointed for the Examination of witnesses on the Slave Trade*

Reported to the House of Commons March 25th 1791
Printed 1791
Paper
335 mm height × 200 mm width (sheet size)
Parliamentary Archives HL/PO/JO/10/7/919

In May 1789 the house of commons appointed a select committee, made up of M.P.s, to investigate the slave trade. As with the privy council investigation of 1788-9, the select committee called witnesses to testify before it. The hearings continued until April 1791. While it was relatively easy to find witnesses who were profiting from the trade and happy to give evidence to support its continuation, witnesses who were employed by plantation and ship owners, and who had more damning evidence, were harder to find, not least because their employers were unlikely to encourage adverse exposure. Thomas Clarkson was central to finding many of the witnesses who could give first-hand evidence of the realities of the trade.

Evidence was heard by the committee on all areas of the trade: the capture and transportation of Africans in Africa; the holding of captives in the coastal forts; conditions and events on board ships during transportation; the selling of captives on arrival in the West Indies; the method of cultivation of sugar; and the conditions and treatment of enslaved workers on plantations. This extract gives an indication of the range of witnesses examined. These included members of the armed forces who had served in the West Indies; plantation owners and managers, and those who had worked as clerks, book keepers and doctors on the plantations and in Africa; a ship's carpenter; a ship builder's clerk; and those who had travelled to the West Indies and mainland America. Although the Commons, and indeed the privy council, committees heard from many witnesses involved directly in the trade, no enslaved or formerly enslaved people seem to have been called.

The range of evidence was substantial and, when printed, was available to abolitionists outside parliament for use in promoting their campaigns.

This report, one of 18 separate reports that were issued by the committee, is contained in a volume that was delivered to the house of lords by the house of commons on 3 May 1792.

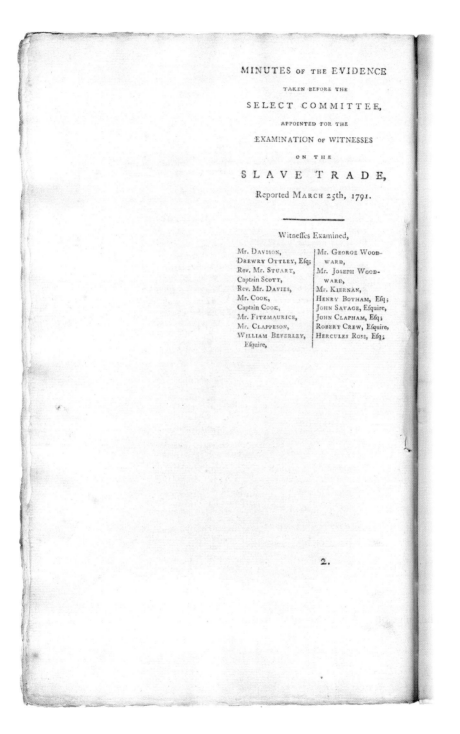

MINUTES of the EVIDENCE

TAKEN BEFORE THE

SELECT COMMITTEE,

APPOINTED FOR THE

EXAMINATION of WITNESSES

ON THE

SLAVE TRADE,

Reported MARCH 25th, 1791.

Witnesses Examined,

Mr. DAVISON,	Mr. GEORGE WOOD-
DREWRY OTTLEY, Esq;	WARD,
Rev. Mr. STUART,	Mr. JOSEPH WOOD-
Captain SCOTT,	WARD,
Rev. Mr. DAVIES,	Mr. KIERNAN,
Mr. COOK,	HENRY BOTHAM, Esq;
Captain COOK,	JOHN SAVAGE, Esquire,
Mr. FITZMAURICE,	JOHN CLAPHAM, Esq;
Mr. CLAPPESON,	ROBERT CREW, Esquire,
WILLIAM BEVERLEY,	HERCULES ROSS, Esq;
Esquire,	

2.

22 Thomas Clarkson's African Box

Various materials
760 mm length × 355 mm height × 280 mm width (chest)
Wisbech and Fenland Museum 1870.13

This exhibit has been variously known as 'Clarkson's West African Collection', 'Clarkson's African Box' and, in latter years, 'Clarkson's Chest'. Clarkson seems to have attached little importance to the chest itself other than as a means of containing his valuable collection of specimens, which supported his arguments for mercantile trading with Africa.

When Thomas Clarkson began to research the slave trade for the London Committee, he started to collect evidence of raw materials and made goods, commodities that were available for a fair and profitable trade with African countries and that did not involve the sale of human beings. He also wanted the British to understand that African peoples had established cultures and traditions as well as advanced craft skills. His attempts to 'humanise' Africans in the minds of the British was all too necessary, as the popular understanding, and indeed the legal position, was of people who were little different from animals and could, therefore, be treated and worked as animals, which is just what the slave trade and slavery did. He collected and bought the contents of his box from sailors and others who had served on ships recently returned from the round trip to Africa and then the West Indies or America.

Clarkson took his 'African Box' with him on his tours of Britain promoting abolition and using its contents as visual aids for his arguments. He also took his chest with him to meetings with Wilberforce and William Pitt to illustrate his arguments against the trade.

The box today does not include all the original contents, and Clarkson does not seem to have ever made an inventory of the box's contents, though certain items are documented in his *History of the Rise, Progress and Accomplishment of the Abolition of the African Slave-Trade by the British Parliament* (2 vols, 1808) and in the evidence he gave to the parliamentary enquiries. Indeed a number of his samples were sent by the committees to experts to establish their trade value (see Catalogue No. 20). The chest and some of its contents are also clearly shown in the portrait watercolour of Clarkson by A. E. Chalon, RA (Wilberforce House Museum, Hull Museums). The inclusion of the chest, or more accurately, since the chest is almost entirely obscured, its contents, in the portrait acknowledges their importance to Clarkson.

Not all the original contents of the box were African. In his *History* Clarkson illustrates some instruments of torture and restraint, which he details buying from a dockside shop in Liverpool, and which are no longer in the collection.

The current contents include samples of seeds, grains, spices and nuts such as tamarind, black eye peas, millet, carob and pepper. The timber samples which featured in the evidence of the parliamentary enquires are today represented only by some campeachey wood chips and unidentified bark samples, along with two samples of wooden cups and three samples of gum (copal, segal and an unidentified sample). There are ten samples of woven cloths, including a woven cotton rug, together with samples of raw cotton and weaving equipment – spindles and a bamboo handloom. Decorative basketry and woven raffia examples include bags of varying sizes, a hat and jewellery. Leather ware is represented by a single sandal and the sheaths to three daggers and a quiver, which holds 15 arrows, though two of the three necklaces with amulets containing charms include seed pods are covered with leather. There are fragments of two pipes, one ceramic and one including some gold filigree work, and there are also some fragments of gold trinkets.

Photography: Graham Howard

There is one ivory trade token, which would have been given as a reference to the African trader, inscribed:

> Obverse: *Sold the Alfred 30 slaves. West India of Grandy Bonney a good trader and an honest man*
> Reverse: *The gift of Captain John Tousdall to young West India of Grandy Bonney*

The only item contained in the collection which appears to be European in origin, is a rope bludgeon, with a large knot at one end. This weapon is similar to one described by Clarkson used in the killing of Peter Green, a steward on the *Alfred*. Clarkson visited Liverpool to investigate this death and was told by a seaman who served with Green of the beating Green had received as a punishment:

> The captain ... beat him [Green] severely ... and ordered his hands to be made fast to some bolts on the starboard side of the ship and under the half deck, and then flogged him himself, using the lashes of the cat-of-nine-tails upon his back at one time, and the *double walled knot at the end of it* upon his head at another [emphasis added] (Clarkson, *History*, I, 400)

Clarkson observed of the sailors involved in the slave trade:

> It was impossible for them to be accustomed to carry away men and women by force, to keep them in chains, to see their tears, to hear their mournful lamentations, to behold the dead and the dying ... without losing their finer feelings, or without contracting those habits of moroseness and cruelty, which would brutalize their nature. (*Ibid.*, I, 395-6)

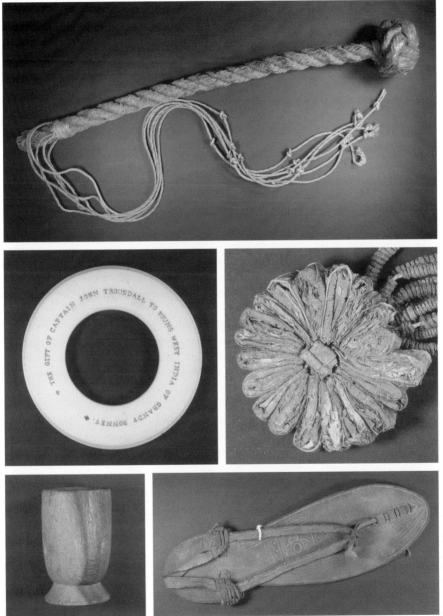

Photography: Graham Howard

23 *William Wilberforce*

George Richmond (1809-96)

1833

Oil on canvas

1410 mm height × 1105 mm width

Palace of Westminster WOA 6071

In 1787 William Wilberforce (1759-1833) was persuaded by his close friend, the prime minister, William Pitt, after a conversation in the garden of Pitt's residence in Kent, to take up the cause of abolition of the slave trade as its parliamentary spokesman. Wilberforce described the moment:

> I well remember, after a conversation in the open air at the root of an old tree at Holwood ... I resolved to give notice on a fit occasion in the House of Commons of my intention to bring the subject forward. (William Hague, *William Pitt* [2005] pp. 291-2)

Wilberforce had entered parliament in 1780. After having undergone a religious conversion in 1785 (and subsequently becoming one of the central figures in the evangelical Clapham Sect), he had taken up the cause of abolition following a meeting with a former slave trader, John Newton. The evangelical Christians, nicknamed 'The Saints', were concerned for the spiritual well-being of the enslaved Africans and the moral health of the British nation, which they felt was put at risk by its involvement with the slave trade.

In March 1789 Wilberforce proposed a debate on the trade which eventually took place in the house of commons on 12 May. Wilberforce, equipped with the results of the privy council report (see Catalogue No. 20), gave his first parliamentary speech on abolition. He ended his epic three-hour-long speech with a statement which showed a common concern with Clarkson:

> Let us make a reparation to Africa so far as we can by establishing a trade upon the commercial principles, and we shall soon find the rectitude of our conduct rewarded by the benefits of a regular and growing commerce. (Terence Brady and Evan Jones, *The Fight Against Slavery* [1975], p. 88)

The outcome of the debate was the establishment under Wilberforce's guidance of a select committee to investigate the trade (see Catalogue No. 21). Wilberforce brought a motion for abolition before the house of commons in April 1791, but it was defeated by the sizeable majority of 75 votes. This first defeat was to prove a foretaste of many more such parliamentary setbacks for the abolitionists over the next 15 years. Wilberforce, however, remained committed to the issue and continued to bring it before the House on an almost annual basis; in conjunction with the Grenville ministry, his role was a key one in the eventual passage of the Abolition Act in 1807.

24 *The humble Petition of the undersigned Inhabitants of the town and Neighbourhood of Manchester*

1806
Parchment
5340 mm height × 786 mm width
Parliamentary Archives HL/PO/JO/10/8/106

One of the purposes of Thomas Clarkson's tours of Britain between 1788 and 1794 was to organise and encourage a new public petitioning campaign. The first campaign reached a peak in 1792. However its failure to result in positive action by parliament was partially responsible for Clarkson's temporary retirement two years later. However he returned to the campaign trail in 1804. In 1805 an abolition bill failed in parliament, for the eleventh time in 15 years. The London Committee decided that a renewal of popular pressure was required and Clarkson was sent on a tour of the committees nationwide to rally support for what became a second petitioning campaign.

The Foreign Slave Trade Abolition Bill of 1806 brought forth a petition from Manchester merchants opposing it (see Catalogue No. 25). In response Clarkson made a desperate plea for an abolitionist counter-petition in support of the bill. Immediately the people of Manchester responded with a petition nearly seven metres long which was despatched to parliament only a day later and was presented to the house of lords on 14 May 1806:

> The town of Manchester perseveres in its former zeal, and preserves its consistency, in its efforts for the abolition of the slave trade. Pending the bill for restricting the importation of slaves into foreign colonies, a petition in its favour was signed by upwards of 2,400 of the most respectable inhabitants, and presented by Lord Derby, who, at the time, observed, that he could, from authority, state, that, had time allowed, at least double the number of signatures would have been obtained. (*The Times*, 2 June 1806)

At a time when only male property owners could vote, petitions provided an opportunity for non-voters to communicate with parliament. Women, who were not able to vote in parliamentary elections were usually excluded from signing petitions, but in spite of this, the signatures of at least five women are included on this petition. (For a full transcript of this petition see www.parliament.uk/slavetrade.)

25 *The humble Petition of the undersigned Manufacturers and Merchants on behalf of themselves and others of the town and Neighbourhood of Manchester*

1806

Parchment

844 mm height × 602 mm width

Parliamentary Archives HL/PO/JO/10/8/106

The Foreign Slave Trade Abolition Bill of 1806 was not introduced to parliament by Wilberforce, but by the attorney-general, Sir Arthur Leary Piggott (1749-1819), as a government bill. The abolitionists inside parliament, led by Wilberforce, seemed to pay little attention to the proposed bill, which passed through its early readings without being much noticed. However, by the third reading, the anti–abolitionists understood that the bill had broad abolitionist implications and that Wilberforce and his colleagues had implemented a clever strategy to get the bill passed without raising awareness of its wider ramifications. Sir Robert Peel M.P. (1750-1830), who saw in it a threat to the cotton industry and to the cotton town of Manchester, raised a petition, highlighting the risk it presented to the merchants and their trade interests. Peel's own firm, Peel, Yates, Halliwell & Co, signed the petition together with 110 other merchants, it was presented to the house of lords by Lord Westmorland on 13 May 1806.

This petition and its abolitionist counterpart (see Catalogue No. 24) are evidence of the public nature of the debate on abolition. Manchester had a strong history of petitioning parliament. It had submitted its first pro-abolition petition, containing over 10,000 signatures, in 1788; this was followed by numerous further petitions throughout the period of the abolition campaign. This is perhaps surprising for a town whose prosperity was based on the textile industry, itself dependant on the slave trade both for raw materials and as a market for finished cloths. Whilst this petition is signed purely by merchants its counterpart has signatures ranging from cloth manufacturers and merchants through shopkeepers and tailors to warehousemen and cutters indicating a broad support for abolition despite the impact it might have on their livelihoods. (For a full transcript of the signatories to these petitions see www. parliament.uk/slavetrade.)

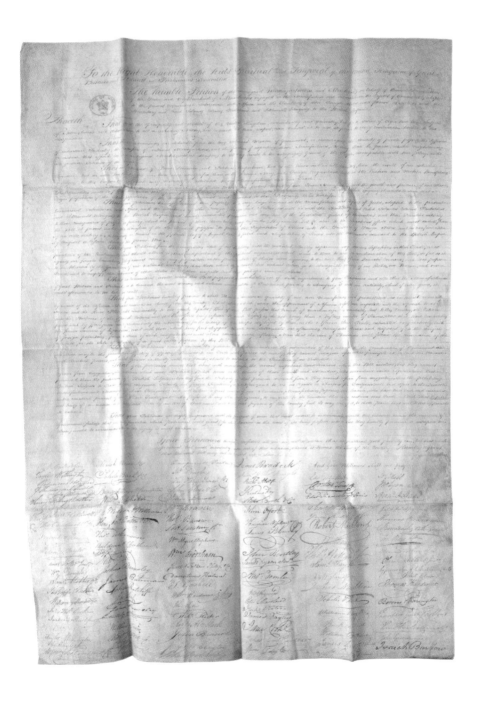

26 *An Act for the Abolition of the Slave Trade*

47 Geo. III sess.1 c. 36

1807

Parchment (animal skin)

72 mm height × 317 mm width when rolled, approx. 5920 mm long unrolled excluding amendment sheets

Parliamentary Archives HL/PO/PU/1/1807/47G3sln60

This act of parliament, as with most historical acts, is made up of a number of sheets or membranes of parchment sewn together to the required length, the final document being rolled for convenience. Once the abolition bill had reached its report stage in the house of lords, where it had been introduced, it was drawn up on parchment by the clerk; however, as it passed through further debates in the house of commons and the house of lords, substantial amendments were made to its wording, and consequently insertions and deletions were made on the membranes, as can be seen here. Further down the roll, additional sheets have been attached, overlaying the original wording to allow for the longer amendments to be inserted. The king did not come to the house of lords to endorse this act in person, but the 'royal assent', which was given on 25 March 1807, is noted at the top in the form 'Le Roy le Veult' (The king wishes it).

The passing of the Foreign Slave Trade Abolition Bill in 1806 paved the way for full abolition of the British trade the following year. The prime minister, Lord Grenville, introduced the general abolition bill in the house of lords at the beginning of the 1807 session of parliament. Its introduction by the head of the government clearly marked it as official policy, and it was passed in the house of lords on its second reading by 100 votes to 34 on 5 February, despite the resistance of the duke of Clarence (the future King William IV) and other peers with West Indian interests.

The debate then moved to the house of commons. Though the house of lords had provided the main opposition to abolition during the past 20 years, the abolitionists were still far from securing victory, since the Commons had also several times proved very resistant to accepting it. The London Committee members rented a house in nearby Downing Street to be close to parliament and allow them to lobby M.P.s in favour of the bill. Wilberforce, after 15 years of promoting abolition, received a standing ovation during the key Commons debate, reducing him to an emotional state - probably tears. The debate on 23 February 1807 lasted ten hours and the vote did not take place until four in the morning of the following day, when the house of commons voted in favour of the abolition bill by 283 votes to 16, a victory far in excess of expectations. (See Stephen Farrell's essay elsewhere in this publication.)

Le Roy le veult

Whereas ~~~ ~~~ ~~~ ~~~
~~~ ~~~ ~~~ ~~~ ~~~ ~~~
~~~ ~~~ ~~~ ~~~ ~~~ ~~~
~~~ ~~~ ~~ ~~~ Two Houses of
Parliament did by their Resolutions
of the Tenth and Twenty fourth Day
of June One thousand eight hundred
and six severally *upon certain Grounds therein mentioned* resolve that they
~~ ~~~ ~~~ ~~~ ~~~ ~~~ ~~~
~~~ ~~~ ~~~ ~~~ ~~~ ~~~ ~~
~~~ ~~~ ~~~ ~~~ ~~ ~~ ~~
would with all practicable Expedition
take effectual Measures for the
Abolition of the *African Slave* Trade in such
Manner and at such Period as
might be deemed adviseable **And
whereas** it is ~~ ~~~ ~~~ ~~~ ~~
fit upon all and each of the Grounds mentioned in the said Resolutions
~~~ ~~~ that the same should be
forthwith abolished and prohibited
and declared to be unlawful **Be it
therefore Enacted** by the King's
Most Excellent Majesty by and with
the advice and consent of the Lords
Spiritual and Temporal and Commons
in this present Parliament Assembled
and by the authority of the same
That from and after the First Day
of May One thousand eight hundred
and seven the African Slave Trade
and all and all manner of Dealing
and Trading in the Purchase Sale
Barter or Transfer of Slaves or of
persons intended to be sold transferred
used or dealt with as Slaves
practised or carried on in at to or
from any part of the Coast or
Countries of Africa shall be and
the same is thereby utterly abolished
prohibited and declared to be unlawful

2 and also that all and all manner of

27 *Abolition of the Slave Trade*

Subtitled *Britannia trampling the emblems of slavery, holding a banner Declaring the Abolition and attending to the voice of Justice and Religion. On the left, the Trade is represented by a Ship freighted with Slaves, and the Standard on which is inscribed the sufferings of the Negroes, and on the right is a bust of Mr Wilberforce with a scroll containing the Names of the Speakers in favour of the ABOLITION in both House of Parliament &c.*

Joseph Collyer (1748-1827) after Henry Moses (1782-1870)
Published London 1808
Broadside
330 mm height × 235 mm width
National Maritime Museum ZBA2644

This engraving is dedicated to His Royal Highness William Frederick, duke of Gloucester. Unlike his uncle, George III, and his cousin, the duke of Clarence, who were opponents of abolition, the duke of Gloucester was a supporter.

As this print illustrates, Britain was in self-congratulatory mode, with 'justice' and 'religion' winning the day over the concerns of 'trade'. The passing of the act led to jubilant celebrations in Britain and by the enslaved workers in the West Indies (see Hilary Beckles' essay elsewhere in the publication). Though the act had no impact on life for the enslaved on the plantations, its passing was perceived as a sign that emancipation would follow swiftly both at home and abroad. Few envisaged it would take a further 20 years before full emancipation was achieved, the Act for the Abolition of Slavery throughout the British Colonies being passed in 1833 and the interim system of apprenticeships being abolished in 1838.

The 1807 act was enforced by the royal navy, which reversed its role from guardian to hunter of British slave ships almost overnight, though ships which had already left (or had been cleared to leave) Britain on the round trip to Africa and the West Indies were allowed to complete their voyages, provided that they had disembarked their captive Africans in the Caribbean by 1 March 1808. The act, however, proved inadequate for the task of halting what was a very lucrative business. The fines imposed did not match the profits which could be earned and, even after an amendment act had been passed in 1811, making trading punishable by transportation to Australia, illegal voyages continued and British-made ships sailed under flags of convenience.

28 Yorkshire election ticket, William Wilberforce

Obverse *WILLIAM WILBERFORCE FOR EVER,*
Reverse *HUMANITY IS THE CAUSE OF THE PEOPLE*
1807
White metal
40 mm diameter
National Maritime Museum ZBA2814

Shown on page 325

29 Yorkshire election ticket, Henry Lascelles

Obverse *LASCELLES FOR EVER*
Reverse *IN MIND INDEPENDENT IN EXERTION INDEFATIGABLE*
1807
White metal
40 mm diameter
National Maritime Museum ZBA2814

Shown on page 327

The abolition of the British slave trade in March 1807 was the last act of Grenville's government before its fall from office and the calling of a general election the following month. Wilberforce had held his Yorkshire seat safely since 1784. Yorkshire returned two members to parliament, and Wilberforce had two opponents, Henry Lascelles, son of Lord Harewood, and Lord Milton, son of Earl Fitzwilliam. Harewood owned

land and plantations in Barbados, while Milton also had close family connexions to the slave trade and the West Indies. Wilberforce, publicly popular after the passing of the act, was expecting an easy victory, leaving his two opponents to fight over the second seat. However, the size of the pro-abolition vote led both of Wilberforce's opponents to align themselves with Wilberforce. Electoral songs were produced by both campaigns – 'Wilberforce and Milton for ever' and 'Wilberforce and Lascelles for ever', both candidates appearing to disown their families' histories and ties. Lascelles went as far as to suggest he would vote for full emancipation of the enslaved, something to which even Wilberforce had refused to commit himself. The campaign degenerated into a series of attacks and counter-attacks, alliances being formed and broken, and mobs were even hired to shout down election addresses. Lascelles's tactics included hiring every carriage that could be obtained in York so as to take his voters to the poll and, equally, to deprive his opponents' supporters of any means of transport. The Yorkshire election was hard fought, Lascelles's campaign, funded by his father, costing a staggering £100,000.

The campaign for abolition was not just relevant to the candidates' manifestos. It also had a direct link to the issuing of these election 'tickets' or tokens, which are evidence of the marketing practices (themselves drawn from early business marketing, see Catalogue No. 2) developed during the abolition campaign, and particularly of the power of collectables as a means of promoting the cause. The production of satirical cartoons, or Wedgwood's cameos of the 'kneeling slave', had allowed supporters to collect, circulate or wear these objects in support of the cause. Similarly, medals, coins and tokens had been produced throughout the campaign for promotional purposes (see Catalogue No. 32). Wilberforce had issued a medal in 1806, when the Foreign Slave Trade Bill had been passed, and circulated it to supporters. He used the same design, amending only the date, for this 1807 election token. Lascelles countered with one of his own, and Milton also issued one. The small hole in each of these 'tickets' was probably to allow the recipient to wear the token on a ribbon or pin.

William Roscoe had used a similar ticket to the Yorkshire examples in his 1806 Liverpool election campaign; however, this cheap electioneering device seems to have been fairly short-lived, suggesting that they were predominately part of the fashion for collectables connected with the campaign for abolition of the slave trade.

30 Button

c.1820
Silver
21 mm diameter
National Maritime Museum ZBA2438

This is an interesting example of the many artefacts produced to show support for abolition. Dated 1820, the button shows the image of a woman's head and, around the edge, there is a broken chain. This is an interesting development from the 'kneeling slave' figure adopted by the London Committee as their official seal in 1787. The image of the kneeling black man with chains and the words, *Am I not a man and a brother?*, was developed by the innovative porcelain producer Josiah Wedgwood (1730-95). Wedgwood was one of the early supporters of the London Committee and became one of its members after the seal was produced. The seal design was marketed widely and successfully by Wedgwood. It became a successful trademark for the abolitionist movement, instantly recognisable and appearing on a wide variety of goods, posters, leaflets and pamphlets, as well as on Wedgwood's cameos, lockets, snuff boxes and buttons. These items were particularly marketed to coincide with the London Committee's petitioning campaigns and the debates on the slave trade and slavery in parliament. The female version of the Wedgwood design, *Am I not a woman and a sister?*, appeared later in the campaign as did this button. Probably they were marketed to reflect the amount of support received from women who were taking a publicly prominent role in the campaign for the abolition of slavery. All-women anti-slavery societies were established around the country from 1825, generally taking a more radical approach to abolition than their male counterparts.

31 *Englishmen! NEGRO APPRENTICESHIP is proved to be but another name for SLAVERY. SIGN THEN WITHOUT DELAY THE PETITION lying within FOR IMMEDIATE ABOLITION*

1830s

Textile banner

2700 mm height × 1200 mm width

Anti-Slavery International

In 1823 a small group of abolitionists, including Thomas Clarkson and Thomas Fowell Buxton, met and established the London Society for the Mitigation and Gradual Abolition of Slavery, the successor to the old London Committee, and which was quickly to become the Anti-Slavery Society. Whilst the trade had been abolished in 1807, illegal trading was still prevalent and slavery continued to be legal. Wilberforce, although included in the membership of the new committee, did not attend the early meetings and was far from convinced that full emancipation was necessary or desirable. In 1823 and 1824, Clarkson, though now 64 years old, embarked on another tour of Britain in support of a petitioning campaign; this was to be the largest yet seen, with 750 petitions submitted to parliament in an 18 month period. The duke of Gloucester (see Catalogue No. 27) became chairman of the Society, adding further status to the campaign. However, it would be ten more years, in which period the petitioning and sugar boycott campaigns continued, before parliament was to act. Women were no longer just supporters, but were now active in the campaign. In 1833 the largest petition received by parliament came from the Ladies' Anti-Slavery Society, made up of 187,000 signatures. The publication of Mary Prince's biography *The History of Mary Prince, A West Indian Slave. Related by Herself*, in 1831, brought a named woman to the attention of the general public for the first time and provided a further focus for the female campaign. In 1833 parliament finally passed the Act Abolishing Slavery within the British Colonies. However, it also included provision for paying £20,000,000 in compensation to the plantation owners, and, rather than granting immediate freedom to the enslaved workers, it established a system of apprenticeships, which it was soon apparent was being abused extensively by the plantation owners, who were treating their apprentices as brutally as they did when they were enslaved. As this banner indicates, the abolitionist campaign continued until 1838, when full emancipation was finally granted in the British empire.

32 General anti-slavery convention medal

Joseph Davis (fl.1828-1857)
1840
White metal
52 mm diameter
National Maritime Museum ZBA2820

Obverse: Draped bust, facing right *THOMAS CLARKSON*
Reverse: An African 'slave' kneeling, his manacled hands raised *AM I NOT A MAN AND A BROTHER, BRITISH & FOREIGN ANTI-SLAVERY SOCIETY. GENERAL ANTI-SLAVERY CONVENTION HELD IN LONDON 1840. PRESIDENT THOMAS CLARKSON AGED 81*

The British and Foreign Anti-Slavery Society, was formed in 1839. The society was committed to the abolition of the slave trade and slavery worldwide. Initially it concentrated on South American slavery, in Brazil and Cuba particularly, and the British colonies of India and Ceylon, which were excluded from the British acts of abolition; by the 1850s it was campaigning for abolition in mainland North America.

The event this medal commemorates was the first world convention, which was held in London in June 1840. Thomas Clarkson was elected president by the five thousand delegates present. The bust on this coin is based on the painting of Clarkson speaking at the convention by Benjamin Robert Haydon (1786-1846) (National Portrait Gallery). Clarkson continued to be actively involved in the abolition movement until his death in 1846.

The British and Foreign Anti-Slavery Society still exists today as Anti-Slavery International.

Select Bibliography

Jill Barber, *Celebrating the Black Presence in Westminster 1500-2000. No. 2 Hidden Lives* (Westminster City Archives, 2000)

Terence Brady and Evan Jones, *The Fight Against Slavery* (1975)

Olaudah Equiano, The Interesting Narrative and Other Writings ed. Vincent Carretta (2003)

Seymour Drescher, 'Whose Abolition? Popular Pressure and the Ending of the British Slave Trade', *Past and Present*, No. 143 (1994), 136-66

Madge Dresser and Sue Giles, *Bristol & Transatlantic Slavery* (Bristol Museums & Art Gallery with the University of the West of England, 2000)

The Life of Olaudah Equiano ed. Paul Edwards (Harlow, 1989)

Michael Graham-Stewart, *Slavery Collection* (unpublished catalogue of collection now in the National Maritime Museum, 2001)

William Hague, *William Pitt the Younger* (2005)

Harry Harmer, *The Longman Companion to Slavery, Emancipation and Civil Rights* (Harlow, 2001)

Michael Jordan, *The Great Abolition Sham. The True Story of the End of the British Slave Trade* (Stroud, 2005)

Reyahn King, Sukhdev Sanduh, James Walvin, Jane Girdham, *Ignatius Sancho. An African Man of Letters* (1997)

Sources for Black and Asian History at the City of Westminster Archives Centre ed. Rory Lalwan (Westminster City Archives, 2005)

J. R. Oldfield, *Popular Politics and British Anti-Slavery. The Mobilisation of Public Opinion against the Slave Trade, 1787-1807* (1998)

Mary Prince, The History of Mary Prince, ed. Sara Salih (2000)

Simon Schama, *Rough Crossings. Britain, the Slaves and the American Revolution* (2005)

Transatlantic Slavery. Against Human Dignity, ed. Anthony Tibbles (National Museums Liverpool, 2005)

James Walvin, *Black Ivory. Slavery in the British Empire* (Oxford, 2001)

INDEX